Rousseau

BASIC POLITICAL WRITINGS
Second Edition

Jean-Jacques Rousseau

BASIC POLITICAL WRITINGS
Second Edition

Discourse on the Sciences and the Arts
Discourse on the Origin and Foundations of Inequality among Men
Discourse on Political Economy
On the Social Contract
The State of War

Translated and Edited by
Donald A. Cress

Introduction and New Annotation by
David Wootton

Hackett Publishing Company, Inc.
Indianapolis / Cambridge

Copyright © 2011 by Hackett Publishing Company, Inc.

Printed in the United States of America

24 23 22 21   3 4 5 6 7

For further information, please address:
    Hackett Publishing Company, Inc.
    P.O. Box 44937
    Indianapolis, IN 46244-0937

    www.hackettpublishing.com

Cover design by Listenberger & Associates
Text design by Meera Dash
Composition by William Hartman

Library of Congress Cataloging-in-Publication Data
Rousseau, Jean-Jacques, 1712–1778.
    [Selections. English. 2011]
    Basic political writings / Jean-Jacques Rousseau ; translated
and edited by Donald A. Cress ; introduction and new annotation
by David Wootton. — 2nd ed.
        p. cm.
    Includes bibliographical references and index.
    ISBN 978-1-60384-673-8 (pbk.) — ISBN 978-1-60384-674-5 (cloth)
    1. Political science. I. Cress, Donald A. II. Title.
    JC179.R7 2011
    320.01—dc23
                                        2011025946

Contents

Translator's Note

With the exception of *The State of War*—my translation of which is new to this edition, and whose textual basis is given in the headnote to that work—the translations contained in this volume are based on the excellent *Oeuvres Complètes de Jean-Jacques Rousseau*, Volume 3 (Paris: Pléiade, 1964). My translations of the *Discourse on the Sciences and the Arts*, *Discourse on the Origin and Foundations of Inequality among Men*, *Discourse on Political Economy*, and *On the Social Contract*—earlier versions of which appeared in the first edition of Jean-Jacques Rousseau: *The Basic Political Writings*—have been revised in light of generous and invaluable suggestions offered by David Wootton, all of which I have considered with enormous gratitude and most of which I have adopted. Any errors or infelicities that remain are my own.

Square brackets [ ] enclose editorial annotations, most of which were provided for this edition by David Wootton; square-bracketed items embedded in the text typically provide the term translated by the rendering that immediately precedes the bracketed item, but occasionally they offer a clarifying editorial comment. In the *Discourse on the Origin and Foundations of Inequality among Men*, angle brackets < > enclose passages added or revised by Rousseau in the 1782 edition.

D.A.C.

Introduction

"We are approaching the state of crisis and the century of revolutions."[1]
—The tutor in Rousseau's novel *Émile* (1762)

Jean-Jacques Rousseau (1712–1778) is a great political theorist, but he is read for the wrong reasons. Three social contract theorists, Thomas Hobbes, John Locke, and Rousseau, are at the center of any introduction to political theory: Hobbes, for his intellectual rigor; Locke, because he is the theorist of the American Revolution; and Rousseau, because he is the theorist of the French Revolution. Locke may or may not have been an important theorist for the American Founding Fathers—the matter is much debated. Rousseau was not regarded as an important political theorist prior to the French Revolution of 1789; his major work of political theory, *On the Social Contract*, was published in French in 1762, but not translated into English until 1791, and his books were not a cause of the revolution. Robespierre and the Jacobins admired him greatly, but they misunderstood him profoundly (their Rousseau was invented to serve their own purposes). It is scarcely worth reading Rousseau if we want to understand eighteenth-century politics, either before or after 1789, but it is certainly worth reading his works if we want to understand ourselves and our own politics. For Rousseau's importance lies, as he always insisted, in his remarkable understanding of the nature of human beings. He, more than any other political theorist, has something important to say about who we are and what politics is for.

In order to understand Rousseau we need to bear three things in mind. First, Rousseau is always writing about Jean-Jacques. The first word of his *Social Contract* is "I"; the last word is "me." In order to understand Hobbes or Locke, it helps to know something about seventeenth-century politics, but one need not know much about their lives. It really does not matter that Hobbes was employed as a tutor, or Locke as a doctor. Rousseau is different. Everything he writes—and not just his *Confessions* or *Rousseau, Judge of Jean-Jacques*—comes directly out of a meditation on his own experience of life and is consequently about himself. Not entirely surprisingly, he was the author of a play, *Narcissus, or the Man Who Fell in Love with Himself* (1752). Who is Rousseau? When he writes about politics he consistently describes himself as "Citizen of Geneva."[2] To understand his politics, we will need to start with his relationship to Geneva.

[1] Jean-Jacques Rousseau, *Émile, or On Education*, trans. Allan Bloom (New York: Basic Books, 1979), 194.

[2] "Citizen of Geneva," title pages of first and second Discourses and *Social Contract*, below, pp. 3, 29, 155.

Second, Rousseau is acutely aware that his contemporaries think that he is the author of "paradoxes."[3] Many of these paradoxes have become famous: "Man is born free, and everywhere he is in chains"; citizens must be "forced to be free."[4] A paradox can be a statement that is contrary to received opinion; or, more strongly, it can be a statement that appears to be self-contradictory or absurd. Rousseau's paradoxes are both. In order to recognize that they are true, readers have to give up conventional ways of thinking, and consequently they have to adopt a way of thinking that appears impractical or irrelevant in most real-life situations. Rousseau's political theory—at least as it appeared in print—is about principle, not practice.[5]

Third, Rousseau was incapable of seeing into the future. He writes often about "revolutions," but even he could not imagine the American and French revolutions. When Rousseau writes of revolutions, he has in mind the major political upheavals described by René-Aubert de Vertot (1655–1735) in his books on the "revolutions" of ancient Rome and of modern Sweden and Portugal—civil wars and coups d'état we would call them, rather than revolutions. Rousseau has been accused of being the author of a totalitarian political theory, but of course Rousseau could never imagine Nazi Germany or Stalinist Russia; he *was* familiar with what he called *despots*, a term that covered ancient Roman emperors such as Caligula, contemporary Ottoman rulers (though Rousseau never explicitly said so), the contemporary ruler of France, Louis XV, and, above all, his predecessor Louis XIV. It seems paradoxical indeed to accuse someone who hated despotism, who described himself as having an "indomitable spirit of liberty," with seeking to establish totalitarianism.[6]

It is easy for us to think that every sensible person is hostile to despotism, but that is because our politics is the long-term product of the English Revolution of 1688 and of the American and French revolutions. In the mid-eighteenth century, the consensus was that some form of despotism represented the political future. David Hume, for example, argued that absolute government could be "civilized" and could represent the likely future for

---

[3] Note xiii to the second Discourse, below, p. 116.

[4] *Social Contract*, Book I, chs. 1 ("... he is in chains"), 7 ("forced to be free"), below, pp. 156, 167. On forcing to be free, see (in English), John Plamenatz, "Ce qui ne signifie autre chose sinon qu'on le forcera d'être libre," in *Hobbes and Rousseau*, ed. Maurice Cranston and Richard S. Peters (New York: Anchor Books, 1972), 318–32, and in *Jean-Jacques Rousseau: Critical Assessments*, ed. John T. Scott (Abingdon, UK: Routledge, 2003), 3:106–16.

[5] He did concern himself with real-life situations in, for example, two works that were not published in his lifetime, *Projet de constitution pour la Corse* and *Considérations sur le gouvernement de Pologne*. The *Social Contract* was a much more realistic text than one might think, but only if read in a Genevan context.

[6] Letter to Malesherbes, January 4, 1762. The classic text, much debated, is J. L. Talmon, *The Origins of Totalitarian Democracy* (London: Secker and Warburg, 1952).

Britain.[7] The leading figures of the French Enlightenment declared their support for despotic rulers such as Frederick the Great of Prussia and Catherine the Great of Russia; their objection to French despotism was not that it was despotic but that it was unenlightened.

The term "Enlightenment" comes from the German *Aufklärung*, and it is not one with which Rousseau was familiar. He often uses the adjective *éclairé*, which means literally "well lit" (an artist's studio should be *éclairé*) and was used metaphorically to mean "well educated." For Rousseau and his contemporaries, *éclairé* does not have the specific meaning of "enlightened." Rousseau knew that he was supposed to live in a *siècle des lumières*, "an age of lights," or an enlightened age. The term seems to have been invented by Pierre Bayle (1647–1706), who, more than anyone, was responsible for one central aspect of the Enlightenment, the attack on the truths of revealed religion. Enlightenment philosophers did not agree on what ought to replace revealed religion. Some, like Baruch de Spinoza, Paul Henri-Thiry (Baron d'Holbach), and Denis Diderot, were atheists or pantheists; some, like Voltaire, were deists; and some, like Locke, wanted a more rational Christianity (Locke wrote *The Reasonableness of Christianity* [1695], and his disciple John Toland wrote *Christianity not Mysterious* [1696]), but, at a time when Protestants were being severely persecuted in France, all favored religious toleration and freedom of debate. A rejection of revealed religion and of a conventional Christian morality (of sexual continence, for example) was one of the first requirements if you were to think of yourself as a *philosophe*—the word means "philosopher," but it was used in France to refer to enlightened philosophers, public intellectuals rather than university professors.

The *philosophes* of the mid-eighteenth century were united by more than a rejection of revealed religion. They had rejected the certainties of both scholastic philosophy (still mainly taught in the universities) and of Cartesianism and had adopted the epistemology and psychology of Locke—a cautious empiricism, a willingness to recognize the intellectual coherence of materialism, and above all a belief that human beings are shaped by their environment and, hence, by their upbringing. Thus, what united the *philosophes* was a conviction that society could be reformed—it could be made more equal, more tolerant, more skeptical.[8] What went with this was a belief in progress—scientific progress, technological progress, economic progress, philosophical progress. The second half of the seventeenth century had seen a debate over whether the "moderns" were the equal of the "ancients." The Enlightenment

---

[7] David Hume, "Whether the British Government Inclines More to Absolute Monarchy, or to a Republic" (1741), in *Essays, Moral, Political, and Literary*, ed. Eugene F. Miller (Indianapolis: Liberty Fund, 1987), 47–53. For his idea of a "civilized European monarchy," see his essays "Of Civil Liberty" (87–96) and "Of the Rise and Progress of the Arts and Sciences" (111–37).

[8] The classic text is Carl L. Becker, *The Heavenly City of the Eighteenth-Century Philosophers* (New Haven: Yale University Press, 1932).

took it for granted that that debate had been settled in favor of the moderns: gunpowder and printing, the science of Newton, the philosophy of Locke, and the new commercial prosperity of the Dutch Republic and of England were irrefutable proof that the moderns had outstripped the ancients.

Rousseau lived in the middle of the age of Enlightenment; for a while at least he counted among his friends some of the greatest *philosophes*—Diderot, Jean d'Alembert, and Hume. But he was never an Enlightenment philosopher. Although he was far from being an orthodox Christian, he was more sympathetic to Christianity than any proper *philosophe* would be. If he did not uphold a conventional Christian morality, he was all in favor of *virtue* (by which he meant old-fashioned pagan virtues, such as courage and frugality, not fashionable "virtues" like politeness and sociability nor Christian virtues such as piety and chastity).[9] He believed strongly that we are shaped by our environment, but he did not believe in progress. In contrast to the leading figures of the Enlightenment, he was systematically hostile to despotism. Rousseau was thus *in* the Enlightenment, but he was not *of* the Enlightenment; indeed, he became one of the Enlightenment's leading critics, placing himself at the opposite pole from the Enlightenment's figurehead, Voltaire, on almost every subject.[10]

CITIZEN OF GENEVA

Rousseau was by birth a citizen of Geneva.[11] His mother died as a consequence of giving birth to him, and his father was an unsuccessful watchmaker who fled Geneva when Rousseau was ten to avoid prosecution for assault. Rousseau became, in effect, an orphan. Just before he turned thirteen, he was apprenticed to an engraver. His master beat him, Rousseau responded by stealing, and his master beat him all the harder. When he was fifteen, Rousseau went out of the city one Sunday on a jaunt. The city gates were closed a little early, and Rousseau and his friends found themselves locked out. Rather than return with his friends the next day for the inevitable beating, Rousseau set out into the unknown. He was homeless, penniless, and friendless. Rousseau was to spend the rest of his life looking for a home, but he was incapable of finding one. Nothing could adequately correspond to his imaginary ideal, the home he would have had if his mother had lived.

---

[9] "J'adore la Vertu": "Observations," in *Oeuvres Complètes*, ed. Bernard Gagnebin and Marcel Raymond (5 vols., Paris: Gallimard, 1959–1995), 3:39.

[10] See Mark Hulliung, *The Autocritique of Enlightenment: Rousseau and the Philosophes* (Cambridge, MA: Harvard University Press, 1998); Graeme Garrard, *Rousseau's Counter-Enlightenment* (Albany: SUNY Press, 2003).

[11] On Rousseau and Geneva, see James Miller, *Rousseau: Dreamer of Democracy* (New Haven: Yale University Press, 1984); Helena Rosenblatt, *Rousseau and Geneva* (Cambridge: Cambridge University Press, 1997).

Rousseau escaped from his immediate predicament by converting to Catholicism. Geneva, the city of John Calvin, was Protestant; converts were welcomed and protected by the authorities of the neighboring Catholic states. By converting, Rousseau automatically forfeited his citizenship; he was no longer a citizen of Geneva. Rousseau was sent (on foot, a hundred fifty miles through the mountains) to Turin, where, after being instructed in his new faith, he found employment as a lackey—a menial servant wearing his employer's uniform. His first employer died, and when her possessions were being inventoried, it turned out a little silver ribbon was missing. Rousseau had stolen it, but he accused an innocent servant girl. Both were dismissed, and for the rest of his life Rousseau was tormented by the thought that Marion, without a reference, faced a future of prostitution, destitution, and early death. Rousseau was more fortunate: he found new employment and was soon being groomed for promotion. But the prospect of spending the rest of his life as a servant was intolerable to him, and after eighteen months in Turin, he set out back toward Geneva. Rousseau had experienced dependence, and for the rest of his life he clung desperately to independence. He had waited on the rich, and he had learned to hate them. Later he would write, "I hate the great; I hate their high status, their harshness, their pettiness, and all their vices, and I would hate them even more if I despised them less."[12]

Rousseau returned, not to Geneva but to Annecy, thirty miles south of Geneva. There, when he first fled Geneva, he had been taken in by Mme de Warens, herself a convert from Protestantism who was paid a pension to encourage others to convert. Mme de Warens, who was separated from her husband, was thirteen years older than Rousseau, and he quickly fell in love with her. For a few years, Rousseau was unsettled: he spent a year wandering, spending time in Lausanne and Neuchâtel, and pretending to be a music teacher, a job for which he was hopelessly ill equipped. He walked three hundred miles to Paris and briefly became a tutor. He walked back to be reunited with Mme de Warens, now in Chambéry, sixty miles south of Geneva. In 1732 Rousseau, now twenty, and Mme de Warens became lovers. Neither took much pleasure in their physical relationship. Rousseau preferred to pretend Mme de Warens was his mother, not his lover (he called her *maman*), and "felt as if I had committed incest,"[13] and Mme de Warens always insisted that she was incapable of erotic feelings (though she had lovers besides Rousseau). Rousseau, who had received no formal education, now had the run of an excellent library and little else but reading to occupy his time.

After six years Rousseau found himself supplanted in Mme de Warens' affections, and two years later he left to become a tutor, first in Lyons, then in Paris. For eighteen months he was secretary to the French ambassador to Venice, but was dismissed for insolence. At the age of thirty-three, he

---

[12] Letter to Malesherbes, January 28, 1762.

[13] Jean-Jacques Rousseau, *The Confessions*, trans. J. M. Cohen (London: Penguin, 1953), 189.

returned to Paris, and there he tried to make a living writing music. He also became a research assistant to a wealthy couple, the Dupins. Louise-Marie-Madelaine was writing an endless feminist tract, and Claude was soon writing a vast, unreadable refutation of Montesquieu. Rousseau also fell in with Diderot and d'Alembert, who were embarking on an ambitious and subversive enterprise, the great *Encyclopédie*, a compendium of progressive thinking. Out of friendship, they commissioned him to write articles on music. Meanwhile Rousseau had taken up with Thérèse Levasseur, a laundress. She was not officially either his mistress or his wife (visitors mistook her for his housekeeper), but their relationship was to last until his death, and they were to have five children—each of which was taken promptly to the Foundling Hospital and abandoned. This was not particularly uncommon (Rousseau himself noted statistics suggesting 25 percent of children born in Paris were abandoned),[14] but the death rate for infants handed in at the Foundling Hospital was very close to 100 percent. Rousseau long kept his abandoned children a secret, and when news of them spread it tarnished his reputation, which has never recovered.

In the summer of 1749, Rousseau was thirty-seven. He was living hand to mouth, with no security; he was one of five hundred or so writers (and perhaps a similar number of musicians) living in Paris, hoping to find some sort of success.[15] He had failed in career after career: a failed notary, engraver, tutor, music teacher, clerk, secretary, composer. Rousseau was on his way (walking again) to visit Diderot, who was locked up in a prison outside Paris for having published a book, the *Letter on the Blind*, a defense of atheism. On his way, he paused to read an advertisement in a newspaper that announced a competition to write a short essay on the topic "Whether the restoration of the sciences and arts has contributed to purifying mores [or morals]." Rousseau later said that he was immediately overcome with a "dizziness like that of drunkenness."[16] "I beheld another universe and became another man."[17] He tells us that a whole system of ideas immediately became apparent to him—and close reading of the Discourse he proceeded to write suggests this is true. The Discourse not only won the prize; when published, it immediately made Rousseau famous—it was even promptly translated into English. Although in the next few years he wrote an opera and a play, he had now embarked on a career as an author, writing several defenses of the first Discourse.

---

[14] *Oeuvres Complètes* 3:528.

[15] Robert Darnton, "Two Paths through the Social History of Ideas," in *The Darnton Debate: Books and Revolution in the Eighteenth Century*, ed. Haydn T. Mason (Oxford: Voltaire Foundation, 1998), 251–94, at p. 256; Darnton, *The Literary Underground of the Old Regime* (Cambridge, MA: Harvard University Press, 1982).

[16] Letter to Malesherbes, January 12, 1762.

[17] Rousseau, *Confessions*, 327.

In 1754 he wrote a second Discourse. This time, before publication, he made a pilgrimage to Geneva, where he rejoined the Protestant church and became a citizen once again. Publication of the second Discourse in 1755 was followed rapidly by publication of volume five of Diderot and d'Alembert's *Encyclopédie*, which included Rousseau's article on political economy or, rather we might say (for his subject is not economics but the administration of the state), on government. It was at this point that Rousseau completed his political theory by adopting (or rather adapting) the idea of the "general will." The next year Rousseau left Paris to take up residence on the country estate of a friend, ten miles north of Paris, in a cottage named The Hermitage. From here he published in 1758 a *Letter to d'Alembert on the Theater*, which represented a sustained attack on the views held by Diderot, d'Alembert, and their associates. The ostensible issue was whether Geneva was right to have a ban on theaters, and Rousseau was once again defending ancient virtue against modern sophistication.

The break with the leading figures of the French Enlightenment, which obliged Rousseau to leave The Hermitage, was crucial in helping him find his own voice. Three works followed in quick succession: *Julie, ou la nouvelle Héloïse* (1761), an epistolary novel about an affair between a young woman and her tutor (the title is a reference to Heloise and Abelard, famous lovers of the twelfth century; Rousseau's book was first published as *Lettres de deux amans* [1761], then as *La nouvelle Héloïse* [1764] and only acquired its final title in the third, authorized edition of 1772), *Émile, ou De l'éducation*, a novel about the education of a young man (May 22, 1762); and *Du contrat social* (May 15, 1762). *Julie* and *Émile* were immediately enormously successful—*Julie* was the best-selling novel of the entire eighteenth century—and turned Rousseau into a "celebrity"; the word was new, and he uses it himself.[18] People traveled long distances just to see him. His appearance in a public place caused crowds to gather.

In order to understand Rousseau's career at this point we have to think about censorship.[19] Diderot and d'Alembert were struggling to publish the *Encyclopédie* legally in France (they wanted the protection of a "privilege," a form of copyright, so that their publisher could recuperate his costs). They were faced with growing hostility from the authorities. In 1757, Robert Damiens had tried to assassinate Louis XV, and the attack on intellectual radicalism, which had been gathering momentum over the previous years, became intense. Censorship was tightened significantly after Claude Adrien Helvétius' *On Mind* (1758), which had been approved for publication, was condemned

---

[18] See the 1781 Foreword to the first Discourse ("What is celebrity?"), below, p. 4. See also Antoine Lilti, "The Writing of Paranoia: Jean-Jacques Rousseau and the Paradoxes of Celebrity," *Representations* 103 (2008): 53–83.

[19] See Robert Darnton, *The Forbidden Best-Sellers of Pre-Revolutionary France* (New York: Norton, 1995).

to be burned by the Paris hangman. Most *philosophes*, however, chose to publish anonymously and abroad; this, for example, was how Voltaire's *Candide* appeared in 1759. Copies were then smuggled into France and sold under the counter, in exactly the same way as pornographic books were. As a consequence, there was no copyright protection for author or publisher—successful works were quickly pirated—and it was almost impossible for an author, even the most successful, to live by writing. (Most successful authors relied on patronage of one sort or another, often in the form of a government pension. Voltaire was rich, but as a result of financial speculation, not royalties.)

Rousseau's approach to publication was different. After the first edition of the first Discourse (which appeared anonymously), he usually published abroad but under his own name. His printer, Marc-Michel Rey in Amsterdam, would then seek permission to bring copies into France; in other words, Rousseau sought to avoid prepublication censorship while still conforming to the law. The case of *Émile* was somewhat different. It was printed with official permission by Nicolas-Bonaventure Duchesne in Paris, although on its title page it claimed to have been printed by Jean Néaulme at The Hague in Holland—a book needed to look as if it had been banned if it was to sell well. Here too, then Rousseau had sought to act within the law.

Rousseau hoped to operate within the law because he had recently acquired the support of powerful aristocrats, the Duke of Luxembourg and the Prince of Conti; and he had their support precisely because he had not signed up to the *philosophes'* program of progress and religious skepticism. In many respects he could be read as a reactionary rather than a progressive writer. This was true even of a key chapter in *Émile*, the profession of faith of the Savoyard vicar. As far as Rousseau and the *philosophes* were concerned, this was an attack on irreligion—even if it could also be read as an attack on orthodox Christianity. Diderot wrote, "He has the religious on his side, and the interest they take in him is due to the bad things he says about the *philosophes*. Since they hate us a thousand times more than they love their God, they don't care that he has dragged their Christ in the mud, so long as he's not one of us."[20] Diderot was wrong. On June 9, 1762, the book was banned by the *parlement* of Paris—the *parlement* being a court of law—and a warrant was issued for Rousseau's arrest. Given the support for Rousseau in the highest quarters, the matter was handled delicately. Duchesne was given time to hide his stock, and he continued to sell copies by the simple device of sticking a new title page on the front, so that he was no longer (ostensibly) selling the book that had been banned. Rousseau was warned that he was about to be arrested. The police passed him on the road but made no attempt to stop him.

Thus Rousseau had to flee France because his religious views—boldly published under his own name—were unacceptable. But a few days later,

---

[20] Letter of July 18, 1762, quoted in Leo Damrosch, *Jean-Jacques Rousseau* (New York: Houghton Mifflin, 2005), 358.

on June 19, both *Émile* and the *Social Contract* were burned in Geneva, the first because it was irreligious, the second because it was subversive. Read in Geneva, the *Social Contract* was subversive because it was an attack on the narrow oligarchy that controlled Genevan politics and an assertion of the rights of all citizens. It is a defense of democracy—one of the first ever written (the ancient Greeks may have invented democracy, but they wrote little in support of it)—but of ancient democracy not modern democracy, of direct democracy not representative government. It is important when reading the *Social Contract* to grasp that Rousseau intended it to be read as a commentary on Genevan politics but that when he wrote it he was living—and expected to continue living—in France. Rousseau is therefore cautious in what he says about monarchy (it is easy to see that his views imply a much more profound hostility to French absolutism than he explicitly states) and keen to make it clear that his arguments are irrelevant to the modern nation-state.

After protests against the banning of his work in Geneva proved futile, Rousseau renounced his Genevan citizenship in 1763. The man who liked to sign himself "Citizen of Geneva" was no longer a citizen—indeed, he had only been one as an adult for nine short years, during which period he had spent only a few weeks in Geneva. Now, once again, he was homeless. He was not to publish another major work during his lifetime. Rousseau moved first to a village near Neuchâtel, Switzerland, but a religious mob drove him out and pressure exerted by the Genevan authorities prevented him from settling anywhere else in Switzerland. Eventually he was forced to take refuge in England. David Hume arranged for him to stay on a country estate in Wootton in Staffordshire. Here Rousseau had a paranoid breakdown—he became convinced that Hume was his enemy and was spying on him. Rousseau's fears were not entirely imaginary: Hume was indeed opening his letters and was trying to obtain a pension for him from the King of England (in Rousseau's eyes a pension represented dependency; he always insisted on earning his own living, and late in his life, when his income from publishing had disappeared, he lived by copying music). Rousseau fled England in disguise, moved around anxiously from one hiding place in France to another, living under an assumed name, and then, readopting his own name, he settled once again in Paris in 1770. Evidently, he was once more receiving official protection, probably because he was playing a part in France's complex engagement in Polish politics.[21] In 1778 his health deteriorated (as a result of being run over by a large dog owned by an aristocrat), and he died in Ermenonville, outside Paris.

During his last years he had been writing a series of autobiographical works—*The Confessions*; *Rousseau, Judge of Jean-Jacques* (a text that is an extended expression of his paranoid delusions); and *The Reveries of the Solitary Walker* (published only after his death). When Rousseau died he was famous

---

[21] See Jean Fabre's introduction to the *Considérations sur le gouvernement de Pologne* in Rousseau, *Oeuvres Complètes* 3:ccxvi–ccxliii.

as the author of *Émile* and *Julie*, and, though to a much lesser extent, as the author of the first and second Discourses. The *Social Contract* had caused a stir in Geneva (where Rousseau had followed it up with a volume of *Letters Written from the Mountain* in 1764) but not elsewhere.

How are we to understand Rousseau as a man and as an author? First, Rousseau was, from the moment he walked away from Geneva, a walker.[22] In *The Confessions*, he describes with delight the long walks of his youth, from Geneva to Turin and to Paris. But he also spent hours walking every day (often searching for botanical specimens). It was while walking that he did his thinking (and daydreaming, for he constructed an elaborate imaginary world for himself), and his last, unfinished work was the *The Reveries of the Solitary Walker*. Walking brought Rousseau close to nature, but it also allowed him to escape from society[23] and from the sense of belonging, of rootedness that goes with calling somewhere home. In Rousseau's view, the natural condition of human beings was to be solitary wanderers. Rousseau never owned a house of his own and was horrified when one critic assumed that he must have land of his own somewhere. He never settled anywhere.

So Rousseau was, by choice, an outsider—a condition he embraced when, at the age of fifteen, he turned away from the locked gates of Geneva. He called himself a citizen of Geneva, but he never lived there as an adult citizen. He did almost all his writing in France, where he constantly emphasized that he was not French. The epigraph of the first Discourse is a pair of lines from the Roman poet Ovid: "Here *I* [my emphasis] am the barbarian because they do not understand me." Ovid had been sent into political exile far from Rome (among the Sarmatians). Literally, a barbarian is someone who speaks incomprehensibly (he says "bababa"; the word is intended to be onomatopoeic). Ovid has no doubt that he is civilized and the Sarmatians are barbarians, but he realizes that they see the world rather differently. Rousseau's epigraph announces that what he has to say will seem outlandish to many—either he is seriously wrong or the established values of the day are topsy-turvy. Either way he is an outsider.

But Rousseau was at odds not just with the rest of the world; he was at odds with himself. He placed enormous emphasis on the responsibilities of parents for their children, but he abandoned his own. He admired antique manliness and insisted on the subordination of women (while Voltaire, for example, wrote in favor of female equality), but his dress seemed effeminate, he took to needlework, and his sexual preferences were masochistic. He attacked the theater but wrote plays. He said the French (unlike the Italians) were incapable

---

[22] For insight into Rousseau's psychology, Ian Hacking, *Mad Travelers: Reflections on the Reality of Transient Mental Illness* (Charlottesville: University Press of Virginia, 1998) is helpful.

[23] "I was born with a natural love of solitude," letter to Malesherbes, January 4, 1762. See Tzvetan Todorov, *Frail Happiness: An Essay on Rousseau* (University Park: Pennsylvania State University Press, 2001), 31–53.

of appreciating good music, but he tried to make a living as a composer in Paris. He praised Geneva but never lived there as an adult. He refused pensions from the kings of France and England, but he accepted the patronage of aristocrats (though he always insisted on paying rent). He submitted his books to the censor (in both France and Geneva), but he wrote books that he knew—or ought to have known—would be banned. He advocated a state religion but could not accept the religion of any state. He claimed that human beings are naturally good but that they are entirely responsible for their own corruption. He made a cult of honesty and integrity but presented himself in *The Confessions* as a liar and a thief. Rousseau did not think he was unfortunate to find himself constantly at odds with himself; his fundamental claim was that this has become an inevitable part of the human condition. Rousseau's work is one extended protest against this internal conflict.

Rousseau the outsider who always aspired to belong, Rousseau the man at odds with himself who always aspired to be undivided and at peace—it is these fundamental contradictions that left Rousseau no choice but to think in paradoxes.

POLITICAL PARADOXES

Rousseau's political theory is straightforward once one grasps the basic principles out of which it is constructed. His starting place is the paradox of the first Discourse: progress is a bad thing because it is morally corrupting. Human beings were better when their lives were simpler and less sophisticated. Underlying this argument—barely stated but already present—is a further paradox, the paradox of the second Discourse: inequality is the root of all evil. Progress requires inequality because it requires some people to have the time to concentrate on literature, philosophy, or science. Free time is one of the luxuries that only come into existence with inequality, and all luxuries are corrupting. Wealth brings about moral corruption, and progress intensifies the process.

We live in societies founded on very different values. We believe—or at least most of us believe (though concern about climate change has led some to question these beliefs)—that progress, economic growth, and prosperity go hand in hand and are fine things. We believe that we should all be equal before the law but that inequalities of wealth are essential in a competitive, free market economy—without them, there would be no progress, economic growth, and prosperity. It is natural for us to think that Rousseau is simply wrong.

Rousseau's contemporaries also thought he was wrong, but for them it was a little more complicated than it is for us.[24] They knew that a number

[24] Christopher J. Berry, *The Idea of Luxury: A Conceptual and Historical Investigation* (Cambridge: Cambridge University Press, 1994).

of previous civilizations, particularly ancient Sparta and republican Rome, had been opposed to luxury, which they had associated with despotism and decadence, and that almost all previous societies thought that trade should be controlled and restricted (by guilds, for example). Free trade, unrestrained economic growth, and the acquisition of luxuries by anyone with money to spare had not been defended before Bernard de Mandeville's *Fable of the Bees, or Private Vices, Public Benefits* (1714; translated into French in 1740).[25] Mandeville's claim was that a society of hardworking, prudent, parsimonious people would be poor, primitive, and easily conquered, while a society of spendthrifts, gamblers, drunkards, and pimps would be rich, civilized, and able to afford a powerful army. Rousseau and Mandeville were in fundamental agreement about the nature of contemporary society, but Mandeville approved of it and Rousseau was opposed to it. After Mandeville, in France, there were Jean-François Melon, author of *A Political Essay on Trade* (1734), and Voltaire, who had defended luxury in a poem titled *Le Mondain* (*The Man of the World*, 1736). In attacking luxury Rousseau could appeal to a long tradition of both moral and economic thinking, but he knew that his contemporaries were for the most part sympathetic—if not to Mandeville, who, like Rousseau, relished unpalatable paradoxes, then at least to Melon and Voltaire—and deeply hostile to traditional critiques of luxury, new wealth, and pleasure-seeking behavior.

In Rousseau's view the critique of progress and luxury—the claim that progress and prosperity are bad for you—opens the way to a more radical claim: human beings are born good but are responsible for all the evil in the world. The word "good" here is very slippery: Rousseau thinks human beings are born good simply because they are God's creation, and God made everything as it should be in the best of all possible worlds. But it is obvious that there is evil in the world, and it is clear that Rousseau does not believe in the orthodox Christian explanation for evil, the Fall, and Original Sin. Rousseau has a quite different explanation. According to him, natural men and women are, in a moral sense, neither good nor bad. They are concerned with their own survival; they are capable of feeling pity, but they have no capacity for moral thought or action. Morality begins only with society, with language, with sustained interaction. Rousseau thinks of society and language as resulting from social evolution, assuming that the first human beings (like, or so he thinks, gorillas and orangutans) lacked both. Our own picture of human evolution is distinctly different from Rousseau's conjectural history, but it is worth remembering that every child does begin without language, without a sense of belonging to a community, and without a moral code— language, society, and morality are indeed things that we have constructed for ourselves and that we are socialized into. (I realize that many people

<hr />

[25] On Mandeville, see E. J. Hundert, *The Enlightenment's Fable: Bernard Mandeville and the Discovery of Society* (Cambridge: Cambridge University Press, 1994).

would insist that this is not true of morality. Rousseau, in this respect like every other Enlightenment philosopher, takes it for granted that we have no innate moral sense. Locke was held to have refuted the idea of an innate conscience. Consequently, we have to construct our moral principles on the basis of our experience.)

So in Rousseau's view we are all born amoral. Two things happen when we enter society: we acquire the capacity for vice, and we acquire the capacity for virtue. Rousseau's analysis of vice is clearer and more developed than his analysis of virtue, and this imbalance has caused a good deal of confusion. Vice is born of competition. Primitive men and women, wandering alone through the woods, think only of food, shelter, and sex. When these needs are satisfied, they have no further concerns. But social men and women are constantly comparing themselves to other people: which of us is the most attractive, successful, admired, and envied? All of these questions involve asking, not how I feel about myself but how others think about me. Thus, social people begin to live outside themselves; what matters to them are the thoughts and feelings that others have about them. Because they have only limited access to these thoughts and feelings, they are forced to imagine what they must be. So they live in a largely imaginary world in which they lose touch with their own thoughts and feelings but become emotionally dependent on the thoughts and feelings they believe others are having about them. (One can readily see how someone who thinks this is how we live might end up having a paranoid breakdown, as Rousseau did.)

This competitive, alienated, imaginary world breeds vanity, which is for Rousseau the fundamental vice. His name for it is *amour propre* (self-love), which he distinguishes from *amour de soi* (love of self).[26] *Amour de soi* is a healthy instinct for self-preservation, neither moral nor immoral, but necessary; *amour propre* is a corrupt, competitive desire to seem better than others, to be envied. People suffering from *amour propre* do not merely have a car to get from A to B; they have a larger car than their neighbors', so that other people will see how important they are, or a faster car, so that others will see how vigorous they are, or a "classic" car, so that others will see what good taste they have. They identify themselves with objects (such as cars) and what they take to be the thoughts of others and lose any authentic sense of who they are. Consequently, even if they are successful—even if they are rich and admired—they are losers, dependent on others, incapable of authenticity. Rousseau's account of how we live in society depends on being able to distinguish between a *true* self and a *false* self, a *real* interest and an *imaginary* interest. I have a real interest in not being hungry or thirsty; I

---

[26] For discussions of Rousseau's understanding of *amour propre*, see N. J. H. Dent, "Rousseau on *Amour Propre*," *Proceedings of the Aristotelian Society: Supplementary Volumes* 72 (1998): 57–73; Frederick Neuhouser, *Rousseau's Theodicy of Self-Love* (Oxford: Oxford University Press, 2008); Niko Kolodny, "The Explanation of *Amour Propre*," *Philosophical Review* 119 (2010): 165–200.

have an imaginary interest in acquiring a reputation as a gourmet cook or an expert on fine wines. Caught up in competition we lose touch with our true selves and our real interests.

But something else happens (or can happen) when we enter society: we acquire the capacity to identify with the society as a whole. Suppose I live on a small island—let's call me an Islander. I decide that what would best improve the lives of my fellow Islanders would be a boat we could use for fishing, so I set about building a boat. Very likely, I hope that when I have finished my boat, people will be grateful to me and will admire me; we often compete to be thought more prudent or more virtuous than our neighbors. But in this case, I am not pursuing an imaginary good, but a real one; and I am not pursuing my own benefit, or not primarily my own benefit, but rather that of my community. It certainly helps that my interests and those of my fellow Islanders coincide—I would be unlikely to build a boat if I did not expect to eat some of the fish that would be caught. It certainly helps that I imagine that one day everyone will be grateful to me, but I work long hours because I know I am not just working for myself but for others. In other words, society makes it possible for me to be virtuous, provided I make an emotional commitment to the community that I belong to.

It will be much easier for me to make this commitment if certain preconditions are met. It helps if my community is small enough for me to feel that I know everyone else in it—a community of strangers is a contradiction in terms. It helps if its members have a great deal in common and live similar lives; they will not be able to identify with each other if some are poor and some are rich, if some are powerful and some are weak, if some live by fishing and some live by hunting, or if they are divided by religion. We can summarize these preconditions as *proximity*, *equality*, and *similarity*. Rousseau's ideal community is a small town; the population of Geneva when Rousseau was growing up there was twenty thousand. Large, anonymous, unequal, diverse societies will foster vice, not virtue, because they will encourage competition, not a sense of solidarity. Rousseau thus offers a sociology of virtue. He also presents us with a profoundly uncomfortable conclusion: to achieve what we are truly capable of as human beings, we need to live in a society characterized by proximity, equality, and similarity; if we do not live in such a society then we will always be at odds with ourselves.

It is often said that Rousseau presents two alternative ideals, that of "man" (the individual) and that of citizen (the member of a community).[27] *Émile*, *Julie*, and *The Confessions* explore the idea of the good life as it can be constructed by one or two people within a larger, far from ideal, community. The *Social Contract* explores the idea of the good life as it can be constructed within the political community of a small city-state (what the ancient Greeks

[27] Judith N. Shklar, *Men and Citizens: A Study of Rousseau's Social Theory* (Cambridge: Cambridge University Press, 1969).

called the *polis*; Rousseau repeatedly uses the word *politie*, which an educated person would have recognized as a French equivalent of *polis* but which was not a word to be found in contemporary dictionaries). Now it is perfectly true that Rousseau tries to tackle these two issues: how can I best live here and now (in eighteenth-century France) and how could I best live if I were fortunate enough to be an Islander? But Rousseau is always clear that true self-fulfillment depends on losing yourself in something bigger than yourself. Aristotle said that human beings are by nature political animals, animals designed to live in a *polis*. Rousseau thinks that human beings are by nature solitary wanderers, but once they enter the world of society, they can achieve true fulfillment only within the *polis*. Outside the *polis* the best we can hope for is some sort of mitigated *amour propre;* inside the *polis* we can hope for virtue. Identifying with an *imagined* community (France or the United States) will not do, because it always leaves unanswered a fundamental question: Which is the real France?[28] The north or the south? Paris or the provinces? It is impossible to *be* French; you always have to be some particular sort of French person. It is even impossible to be a Parisian. If you live in Paris you cannot possibly know your fellow Parisians or feel for them (the population of Paris in Rousseau's day was more than half a million); but you can if you live in Paris, Texas (population in the 2000 census, 25,898). Rousseau is a small-town boy trying to make it in the big city while insisting that to succeed you have to betray everything you believe in.

We are now in a position to grasp the central paradox of Rousseau's political theory: that we can find freedom in obedience. Human beings are, Rousseau believes (following Locke), born free; in most political communities they are subjected to a form of dependence that amounts to slavery. We cannot go back to a presocial world, so how can we recover our freedom? This is the crucial puzzle that Rousseau believed he had solved in the *Social Contract*. Rousseau's answer depends on a basic distinction between sovereignty and government—this is very close to the distinction between legislative and executive that would later become important for the U.S. Constitution. Sovereignty expresses itself through laws, and government expresses itself through decisions. The law says murder is a crime; the government prosecutes a particular individual for murder. The law says there shall be a national currency; the government decides that the face of George Washington shall appear on the dollar bill. The law says there shall be an army and a navy; the government appoints generals and admirals. The law gives the government the authority to impose speed limits; the government decides which particular roads will be limited to which particular speeds.

Sovereignty, Rousseau believes, should be exercised by the people (or at least all the adult males) as a whole. Let them gather at a town hall meeting

---

[28] Benedict Anderson, *Imagined Communities: Reflections on the Origin and Spread of Nationalism* (London: Verso, 1983).

and make decisions together. But when they think about what to do they must never ask themselves, "What would be good for me?" but only "What would be good for us?" In other words—Rousseau never puts it like this, but the thought is one he would have agreed with—they must vote as if from behind a veil of ignorance where they have no knowledge of their own particular circumstances and interests.[29] If they do this, their decision will embody what Rousseau calls "the general will." Rousseau tells us that the general will is infallible, that it is always right. This seems very strange to us because we are used to thinking that the majority decisions of assemblies are often wrong. But in other contexts we are quite happy using concepts in which the ideal and the actual are inextricably confused: we believe that all laws must be just, and once a jury has declared someone to be guilty or innocent we think it is nearly always wrong to second guess the jury's decision. Suppose the general assembly votes to ban cigarettes. I have spoken and voted against the ban because I think it will give rise to an illegal trade in cigarettes. But once the decision is made—once the general will is known—I must say to myself, "Now that we have a ban, I must help make sure it works." Far from adopting an oppositional mentality, I must join in and identify with the majority. It is an indication of the novelty of Rousseau's argument that he has to invent a new word, *identification*, to explain his thinking.[30]

Rousseau's argument may be new, but there is nothing psychologically odd about this "joining in" process. We do it all the time. When the coach picks a team we want the team to win, even if we do not agree with all the coach's choices. When a business decides on a future strategy, all the executives work to make it succeed, even if some of them previously advocated a quite different strategy. In the British political system, when the cabinet makes a decision its members are bound by "cabinet responsibility." They must defend, and accept joint responsibility for, a policy that some of them may have been actively opposing only a few hours before. All Rousseau requires of his citizens is that they engage in team thinking of this sort, and this will only be possible if they think of themselves as plain citizens, not as rich or poor, old or young, sailors, soldiers, or candlestick makers. If they vote on the basis of their individual interests, then the vote will simply establish which interest group is biggest; if they vote for what will benefit the community as a whole, then the vote ought to establish the general will. But of course circumstances change and people make mistakes, which is why Rousseau insists that the community cannot be bound by its previous decisions. There can be no fundamental law, no constitution, because every law is a new and complete act of sovereignty. Moreover, since we are all born free, we can only become citizens by an act of choice: we must freely choose to give priority to

[29] John Rawls, *A Theory of Justice* (Cambridge, MA: Belknap Press, 1971).

[30] Pierre Force, *Self-Interest before Adam Smith* (Cambridge: Cambridge University Press, 2003), 24–34.

our membership of a particular community. Then when we obey the general will we are living out our own free choice; even the minority, outvoted when a new law is enacted, obeys its own choice when it obeys the law.

It should now be apparent how human beings can be born free and be everywhere in chains: they are in chains whenever a will is imposed upon them that is at odds with the general will. It should also be apparent that people can be forced to be free. Suppose I decide to become an Islander, and we Islanders find ourselves at war with the Mainland. Then, as an Islander, I should be prepared to die for my community; while as an ordinary human being, of course, I would rather run away than fight. If I am conscripted I am being forced to be free, for no one can be free if we all put our particular interests ahead of our interests as a community. Rousseau is thus particularly concerned to overcome the free rider problem.[31] I want other people to fight for my country, but I don't want to fight (and die) for it myself. I want other people to pay taxes, but I don't want to pay taxes myself. The solution is simple: I must be required to do what I want other people to do. It would be unfair to allow me to avoid paying the price (both in blood and money) for my freedom but to expect everyone else to pay.

It should also now be apparent that there is a fundamental ambiguity in Rousseau's theory of virtue. If I identify with the welfare of society as a whole and am prepared to put my own interests to one side, then I am virtuous. But in a society where everyone identifies with the whole, having a team spirit is precisely what will be rewarded by the approval of others. In extended, unequal societies *amour propre* results in the vice of vanity; in tight-knit, egalitarian societies *amour propre* results in something indistinguishable from virtue. How could one recognize true virtue and distinguish it from benign *amour propre*? Only by finding it in someone who pursued the good of humanity in face of the opposition, rather than the admiration, of his fellow citizens—in Rousseau, for example.[32] But such cases will be rare exceptions that prove the rule that we are shaped by the communities in which we live.

It is striking that it is very difficult to give an account of Rousseau's political theory without employing terminology—for example, "imagined communities," "veils of ignorance," "free riders"—that was completely unknown to him. This terminology reflects late-twentieth-century efforts to come to grips with paradoxical aspects of the relationship between individuals and communities, but Rousseau would be entitled to say that he had already thought these issues through.

---

[31] Mancur Olson, Jr., *The Logic of Collective Action* (Cambridge, MA: Harvard University Press, 1965).

[32] See, for example, Rousseau's self-description in "Préface d'une seconde lettre à Bordes," *Oeuvres Complètes* 3:103–5. But see also how Rousseau attributes even his own love of truth to the hidden working of *amour propre*: letter to Malesherbes, January 12, 1762.

ROUSSEAU'S SOURCES

Rousseau never received a day of formal education in his life. As a child he received his education from his relatives, and as a young man he was self-educated. But it would be a mistake to think that this means he was in any way ill informed. Indeed not only is he exceptionally well informed, but he generally demonstrates excellent judgment; the texts Rousseau refers to when outlining his political theory are nearly all texts still read today (Grotius, Hobbes, Locke, Pufendorf—the great contract theorists—and, of course, Montesquieu). The judgment here is not so much Rousseau's as Jean Barbeyrac's. Barbeyrac (1674–1744) had produced important editions of Hugo Grotius and Samuel Pufendorf, was an admirer of Locke, and had edited and translated an important refutation of Hobbes by Richard Cumberland. Rousseau did not consistently exercise such good judgment; he wrote at length on the political theory of the Abbot of Saint-Pierre, who is now almost entirely forgotten. He did so partly to satisfy Mme Dupin, and writing about Saint-Pierre was an excuse for writing about a much less respectable figure, Hobbes.

Of all political theorists, Hobbes (the Hobbes of *De Cive*, for there is no evidence that Rousseau ever read *Leviathan*) is much the most important for understanding Rousseau, for Rousseau's political theory is fundamentally a reworking of Hobbes'. Rousseau thinks that Hobbes' intellectual system is "horrible," but Hobbes himself is "one of the finest geniuses who ever lived."[33] Hobbes argues that there is no law governing individuals in the state of nature and that they have a right to do anything to protect themselves. Rousseau agrees. Hobbes argues that a political community is constructed by all individuals coming together and agreeing that their own wills will conform to those of the majority. Rousseau agrees. Hobbes expects this initial democracy to choose to be represented by a sovereign other than itself, whereas Rousseau argues that the sovereign can never be represented, although he does expect it to hand over much power to the government. Where Hobbes replaces popular sovereignty with despotism, Rousseau supplements popular sovereignty with an executive that is answerable to the people. Rousseau thus seeks to halt Hobbes' argument at the point where popular sovereignty has been established, and he reads Hobbes as if he were a democratic theorist.

Rousseau's account of the place of religion in politics should also be seen as a reworking of Hobbes'. Hobbes thought that in all modern Christian

---

[33] For Rousseau's words ("horrible" and "one of the finest geniuses . . ."), see *The State of War*, below, p. 256. On Rousseau and Hobbes, see Grace G. Roosevelt, *Reading Rousseau in the Nuclear Age* (Philadelphia: Temple University Press, 1990), 21–42; Zev Trachtenberg, "Subject and Citizen: Hobbes and Rousseau on Sovereignty and the Self," in *Jean-Jacques Rousseau and the Sources of the Self*, ed. Timothy O'Hagan (Aldershot: Avebury, 1997), 85–105; Peter J. Steinberger, "Hobbes, Rousseau and the Modern Conception of the State," *Journal of Politics* 70 (2008): 595–611.

societies political authority and religious authority were at odds and that the church must be made subordinate to the state. Rousseau agreed. Hobbes went further; he advocated a rigorous materialism, while Rousseau wanted to preserve a belief in God's beneficence and the soul's immortality, partly because he held that these beliefs encouraged virtue. And Rousseau, with a typical love of paradox, argued that religious intolerance is never justified— except as a response to intolerance.[34]

Where Hobbes and Rousseau fundamentally disagree is on war. Hobbes thinks that in the state of nature there is a war of all against all; Rousseau argues that human beings' interests start to conflict only when some individuals lay claim to so much property that there is not enough and as good left for others (an argument derived from Locke). The state, which should have been invented to further the interests of all, is (by a cunning sleight of hand) actually employed by property owners to protect their interests and disarm those without property. Thus war does not lead to the construction of the state; rather, the construction of the state leads to conflict between states (the conflict of all against all that Hobbes had read back into the state of nature), and it leads to conflict within the state (the exploitation of the poor by the powerful and the rich). As a consequence we live in an unending state of war. Violence between states, and between rulers and subjects, may break out only occasionally, but the state is always preparing for violence. In Sparta, the ruling elite regularly declared war on its subservient underclass, the helots. Rousseau thinks that an undeclared war of the rich against the poor takes place in every modern society. Carl von Clausewitz was later to say that war is the continuation of politics by other means; Rousseau's idea of a "state of war" implies rather that politics is the continuation of war by other means. Thus Hobbes is right: we need to find a way of escaping from a war in which we are all caught up, but we are only caught up in this war *because* we live in political communities. How, then, to escape? The Abbot of Saint-Pierre had a utopian solution to this problem: the governments of Europe must get together and impose limits on each other (much as the United Nations seeks to use the collective force of all states to discipline some states). Rousseau thought it ridiculous to imagine that despotic governments would give up the quest for ever more power. How then could the small city-states he advocated defend themselves? Only by forming confederations. Rousseau is an early advocate of a federation of independent republics (perhaps the only respect in which he is a significant influence on the American Founding Fathers).

In addition to Mandeville (to whom Rousseau owes his account of the hypocrisy at the heart of commercial society), Hobbes (to whom he owes his account of popular sovereignty and of the state of war), and Locke (to whom

---

[34] Rousseau hesitated over whether to mount a direct attack in the *Social Contract* on the religious intolerance of contemporary France and eventually decided not to. See *Social Contract*, note 156 (below, p. 251).

he owes his account of the proper limits on private property in a state of nature), there is one other political theorist we need to have in mind when reading the *Social Contract:* Diderot. In volume five of the *Encyclopédie* (the volume in which Rousseau's article "Political Economy" appeared), Diderot published an article on *droit naturel* (natural right). There Diderot argued that in principle we have a moral obligation to the whole of humanity to do those things that humanity as a whole would want us to do. Thus, Diderot ultimately grounds our obligations toward other human beings in what he calls the "general will." Diderot's general will seems pretty pointless: it is infallible, but it is hard to know what it says, and if we disobey it nothing happens to us. It is this theory that Rousseau adopts and adapts in the *Social Contract*. Rousseau localizes Diderot's universal general will; in place of the whole of humanity, he substitutes the members of a particular city-state. We can usually discover the general will, he thinks, through a democratic vote of all citizens. If we disobey the general will, we break the law and can be punished—and indeed, we can be forced to be free. Rousseau thus takes the idea of the general will and turns it from a moral concept into a political concept—and claims that this concept solves the problem of how we can belong to a political community while retaining our freedom.[35]

There is of course a further source for Rousseau's political theory: the real constitutions of city-states. Rousseau made a careful study of ancient Greece and ancient Rome, of contemporary Venice (where he worked for eighteen months), and of his own city of Geneva.[36] In Geneva there was a general assembly that embodied the community as a whole, but it had lost the power to meet unless it was summoned, and its agenda was controlled by the oligarchy. In Rousseau's eyes Geneva was a degenerate city-state, and if power could be wrested from the oligarchy and returned to the general assembly it might become once more a true republic. His own interventions in Genevan politics, particularly after the banning of the *Social Contract* and *Émile*, were designed to bring about this transformation.

THE FRENCH REVOLUTION

In the years immediately before the French Revolution everyone was reading Rousseau (particularly the newly published *Confessions*), but no one was reading the *Social Contract*. In 1910 Daniel Mornet surveyed the catalogues of five hundred French private libraries for the years 1750–1780. He found 185 copies of *Julie* and one solitary copy of the *Social Contract*. A hundred years of further

---

[35] Patrick Riley, "Rousseau's General Will," in *The Cambridge Companion to Rousseau*, ed. Riley (Cambridge: Cambridge University Press, 2001), 124–53; Roosevelt, *Reading Rousseau*, 69–89.

[36] Sparta had a particular influence on Rousseau. See Elizabeth Rawson, *The Spartan Tradition in European Thought* (Oxford: Clarendon Press, 1969), 231–41.

research has done nothing to alter the picture Mornet drew.[37] So if Rousseau was a cause of the French Revolution, it was not through his political theory; it was through his fundamental claim that human beings are naturally good and that consequently there is no excuse for injustice—a claim readers would have encountered in *Julie* and *Émile* rather than in the *Social Contract*.

Almost overnight, the French Revolution changed everything. Between 1789 and 1799 there were thirty-two editions of the *Social Contract* in French—eight in 1792 alone.[38] When people were looking for a philosopher who advocated political revolution, they turned at once to Rousseau—partly because he was widely believed to have been the inspiration behind a democratic uprising that had taken place in Geneva in 1782.[39] One man above all constantly called on Rousseau as the guiding spirit of the revolution: the leader of the Jacobins, Maximilien Robespierre. He found in Rousseau much that served his purposes—a belief in the goodness of human nature, a love of virtue, a hatred of inequality, and the outline of a civil religion.

The question of Rousseau's significance for the French Revolution is so central to any understanding of the revolution that it cannot be answered without committing oneself to a theory of what the revolution was really all about. Much recent literature has taken Rousseau as the emblem of a new type of language, a language that constantly rejected moderation and treated the revolution as if it were a series of speeches. On this view, Rousseau shaped the rhetoric of revolutionary extremism. An older literature argued that the revolution stumbled from crisis to crisis, and Rousseau became the philosopher of the revolution as it became, almost accidentally, driven to more and more radical expedients.[40] Neither approach seems to me to capture the central feature of the role of Rousseau's books in the revolution.

On May 31, 1793, an armed insurrection of the *sans-culottes* brought Robespierre and his allies to power. Their power base was the Jacobin Club, which sought to control the National Assembly by claiming to speak for the people, to be an organ of direct democracy; its power depended on its ability to take control of the streets of Paris. This power lasted less than a year, for Robespierre himself was taking power away from the Jacobins and the *sans-culottes* before his own fall. He was executed on July 28, 1794. This brief year was the heyday of Rousseauism during the revolution, and the reason for this is very simple: Rousseau had rejected the principle of representation in favor of the principle of direct democracy, and he had accepted the logic of this position by turning back in his mind to the city-states of the ancient world. Fundamentally, the French Revolution was not French: the revolution took place in Paris, and Paris claimed the right to determine the fate of France. The

---

[37] Miller, *Rousseau: Dreamer of Democracy*, 134; Darnton, *Forbidden Best-Sellers*, xvii–xviii, 67.

[38] Miller, *Rousseau: Dreamer of Democracy*, 143.

[39] Miller, *Rousseau: Dreamer of Democracy*, 140–42.

[40] Darnton, "Diffusion vs. Discourse," in *Forbidden Best-Sellers*, 169–80.

sans-culottes and the Jacobins claimed to speak for Paris and for France and thereby claimed the right to control the National Assembly of representatives. They backed up their claim with armed force. Rousseau was the only theorist who could be made to speak for a revolution that took place in the streets and squares of a single city. What mattered about Rousseau, then, was that he was a theorist of *civic* politics, of urban politics, not national politics.

Here the contrast with the American Revolution is crystal clear. The American Revolution stretched across thirteen colonies; no one city had a dominant position, which is why the government eventually had to be located in a brand new city, Washington, D.C. From its beginning the American Revolution was rooted, inevitably, in the principle of representation. Radicals like Paine wanted democratic, unicameral representative assemblies with unlimited powers; the Founding Fathers wanted the separation of powers, bicameralism, and an entrenched constitution. But nobody questioned the underlying principle of representation; and nobody in America took Rousseau's *Social Contract* seriously.

So the place of Rousseau in the French Revolution comes down to the relationship between Paris and the Provinces:[41] Rousseau, as an advocate of direct democracy, provided a spurious justification for the idea that the course of the revolution should be decided on the streets of the capital city. I say a spurious justification because if Robespierre exploited one key feature of Rousseau's political philosophy, he also misrepresented him utterly. Rousseau had made clear that the people—all the people—must choose. The revolution substituted Paris for the nation, the *sans-culottes* for Paris, the Jacobin Club for the National Assembly, the Committee of Safety for the executive, terror for justice. Rousseau had never intended to justify substitutions of this sort, substitutions that made possible the concentration of absolute power in the hands of a few, and the sacrifice of the lives of vast numbers of innocent individuals to a revolutionary government claiming to act on behalf of a people whose wishes it had no intention of respecting. Rousseau had done his utmost to insist both on the rights of *all*, not of some faction or mob, and on the rights of *each*—the right of each individual to a fair trial according to the law.

In short, Rousseau would have been horrified by the revolution and he would have loathed Robespierre. He saw civil conflict in Geneva in 1737; he called it a "hideous spectacle." He saw a father and son preparing to fight on opposite sides. He resolved, he would later say, "never to take part in any civil war, and never to uphold freedom by arms."[42] When conflict broke out again in Geneva in 1765, in large part provoked by Rousseau's own publications, Rousseau hastily detached himself from the radical cause and called for restraint. Rousseau provided ammunition for revolutionaries, but he had no stomach for revolution. This does not, of course, absolve him of all

---

[41] Richard Cobb, *Paris and Its Provinces, 1792–1802* (Oxford: Oxford University Press, 1975).

[42] Miller, *Rousseau: Dreamer of Democracy*, 20, 126.

responsibility. Above all, by consistently giving priority to the community over the individual, the general will over the wishes of individuals, Rousseau invited misinterpretation and misrepresentation. But we can hardly blame him for failing to foresee an event without parallel in previous history.

Shortly after the fall of Robespierre, a report to the National Convention recommending that Rousseau's remains be transferred to the Panthéon captured well the complex and ambiguous relationship between Rousseau's political theory and the revolution:

> The Social Contract seems to have been made to be read in the presence of the human species assembled in order to learn what it has been and what it has lost. . . . But the great maxims developed in The Social Contract, as evident and simple as they seem to us today, then [on first publication] produced little effect; people did not understand them enough to profit from them, or to fear them, they were too much beyond the reach of common minds, even of those who were or were believed to be superior to the vulgar mind; in a way, it is the Revolution that has explained to us The Social Contract.[43]

Of course we can go on reading the Social Contract as the handbook for political revolution, but when we do so we are not reading the book that Rousseau intended to write; we are reading Robespierre's Social Contract, not Rousseau's.

ROUSSEAU'S FRENCH

What is a good translation? One view is that the text should read so well that one can almost forget that one is reading a translation: Rousseau should be turned into a writer of twenty-first–century English. Another view is that, as far as possible, the language and sentence structure of the original should be retained: we should be constantly reminded that we are reading a text written in a different language in a different era. Translations of classic texts are of necessity always something of a compromise between these two approaches.

No translation, however brilliant, can give us information that is essential for the understanding of any classic text. In the first place, a good translation will often avoid what seems to be the obvious equivalent English word for reasons that at first seem puzzling. For example, industrieux does not mean "industrious" in eighteenth-century French; it means "skillful," as "industrious" did in Shakespeare's English. It only comes to mean "industrious" in nineteenth-century French. It would therefore be simply misleading to translate industrieux as "industrious." Sometimes words in French are

---

[43] Quoted in Miller, Rousseau: Dreamer of Democracy, 163.

ambiguous, so that their English equivalent is unclear. Thus, eighteenth-century French has no word for "parental," so *paternel* sometimes means gender-specific "paternal" and sometimes gender-neutral "parental" (just as the masculine pronoun sometimes refers only to males and sometimes to any human being).

Where translations inevitably fall short is in failing to alert us when words are new (Rousseau's words "identification" and "perfectibility," for example) or being used in a new sense (Rousseau gives new meanings to the words "city," "sovereign," and "government"),[44] and they give us no sense of which words are simply missing from the language (Rousseau complains at one point that he might appear to contradict himself, but this is only because he lacks the right words to convey his meaning).[45] In Russian, for example, there are no definite or indefinite articles (no words for "the" or "a"), yet every translation from Russian inevitably conveys the impression that there are, and obscures the choices the translator has had to make. Every reader of Rousseau needs to know that "social" was an unfamiliar word when he used it in the title of the *Social Contract*.[46] Three years later Diderot wrote the article "Social" for the *Encyclopédie*, which begins, "SOCIAL, adj. (Gramm.) a word recently introduced into the language." We talk about social contract theories, but we do so only because Rousseau put the word "social" in the title of his book; neither Hobbes nor Locke writes of a "social contract." Rousseau was in the forefront of a movement to isolate what he called (in words that seem straightforward to us) the "social system."[47]

We have already seen another example of Rousseau's innovative use of language: Rousseau uses the word *politie*, and the obvious translation is "polity," but no translation is going to tell you that the word is unusual in the French of Rousseau's day, so unusual that Rousseau wrote to his publisher warning him not to let the copyeditors correct it to *politique*.[48] He needs the word because he has no word for a city-state; he makes do with the word *cité* (city), which he redefines as a community of citizens rather than an urban conglomeration. This example brings us to the very heart of Rousseau's political theory. *Politie* and *cité* are nouns. For Rousseau the equivalent adjective is *civil*, as in *société civile* and *religion civile*. The standard English translations are "civil society" and "civil religion." These are terms commonly used in English, and so these are the translations one should prefer. But *société civile* is the French translation of the Latin *societas civilis*, and the standard English translation

---

[44] On "city," Rousseau was presumably following Diderot's article for the *Encyclopédie*, vol. 3 (1753).

[45] See *Social Contract*, note 41 (below, p. 174).

[46] John Lough, "The *Encyclopédie* and the *Contrat social*," in *Reappraisals of Rousseau*, ed. Simon Harvey et al. (Manchester, UK: Manchester University Press, 1980), 64–74.

[47] *Social Contract*, Book I, Chapter 9 (below, p. 169). Letter to Malesherbes, January 12, 1762.

[48] Letter to Rey, December 23, 1761.

for this in modern English would be "civic society." In eighteenth-century French there is no word for "civic," and *civil* conveys a range of meanings from "urban" to "civilized." When Rousseau writes of *société civile*, we have to decide whether he means urban society, civilized society, or (its root meaning) a society characterized by having citizens (a self-governing society, a civic society). Certainly he never defines "civil society" as being something different from the political community, as we would. So too when he writes of *religion civile* we have to remember that *civil* for Rousseau refers back to the city-states of ancient Greece and Italy; the civil religion is, in the first place, the religion of a *polis*. We say the United States has a civil society and a civil religion. Rousseau would have found this usage puzzling, as the United States is not a *polis*. In his view there can be no "civil society," and perhaps no "civil religion," in a nation-state.

How we understand *politie* and *civil* is thus central to how we understand Rousseau's political theory. Central to his moral theory is another problematic term: *amour propre*—commonly translated as "vanity," but vanity is always a vice, and as we have seen, *amour propre* can sometimes be virtuous. "Vanity" is a good translation if it reminds us that *amour propre* had standardly been a vice in writers prior to Rousseau, a bad translation if it makes us think it is always a vice in Rousseau's own writing and thus obscures the way in which his argument differs from that of his predecessors. Another key term is *moeurs*, which means "customs" or "habits" and, more broadly, everything that a modern anthropologist might include within the term "culture."[49] *Moeurs* has an English equivalent in "mores," but it also bears on our understanding of Rousseau's words *moral* (adjective) and *morale* (noun). It is easy to regard these as straightforwardly equivalent to "moral" and "morality," but in the French of Rousseau's day *moral* and *morale* refer to *moeurs* in general as well as to morality in particular. The words "culture" and "civilization" do not yet exist in the French of Rousseau's day; Rousseau's equivalent terms are *moeurs* and *morale*.

So when Rousseau answers the question posed by the Academy of Dijon, "Si le rétablissement des sciences et des arts a contribué à épurer les *moeurs*" (Whether the restoration of the sciences and the arts contributed to the purification of mores), *moeurs* can mean "morals," "culture," or both. Equally problematic are the apparently simple words "sciences" and "arts." In the French of Rousseau's day a *science* is any system of knowledge (including philosophy, even theology), and an *art* is any skilled activity, including metallurgy and shipbuilding as well as poetry and painting. Broadly speaking, Rousseau's *sciences* are theoretical, and his *arts* are practical, and between them they include knowledge in all its many forms. As for "restoration," the implicit reference is to the restoration (or rebirth) of knowledge that we call the

[49] "I argue that Rousseau invented anthropology," says Darnton, "Two Paths through the Social History of Ideas," 273.

Renaissance. Since the Renaissance is above all about the restoration of classical learning, Rousseau's answer is doubly paradoxical. He argues that progress is bad for us and that the recovery of classical learning in particular may make us apparently civilized, but it prevents us from being citizens. We have civility but we do not have civic virtue; we have culture but we do not have morality; we have politics but we do not have citizenship. Rousseau's whole argument depends on distinctions that we would express by contrasting "civil" and "civic," "culture" and "morality," and "politics" and "citizenship."

Is it possible to sum up in a sentence or two the difference between the language available to Rousseau for discussing politics and society and our language? It is. The rise of the social sciences has meant that our language provides a whole range of ways of distinguishing empirical from normative arguments. Rousseau's vocabulary—terms like "moral" and "civil"—encourages a constant slippage back and forth between the two. Even "social," which we normally use to provide descriptions of how things *are* rather than how they *should be*, is defined by Diderot in a way that elides the normative and the descriptive: "a word recently introduced into the language to designate the qualities which make a man useful in society, well-equipped to engage with other men: the *social* virtues."[50] David Hume had defined what we call "the fact-value distinction" or "the is-ought problem" in his *Treatise of Human Nature* (1739), but this book, as Hume put it in "My Own Life," "fell dead-born from the press."[51] Rousseau would never have encountered "the fact-value distinction."

Rousseau does not distinguish, as we would, between normative and empirical arguments, not because he is writing in French but because he is writing in the eighteenth century. He would have had equal difficulty making the distinction in eighteenth-century English, and when Hume did make the distinction it was scarcely noticed (or understood) by his contemporaries. However, by attacking the conventional values of his age, by exposing what he called "the contradictions of the social system,"[52] by using "nature" as a normative concept to criticize society, Rousseau made it peculiarly difficult for everyone else to carry on taking their own value system for granted. If a whole range of distinctions—between morality and culture, principle and practice, values and facts—have come to seem obvious distinctions to us, that is a measure of the extent to which Rousseau's way of thinking provoked an intellectual crisis, a crisis that has profoundly shaped our modern culture.

---

[50] Quoted in Lough, "The *Encyclopédie* and the *Contrat social*," 70.

[51] Hume, *Essays*, ed. Miller, xxxi–xli, at xxxiv.

[52] Letter to Malesherbes, January 12, 1762.

Suggestions for Further Reading

The classic edition of Rousseau's political writings is Jean-Jacques Rousseau, *The Political Writings*, ed. C. E. Vaughan (Cambridge: Cambridge University Press, 1915)—now out of copyright and so available on the Internet. The standard modern edition is volume 3 of the Pléiade edition of Rousseau's *Oeuvres Complètes* (Paris: Gallimard, 1964). For "The State of War" it is necessary to consult the appendix that appears in the 1975 reprint of that work (pp. 1891–1904) and Grace G. Roosevelt, *Reading Rousseau in the Nuclear Age* (Philadelphia: Temple University Press, 1990).

The major sources for Rousseau's biography are the letters to Malesherbes of 1762 (which have been repeatedly translated into English) and the posthumous *Confessions*. An excellent modern biography is Leo Damrosch, *Jean-Jacques Rousseau: Restless Genius* (Boston: Houghton Mifflin, 2005). The classic study of Rousseau is Jean Starobinski, *Jean-Jacques Rousseau: Transparency and Obstruction* (1957; English translation, Chicago: University of Chicago Press, 1988). A valuable introduction is provided by Patrick Riley, ed., *The Cambridge Companion to Rousseau* (Cambridge: Cambridge University Press, 2001), and a brief survey is found in Tzvetan Todorov, *Frail Happiness: An Essay on Rousseau* (University Park: Pennsylvania State University Press, 2001).

The two classic texts on Rousseau's political theory are Ernst Cassirer, *The Question of Jean-Jacques Rousseau* (1932; English translation, New York: Columbia University Press, 1954) and Judith N. Shklar, *Men and Citizens: A Study of Rousseau's Social Theory* (Cambridge: Cambridge University Press, 1969). Admirable are James Miller, *Rousseau: Dreamer of Democracy* (New Haven: Yale University Press, 1984) and Arthur M. Melzer, *The Natural Goodness of Man: On the System of Rousseau's Thought* (Chicago: Chicago University Press, 1990). For a recent account of Rousseau's political thought by an English-language political philosopher, there is Joshua Cohen, *Rousseau: A Free Community of Equals* (Oxford: Oxford University Press, 2010). On gender and politics, see Joel Schwartz, *The Sexual Politics of Jean-Jacques Rousseau* (Chicago: University of Chicago Press, 1984) and Lynda Lange, ed., *Feminist Interpretations of Jean-Jacques Rousseau* (University Park: Pennsylvania State University Press, 2002). Good starting points for thinking about two of Rousseau's key concepts are Patrick Riley, "Rousseau's General Will," in *The Cambridge Companion to Rousseau*, ed. Riley (which should be supplemented by a reading of Diderot's essay "Droit naturel," translated in Diderot, *Political Writings*, ed. John Hope Mason and Robert Wokler [Cambridge: Cambridge University Press, 1992]) and N. J. H. Dent, "Rousseau on *Amour Propre*," *Proceedings of the Aristotelian Society: Supplementary Volumes* 72 (1998): 57–73.

Chronology

1749   Rousseau conceives the argument of the first Discourse (*Discourse on the Sciences and the Arts*) on the road to Vincennes

1750   The first Discourse wins the Academy of Dijon's prize and appears in print

1751   First volume of Diderot and d'Alembert's *Encyclopédie* is published

1754   Rousseau visits Geneva and converts back to Protestantism

1755   Publication of the second Discourse, *Discourse on the Origin and Foundations of Inequality among Men*, and of the third, *Discourse on Political Economy*

1756   Rousseau and Levasseur move to The Hermitage

1757   Rousseau breaks with Diderot and other leading *philosophes*

1758   Rousseau moves to Montmorency; publishes *Letter to d'Alembert on the Theater*, completing his break with the leading figures of the French Enlightenment; Helvétius publishes *De l'esprit*, which is promptly condemned

1759   Rousseau becomes friends with the Duke and Duchess of Luxembourg; Voltaire publishes *Candide;* the *Encyclopédie* is officially suppressed

1761   Rousseau publishes *Julie, or the New Héloïse*

1762   Rousseau publishes the *Social Contract* and *Émile;* both are condemned in Paris and Geneva; he flees France and settles near Neuchâtel, Switzerland

1763   Rousseau renounces his Genevan citizenship

1764   Rousseau publishes an attack on the Genevan authorities, *Letters Written from the Mountain;* Voltaire reveals the secret of Rousseau's abandoned children

1765   Rousseau is driven from Neuchâtel and finds temporary refuge on the Île de Saint-Pierre; last volume of Diderot and d'Alembert's *Encyclopédie* is published

1766   Rousseau moves to England (to Wootton in Staffordshire) and begins writing *The Confessions*

1767   Rousseau flees to France, living here and there under an assumed name, protected by the Prince of Conti

1768   Rousseau goes through a form of marriage (which is not legally valid) with Levasseur

1770   Rousseau resumes his real name and moves to Paris

1771   Rousseau gives readings from *The Confessions* but is ordered by the authorities to stop

1772   Rousseau begins work on *Rousseau, Judge of Jean-Jacques*

1776   Rousseau begins work on *The Reveries of the Solitary Walker;* is knocked over in the street by a huge dog and never fully recovers

1778   Rousseau moves to Ermenonville, outside Paris, where he dies July 2

1780   *Rousseau, Judge of Jean-Jacques* is published

1782   First half of *The Confessions* is published; democratic uprising in Geneva

1789   Second half of *The Confessions* is published; the French Revolution begins

1793   Execution of King Louis XVI (January 21)

1794   Execution of Robespierre, followed by the transfer of Rousseau's remains to the Panthéon in Paris

1801   Death of Thérèse Levasseur

Discourse on the Sciences and the Arts

Rousseau read the advertisement announcing the competition established by the Academy of Dijon in October 1749 while on his way to visit Diderot in prison in Vincennes, outside Paris. Immediately the whole of his Discourse flashed through his mind, and he quickly wrote down a key section, the speech of Fabricius. This moment of revelation transformed his life. By March 1750, the Discourse was finished, in July it was awarded the prize, by December it was in print. Rousseau felt obliged to publish the text he had submitted, although he had been working on revisions (he added only two brief passages). At once everyone was talking about it. Rousseau had acquired an unshakeable reputation as an author addicted to paradox. Rousseau spent much of 1751 and 1752 writing replies to his many critics (seventy-five reviews and critiques were published within three years). Naturally he was well aware from the beginning of the contradiction in being an educated person (albeit self-educated) attacking education, a modern author arguing that the world would be better off without books, a man of letters praising action and condemning words, and a resident of France praising liberty and equality. His epigraph from Ovid predicts the whole of his future.

D.W.

DISCOURSE
THAT WON THE PRIZE
ON THE ACADEMY OF DIJON[1]
IN THE YEAR 1750

On this Question Proposed by that Academy:

Whether the Restoration of the Sciences and the Arts
Contributed to the Purification of Mores[2]

BY A CITIZEN OF GENEVA

"Here I am the barbarian because they do not understand me."
—Ovid[3]

---

[1] [The Academy of Dijon was founded by Hector-Bernard Pouffier, dean of the Parliament of Bourgogne. In the October 1749 issue of *Mercure de France*, the academy announced the topic of its 1750 essay competition: whether the restoration of the sciences and the arts contributed to the purification of mores. The prize consisted of a gold medallion.]

[2] [Throughout this translation, *moeurs* is rendered as "mores." No one word can capture the range of meanings of *moeurs*, which can include "morals" and "culture" (see Introduction, p. xxxiii, at "Another key term is *moeurs*"), but the consistent rendering here has the added advantage of drawing the reader's attention to the original French word behind the translation.]

[3] [*Tristia*, bk. 5, 10:37. Rousseau quotes the Latin: "Barbarus hic ego sum quia non intelligor illis."]

FOREWORD[4]

What is celebrity? Here is the unhappy work to which I owe mine. Certainly this piece, which earned me a prize and made a name for me, is at best mediocre, and I dare to add that it is one of the least of this collection.[5] What an abyss of miseries the author would have avoided, had his first work been received as it deserved to be! But it was inevitable that a favor, unjust from the beginning, visited upon me by degrees a stiff penalty that is even more unjust.

DISCOURSE ON THE SCIENCES AND THE ARTS[6]

PREFACE

Here is one of the great and finest questions ever debated. This discourse is not concerned with those metaphysical subtleties that have found their way into every branch of learning and from which academy-sponsored competitions are not always exempt. Rather, it is concerned with one of those truths that are bound up with the happiness of mankind.

I foresee that I will not easily be forgiven for the side I have dared to choose. Running head-on into everything that men admire today, I can expect only universal blame; and the fact of having been honored by the approval of a few wise men does not lead me to count on the approval of the public. Thus I have taken my stand. I do not care about pleasing either the witty or the fashionable. There will always be men destined to be subjugated by the opinions of their century, their country, their society. A man who plays the freethinker and the philosopher today would, for the same reason, have merely been a fanatic at the time of the League.[7] One should not write for such readers when one wants to live beyond one's century.

One more word and I have finished. Counting little on the honor that I have received, I had, since sending it, recast and enlarged this discourse to the point of, in a sense, making another work of it. Today I believe I am obliged to restore it to the state in which it was awarded the prize. I have merely inserted some notes and allowed two easily recognized additions to remain,

---

[4] [This foreword did not appear in print until 1781.]

[5] [The reference is to an edition of Rousseau's collected works that the author himself was preparing for publication.]

[6] [The terms *sciences* and *arts* are translated throughout as "sciences" and "arts," but the French *science* includes almost all forms of knowledge, and the French *art* refers to specialized skills as well as what we call "the arts."]

[7] [Founded in 1576 by Henry, third Duke of Guise, the Holy League was an organization of Catholics dedicated to the suppression of French Protestantism.]

of which the Academy might perhaps not have approved. I thought that fair-mindedness, respect, and gratitude demanded this notice from me.

DISCOURSE

"We are deceived by the appearance of right."[8]

Has the restoration of the sciences and the arts contributed to the purification of mores or to their corruption? That is what is to be examined. Which side should I take in this question? The one, gentlemen, that is appropriate to an honest man who knows nothing and who thinks no less of himself for it.

It will be difficult, I feel, to adapt what I have to say to the tribunal before which I appear. How can I dare to blame the sciences before one of Europe's most learned societies, praise ignorance in a famous academy, and reconcile contempt for study with respect for the truly learned? I have seen these points of conflict, and they have not daunted me. I am not abusing science, I told myself; I am defending virtue before virtuous men. Integrity is dearer to good men than erudition is to the studious. What then have I to fear? The enlightenment of the assembly that listens to me? I admit it; but this is owing to the composition of the discourse and not to the sentiment of the speaker. Fair-minded sovereigns have never hesitated to pass judgments against themselves in disputes whose outcomes are uncertain; and the position most advantageous for a just cause is to have to defend oneself against an upright and enlightened opponent who is judge in his own case.

To this motive that heartens me is joined another that determines me, namely that, having upheld, according to my natural light, the side of truth, whatever my success, there is a prize that I cannot fail to receive; I will find it within the depths of my heart.

PART ONE

It is a grand and beautiful sight to see man emerge somehow from nothing by his own efforts; dissipate, by the light of his reason, the shadows in which nature had enveloped him; rise above himself; soar by means of his mind into the heavenly regions; traverse, like the sun, the vast expanse of the universe with giant steps; and, what is even grander and more difficult, return to himself in order to study man and know his nature, his duties, and his end. All of these marvels have been revived in the past few generations.

Europe had relapsed into the barbarism of the first ages. A few centuries ago the peoples of that part of the world, who today live such enlightened

---

[8] [Horace, *On the Art of Poetry*, line 25. Rousseau here quotes the Latin.]

lives, lived in a state worse than ignorance. An incomprehensible scientific jargon, even more contemptible than ignorance, had usurped the name of knowledge and posed a nearly invincible obstacle to its return. A revolution was needed to bring men back to common sense; it finally came from the least expected quarter. It was the stupefied Moslem, the eternal scourge of letters, who caused them to be reborn among us. The fall of the throne of Constantinople[9] brought into Italy the debris of ancient Greece. France in turn was enriched by these precious spoils. Soon the sciences followed letters. To the art of writing was joined the art of thinking—a sequence of events that may seem strange, but which perhaps is only too natural. And the chief advantage of commerce with the Muses began to be felt, namely, that of making men more sociable by inspiring in them the desire to please one another with works worthy of their mutual approval.

The mind has its needs, as does the body. The needs of the latter are the foundations of society; the needs of the former make it pleasant. While the government and the laws see to the safety and well-being of assembled men, the sciences, letters, and the arts, less despotic and perhaps more powerful, spread garlands of flowers over the iron chains with which they are burdened, stifle in them the sense of that original liberty for which they seem to have been born, make them love their slavery, and turn them into what are called civilized peoples.[10] Need raised up thrones; the sciences and the arts have strengthened them. Earthly powers, love talents and protect those who cultivate them![11] Civilized peoples, cultivate them! Happy slaves, you owe them that delicate and refined taste on which you pride yourselves, that sweetness of character and that urbanity in mores that make relationships among you so cordial and easy, in a word, the appearances of all the virtues without having any.

By this sort of civility, all the more agreeable as it puts on fewer airs, Athens and Rome once distinguished themselves in the much vaunted days of their magnificence and splendor. By it our century and our nation will doubtlessly surpass all times and all peoples. A philosophic tone without pedantry,

---

[9] [Constantinople (present-day Istanbul) was the former capital of the Byzantine Empire. It was captured by Sultan Mohammed II and the Turks in 1453.]

[10] [This sentence may be one of the two passages added by Rousseau after his Discourse was awarded the prize. See the headnote.]

[11] Princes always view with pleasure the spread, among their subjects, of the taste for pleasant arts and luxuries as long as they do not result in the exporting of money. For, in addition to nurturing in them that pettiness of soul so appropriate to servitude, they know very well that all the needs the populace imposes on itself are so many chains that burden it. Alexander, wishing to keep the Ichthyophagi in a state of dependency, forced them to renounce fishing and eat foods common to other peoples. And the savages of America, who go totally naked and who live off the product of their hunting, have never been tamed. Indeed, what yoke could be imposed upon men who need nothing?

manners natural yet engaging, equally removed from Teutonic rusticity as from Italian pantomime, these are the fruits of the taste acquired by good schooling and perfected in social interaction.

How sweet it would be to live among us, if outer appearances were always the likeness of the heart's dispositions, if decency were virtue, if our maxims served as our rules, if true philosophy were inseparable from the title of philosopher! But so many qualities are all too rarely found in combination, and virtue seldom goes forth in such great pomp. Expensive finery can betoken a wealthy man, and elegance a man of taste. The healthy and robust man is recognized by other signs. It is in the rustic clothing of the fieldworker and not underneath the gilding of the courtier that one will find bodily strength and vigor. Finery is no less alien to virtue, which is the strength and vigor of the soul. The good man is an athlete who enjoys competing in the nude.[12] He is contemptuous of all those vile ornaments that would impair the use of his strength, most of which were invented merely to conceal some deformity.

Before art had fashioned our manners and taught our passions to speak an affected language, our mores were rustic but natural, and differences in behavior heralded, at first glance, differences of character. At base, human nature was no better, but men found their safety in the ease with which they saw through each other, and that advantage, which we no longer value, spared them many vices.

Today, when more subtle inquiries and a more refined taste have reduced the art of pleasing to established rules, a vile and deceitful uniformity reigns in our mores, and all minds seem to have been cast in the same mold. Without ceasing, politeness makes demands, propriety gives orders; without ceasing, common customs are followed, never one's own lights. One no longer dares to seem what one really is; and in this perpetual constraint, the men who make up this herd we call society will, if placed in the same circumstances, do all the same things unless stronger motives deter them. Thus no one will ever really know those with whom he is dealing. Hence in order to know one's friend, it would be necessary to wait for critical occasions, that is, to wait until it is too late, since it is for these very occasions that it would have been essential to know him.

What a retinue of vices must attend this incertitude! No more sincere friendships, no more real esteem, no more well-founded confidence. Suspicions, offenses, fears, coldness, reserve, hatred, betrayal will unceasingly hide under that uniform and deceitful veil of politeness, under that much vaunted urbanity that we owe to the enlightenment of our century. The name of the master of the universe will no longer be profaned with oaths; rather it will be insulted with blasphemies without our scrupulous ears being offended by them. No one will boast of his own merit, but will disparage that of others. No one will crudely wrong his enemy, but will skillfully slander him. National

[12] [In ancient Greece athletes competed in the nude.]

hatreds will die out, but so will love of country. Scorned ignorance will be replaced by a dangerous Pyrrhonism. Some excesses will be forbidden, some vices held in dishonor, but others will be adorned with the name of virtues. One must either have them or affect them. Let those who wish extol the sobriety of the wise men of the present. For my part, I see in it merely a refinement of intemperance as unworthy of my praise as their artful simplicity.[13]

Such is the purity that our mores have acquired. Thus have we become decent men. It is for letters, the sciences, and the arts to claim their part in so wholesome an achievement. I will add but one thought: an inhabitant of some distant lands who sought to form an idea of European mores on the basis of the state of the sciences among us, the perfection of our arts, the seemliness of our theatrical performances, the civilized quality of our manners, the affability of our speech, our perpetual displays of goodwill, and that tumultuous competition of men of every age and circumstance who, from morning to night, seem intent on being obliging to one another—that foreigner, I say, would guess our mores to be exactly the opposite of what they are.

Where there is no effect, there is no cause to seek out. But here the effect is certain, the depravation real, and our souls have become corrupted in proportion as our sciences and our arts have advanced toward perfection. Will it be said that this is a misfortune peculiar to our age? No, gentlemen, the evils caused by our vain curiosity are as old as the world. The daily rise and fall of the ocean's waters have not been more unvaryingly subjected to the celestial body that provides us with light during the night than has the fate of mores and integrity been to the progress of the sciences and the arts. Virtue has been seen taking flight in proportion as their light rose on our horizon, and the same phenomenon has been observed in all times and in all places.

Consider Egypt, that first school of the universe, that climate so fertile beneath a brazen sky, that famous country from which Sesostris[14] departed long ago to conquer the world. She became the mother of philosophy and the fine arts and soon thereafter was conquered by Cambyses,[15] then by Greeks, Romans, Arabs, and finally Turks.

Consider Greece, formerly populated by heroes who twice conquered Asia, once at Troy and once on their own home ground. Nascent letters had not yet brought corruption into the hearts of her inhabitants; but the progress of the arts, the dissolution of mores, and the Macedonian's yoke followed

---

[13] "I love," says Montaigne, "to debate and discuss, but only with a few men and for my own sake. For I find it an especially unworthy profession for a man of honor to serve as a spectacle to the great and shamelessly parade one's mind and one's prattling." It is the profession of all our wits, save one. [This citation is from Montaigne's "On the Art of Discussion," *Essays*, bk. 3, ch. 8. The exception is presumably Diderot, who took charge of the publication of the Discourse.]

[14] [A fairly common name among Egyptian pharaohs. The Sesostris in question here seems to be legendary.]

[15] [Cambyses, king of Persia, conquered Egypt in 525 BC.]

closely upon one another; and Greece, ever learned, ever voluptuous, and ever the slave, experienced nothing in her revolutions but changes of masters. All the eloquence of Demosthenes could never revive a body that luxury and the arts had enervated.

It is at the time of the likes of Ennius and Terence[16] that Rome, founded by a shepherd and made famous by fieldworkers, began to degenerate. But after the likes of Ovid, Catullus, Martial,[17] and that crowd of obscene writers whose names alone offend modesty, Rome, formerly the temple of virtue, became the theater of crime, the disgrace of nations, and the plaything of barbarians. Finally, that capital of the world falls under the yoke that she had imposed on so many peoples, and the day of her fall was the eve of the day when one of her citizens was given the title of Arbiter of Good Taste.[18] What shall I say about that capital of the Eastern Empire, which, by virtue of its location, seemed destined to be the capital of the entire world, that refuge of the sciences and the arts banished from the rest of Europe—more perhaps out of wisdom than barbarism. All that is most shameful about debauchery and corruption; blackest in betrayals, assassinations, and poisons; most atrocious in the coexistence of every sort of crime, that is what constitutes the fabric of the history of Constantinople, that is the pure source whence radiates to us the enlightenment on which our century prides itself.

But why seek in remote times proofs of a truth for which we have existing evidence before our eyes? In Asia there is an immense country where acknowledgment in the field of letters leads to the highest offices of the state. If the sciences purified mores, if they taught men to shed their blood for their country, if they enlivened their courage, the peoples of China should be wise, free, and invincible. But if there is not a single vice that does not have mastery over them, not a single crime that is unfamiliar to them; if neither the enlightenment of the ministers, nor the alleged wisdom of the laws, nor the multitude of the inhabitants of that vast empire have been able to shield her from the yoke of the ignorant and coarse Tartar, what purpose have all her learned men served? What benefit has been derived from the honors bestowed upon them? Could it be to be peopled by slaves and wicked men?

[16] [Quintus Ennius (239–c. 170 BC) was an early Latin poet revered as the father of Roman poetry. Publius Terentius Afer (c. 190–c. 159 BC) was a famous Roman playwright.]

[17] [Publius Ovidius Naso (43 BC–AD 18) was a Roman writer, among whose works were *Metamorphoses* and *Ars Amatoria* (see also note 3). Gaius Valerius Catullus (c. 84–c. 54 BC) is generally considered one of the greatest of the lyric poets of ancient Rome. Marcus Valerius Martialis (c. AD 40–c. 104) was a Roman satirist and epigrammatist. All three writers are perhaps best known for their graphically erotic poetry.]

[18] [Tacitus, in his *Annals*, bk. 16, ch. 18, states that this title was given to Petronius (d. AD 66), a satirist and courtier to the emperor Nero. An indolent and profligate lover of comfort and luxury, Petronius enjoyed a reputation as a man of elegant and refined taste. In recognition of these traits, Petronius was made the "Arbiter of Good Taste," responsible for orchestrating the emperor's entertainment.]

Contrast these scenes with that of the mores of the small number of peoples who, protected against this contagion of vain knowledge, have by their virtues brought about their own happiness and the model for other nations. Such were the first Persians, a singular nation in which virtue was learned just as science is among us, that subjugated Asia so easily, and that alone has enjoyed the distinction of having the history of its institutions taken for a philosophical novel.[19] Such were the Scythians, about whom we have been left such magnificent praises. Such were the Germans, whose simplicity, innocence, and virtues a pen—weary of tracing the crimes and atrocities of an educated, opulent, and voluptuous people—found relief in depicting.[20] Such had been Rome herself in the times of her poverty and ignorance. Such, finally, has that rustic nation shown herself to this day—so vaunted for her courage, which adversity could not overthrow, and for her faithfulness, which example could not corrupt.[21]

It is not out of stupidity that these people have preferred other forms of exercise to those of the mind. They were not unaware of the fact that in other lands idle men spent their lives debating about the sovereign good, about vice and about virtue, and that arrogant reasoners, bestowing on themselves the highest praises, grouped other peoples under the contemptuous name of barbarians. However, they considered their mores and learned to disdain their teaching.[22]

Could I forget that it was in the very bosom of Greece that there was seen to arise that city as famous for her happy ignorance as for the wisdom of her laws, that republic of demigods rather than men, so superior to humanity did their virtues seem? O Sparta! Eternal shame to a vain doctrine! While the vices, led by the fine arts, intruded themselves together into Athens, while

---

[19] [An apparent reference to Xenophon's (430–354 BC) *Education of Cyrus*.]

[20] [A reference to Tacitus' *Germania*.]

[21] I dare not speak of those happy nations that do not know even by name the vices that we have so much trouble repressing, those savages in America whose simple and natural polity Montaigne unhesitatingly prefers not only to Plato's *Laws* but even to everything philosophy could ever imagine as the most perfect for the government of peoples. He cites a number of examples that are striking for someone who would know how to admire them. "What!" he says, "why they don't wear pants!" [This citation is from Montaigne's "Of Cannibals," *Essays*, bk. 1, ch. 31. The "rustic nation" refers to the Swiss.]

[22] Will someone honestly tell me what opinion the Athenians themselves must have held regarding eloquence, when they were so fastidious about banning it from that upright tribunal whose judgments the gods themselves did not appeal? What did the Romans think of medicine, when they banished it from their republic? And when a remnant of humanity led the Spanish to forbid their lawyers to enter America, what idea must they have had of jurisprudence? Could it not be said that they believed that by this single act they had made reparation for all the evils they had brought upon those unfortunate Indians?

a tyrant there gathered so carefully the works of the prince of poets,[23] you drove out from your walls the arts and artists, the sciences and scientists.

The event confirmed this difference. Athens became the abode of civility and good taste, the country of orators and philosophy. The elegance of her buildings paralleled that of the language. Marble and canvas, animated by the hands of the most capable masters, were to be seen everywhere. From Athens came those astonishing works that will serve as models in every corrupt age. The picture of Lacedaemon is less brilliant. "There," said the other peoples, "men are born virtuous, and the very air of the country seems to inspire virtue." Nothing of her inhabitants is left to us except the memory of their heroic actions. Are such monuments worth less to us than the curious marbles that Athens has left us?

Some wise men, it is true, had resisted the general torrent and protected themselves from vice in the abode of the Muses. But listen to the judgment that the first and unhappiest of them made of the learned men and artists of his time. "I have," he says, "examined the poets, and I view them as people whose talent makes an impression on them and on others who claim to be wise, who are taken to be such, and who are nothing of the sort.

"From poets," continues Socrates, "I moved on to artists.[24] No one knew less about the arts than I; no one was more convinced that artists possessed some especially fine secrets. Still, I perceived that their condition is no better than that of the poets and that they are both laboring under the same prejudice. Because the most skillful among them excel in their specialty, they view themselves as the wisest of men. To my way of thinking, this presumption has completely tarnished their knowledge. From this it follows that, as I put myself in the place of the oracle and ask myself whether I would prefer to be what I am or what they are, to know what they have learned or to know that I know nothing, I answered myself and God: I want to remain what I am.

"We do not know—neither the sophists, nor the poets, nor the orators, nor the artists, nor I—what is the true, the good, and the beautiful. But there is this difference between us: that although these people know nothing, they all believe they know something. I, however, if I know nothing, at least am not in doubt about it. Thus all that superiority in wisdom accorded me by the oracle reduces to being convinced that I am ignorant of what I do not know."[25]

Here then is the wisest of men in the judgment of the gods and the most learned of Athenians in the opinion of all Greece, Socrates, speaking in praise of ignorance! Does anyone believe that, were he to be reborn among us, our

---

[23] [Pisistratus (c. 605–527 BC) was said to have directed the collection, transcription, and organization of the works of Homer.]

[24] [Rousseau uses the words *artistes* and *arts*, translated here for consistency as "artists" and "arts," though modern translations of Plato have "artisans" and "crafts."]

[25] [Rousseau is paraphrasing Plato's *Apology*, 22a–23b.]

learned men and our artists would make him change his mind? No, gentlemen, this just man would continue to hold our vain sciences in contempt. He would not aid in the enlargement of that mass of books that inundate us from every quarter; and the only precept he would leave is the one left to his disciples and to our descendants: the example and the memory of his virtue. Thus is it noble to teach men!

Socrates had begun in Athens, Cato[26] the Elder continued in Rome to rail against those artful and subtle Greeks who seduced the virtue and enervated the courage of his fellow citizens. But the sciences, the arts, and dialectic prevailed once again. Rome was filled with philosophers and orators; military discipline was neglected, agriculture scorned, sects embraced, and the homeland forgotten. The sacred names of liberty, disinterestedness, obedience to the laws were replaced by the names of Epicurus, Zeno, Arcesilaus.[27] "Ever since learned men have begun to appear in our midst," their own philosophers said, "good men have vanished." Until then the Romans had been content to practice virtue; all was lost when they began to study it.

O Fabricius![28] What would your great soul have thought if, had it been your misfortune to be returned to life, you had seen the pompous countenance of that Rome saved by your arm and honored more by your good name than by all her conquests? "Gods!" you would have said, "what has become of those thatched roofs and those rustic hearths where moderation and virtue once dwelt? What fatal splendor has followed upon Roman simplicity? What is this strange speech? What are these effeminate mores? What is the meaning of these statues, these paintings, these buildings? Fools, what have you done? You, the masters of nations, have you made yourselves the slaves of the frivolous men you conquered? Do rhetoricians govern you? Was it to enrich architects, painters, sculptors, and actors that you soaked Greece and Asia with your blood? Are the spoils of Carthage the prey of a flute player?[29] Romans make haste to tear down these amphitheaters, shatter these marbles, burn these paintings, drive out these slaves who subjugate you and whose fatal arts corrupt you. Let others achieve notoriety by vain talents; the only talent worthy of Rome is that of conquering the world and making virtue reign in

---

[26] [Marcus Porcius Cato (Cato the Elder, 234–149 BC) was a Roman general and statesman renowned for his devotion to the old Roman ideals of simplicity, honesty, courage, loyalty, and steadfastness.]

[27] [Epicurus (c. 341–270 BC) was the founder of the Epicurean school of philosophy. Zeno of Citium (c. 336–264 BC) was the founder of the Stoic school of philosophy. Arcesilaus (c. 316–241 BC) was a figure in the Middle Academy who played a pivotal role in the transmission and development of philosophical skepticism.]

[28] [Gaius Fabricius Luscinus (d. 250 BC) was a Roman general and statesman renowned for his uncomplicated integrity and dignity.]

[29] [The flute player is the emperor Nero.]

it. When Cineas[30] took our Senate for an assembly of kings, he was dazzled neither by vain pomp nor by studied elegance. There he did not hear that frivolous eloquence, the focus of study and delight of futile men. What then did Cineas see that was so majestic? O citizens! He saw a sight that neither your riches nor all your arts could ever display, the most beautiful sight ever to have appeared under the heavens: the assembly of two hundred virtuous men worthy of commanding in Rome and of governing the earth."

But let us leap over the distance of place and time and see what has happened in our countries and before our eyes; or rather, let us set aside odious pictures that offend our delicate sensibilities and spare ourselves the trouble of repeating the same things under different names. It was not in vain that I summoned the shade of Fabricius; and what did I make that great man say that I could not have placed in the mouth of Louis XII or Henry IV? Among us, it is true. Socrates would not have drunk the hemlock; but he would have drunk from a cup more bitter still: the insulting ridicule and scorn that are a hundred times worse than death. That is how luxury, dissolution, and slavery have at all times been the punishment for the arrogant efforts that we have made to leave the happy ignorance where eternal wisdom had placed us. The heavy veil with which she had covered all her operations seemed to give us sufficient warning that she had not destined us for vain inquiries. But is there even one of her lessons from which we have learned to profit or that we have neglected with impunity? Peoples, know then once and for all that nature wanted to protect you from science just as a mother wrests a dangerous weapon from the hands of her child, that all the secrets she hides from you are so many evils from which she is protecting you, and that the difficulty you find in teaching yourselves is not the least of her kindnesses. Men are perverse; they would be even worse if they had had the misfortune of being born learned.

How humiliating are these reflections for humanity! How mortified our pride must be! What! Could probity be the daughter of ignorance? Science and virtue incompatible? What consequences might not be drawn from these prejudices? But to reconcile these apparent points of conflict, one need merely examine at close range the vanity and the emptiness of those proud titles that overpower us and that we so gratuitously bestow upon human knowledge. Let us then consider the sciences and the arts in themselves; let us see what must result from their progress; and let us no longer hesitate to be in agreement on all the points where our reasoning will be found to be in accord with historical inductions.

---

[30] [Cineas, a Thessalian, was an ambassador of King Pyrrhus. Reputed to be possessed of good sense, he was also the student of Demosthenes who most reminded people of his teacher.]

PART TWO

It was an ancient tradition, passed from Egypt to Greece, that a god who was antagonistic toward the tranquility of men was the inventor of the sciences.[31] What opinion then must have been held about them by the Egyptians themselves, among whom the sciences were born? They saw at close quarters the sources that had produced them. Indeed, whether one leafs through the annals of the world or supplements uncertain chronicles with philosophical inquiries, one will not find an origin for human knowledge corresponding to the idea that one wants to form of it. Astronomy was born of superstition, eloquence of ambition, hatred, flattery, lying; geometry of avarice; physics of vain curiosity; all of them, even moral philosophy, of human pride. Thus the sciences and the arts owe their birth to our vices; we would be less in doubt about their advantages if they owed it to our virtues.

The defect of their origin is only too clearly called to mind for us in their objects. What would we do with the arts without the luxury that feeds them? What purposes would jurisprudence serve without the injustices of men? What would history become if there were no tyrants, no wars, no conspirators? In a word, who would want to spend his life in fruitless speculations if each person, consulting only the duties of man and the needs of nature, had time for nothing but the homeland, the unfortunate, and his friends? Are we destined then to die fastened to the edge of the well where truth has retreated?[32] This reflection alone should block from the start any man who would seriously seek to teach himself through the study of philosophy.

What dangers! What false pathways in the investigation of the sciences! How many errors, a thousand times more dangerous than the truth is useful, must be endured in order to reach it? The disadvantage is apparent, for falsity is susceptible to an infinity of combinations; but truth has but one mode of being. Besides, who seeks it sincerely? Even with the best will, by what marks is one sure of recognizing it? In this crowd of different opinions, what will be our criterion for judging it properly.[33] And, what is most difficult,

---

[31] The allegory of the fable of Prometheus is easy to recognize; and it does not appear that the Greeks who nailed him to the Caucasus thought any more favorably of him than the Egyptians did of their god Theuth. "The satyr," says an ancient fable, "wanted to kiss and embrace fire the first time he saw it. But Prometheus cried out to him, 'Satyr, you will mourn the loss of the beard on your chin, for it burns when touched.'" It is the subject of the frontispiece.

[32] [The suggestion that truth is as unobtainable as it would be if it had been thrown into a well originates with Democritus (c. 460–c. 370 BC).]

[33] The less one knows, the more one believes one knows. Did the Peripatetics doubt anything? Did Descartes not construct the universe with cubes and vortices? And is there in Europe even today a physicist, however humble, who does not boldly explain the profound mystery of electricity, which will perhaps forever be the despair of true

if perchance we finally find it, who among us will know how to make good use of it?

If our sciences are vain in the objects they have in view, they are even more dangerous in the effects they produce. Born in idleness, they nourish it in turn; and the irreparable loss of time is the first injury they necessarily cause society. In politics, as in moral philosophy, it is a great evil not to do good, and every useless citizen may be viewed as a pernicious man. Answer me, then, illustrious philosophers, you thanks to whom we know the ratios in which bodies attract one another in a vacuum; the relationships of areas covered in equal periods of time in the revolutions of the planets; what curves have conjugate points, which have points of inflection, and which have cusps; how man sees everything in God; how the soul and the body are in harmony with one another, like two clocks, without communicating; what heavenly bodies can be inhabited; what insects reproduce in some extraordinary manner?[34] Answer me, I say, you from whom we have received so much sublime knowledge; if you had never taught us any of these things, would we therefore have been any less numerous, less well governed, less formidable, less flourishing or more perverse? Reconsider, then, the importance of your productions; and if the labors of the most enlightened of our learned men and our best citizens obtain for us so little that is useful, tell us what we should think about that crowd of obscure writers and idle men of letters who to no purpose devour the substance of the state.

What did I say? Idle? Would to God they really were! Mores would then be healthier and society would be more peaceful. But these vain and futile declaimers go off in every direction, armed with their deadly paradoxes, undermining the foundations of faith and annihilating virtue. They smile contemptuously at such old-fashioned words as *homeland* and *religion* and dedicate their talents and their philosophy to destroying and degrading all that is sacred among men. Not that at bottom they hate either virtue or our dogmas; they are enemies of public opinion, and to bring them back to the feet of the altars it would be enough to consign them among the atheists. O fury to gain distinction, of what are you not capable?

The misuse of time is a great evil. Other evils that are even worse follow after letters and the arts. Luxury, born like them of idleness and men's vanity, is one such. Luxury seldom thrives without the sciences and the arts, and they never thrive without it. I know that our philosophy, ever fecund with singular maxims, claims, contrary to the experience of all centuries,

---

philosophers? [Peripatetics were followers of the philosophy of Aristotle. René Descartes (1596–1650), French mathematician and philosopher, is often cited as "the father of modern philosophy." He is the author of the *Discourse on Method*, *Meditations on First Philosophy*, and *Principles of Philosophy*.]

[34] [In the eighteenth century, "philosophy" included natural philosophy, or what we call "science." The philosophers Rousseau refers to here include Newton, Kepler, Malebranche, Leibniz, Fontenelle, and Réaumur.]

that luxury causes the splendor of states.[35] But after having forgotten the need for sumptuary laws, will it still dare deny that good mores are essential to the continuance of empires and that luxury is diametrically opposed to good mores? Granted luxury is a sure sign of wealth; it even serves, if you will, to increase wealth. What conclusion must we draw from this paradox so worthy of being born in our times; and what will become of virtue when one must become wealthy at any cost? Ancient politicians spoke incessantly about mores and virtue; ours speak only of commerce and money. One will tell you that in a given country a man is worth the price he would sell for in Algiers; another, following this calculation, will find some countries where a man is worth nothing and others where he is worth less than nothing. They value men the way they would herds of cattle. According to them, a man is worth no more to the state than what he consumes. Thus one Sybarite would have been worth at least thirty Lacedaemonians. So guess which of these two republics, Sparta and Sybaris,[36] was subjugated by a handful of peasants and which caused Asia to tremble.

The monarchy of Cyrus[37] was conquered with thirty thousand men by a prince who was poorer than the humblest of Persian satraps; and the Scythians, the most miserable of all peoples, resisted the most powerful monarchs in the universe. Two famous republics competed for world domination. One was very rich and the other had nothing, and it was the latter that destroyed the former. The Roman Empire, in turn, after having swallowed up all the wealth of the universe, fell prey to men who did not even know what wealth was. The Franks conquered the Gauls, the Saxons conquered England—with no other treasures than their bravery and their poverty. A band of poor mountaineers, all of whose greed was limited to a few sheepskins, after having tamed Austrian arrogance, crushed that opulent and formidable house of Burgundy that caused the potentates of Europe to tremble. Finally, all the power and wisdom of Charles V's heir, supported by all the treasures of the Indies, were beaten by a handful of herring fishers.[38] Let our politicians deign to suspend their calculations in order to reflect on these examples, and let them learn for once that with money one has everything but mores and citizens.

---

[35] [The most important contemporary text in defense of luxury was Voltaire's *Le Mondain* (1736). Rousseau refers later to Mandeville's *Fable of the Bees* (1714), which he may have already read when writing the first Discourse.]

[36] [Sybaris was a city in Magna Graecia (now southern Italy), founded in 770 BC. It was a wealthy city whose citizens were reputed to have pursued lives of pleasure and luxury—"sybaritic" pastimes. The city was destroyed in 510 BC. *Lacedaemonians* is another word for Spartans. Sparta, which emphasized military discipline and frugality, repeatedly defeated the Persians during the Greco-Persian wars (499–449 BC).]

[37] [Cyrus the Great (d. 529 BC), king of Persia and founder of the Achaemenian dynasty and the Persian Empire. The military defeat mentioned here did not involve Cyrus himself but one of his successors.]

[38] [By the Dutch in their war for independence from Spain, 1568–1648.]

Precisely what, then, is at issue in this question of luxury? To know whether it is more important for empires to be brilliant and fleeting or virtuous and long lasting. I say brilliant, but by what luster? The taste for ostentation is hardly ever combined in the same souls with the taste for honesty. No, it is not possible for minds degraded by a multitude of futile needs ever to rise to anything great; and even if they had the strength, they would lack the courage.

Every artist wants to be applauded. The praises of his contemporaries are the most precious part of his reward. What then will he do to obtain praise if he has the misfortune to be born among a people and at a time when learned men, having become fashionable, have placed a frivolous youth in a position to set the tone; when men have sacrificed their taste to the tyrants of their liberty;[39] when, because one of the sexes dares approve only what is a match for the other's pusillanimity, masterpieces of dramatic poetry are dropped and harmonic prodigies rejected? What will he do, gentlemen? He will lower his genius to the level of his century and will prefer to compose popular works that are admired during his lifetime instead of marvels that would not be admired until long after his death. Tell us, famed Arouet,[40] how many manly and strong beauties you have sacrificed to our false delicacy, and how many great things has the spirit of gallantry, so fertile in small things, cost you?

In this way the dissolution of mores, a necessary consequence of luxury, leads in turn to the corruption of taste. If perchance there is, among men of extraordinary talents, someone who has firmness of soul and who refuses to yield to the genius of his century and to degrade himself by childish productions, woe to him! He will die in poverty and oblivion. Would that I were making a prediction and not reporting an experience! Carle, Pierre;[41] the moment has come when that brush destined to enhance the majesty of our temples with sublime and saintly images will either fall from your hands or

[39] I am very far from thinking that this ascendancy of women is itself an evil. It is a gift bestowed on them by nature for the happiness of mankind. Better directed, it could produce as much good as today it does harm. We are not sufficiently aware of the advantages that would come to pass in society if a better education were given to that half of mankind that governs the other. Men will always be what is pleasing to women. Thus if you want men to become great and virtuous, teach women what greatness of soul and virtue are. The reflections afforded by this subject and made long ago by Plato richly deserve a better development by a pen worthy of writing in the tradition of such a teacher and of defending so great a cause.

[40] [François Marie Arouet de Voltaire (1694–1778), better known simply as Voltaire, was a French poet, dramatist, essayist, historian, philosopher, and scientist, and the dominant figure in French literary culture of the day. Since he had invented for himself the title "de Voltaire" in 1718, it was a hostile gesture on Rousseau's part to demote him once again to the ranks of commoners.]

[41] [Charles-André (Carle) Vanloo (1705–1765) and Jean-Baptiste-Marie Pierre (1713–1789) enjoyed international reputations as painters.]

be prostituted to embellish carriage panels with lascivious pictures. And you, rival of the likes of Praxiteles and Phidias,[42] you whose chisel the ancients would have employed to make them gods capable of excusing their idolatry in our eyes; inimitable Pigalle,[43] either your hand will be determined to rough out the belly of a grotesque or it will have to remain idle.

One cannot reflect on mores without taking delight in recalling the image of the simplicity of the earliest times. It is a beautiful shore, adorned by the hands of nature alone, toward which one continually turns one's eyes and from which one regretfully feels oneself moving away. When innocent and virtuous men wanted to have the gods as witnesses of their actions, they lived together in the same huts. But having soon become wicked, they wearied of these inconvenient spectators and banished them to magnificent temples. Finally, they chased them from the temples in order to take up residence in them themselves, or at least the temples of the gods were no longer distinguishable from the homes of the citizens. That period was the height of depravity, and vices were never given freer rein than when they were, so to speak, seen standing on columns of marble and carved on Corinthian capitals at the entrance to the palaces of the great.

While the conveniences of life increase, the arts are perfected and luxury spreads, true courage is enervated, military virtues disappear, and this too is the work of the sciences and of all those arts that are practiced in the darkness of the study. When the Goths ravaged Greece, all of the libraries were saved from fire only because of the opinion, spread by one of them, that the enemy should be left the furnishings so well suited to distracting them from military exercise and to amusing them with idle and sedentary occupations. Charles VIII found himself master of Tuscany and the kingdom of Naples practically without having drawn his sword, and his entire court attributed this unexpected ease to the fact that the princes and the nobility of Italy had a good time becoming ingenious and learned more than they exerted themselves trying to become vigorous and warlike. In fact, says the sensible man who reports these two cases,[44] all examples teach us that in this martial polity and in all those that resemble it, the study of the sciences is much more apt to soften and enervate courage than to strengthen and enliven it.

The Romans admitted that military virtue died out among them in so far as they had begun to become connoisseurs of paintings, engravings, goldsmiths' vessels, and to cultivate the fine arts. And, as if that famous country were destined to serve unceasingly as an example to other peoples, the rise of the Medici and the revival of letters brought down once again and perhaps forever

---

[42] [Praxiteles (fl. c. 370–300 BC) and Phidias (c. 500–c. 432 BC) are among the most famous of ancient Greek sculptors.]

[43] [Jean-Baptiste Pigalle (1714–1785) was a French sculptor who achieved fame through a life of hardship and sacrifice.]

[44] [Montaigne, *Essays*, bk. 1, ch. 24.]

that warlike reputation that Italy seemed to have recovered a few centuries ago. The ancient republics of Greece, with that wisdom that radiated through most of their institutions, had forbidden their citizens to engage in all those tranquil and sedentary professions that, by weighing down and corrupting the body, soon enervate the vigor of the soul. Indeed, with what eye does one think that men who are crushed by the smallest need and stopped cold by the least pain could face hunger, thirst, periods of fatigue, dangers, and death? With what courage will soldiers stand up under excessive labors to which they are unaccustomed? With what fervor will they go on forced marches under officers who lack even the strength to travel on horseback? Let no one raise as an objection against me the renowned valor of all those modern warriors who are so scientifically disciplined. People brag to me of their bravery on a day of battle, but they do not tell me how they handle overwork, how they withstand the harshness of the seasons and the inclemency of the weather. All that is needed is a bit of sunshine or snow, a lack of a few superfluities, to melt and destroy the best of our armies in a few days. Intrepid warriors, suffer for once the truth you so rarely hear: you are brave. I know: you would have triumphed with Hannibal at Cannae and at Trasimene; with you Caesar would have crossed the Rubicon and enslaved his country; but it was not with you that the former would have crossed the Alps, and the latter would have vanquished your ancestors.

Battles do not always make for success in war, and for generals there is an art superior to that of winning battles. A man who runs intrepidly into the line of fire is still a very bad officer. Even in a soldier, a little more strength and vigor would perhaps be more necessary than that sort of bravery, which does not protect him from death; and what difference does it make to the state whether its troops die from fever and cold or by the enemy's sword?

If the cultivation of the sciences is harmful to warlike qualities, it is even more so to moral qualities. From our earliest years a foolish education adorns our mind and corrupts our judgment. Everywhere I see immense establishments where youths are brought up at great expense to learn everything but their duties. Your children will not know their own language but will speak others that are nowhere in use.[45] They will know how to compose verses they will scarcely be capable of comprehending. Without knowing how to separate error from truth, they will possess the art of making them unrecognizable to others by means of specious arguments. But they will not know the meaning of the words magnanimity, fair-mindedness, temperance, humanity, courage. That sweet name *homeland* will never strike their ear; and if they hear God spoken of at all, it will be less to be in awe of him than to be in fear of him.[46] I would just as soon, said a wise man, my pupil had passed time on the tennis court; at least his body would have been more fit because of it. I

---

[45] [Latin and Greek.]

[46] *Pens. Philosoph.* [The reference is to Diderot, *Pensées philosophiques*, no. 8.]

know that children need to be kept occupied and that, for them, idleness is the greatest danger to fear. What then should they learn? That is certainly a fine question! Let them learn what they ought to do when they are men[47] and not what they ought to forget.

Our gardens are decorated with statues and our galleries with pictures. What would you think these masterpieces of art, exhibited for public admiration, represent? The defenders of the homeland? Or those even greater men who have enriched it with their virtues? No. They are images of all the aberrations of the heart and reason, carefully drawn from ancient mythology and presented at an early age to the curiosity of our children, doubtless so that they may have models of bad actions before their eyes even before they know how to read.

Where do all these abuses come from, if not from the fatal inequality introduced among men by the distinction of talents and the degradation of virtues?[48] That is the most evident effect of all our studies and the most dangerous of all their consequences. One no longer asks whether a man has

[47] Such was the education of the Spartans according to the greatest of their kings. It is, says Montaigne [*Essays*, bk. 1, ch. 24], well worth considering that in that excellent administration of Lycurgus (in truth monstrously perfect), which was preoccupied with the diet of children, as if this were its chief responsibility, and although it was in the very home of the Muses [i.e., Mount Helicon], so little mention was made of the content of their education, as if those great-souled youths, disdaining every other yoke, required only the teachers of valor, prudence, and justice, instead of our teachers of science.

Let us now see how the same author speaks of the ancient Persians. Plato, he says, relates that the eldest son of their royal line was brought up as follows. After his birth he was given over not to women but to eunuchs who, because of their virtue, had the greatest influence with the king. They took charge of making his body fair and healthy, and after seven years they taught him to ride and hunt. When he turned fourteen, they placed him in the hands of four people: the most wise, the most just, the most temperate, the most valiant in the nation. The first taught him religion; the second always to be truthful; the third to conquer his appetites; the fourth to fear nothing. All, I would add, to make him good, none to make him learned.

Astyages, in Xenophon, asks Cyrus for an account of his last lesson. It was, he says, that in our school a large boy who had a small tunic gave it to one of his companions who was smaller and took from him his tunic, which was larger. When our tutor made me the judge of this dispute, I judged that things should be allowed to stand as they were, and that they both seemed to be better taken care of in this matter. Whereupon he chastised me for having done wrong, for I had stopped to consider seemliness, and one ought first to have taken justice into account, which requires that no one be subjected to force in matters pertaining to what belongs to him. And he said that he was punished, just as we are punished in our villages for having forgotten the first aorist of τύπτω ["I beat"]. My schoolmaster would have to give me a fine harangue *in genere demonstrativo*, before he persuaded me that his school is as good as that one.

[48] [This sentence may be the second passage added by Rousseau to his original text.]

integrity, but whether he has talents; not whether a book is useful, but whether it is well written. Rewards are showered upon the wit, and virtue is left without honors. There are a thousand prizes for fine discourses, none for fine actions. Meanwhile, would someone tell me whether the glory attached to the best of discourses that will be crowned in this academy is comparable to the merit of having established the prize?

The wise man does not chase after fortune, but he is not insensitive to glory; and he sees it so ill distributed that his virtue, which a little emulation would have enlivened and made advantageous to society, languishes and dies out in misery and oblivion. This is what, in the long run, the preference for congenial talents over useful ones must everywhere produce, and what experience since the revival of the sciences and the arts has only too well confirmed. We have physicists, geometers, chemists, astronomers, poets, musicians, painters; we no longer have citizens. Or if there still are some left to us, dispersed in our abandoned countryside, they perish there indigent and despised. Such is the state to which those who give us bread and our children milk are reduced; such are the values they get from us.

Nevertheless, I confess that the evil is not as great as it could have become. By placing health-restoring herbs next to various harmful plants, and by placing the remedy for their bites in the flesh of various injurious animals, eternal foresight has taught sovereigns, who are its ministers, to imitate its wisdom. By following this example, that great monarch, whose glory will only acquire a new luster from one age to another, drew from the very bosom of the sciences and the arts sources of a thousand disorders, those famed societies which are charged simultaneously with the dangerous trust of human knowledge and the sacred trust of mores, by the attention they pay to maintaining them in all their purity, and to requiring it in the members they admit.[49]

These wise institutions, strengthened by his august successor and imitated by all the kings of Europe, will at least serve as a restraint on men of letters, who, since they all aspire to the honor of being admitted to the academies, will keep watch over themselves and try to make themselves worthy by means of useful works and irreproachable mores. Those among these organizations that will select, for the prize competitions honoring literary merit, subjects suitable for reviving the love of virtue in the hearts of citizens will show that such love reigns among them and will give the people that very rare and sweet pleasure of seeing learned societies devote themselves to spreading throughout mankind not only congenial enlightenment but also salutary teachings.

Do not therefore raise an objection against me that for me is merely a new proof. So many precautions show all too well the necessity for taking them, and no one seeks remedies for nonexistent evils. Why is it inevitable that these, by their inadequacy, should prove to be just like ordinary remedies?

---

[49] [A reference to the various academies, including the Academy of Sciences, founded by Louis XIV.]

So many establishments brought into being for the benefit of the learned are, after all, all the more capable of causing deception in regard to the objects of the sciences and of turning minds toward their cultivation. To judge from the precautions that have been taken, it would seem that there are too many field hands and that a shortage of philosophers is feared. I have no desire to venture here a comparison between agriculture and philosophy; it would not be tolerated. I will ask merely, what is philosophy? What do the writings of the best-known philosophers contain? What are the lessons of these friends of wisdom? To listen to them, would one not take them for a troop of charlatans, each crying from his own place on a public square, "Come to me; I alone do not deceive?" One claims there are no bodies and that everything is appearance; another that there is no substance but matter, nor any God but the world. This one proposes that there are neither virtues nor vices and that moral good and evil are chimeras; that one that men are wolves and can devour one another with a clear conscience.[50] O great philosophers! Why do you not save these useful lessons for your friends and for your children? You would soon reap the reward for them, and we would have no fear of finding one of your followers among our own.

These then are the wonderful men on whom the esteem of their contemporaries was squandered during their lifetimes and who alone were judged worthy of immortality after their deaths! These are the wise maxims that we have received from them and that we will transmit to our descendants from generation to generation. Paganism was given over to all the aberrations of human reason, but has it left to posterity anything comparable to the shameful monuments prepared for it by the printing press under the reign of the Gospel? The impious writings of the likes of Leucippus and Diagoras[51] perished with them. The art of immortalizing the extravagances of the human mind had not yet been invented. But thanks to typography[52] and the use we

---

[50] [Rousseau is referring to Berkeley, Spinoza, Mandeville, and Hobbes.]

[51] [Leucippus (fl. fifth century BC) was an ancient Greek philosopher reputed by Aristotle to have been the inspiration for the atomistic theory associated with Democritus. Diagoras of Melos (fl. fifth century BC) was a Greek poet and philosopher. When Spartan forces overran Melos, he fled to Athens, where he gained a reputation for his outspoken skepticism and atheism. He was an ardent follower of the atomistic philosophy of Democritus.]

[52] Considering the frightful disorders that the printing press has already caused in Europe, and judging the future by the progress that the evil makes from one day to the next, it is easy to foresee that sovereigns will not delay in taking as many pains to banish this terrible art from their states as they took to establish it in them. The Sultan Achmed, yielding to the importunities of some alleged men of taste, had consented to establish a printing press in Constantinople. But the press had hardly begun operations when it had to be destroyed and the equipment thrown into a well. It is said that the Caliph Omar, when asked what ought to be done with the library of Alexandria, answered in these terms: "If the books in this library contain things opposed to the Koran, they are bad and should be burned. If they contain

make of it, the dangerous reveries of the likes of Hobbes and Spinoza[53] will remain forever. Go, famed writings of which the ignorance and rusticity of our forefathers would have been incapable. Go among our descendants in company with those even more dangerous works that reek of the corruption of the mores of our century; and together send on to future centuries a faithful history of the progress and advantages of our sciences and our arts. If they read you, you will not leave them in any doubt about the question we are dealing with today; and unless they are more foolish than we, they will raise their hands to heaven and will say with bitterness of heart, "Almighty God, you who hold minds in your hands, deliver us from the enlightenment and the deadly arts of our fathers, and give back to us ignorance, innocence, and poverty—the only goods that can bring about our happiness and that are precious in your sight."

But if the progress of the sciences and the arts has added nothing to our genuine felicity, if it has corrupted our mores, and if the corruption of mores has damaged the purity of taste, what are we to think of that crowd of elementary-level writers who have removed from the temple of the Muses the difficulties that protected its approach and that nature had spread out before it as a test of strength for those who might be tempted to know? While it would be desirable for all those who could not go far in a career in letters to be deterred from the outset and become involved with arts useful to society, what are we to think of those compilers of works who have indiscreetly broken down the door of the sciences and ushered into their sanctuary a populace unworthy of approaching it? Someone who will be a bad versifier or an inferior geometer all his life might perhaps have become a great cloth maker. Those whom nature destined to be her disciples had no need of teachers. The likes of Verulam, Descartes, Newton,[54] these tutors of mankind had

---

nothing but the doctrine of the Koran, burn them anyway; they are superfluous." Our learned men have cited this reasoning as the height of absurdity. Nevertheless, imagine Gregory the Great in place of Omar and the Gospel in place of the Koran. The library would still have been burned, and this perhaps would be the finest deed in the life of that illustrious pontiff. [Achmed II (1673–1736), Ottoman sultan who ruled from 1703 until 1730, when he was overthrown and later died in prison. Omar (c. 581–644) became caliph in 634 and was assassinated ten years later. He is largely responsible for the early spread of Mohammedanism in the Near East. Pope Gregory I, also known as Gregory the Great (c. 540–604), ruled as pope from 590 to 604. He is best known for his establishment of the supremacy and temporal power of the papacy.]

[53] [Thomas Hobbes (1588–1679) was an English philosopher who espoused the doctrine of mechanistic materialism. He was the author of *De Cive*, *Leviathan*, and *De Homine*. Baruch (or Benedict) de Spinoza (1632–1677) was a member of the community of Sephardic Jews living in Holland who had fled persecution in Spain and Portugal. His chief writings were the *Ethics*, *On the Improvement of the Understanding*, and *Theological-Political Treatise*.]

[54] [Francis Bacon (1561–1626), English statesman and philosopher, was created Baron Verulam in 1618 and Viscount of St. Albans in 1621. He is the author of *The Advancement of Learning* and *Novum Organum*. Descartes is described in note 33. Isaac Newton (1642–1727), English physicist

none themselves. Indeed, what guides would have led them as far as their own vast genius has carried them? Ordinary teachers could only have constricted their understanding by confining it to the narrow capacity of their own. The very first obstacles they encountered taught them to work hard and to exert themselves in order to cover the immense area they traversed. If a few men must be permitted to devote themselves to the study of the sciences and the arts, it should only be those who feel the strength to venture forth alone in their footsteps and to overtake them. It is for this small number to raise monuments to the glory of the human mind. But if we want nothing to be beyond their genius, nothing must be beyond their hopes. That is the only encouragement they need. The soul imperceptibly proportions itself to the objects that occupy it, and it is great events that make great men. The prince of eloquence was consul of Rome, and perhaps the greatest of philosophers, chancellor of England.[55] Does anyone believe that if the one had merely occupied a chair at some university and the other had obtained only a modest pension from an academy, does anyone, say, believe that their works would not have felt the effects of their condition? Therefore let kings not disdain to admit into their councils the men most capable of counseling them well. Let them renounce the old prejudice invented by the pride of the great, that the art of leading peoples is more difficult than that of enlightening them, as if it were easier to induce men to act well of their own accord than to compel them to do it by force. May learned men of the first rank find honorable asylum in their courts. May they obtain the only recompense worthy of them: that of contributing by their influence to the happiness of the peoples to whom they have taught wisdom. Only then will we see what can be done by virtue, science, and authority, enlivened by a noble emulation and working in concert for the felicity of mankind. But as long as power is alone on one side, with enlightenment and wisdom alone on the other, learned men will rarely think about great things, princes will even more rarely perform noble deeds, and peoples will continue to be vile, corrupt, and unhappy.

As for us—ordinary men to whom heaven has not distributed such great talents and whom it does not destine for so much glory—let us remain in our obscurity. Let us not chase after a reputation that would escape us and that, in the present state of things, would never repay us what it would have cost us, even if we had all the qualifications to obtain it. What good is it to seek our happiness in the opinion of another if we can find it in ourselves? Let us leave to others the care of instructing peoples in their duties and confine ourselves to fulfilling our own duties well. We have no need to know more than this.

---

and philosopher, invented the reflecting telescope and is best known for his formulation of the laws of motion and gravitation. His principal works were *Philosophiae naturalis principia mathematica* and *Opticks*.]

[55] [Cicero and Francis Bacon, respectively.]

O virtue! Sublime science of simple souls, are there so many difficulties and so much preparation necessary in order to know you? Are your principles not engraved in all hearts, and is it not enough, in order to learn your laws, to commune with oneself and, in the silence of the passions, to listen to the voice of one's conscience? That is the true philosophy. Let us know how to be satisfied with it. And without envying the glory of those famous men who are immortalized in the republic of letters, let us try to place between them and ourselves that glorious distinction observed long ago between two great peoples: that the one knew how to speak well, the other how to act well.[56]

---

[56] [Athens and Sparta, respectively. The Spartans were famously laconic, an adjective from Laconia, their home region.]

Discourse on the Origin and Foundations of Inequality among Men

The second Discourse, like the first, was an entry to a competition organized by the Academy of Dijon (November 1753)—but its length ensured that it had no chance of winning, since entries were supposed to be short enough to be read in half an hour, and its intended audience was not so much the academy as the citizens of Geneva, Rousseau's homeland. It was written before he left for Geneva (June 1, 1754), and presumably in time to meet the competition's closing date of April 21. The dedication is dated Chambéry, June 12, 1754—Chambéry was in neither French nor Genevan territory, which Rousseau thought was important. His original intention, however, was to publish in Paris on August 25—the day St. Louis, king of France, died in 1270, and so a symbolic date for the French. But in Geneva, Rousseau met Marc-Michel Rey, a Genevan with a publishing business in Amsterdam, who became his regular publisher. Rey received the manuscript in October and promised to publish in January— but it was only at the end of April that publication was complete. On May 12, permission was given for copies to be legally imported into Paris. As he wrote, Rousseau therefore had a number of distinct audiences in mind: the Academy of Dijon, the citizens and government of Geneva, and the intellectuals of Paris. As he revised his text in the winter of 1754–1755, he would also have had in mind the cosmopolitan audience that read books published in Protestant Holland. Some additions appeared in the posthumous edition of 1782. The second Discourse belongs (like Hume's Natural History of Religion*) to a literary genre that no longer exists— hypothetical or speculative history. In social contract theory before Rousseau the "state of nature" is a theoretical, not a historical, condition—it exists wherever there is no government (on the open ocean, for example). Rousseau set out to reconceptualize the transition from nature to society in historical terms—to ask how (putting aside the biblical narrative) human beings ceased being animals (without language or politics) and became "civilized." He thus opened up a whole new type of historical enquiry into the early history of humanity.*

D.W.

DISCOURSE
ON THE ORIGIN AND FOUNDATIONS
OF INEQUALITY AMONG MEN

By JEAN-JACQUES ROUSSEAU

CITIZEN OF GENEVA

"Not in depraved things,
but in those well oriented according to nature,
are we to consider what is natural."
— Aristotle, *Politics*, II.[1]

---

[1] [*Politics*, bk. 1, ch. 5, 1254a. Aristotle goes on to argue that it is natural that some should be slaves.]

To
THE REPUBLIC OF GENEVA[2]

MAGNIFICENT, MOST HONORED, AND SOVEREIGN LORDS:

Convinced that only a virtuous man may bestow on his homeland those honors that it can acknowledge, I have labored for thirty years to earn the right to offer you public homage.[3] And since this happy occasion supplements to some extent what my efforts have been unable to accomplish, I believed I might be allowed here to give heed to the zeal that urges me on, instead of the right that ought to have given me authorization. Having had the good fortune to be born among you, how could I meditate on the equality that nature has established among men and upon the inequality they have instituted without thinking of the profound wisdom with which both, felicitously combined in this state, cooperate in the manner that most closely approximates the natural law and that is most favorable to society, to the maintenance of public order and to the happiness of private individuals? In searching for the best maxims that good sense could dictate concerning the constitution of a government, I have been so struck on seeing them all in operation in your own, that even if I had not been born within your walls, I would have believed myself incapable of exempting myself from the obligation of offering this picture of human society to that people which, of all peoples, seems to me to be in possession of the greatest advantages, and to have best prevented its abuses.

If I had had to choose my birthplace, I would have chosen a society of a size limited by the extent of human capacities, that is to say, limited by the possibility of being well governed, and where, with each being equipped to perform his task, no one would have been forced to delegate to others the functions with which he was charged; a state where, with all private individuals being known to one another, neither the obscure maneuvers of vice nor the modesty of virtue could be hidden from the notice and the judgment of the public, and where that pleasant habit of seeing and knowing one another turned love of homeland into love of the citizens rather than into love of the land.[4]

I would have wanted to be born in a country where the sovereign and the people could have but one and the same interest, so that all the movements of the machine always tended only to the common happiness. Since this could not have taken place unless the people and the sovereign were one and the same person, it follows that I would have wished to be born under

---

[2] [Rousseau did not obtain (as he knew he should have) the republic's permission before dedicating his book to it; he sent the council a copy of his book and received what he later described as "cold" thanks.]

[3] [Rousseau dates his ambition to serve Geneva to the year he started work as an apprentice notary.]

[4] [Rousseau follows Montesquieu in insisting that a republic must be limited in size.]

a democratic government, wisely tempered.[5] I would have wanted to live and die free, that is to say, subject to the laws in such wise that neither I nor anyone else could shake off their honorable yoke: that pleasant and salutary yoke, which the most arrogant heads bear with all the greater docility, since they are made to bear no other.

I would therefore have wanted it to be impossible for anyone in the state to say that he was above the law and for anyone outside it to insist that the state be obliged to give him recognition. For whatever the constitution of a government may be, if a single man is found who is not subject to the law, all the others are necessarily at his discretion.[i] And if there is a national leader and a foreign leader as well, whatever division of authority they may make, it is impossible for both of them to be strictly obeyed and for the state to be well governed.[6]

I would not have wanted to dwell in a newly constituted republic, however good its laws might be, out of fear that, with the government perhaps constituted otherwise than would be required for the moment and being unsuited to the new citizens or the citizens to the new government, the state would be subject to being overthrown and destroyed almost from its inception. For liberty is like those solid and tasty foods or those full-bodied wines which are appropriate for nourishing and strengthening robust constitutions that are used to them, but which overpower, ruin, and intoxicate the weak and delicate who are not suited for them. Once peoples are accustomed to masters, they are no longer in a position to get along without them.[7] If they try to shake off the yoke, they put all the more distance between themselves and liberty, because, in mistaking for liberty an unbridled license that is its opposite, their revolutions nearly always deliver them over to seducers who simply make their chains heavier. The Roman people itself—that model of all free peoples—was in no position to govern itself when it emerged from the oppression of the Tarquins. Debased by slavery and the ignominious labors the Tarquins had imposed on it, at first it was but a stupid rabble that needed to be managed and governed with the greatest wisdom, so that, as it gradually became accustomed to breathe the salutary air of liberty, these souls, enervated or rather brutalized under tyranny, acquired by degrees that severity of mores and that high-spirited courage that eventually made them, of all the peoples, most worthy of respect. I would therefore have sought for my homeland a happy and tranquil republic, whose antiquity was somehow

[5] [According to the long tradition descending from Aristotle, democracy was, like tyranny and oligarchy, a perverted form of government. Few writers before Rousseau used the term in a favorable sense; and even he acknowledges that democracy must be "tempered."]

[6] [Rousseau probably has in mind the claim by the Dukes of Savoy to have sovereignty over Geneva, although he may also be thinking of the papacy's claim to an overarching authority above all secular sovereigns.]

[7] [This is an argument to be found in Machiavelli's *Discourses*, bk. 1, ch. 16.]

lost in the dark recesses of time, which had experienced only such attacks as served to manifest and strengthen in its inhabitants courage and love of homeland, and where the citizens, long accustomed to a wise independence, were not only free but worthy of being so.

I would have wanted to choose for myself a homeland diverted by a fortunate impotence from the fierce love of conquest, and protected by an even more fortunate position from the fear of becoming itself the conquest of another state; a free city, situated among several peoples none of whom had any interest in invading it, while each had an interest in preventing the others from invading it themselves; in a word, a republic that did not tempt the ambition of its neighbors and that could reasonably count on their assistance in time of need. It follows that in so fortunate a position, it would have had nothing to fear except from itself, and that, if its citizens were trained in the use of arms, it would have been more to maintain in them that martial fervor and that high-spirited courage that suit liberty so well and whet the appetite for it, than out of the necessity to provide for their defense.

I would have searched for a country where the right of legislation was common to all citizens, for who can know better than they the conditions under which it suits them to live together in a single society? But I would not have approved of plebiscites like those of the Romans where the state's leaders and those most interested in its preservation were excluded from the deliberations on which its safety often depended, and where, by an absurd inconsistency, the magistrates were deprived of the rights enjoyed by ordinary citizens.

On the contrary, I would have desired that, in order to stop the self-centered and ill-conceived projects and the dangerous innovations that finally ruined Athens, no one would have the power to propose new laws according to his fancy; that this right belonged exclusively to the magistrates;[8] that even they used it with such caution that the populace, for its part, was so hesitant about giving its consent to these laws, and that their promulgation could only be done with such solemnity, that before the constitution was overturned one had time to be convinced that it is above all the great antiquity of the laws that makes them holy and venerable; that the populace soon holds in contempt those laws that it sees change daily; and that in becoming accustomed to neglect old usages on the pretext of making improvements, great evils are often introduced in order to correct the lesser ones.

Above all, I would have fled, as necessarily ill-governed, a republic where the people, believing it could get along without its magistrates or permit them but a precarious authority, would imprudently have held on to the administration of civil affairs and the execution of its own laws. Such must have been the rude constitution of the first government, immediately emerging from the state of nature, and such too was one of the vices that ruined the republic of Athens.

[8] [This was the case in Geneva.]

But I would have chosen that republic where private individuals, being content to give sanction to the laws and to decide as a body and upon the recommendation of their leaders the most important public affairs, would establish respected tribunals, distinguish with care their various departments, annually elect the most capable and most upright of their fellow citizens to administer justice and to govern the state; and where, with the virtue of the magistrates thus bearing witness to the wisdom of the people, they would mutually honor one another. Thus if some fatal misunderstandings were ever to disturb public concord, even those periods of blindness and errors were marked by indications of moderation, reciprocal esteem, and a common respect for the laws: presages and guarantees of a sincere and perpetual reconciliation.

Such, MAGNIFICENT, MOST HONORED, AND SOVEREIGN LORDS, are the advantages that I would have sought in the homeland that I would have chosen for myself. And if in addition providence had joined to it a charming location, a temperate climate, a fertile country, and the most delightful appearance there is under the heavens, to complete my happiness I would have desired only to enjoy all these goods in the bosom of that happy homeland, living peacefully in sweet society with my fellow citizens, and practicing toward them (following their own example), humanity, friendship, and all the virtues; and leaving behind me the honorable memory of a good man and a decent and virtuous patriot.

If, less happy or too late grown wise, I had seen myself reduced to end an infirm and languishing career in other climates, pointlessly regretting the repose and peace of which an imprudent youth deprived me, I would at least have nourished in my soul those same sentiments, even though I could not have used them in my native country; and penetrated by a tender and disinterested affection for my distant fellow citizens, I would have addressed them from the bottom of my heart more or less along the following lines:

My dear fellow citizens, or rather my brothers, since the bonds of blood as well as the laws unite almost all of us, it gives me pleasure to be incapable of thinking of you without at the same time thinking of all the good things you enjoy, and of which perhaps none of you appreciates the value more deeply than I who have lost them. The more I reflect upon your political and civil situation, the less I am capable of imagining that the nature of human affairs could admit of a better one. In all other governments, when it is a question of assuring the greatest good of the state, everything is always limited to imaginary projects, and at most to mere possibilities. As for you, your happiness is complete; it remains only to enjoy it. And to become perfectly happy you are in need of nothing more than to know how to be satisfied with being so. Your sovereignty, acquired or recovered at the point of a sword, and preserved for two centuries by dint of valor and wisdom, is at last fully and universally recognized. Honorable treaties fix your boundaries, secure your rights, and strengthen your repose. Your constitution is excellent, since it is dictated by the most sublime reason and is guaranteed by friendly powers deserving of respect.[9] Your state is tranquil; you have neither wars nor conquerors to fear. You have no other masters but the wise laws you have made, administered by upright magistrates of your own choosing. You are neither rich enough to enervate yourself with softness and lose in vain delights the taste for true happiness and solid virtues, nor poor enough to need more foreign assistance than your skills[10] procure for you. And this precious liberty, which in large nations is maintained only by exorbitant taxes, costs you almost nothing to preserve.

For the happiness of its citizens and the examples of the peoples, may a republic so wisely and so happily constituted last forever! This is the only wish left for you to make, and the only precaution left for you to take. From here on, it is for you alone, not to bring about your own happiness, your ancestors having saved you the trouble, but to render it lasting by the wisdom of using it well. It is upon your perpetual union, your obedience to the laws, your respect for their ministers that your preservation depends. If there remains among you the slightest germ of bitterness or distrust, hasten to destroy it as a ruinous leaven[11] that sooner or later results in your misfortunes and the ruin of the state. I beg you all to look deep inside your hearts and to heed the secret voice of your conscience. Is there anyone among you who knows of a body that is more upright, more enlightened, more worthy of respect than that of your magistracy? Do not all its members give you the example of moderation, of simplicity of mores, of respect for the laws, and of the most sincere reconciliation? Then freely give such wise chiefs that salutary confidence that reason owes virtue. Bear in mind that they are of your choosing, that they justify it, and that the honors due to those whom you have established in dignity necessarily reflect back upon yourselves. None of you is so unenlightened as to be ignorant of the fact that where the vigor of laws and the authority of their defenders cease, there can be neither security nor freedom for anyone. What then is the point at issue among you except to do wholeheartedly and with just confidence what you should always be obliged to do by a true self-interest, by duty and for the sake of reason? May a sinful and ruinous indifference to the maintenance of the constitution never make you neglect in time of need the wise teachings of the most enlightened and most zealous among you. But may equity, moderation, and the most respectful firmness continue to regulate all your activities and display in you, to the entire universe, the example of a proud and modest people, as jealous of its

---

[9] [In 1738, France had stepped in to mediate between conflicting democratic and oligarchic forces in Geneva and had underwritten the resulting compromise.]

[10] [Rousseau's word is *industrie*, but to translate this as "industry" would be misleading. The *Dictionnaire de l'Académie française* gives as its core meaning "dexterity or skill [*adresse*] in making something." From here on, *industrie* is translated as "skills."]

[11] [The implicit reference is to Matthew 15:6.]

glory as of its liberty. Above all, beware (and this will be my last counsel) of ever listening to sinister interpretations and venomous speeches whose secret motives are often more dangerous than the actions that are their object. An entire household awakens and takes warning at the first howls of a good and faithful watchdog who never barks except at the approach of burglars. But people hate the nuisance caused by those noisy animals that continually disturb the public repose and whose continual and ill-timed warnings are not heeded even at the moment when they are necessary.

And you, MAGNIFICENT AND MOST HONORED LORDS, you upright and worthy magistrates of a free people, permit me to offer you in particular my compliments and my respects. If there is a rank in the world suited to conferring honor on those who hold it, it is without doubt the one that is given by talents and virtue, that of which you have made yourselves worthy, and to which your fellow citizens have raised you. Their own merit adds still a new luster to yours. And I find that you, who were chosen by men capable of governing others in order that they themselves may be governed, are as much above other magistrates as a free people—and above all the one which you have the honor of leading—is, by its enlightenment and reason, above the populace of other states.

Permit me to cite an example of which better records ought to remain, and which will always be near to my heart. I never call to mind without the sweetest emotion the memory of the virtuous citizen to whom I owe my being, and who often spoke to me in my childhood of the respect that was owed you. I still see him living from the work of his hands, and nourishing his soul on the most sublime truths. I see Tacitus, Plutarch, and Grotius mingled with the instruments of his craft before him.[12] I see at his side a beloved son receiving with too little profit the tender instruction of the best of fathers. But if the aberrations of foolish youth made me forget such wise lessons for a time, I have the happiness to sense at last that whatever the inclination one may have toward vice, it is difficult for an education in which the heart is involved to remain forever lost.

Such, MAGNIFICENT AND MOST HONORED LORDS, are the citizens and even the simple inhabitants born in the state you govern. Such are those educated and sensible men concerning whom, under the name of

---

[12] [Tacitus (AD 56–117), a Roman historian, was admired by lovers of liberty for his unsparing description of despotism. Plutarch (AD 46–120), a Greek historian, provided in his *Lives* an account of the key political leaders of ancient Greece and Rome. Since Rousseau is portraying his father as a model citizen and lover of liberty, it seems likely that the work of Hugo Grotius (1583–1645) that he has in mind is not *On the Law of War and Peace* (1625) or *On the Truth of the Christian Religion* (1627) but *The Annals and History of the Affairs of the Low Countries*, a history of the Protestant Dutch Revolt against Catholic Spain covering the period 1559–1609, published posthumously in Latin in 1657 and translated into French in 1662. Rousseau was thus raised by his father, he would have the reader understand, in the principles of both ancient and modern liberty.]

workers and people, such base and false ideas are entertained in other nations. My father, I gladly acknowledge, was in no way distinguished among his fellow citizens; he was only what they all are; and such as he was, there was no country where his company would not have been sought after, cultivated, and profitably too, by the most upright men. It does not behoove me, nor, thank heaven, is it necessary to speak to you of the regard which men of that stamp can expect from you: your equals by education as well as by the rights of nature and of birth; your inferiors by their will and by the preference they owe your merit, which they have granted to it, and for which you in turn owe them some sort of gratitude. It is with intense satisfaction that I learn how much, in your dealings with them, you temper with gentleness and coopera-tiveness the gravity suited to the ministers of the law; how much you repay them in esteem and attention for the obedience and respect they owe you; conduct full of justice and wisdom, suited to putting at a greater and greater distance the memory of unhappy events that must be forgotten so as never to see them again;[13] conduct all the more judicious because this equitable and generous people makes a pleasure out of its duty, because it naturally loves to honor you, and because those who are most zealous in upholding their rights are the ones who are most inclined to respect yours.

It should not be surprising that the leaders of a civil society love its glory and happiness; but, unfortunately for the tranquility of men, it really is quite astonishing that those who consider themselves as the magistrates, or rather as the masters, of a more holy and more sublime homeland[14] manifest some love for the earthly homeland that nourishes them. How sweet it is for me to be able to make such a rare exception in our favor, and to place in the rank of our best citizens those zealous trustees of the sacred dogmas authorized by the laws, those venerable pastors of souls, whose lively and sweet eloquence the better instills the maxims of the Gospel into people's hearts because they themselves always begin by practicing them. Everyone knows the success with which the great art of preaching is cultivated in Geneva. But since people are too accustomed to seeing things said in one way and done in another, few of them know the extent to which the spirit of Christianity, the saintliness of mores, severity to oneself, and gentleness to others reign in the general run of our ministers. Perhaps it behooves only the city of Geneva to provide the edifying example of such a perfect union between a society of theologians and of men of letters. It is in large part upon their wisdom and their acknowledged moderation and upon their zeal for the prosperity of the state that I base my hopes for its eternal tranquility. And I note, with a pleasure mixed with amazement and respect, how much they abhor the atrocious maxims of those sacred and barbarous men of whom history provides more than one example, and who, in order to uphold the alleged rights of God—that is to say, their

[13] [The internal conflicts of 1734–1738 that led to French intervention.]
[14] [The clergy.]

own interests—were all the less sparing of human blood because they hoped their own would always be respected.[15]

Could I forget that precious half of the republic that produces the happiness of the other and whose gentleness and wisdom maintain peace and good mores? Amiable and virtuous women citizens, it will always be the fate of your sex to govern ours. Happy it is when your chaste power, exercised only within the conjugal union, makes itself felt only for the glory of the state and the public happiness! Thus it was that in Sparta women were in command, and thus it is that you deserve to be in command in Geneva. What barbarous man could resist the voice of honor and reason in the mouth of an affectionate wife? And who would not despise vain luxury on seeing your simple and modest attire, which, from the luster it derives from you, seems the most favorable to beauty? It is for you to maintain always, by your amiable and innocent dominion and by your insinuating wit, the love of laws in the state and concord among the citizens; to reunite, by happy marriages, divided families; and above all, to correct, by the persuasive sweetness of your lessons and by the modest graces of your conversation, those extravagances that our young people come to acquire in other countries, whence, instead of the many useful things they could profit from, they bring back, with a childish manner and the ridiculous airs adopted among fallen women, nothing more than an admiration for who knows what pretended grandeurs, frivolous compensations for servitude, which will never be worth as much as august liberty. Therefore always be what you are, the chaste guardians of mores and the gentle bonds of peace, and continue to assert on every occasion the rights of the heart and of nature for the benefit of duty and virtue.

I flatter myself that events will not prove me wrong in basing upon such guarantees hope for the general happiness of the citizens and for the glory of the republic. I admit that with all these advantages it will not shine with that brilliance which dazzles most eyes; and the childish and fatal taste for this is the deadliest enemy of happiness and liberty. Let a dissolute youth go elsewhere in search of easy pleasures and lengthy repentances. Let the alleged men of taste admire someplace else the grandeur of palaces, the beauty of carriages, the sumptuous furnishings, the pomp of spectacles, and all the refinements of softness and luxury. In Geneva we will find only men; but such a sight has a value of its own, and those who seek it are well worth the admirers of the rest.

May you all, MAGNIFICENT, MOST HONORED, AND SOVEREIGN LORDS, deign to receive with the same goodness the respectful testimonies of the interest I take in your common prosperity. If I were unfortunate enough to be guilty of some indiscreet rapture in this lively effusion of my heart, I beg you to pardon it as the tender affection of a true patriot, and as the ardent

---

[15] [This is an indirect blow against Jean Cauvin (John Calvin), who had Miguel Servet (Servetus) executed.]

and legitimate zeal of a man who envisages no greater happiness for himself than that of seeing all of you happy. With the most profound respect, I am, MAGNIFICENT, MOST HONORED, AND SOVEREIGN LORDS, your most humble and most obedient servant and fellow citizen.

JEAN-JACQUES ROUSSEAU

Chambéry
June 12, 1754

PREFACE

Of all the branches of human knowledge, the most useful and the least advanced seems to me to be that of man;[ii] and I dare say that the inscription on the temple at Delphi[16] alone contained a precept more important and more difficult than all the huge tomes of the moralists. Thus I regard the subject of this discourse as one of the most interesting questions that philosophy is capable of proposing, and unhappily for us, one of the thorniest that philosophers can attempt to resolve. For how can the source of the inequality among men be known unless one begins by knowing men themselves? And how will man be successful in seeing himself as nature formed him, through all the changes that the succession of time and things must have produced in his original constitution, and in separating what he derives from his own essential nature from what circumstances and his progress have added to or changed in his primitive state? Like the statue of Glaucus,[17] which time, sea, and storms had disfigured to such an extent that it looked less like a god than a wild beast, the human soul, altered in the midst of society by a thousand constantly recurring causes, by the acquisition of endless bits of information and of errors, by changes that took place in the constitution of the human body, by the constant impact of the passions, has, as it were, changed its appearance to the point of being nearly unrecognizable. And instead of a being who acts always by fixed and invariable principles, instead of that heavenly and majestic simplicity whose mark its author had left on it, one no longer finds anything but the grotesque conflict of passion that thinks it reasons and an understanding in a state of delirium.

What is even more cruel is that, since all the progress of the human species continually moves away from its primitive state, the more we accumulate new knowledge, the more we deprive ourselves of the means of acquiring the most important knowledge of all. Thus, in a sense, it is by dint of studying man that we have rendered ourselves incapable of knowing him.

---

[16] ["Know thyself."]

[17] [Plato, *Republic*, bk. 10, 611c–d.]

It is easy to see that it is in these successive changes of the human constitution that we must seek the first origin of the differences that distinguish men, who, by common consensus, are naturally as equal among themselves as were the animals of each species—at least before various physical causes had introduced into certain species the varieties we now observe among some of them. In effect, it is inconceivable that these first changes, by whatever means they took place, should have altered all at once and in the same manner all the individuals of the species. But while some improved or declined and acquired various good or bad qualities that were not inherent in their nature, the others remained longer in their original state. And such was the first source of inequality among men, which it is easier to demonstrate thus in general than it is to assign with precision its true causes.

Let my readers not imagine, then, that I dare flatter myself with having seen what appears to me so difficult to see. I have begun some lines of reasoning; I have hazarded some guesses, less in the hope of resolving the question than with the intention of clarifying it and of reducing it to its true state. Others will easily be able to go farther on this same route, though it will not be easy for anyone to reach the end of it. For it is no light undertaking to separate what is original from what is artificial in the present nature of man, and to have a proper understanding of a state that no longer exists, that perhaps never existed, that probably never will exist, and yet about which it is necessary to have accurate notions in order to judge properly our own present state. He who would attempt to determine precisely which precautions to take in order to make solid observations on this subject would need even more philosophy than is generally supposed; and a good solution of the following problem would not seem to me unworthy of the Aristotles and Plinys of our century: *What experiments would be necessary to achieve knowledge of natural man? And what are the means of carrying out these experiments in the midst of society?* Far from undertaking to resolve this problem, I believe I have meditated sufficiently on the subject to dare to respond in advance that the greatest philosophers will be scarcely good enough to direct these experiments, and the most powerful sovereigns to carry them out. It is hardly reasonable to expect such a combination, especially with the perseverance or rather the succession of understanding and goodwill needed on both sides in order to achieve success.

These investigations, so difficult to carry out and so little thought about until now, are nevertheless the only means we have left of removing a multitude of difficulties that conceal from us the knowledge of the real foundations of human society. It is this ignorance of the nature of man that throws so much uncertainty and obscurity on the true definition of natural right. For the idea of right, says Mr. Burlamaqui,[18] and even more that of natural right

---

[18] [Jean-Jacques Burlamaqui (1694–1748), author of *Principles of Natural Right* (1747) and *Principles of Political Right* (1751).]

are manifestly ideas relative to the nature of man. Therefore, he continues, the principles of this science must be deduced from this very nature of man, from man's constitution and condition.

It is not without surprise and a sense of outrage that one observes the paucity of agreement on this important matter that prevails among the various authors who have treated it. Among the most serious writers, one can hardly find two who are of the same opinion on this point. The Roman jurists—not to mention the ancient philosophers who seem to have done their best to contradict each other on the most fundamental principles—subject man and all other animals indifferently to the same natural law, because they take this expression to refer to the law that nature imposes on itself rather than the law it prescribes, or rather because of the particular sense in which those jurists understood "law," which on this occasion they seem to have taken only for the expression of the general relations established by nature among all animate beings for their common preservation. The moderns, in acknowledging under the word "law" merely a rule prescribed to a moral being, that is to say, intelligent, free, and considered in his relations with other beings, consequently limit the competence of the natural law to the only animal endowed with reason, that is, to man. But with each one defining this law in his own fashion, they all establish it on such metaphysical principles that even among us there are very few people in a position to grasp these principles, and they are far from being able to find them by themselves. Thus all the definitions of these wise men, otherwise in perpetual contradiction with one another, agree on this alone, that it is impossible to understand the law of nature and consequently to obey it without being a great reasoner and a profound metaphysician, which means precisely that for the establishment of society, men must have used an enlightenment that develops only with great difficulty and only among a very small number of people, even within society itself.

Knowing nature so little and agreeing so poorly on the meaning of the word "law," it would be quite difficult to come to some common understanding regarding a good definition of natural law. Thus all those definitions that are found in books have, over and above a lack of uniformity, the added fault of being drawn from several branches of knowledge that men do not naturally have, and from advantages the idea of which they cannot conceive until after having left the state of nature. Writers begin by seeking the rules on which, for the common utility, it would be appropriate for men to agree among themselves; and then they give the name *natural law* to the collection of these rules, with no other proof than the good that presumably would result from their universal observance. Surely this is a very convenient way to compose definitions and explain the nature of things by virtually arbitrary views of what is seemly.

But as long as we are ignorant of natural man, it is futile for us to attempt to determine the law he has received or that is best suited to his constitution. All that we can see very clearly regarding this law is that, for it to be law, not only must the will of him who is obliged by it be capable of a discerning submission to it, but also, for it to be natural, it must speak directly by the voice of nature.

Leaving aside therefore all the scientific books that teach us only to see men as they have made themselves, and meditating on the first and most simple operations of the human soul, I believe I perceive in it two principles that are prior to reason, of which one makes us ardently interested in our well-being and our self-preservation, and the other inspires in us a natural repugnance to seeing any sentient being, especially our fellowman, perish or suffer. It is from the conjunction and combination that our mind is in a position to make of these two principles, without the need for introducing that of sociability, that all the rules of natural right appear to me to flow; rules that reason is later forced to reestablish on other foundations, when, by its successive developments, it has succeeded in smothering nature.

In this way, one is not obliged to make a man a philosopher before making him a man. His duties toward others are not uniquely dictated to him by the belated lessons of wisdom; and as long as he does not resist the inner impulse of compassion, he will never harm another man or even another sentient being, except in the legitimate instance where, if his preservation is involved, he is obliged to give preference to himself. By this means, an end can also be made to the ancient disputes regarding the participation of animals in the natural law. For it is clear that, lacking intelligence and liberty, they cannot recognize this law; but since they share to some extent in our nature by virtue of the sentient quality with which they are endowed, one will judge that they should also participate in natural right, and that man is subject to some sort of duties toward them. It seems, in effect, that if I am obliged not to do any harm to my fellowman, it is less because he is a rational being than because he is a sentient being: a quality that, since it is common to both animals and men, should at least give the former the right not to be needlessly mistreated by the latter.

This same study of original man, of his true needs and the fundamental principles of his duties, is also the only good means that can be used to remove those multitudes of difficulties that present themselves regarding the origin of moral inequality,[19] the true foundations of the body politic, the reciprocal rights of its members, and a thousand other similar questions that are as important as they are poorly explained.

In considering human society from a tranquil and disinterested point of view, it seems at first to manifest merely the violence of powerful men and the oppression of the weak. The mind revolts against the harshness of the

[19] [Rousseau's phrase is *inégalité morale* (inequality with regard to mores). There is no word in the French or English of Rousseau's day for "culture" in the sense of the customs or way of life of a particular society. So it would be slightly anachronistic, but not misleading, to translate *inégalité morale* as "cultural inequality."]

former; one is inclined to deplore the blindness of the latter. And since nothing is less stable among men than those external relationships that chance brings about more often than wisdom, and that are called weakness or power, wealth or poverty, human establishments appear at first glance to be based on piles of shifting sand. It is only in examining them closely, only after having cleared away the dust and sand that surround the edifice, that one perceives the unshakeable base on which it is raised and one learns to respect its foundations. Now without a serious study of man, of his natural faculties and their successive developments, one will never succeed in making these distinctions and in separating in the present constitution of things what the divine will has done from what human art has pretended to do. The political and moral investigations occasioned by the important question I am examining are therefore useful in every way; and the hypothetical history of governments is an instructive lesson for man in every respect. In considering what we would have become, left to ourselves, we ought to learn to bless him whose beneficent hand, in correcting our institutions and giving them an unshakeable foundation, has prevented the disorders that must otherwise result from them, and has brought about our happiness from the means that seemed likely to add to our misery.

"Learn whom God has ordered you to be,
and in what part of human affairs you have been placed."[20]

Notice on the Notes

I have added some notes to this work, following my indolent custom of working in fits and starts. Occasionally these notes wander so far from the subject that they are not good to read with the text. I therefore have consigned them to the end of the Discourse, in which I have tried my best to follow the straightest path. Those who have the courage to begin again will be able to amuse themselves the second time as they beat the bushes and try to run through the notes. There will be little harm done if others do not read them at all.

[These notes are presented at the end of this Discourse. Significant additions and revisions to the original text of the Discourse and notes that Rousseau made for the 1782 edition appear in the text in angle < > brackets.]

[20] [Persius, *Satire 3*, lines 71–73.]

QUESTION
Proposed by the Academy of Dijon

*What is the origin of inequality
among men, and is it authorized by the natural law?*

DISCOURSE
ON THE ORIGIN AND FOUNDATIONS OF
INEQUALITY AMONG MEN

It is of man that I have to speak, and the question I am examining indicates to me that I am going to be speaking to men, for such questions are not proposed by those who are afraid to honor the truth. I will therefore confidently defend the cause of humanity before the wise men who invite me to do so, and I will not be displeased with myself if I make myself worthy of my subject and my judges.

I conceive of two kinds of inequality in the human species: one that I call natural or physical, because it is established by nature and consists in the difference of age, health, bodily strength, and qualities of mind or soul. The other may be called moral[21] or political inequality, because it depends on a kind of convention and is established, or at least authorized, by the consent of men. This latter type of inequality consists in the different privileges enjoyed by some at the expense of others, such as being richer, more honored, more powerful than they, or even causing themselves to be obeyed by them.

There is no point in asking what the source of natural inequality is, because the answer would be found enunciated in the simple definition of the word. There is still less of a point in asking whether there would not be some essential connection between the two inequalities, for that would amount to asking whether those who command are necessarily better than those who obey, and whether strength of body or mind, wisdom or virtue, are always found in the same individuals in proportion to power or wealth. Perhaps this is a good question for slaves to discuss within earshot of their masters, but it is not suitable for reasonable and free men who seek the truth.

Precisely what, then, is the subject of this discourse? To mark, in the development of things, the moment when, right taking the place of violence, nature was subjected to the law. To explain the sequence of wonders by which the strong could resolve to serve the weak, and the people to buy imaginary repose at the price of real felicity. The philosophers who have examined the foundations of society have all felt the necessity of returning to the state of nature, but none of them has reached it. Some have not hesitated to ascribe to man in that state the notion of just and unjust, without bothering to show that he had to have that notion, or even that it was useful to him.[22] Others have spoken of the natural right that everyone has to preserve what belongs to him, without explaining what they mean by "belonging."[23] Others started

[21] [Rousseau's phrase is *inégalité morale;* see note 19.]

[22] [E.g., Hugo Grotius.]

[23] [E.g., John Locke, *Two Treatises of Government*, Second Treatise, ch. 2, §4.]

out by giving authority to the stronger over the weaker, and immediately brought about government, without giving any thought to the time that had to pass before the meaning of the words "authority" and "government" could exist among men.[24] Finally, all of them, speaking continually of need, avarice, oppression, desires, and pride, have transferred to the state of nature the ideas they themselves acquired in society. They spoke about savage man, and it was civilized man they depicted. It did not even occur to most of our philosophers to doubt that the state of nature had existed, even though it is evident from reading the Holy Scriptures that the first man, having received enlightenment and precepts immediately from God, was not himself in that state; and if we give the writings of Moses the credence that every Christian owes them, we must deny that, even before the flood, men were ever in the pure state of nature, unless they had fallen back into it because of some extraordinary event: a paradox that is quite awkward to defend and utterly impossible to prove.

Let us therefore begin by putting aside all the facts, for they have no bearing on the question.[25] The investigations that may be undertaken concerning this subject should not be taken for historical truths, but only for hypothetical and conditional reasonings, better suited to shedding light on the nature of things than on pointing out their true origin, like those our physicists make every day with regard to the formation of the world. Religion commands us to believe that since God himself drew men out of the state of nature, they are unequal because he wanted them to be so; but it does not forbid us to form conjectures, drawn solely from the nature of man and the beings that surround him, concerning what the human race could have become, if it had been left to itself. That is what I am asked, and what I propose to examine in this discourse. Since my subject concerns man in general, I will attempt to speak in terms that suit all nations, or rather, forgetting times and places in order to think only of the men to whom I am speaking, I will imagine I am in the Lyceum in Athens, reciting the lessons of my masters, having men like Plato and Xenocrates[26] for my judges, and the human race for my audience.

O man, whatever country you may be from, whatever your opinions may be, listen: here is your history, as I have thought to read it, not in the books of your fellowmen, who are liars, but in nature, which never lies. Everything that comes from nature will be true; there will be nothing false except what I have unintentionally added. The times about which I am going to speak are quite remote: how much you have changed from what you were! It is, as it were, the life of your species that I am about to describe to you according to the qualities you have received, which your education and your habits have

---

[24] [E.g., Thomas Hobbes.]

[25] [The "facts" here are the history of humanity as recorded in the Bible.]

[26] [394–314 BC, a disciple of Plato.]

been able to corrupt but have been unable to destroy. There is, I feel, an age at which an individual man would want to stop. You will seek the age at which you would want your species to have stopped. Dissatisfied with your present state for reasons that portend even greater grounds for dissatisfaction for your unhappy posterity, perhaps you would like to be able to go backward in time. This thought should be a hymn in praise of your first ancestors, a critique of your contemporaries, and should strike dread into those who have the unhappiness of living after you.

PART ONE

However important it may be, in order to render sound judgments regarding the natural state of man, to consider him from his origin and to examine him, so to speak, in the first embryo of the species, I will not follow his nature through its successive developments. I will not stop to investigate in the animal kingdom what he might have been at the beginning so as eventually to become what he is. I will not examine whether, as Aristotle thinks, man's elongated nails were not at first hooked claws, whether man was not furry like a bear, and whether, if man walked on all fours,[iii] his gaze, directed toward the ground and limited to a horizon of a few steps, did not provide an indication of both the character and the limits of his ideas. On this subject I could form only vague and almost imaginary conjectures. Comparative anatomy has as yet made too little progress; the observations of naturalists are as yet too uncertain for one to be able to establish the basis of solid reasoning on such foundations. Thus, without having recourse to the supernatural knowledge we have on this point, and without taking note of the changes that must have occurred in the internal as well as the external conformation of man, as he applied his limbs to new purposes and nourished himself on new foods, I will suppose him to have been formed from all time as I see him today: walking on two feet, using his hands as we use ours, directing his gaze over all of nature, and measuring with his eyes the vast expanse of the heavens.

When I strip that being, thus constituted, of all the supernatural gifts he could have received, and of all the artificial faculties he could have acquired only through a lengthy process; when I consider him, in a word, as he must have left the hands of nature, I see an animal less strong than some, less agile than others, but all in all, the most advantageously organized of all. I see him satisfying his hunger under an oak tree, quenching his thirst at the first stream, finding his bed at the foot of the same tree that supplied his meal; and thus all his needs are satisfied.

When the earth is left to its natural fertility[iv] and covered with immense forests that were never mutilated by the axe, it offers storehouses and shelters at every step to animals of every species. Men, dispersed among the animals, observe and imitate their skills, and thereby raise themselves to the level of animal instinct, with the advantage that, whereas each species has only its own instincts, man, who may perhaps have none that belongs to him, appropriates all of them to himself, feeds himself equally well on most of the various foods[v] that the other animals divide among themselves, and consequently finds his sustenance more easily than any of the rest can.

Accustomed from childhood to inclement weather and the rigors of the seasons, acclimated to fatigue, and forced, naked and without arms, to defend their lives and their prey against other ferocious beasts, or to escape them by taking flight, men develop a robust and nearly unalterable temperament. Children enter the world with the excellent constitution of their parents and strengthen it with the same exercises that produced it, thus acquiring all the vigor that the human race is capable of having. Nature treats them precisely the way the law of Sparta treated the children of its citizens: it renders strong and robust those who are well constituted and makes all the rest perish, thereby differing from our present-day societies, where the state, by making children burdensome to their parents, kills them indiscriminately before their birth.[27]

Since the savage man's body is the only instrument he knows, he employs it for a variety of purposes that, for lack of practice, ours are incapable of serving. And our skills deprive us of the force and agility that necessity obliges him to acquire. If he had had an axe, would his wrists break such strong branches? If he had had a sling, would he throw a stone with so much force? If he had a ladder, would he climb a tree so nimbly? If he had a horse, would he run so fast? Give a civilized man time to gather all his machines around him, and undoubtedly he will easily overcome a savage man. But if you want to see an even more unequal fight, pit them against each other naked and disarmed, and you will soon realize the advantage of constantly having all of one's forces at one's disposal, of always being ready for any event, and of always carrying one's entire self, as it were, with one.[vi]

Hobbes maintains that man is naturally intrepid and seeks only to attack and fight. On the other hand, an illustrious philosopher thinks, and Cumberland and Pufendorf also affirm, that nothing is as timid as man in the state of nature, and that he is always trembling and ready to take flight at the slightest sound he hears or at the slightest movement he perceives.[28] That may be the case with regard to objects with which he is not acquainted. And I do not doubt that he is frightened by all the new sights that present themselves to him every time he can neither discern the physical good and evil he may expect from them nor compare his forces with the dangers he

[27] [Judging from what Rousseau says later in the Discourse ("multiply the number of abortions," p. 66), he would seem to have abortion in mind.]

[28] [The illustrious philosopher is Montesquieu: *The Spirit of the Laws*, bk. 1, ch. 2. Richard Cumberland is the author of a refutation of Hobbes, *On the Laws of Nature* (1672). Samuel Pufendorf (1632–1694) was widely regarded as the leading authority on the law of nature.]

must run: rare circumstances in the state of nature, where everything takes place in such a uniform manner and where the face of the earth is not subject to those sudden and continual changes caused by the passions and inconstancy of peoples living together. But a savage man lives dispersed among the animals and, finding himself early on in a position to measure himself against them, he soon makes the comparison; and, aware that he surpasses them in skillfulness more than they surpass him in strength, he learns not to fear them anymore. Pit a bear or a wolf against a savage who is robust, agile, and courageous, as they all are, armed with stones and a hefty cudgel, and you will see that the danger will be at least equal on both sides, and that after several such experiences, ferocious beasts, which do not like to attack one another, will be quite reluctant to attack a man, having found him to be as ferocious as themselves. With regard to animals that actually have more strength than man has skillfulness, he is in the same position as other weaker species, which nevertheless subsist. Man has the advantage that, since he is no less adept than they at running and at finding almost certain refuge in trees, he always has the alternative of accepting or leaving the encounter and the choice of taking flight or entering into combat. Moreover, it appears that no animal naturally attacks man, except in the case of self-defense or extreme hunger, or shows evidence of those violent antipathies toward him that seem to indicate that one species is destined by nature to serve as food for another.

<No doubt these are the reasons why Negroes and savages bother themselves so little about the ferocious beasts they may encounter in the woods. In this respect, the Caribs of Venezuela, among others, live in the most profound security and without the slightest inconvenience. Although they are practically naked, says Francisco Coreal, they boldly expose themselves in the forest, armed only with bow and arrow, but no one has ever heard of one of them being devoured by animals.>[29]

There are other, more formidable enemies, against which man does not have the same means of self-defense: natural infirmities, childhood, old age, and illnesses of all kinds—sad signs of our weakness, of which the first two are common to all animals, with the last belonging principally to man living in society. On the subject of childhood, I even observe that a mother, by carrying her child everywhere with her, can feed it much more easily than females of several animal species, which are forced to be continually coming and going, with great fatigue, to seek their food and to suckle or feed their young. It is true that if a woman were to perish, the child runs a considerable risk of perishing with her. But this danger is common to a hundred other species, whose young are for quite some time incapable of going off to seek their nourishment for themselves. Moreover, although childhood is longer among us, our life span is also longer; thus things are more or less

[29] [Francisco Coreal (1648–1708) wrote an account of his voyages to the West Indies.]

equal in this respect,[vii] although there are other rules, not relevant to my subject, that are concerned with the duration of infancy and the number of young.[viii] Among the elderly, who are less active and perspire little, the need for food diminishes with the capacity to provide for it. In addition, since savage life shields them from gout and rheumatism, and since old age is, of all ills, the one that human assistance can least alleviate, they eventually die without anyone being aware that they are ceasing to exist, and almost without being aware of it themselves.

With regard to illnesses, I will not repeat the vain and false pronouncements made against medicine by the majority of people in good health. Rather, I will ask whether there is any solid observation on the basis of which one can conclude that the average life span is shorter in those countries where the art of medicine is most neglected than in those where it is cultivated most assiduously. And how could that be the case, unless we give ourselves more ills than medicine can furnish us remedies? The extreme inequality in our lifestyle: excessive idleness among some, excessive labor among others; the ease with which we arouse and satisfy our appetites and our sensuality; the overly refined foods of the wealthy, which nourish them with irritating juices and overwhelm them with indigestion; the bad food of the poor, who most of the time do not have even that, and who, for want of food, are inclined to stuff their stomachs greedily whenever possible; staying up until all hours, excesses of all kinds, immoderate outbursts of every passion, bouts of fatigue and mental exhaustion; countless sorrows and afflictions, which are felt in all levels of society and which perpetually gnaw away at souls: these are the fatal proofs that most of our ills are of our own making, and that we could have avoided nearly all of them by preserving the simple, regular, and solitary lifestyle prescribed to us by nature. If nature has destined us to be healthy, I almost dare to affirm that the state of reflection is a state contrary to nature and that the man who meditates is a depraved animal. When one thinks about the stout constitutions of the savages, at least of those whom we have not ruined with our strong liquors; when one becomes aware of the fact that they know almost no illnesses but wounds and old age, one is strongly inclined to believe that someone could easily write the history of human maladies by following the history of civil societies. This at least was the opinion of Plato, who believed that, from certain remedies used or approved by Podalirius and Machaon at the siege of Troy, various illnesses which these remedies should exacerbate were as yet unknown among men, <And Celsus reports that diet, so necessary today, was only an invention of Hippocrates.>[30]

With so few sources of ills, man in the state of nature hardly has any need therefore of remedies, much less of physicians. The human race is in

[30] [Podalirius and Machaon are the sons of Asclepius, the god of medicine in ancient Greece. Celsus (c. 25 BC–c. AD 50) was the Roman author of a treatise on medicine. Hippocrates (c. 460–c. 370 BC) was regarded by the Greeks as the founder of medicine.]

no worse condition than all the others in this respect; and it is easy to learn from hunters whether in their pursuit they find many sick animals. They find quite a few that have received serious wounds that healed quite nicely, that have had bones or even limbs broken and reset with no other surgeon than time, no other regimen than their everyday life, and that are no less perfectly cured for not having been tormented with incisions, poisoned with drugs, or exhausted with fasting. Finally, however correctly administered medicine may be among us, it is still certain that although a sick savage, abandoned to himself, has nothing to hope for except from nature, on the other hand, he has nothing to fear except his illness. This frequently makes his situation preferable to ours.

Therefore we must take care not to confuse savage man with the men we have before our eyes. Nature treats all animals left to its care with a tenderness that seems to show how jealous it is of that right. The horse, the cat, the bull, even the ass, are usually taller, and all of them have a more robust constitution, more vigor, more strength, and more courage in the forests than in our homes. They lose half of these advantages in becoming domesticated; it might be said that all our efforts at feeding them and treating them well only end in their degeneration. It is the same for man himself. In becoming habituated to the ways of society and a slave, he becomes weak, fearful, and servile; his soft and effeminate lifestyle completes the enervation of both his strength and his courage. Let us add that the difference between the savage man and the domesticated man should be still greater than that between the savage animal and the domesticated animal; for while animal and man have been treated equally by nature, man gives more comforts to himself than to the animals he tames, and all of these comforts are so many specific causes that make him degenerate more noticeably.

It is therefore no great misfortune for those first men, nor, above all, such a great obstacle to their preservation, that they are naked, that they have no dwelling, and that they lack all those useful things we take to be so necessary. If they do not have furry skin, they have no need for it in warm countries, and in cold countries they soon learn to help themselves to the skins of animals they have vanquished. If they have but two feet to run with, they have two arms to provide for their defense and for their needs. Perhaps their children learn to walk late and with difficulty, but mothers carry them easily: an advantage that is lacking in other species, where the mother, on being pursued, finds herself forced to abandon her young or to conform her pace to theirs. <It is possible there are some exceptions to this. For example, the animal from the province of Nicaragua which resembles a fox and which has feet like a man's hands, and, according to Coreal, has a pouch under its belly in which the mother places her young when she is forced to take flight. No doubt this is the same animal that is called *tloquatzin* in Mexico; the female of the species Laët describes as having a similar pouch for the

same purpose.>[31] Finally, unless we suppose those singular and fortuitous combinations of circumstances of which I will speak later, and which might very well have never taken place, at any rate it is clear that the first man who made clothing or a dwelling for himself was giving himself things that were hardly necessary, since he had done without them until then and since it is not clear why, as a grown man, he could not endure the kind of life he had endured ever since he was a child.

Alone, idle, and always near danger, savage man must like to sleep and be a light sleeper, like those animals that do little thinking and, as it were, sleep the entire time they are not thinking. Since his self-preservation was practically his sole concern, his best-trained faculties ought to be those that have attack and defense as their principal object, either to subjugate his prey or to prevent his becoming the prey of another animal. On the other hand, the organs that are perfected only by softness and sensuality must remain in a state of crudeness that excludes any kind of refinement in him. And with his senses being divided in this respect, he will have extremely crude senses of touch and taste; those of sight, hearing, and smell will have the greatest subtlety. Such is the state of animals in general, and, according to the reports of travelers, such also is that of the majority of savage peoples. Thus we should not be surprised that the Hottentots of the Cape of Good Hope can sight ships with the naked eye as far out at sea as the Dutch can with telescopes; or that the savages of America were as capable of trailing Spaniards by smell as the best dogs could have done; or that all these barbarous nations endure their nakedness with no discomfort, whet their appetites with hot peppers, and drink European liquors like water.[32]

So far I have considered only physical man. Let us now try to look at him from a metaphysical and moral point of view.

In any animal I see nothing but an ingenious machine to which nature has given senses in order for it to renew its strength and to protect itself, to a certain point, from all that tends to destroy or disturb it. I am aware of precisely the same things in the human machine, with the difference that nature alone does everything in the operations of an animal, whereas man contributes as a free agent to his own operations. The former chooses or rejects by instinct and the later by an act of freedom. Hence an animal cannot deviate from the rule that is prescribed to it, even when it would be advantageous to do so, while man deviates from it, often to his own detriment. Thus a pigeon would die of hunger near a bowl filled with choice meats, and so would a cat perched atop a pile of fruit or grain, even though both could nourish themselves quite

---

[31] [Jean Laët (1593–1646) published an account of the West Indies that was translated into French in 1650.]

[32] [Rousseau's major source for his knowledge of "savage man" is the *General History of Voyages* published by the Abbot Prévost in a multivolume series, of which the first eleven volumes appeared in 1746 and the twelfth in 1754.]

well with the food they disdain, if they were of a mind to try some. And thus dissolute men abandon themselves to excesses that cause them fever and death, because the mind perverts the senses and because the will still speaks when nature is silent.

Every animal has ideas, since it has senses; up to a certain point it even combines its ideas, and in this regard man differs from an animal only in degree. Some philosophers have even suggested that there is a greater difference between two given men than between a given man and an animal. Therefore it is not so much understanding that causes the specific distinction of man from all other animals as it is his being a free agent. Nature commands every animal, and the beasts obey. Man feels the same impetus, but he knows he is free to go along or to resist; and it is above all in the awareness of this freedom that the spirituality of his soul is made manifest. For physics explains in some way the mechanism of the senses and the formation of ideas; but in the power of willing, or rather of choosing, and in the feeling of this power, we find only purely spiritual acts, about which the laws of mechanics explain nothing.

But if the difficulties surrounding all these questions should leave some room for dispute on this difference between man and animal, there is another very specific quality that distinguishes them and about which there can be no argument: the faculty of self-perfection, a faculty that, with the aid of circumstances, successively develops all the others, and resides among us as much in the species as in the individual. On the other hand, an animal, at the end of a few months, is what it will be all its life; and its species, at the end of a thousand years, is what it was in the first of those thousand years. Why is man alone subject to becoming an imbecile? Is it not that he thereby returns to his primitive state, and that, while the animal which has acquired nothing and which also has nothing to lose, always retains its instinct, man, in losing through old age or other accidents all that his *perfectibility*[33] has enabled him to acquire, thus falls even lower than the animal itself? It would be sad for us to be forced to agree that this distinctive and almost unlimited faculty is the source of all man's misfortunes; that this is what, by dint of time, draws him out of that original condition in which he would pass tranquil and innocent days; that this is what, through the centuries unfolds both his enlightenment and his errors, his vices and his virtues, and eventually makes him a tyrant over himself and nature.[ix] It would be dreadful to be obliged to praise as a beneficent being the one who first suggested to the inhabitant on the banks of the Orinoco the use of boards that he binds to his children's temples, and that assure them of at least part of their imbecility and their original happiness.

Savage man, left by nature to instinct alone, or rather compensated for the instincts he is perhaps lacking by faculties capable of first replacing them and then of raising him to the level of instinct, will therefore begin with purely

[33] [Rousseau places *perfectibility* in italics because it is a word of his own invention.]

animal functions.[x] Perceiving and feeling will be his first state, which he will have in common with all animals. Willing and not willing, desiring, and fearing will be the first and nearly the only operations of his soul until new circumstances bring about new developments in it.

Whatever the moralists may say about it, human understanding owes much to the passions, which, by common consensus, also owe a great deal to it. It is by their activity that our reason is perfected. We seek to know only because we desire to find enjoyment; and it is impossible to conceive why someone who had neither desires nor fears would go to the bother of reasoning. The passions in turn take their origin from our needs, and their progress from our knowledge. For one can desire or fear things only by virtue of the ideas one can have of them, or from the simple impulse of nature; and savage man, deprived of every sort of enlightenment, feels only the passions of this latter sort. His desires do not go beyond his physical needs.[xi] The only goods he knows in the universe are nourishment, a woman, and rest; the only evils he fears are pain and hunger. I say pain and not death because an animal will never know what it is to die; and knowledge of death and its terrors is one of the first acquisitions that man has made in withdrawing from the animal condition.

Were it necessary, it would be easy for me to support this view with facts and to demonstrate that, among all the nations of the world, the progress of the mind has been precisely proportionate to the needs received by peoples from nature or to those needs to which circumstances have subjected them, and consequently to the passions that inclined them to provide for those needs. I would show the arts[34] coming into being in Egypt and spreading with the flooding of the Nile. I would follow their progress among the Greeks, where they were seen to germinate, grow, and rise to the heavens among the sands and rocks of Attica, though never being able to take root on the fertile banks of the Eurotas.[35] I would point out that in general the peoples of the north are more industrious than those of the south, because they cannot get along as well without being so, as if nature thereby wanted to equalize things by giving to their minds the fertility it refuses their soil.[36]

But without having recourse to the uncertain testimonies of history, does anyone fail to see that everything seems to remove savage man from the temptation and the means of ceasing to be savage? His imagination depicts nothing to him; his heart asks nothing of him. His modest needs are so easily found at hand, and he is so far from the degree of knowledge necessary to make him desire to acquire greater knowledge, that he can have neither foresight nor curiosity. The spectacle of nature becomes a matter of indifference

---

[34] [Rousseau's word *arts* includes the mechanical arts or technology; indeed, here it refers specifically to technology.]

[35] [The Eurotas runs through Sparta.]

[36] [Cf. Montesquieu, *Spirit of the Laws*, bk. 18, ch. 4.]

to him by dint of its becoming familiar to him. It is always the same order, always the same succession of changes. He does not have a mind for marveling at the greatest wonders; and we must not seek in him the philosophy that a man needs in order to know how to observe once what he has seen every day. His soul, agitated by nothing, is given over to the single feeling of his own present existence, without any idea of the future, however near it may be, and his projects, as limited as his views, hardly extend to the end of the day. Such is, even today, the extent of the Carib's foresight. In the morning he sells his bed of cotton and in the evening he returns in tears to buy it back, for want of having foreseen that he would need it that night.[37]

The more one meditates on this subject, the more the distance from pure sensations to the simplest knowledge increases before our eyes; and it is impossible to conceive how a man could have crossed such a wide gap by his forces alone, without the aid of communication and without the provocation of necessity. How many centuries have perhaps gone by before men were in a position to see any fire other than that from the heavens? How many different risks did they have to run before they learned the most common uses of that element? How many times did they let it go out before they had acquired the art of reproducing it? And how many times perhaps did each of these secrets die with the one who had discovered it? What will we say about agriculture, an art that requires so much labor and foresight, that depends on so many other arts, that quite obviously is practicable only in a society which is at least in its beginning stages, and that serves us not so much to derive from the earth food it would readily provide without agriculture, as to force from it those preferences that are most to our taste? But let us suppose that people multiplied to the point where the natural productions were no longer sufficient to nourish them: a supposition that, it may be said in passing, would show a great advantage for the human species in that way of life. Let us suppose that, without forges or workshops, farm implements had fallen from the heavens into the hands of the savages; that these men had conquered the mortal hatred they all have for continuous work; that they had learned to foresee their needs far enough in advance; that they had guessed how the soil is to be cultivated, grains sown, and trees planted; that they had discovered the arts of grinding wheat and fermenting grapes: all things they would need to have been taught by the gods, for it is inconceivable how they could have picked these things up on their own. Yet, after all this, what man would be so foolish as to tire himself out cultivating a field that will be plundered by the first comer, be it man or beast, who takes a fancy to the crop? And how could each man resolve to spend his life in hard labor, when, the more necessary to him the fruits of his labor may be, the surer he is of not realizing them? In a word, how could this situation lead men to cultivate the soil as long as

[37] [Rousseau's source is Jean Baptiste Du Tertre, *General History of the Islands of St. Christophe [St. Kitts], Guadeloupe and Martinique* (1654).]

it is not divided among them, that is to say, as long as the state of nature is not wiped out?

Were we to want to suppose a savage man as skilled in the art of thinking as our philosophers make him out to be; were we, following their example, to make him a full-fledged philosopher, discovering by himself the most sublime truths, and, by chains of terribly abstract reasoning, forming for himself maxims of justice and reason drawn from the love of order in general or from the known will of his creator; in a word, were we to suppose there was as much intelligence and enlightenment in his mind as he needs, and as he is in fact found to have been possessed of dullness and stupidity, what use would the species have for all that metaphysics, which could not be communicated and which would perish with the individual who would have invented it? What progress could the human race make, scattered in the woods among the animals? And to what extent could men mutually perfect and enlighten one another, when, with neither a fixed dwelling nor any need for one another, they would hardly encounter one another twice in their lives, without knowing or talking to one another?

Let us consider how many ideas we owe to the use of speech; how much grammar trains and facilitates the operations of the mind. And let us think of the inconceivable difficulties and the infinite amount of time that the first invention of languages must have cost. Let us join their reflections to the preceding ones, and we will be in a position to judge how many thousands of centuries would have been necessary to develop successively in the human mind the operations of which it was capable.

May I be permitted to consider for a moment the obstacles to the origin of languages. I could be content here to cite or repeat the investigations that the abbot de Condillac has made on this matter, all of which completely confirm my view, and may perhaps have given me the idea in the first place.[38] But since the way in which this philosopher resolves the difficulties he himself raises concerning the origin of conventional signs shows that he assumed what I question (namely, a kind of society already established among the inventors of language), I believe that in referring to his reflections I must add to them my own, in order to present the same difficulties from a standpoint that is pertinent to my subject. The first that presents itself is to imagine how languages could have become necessary; for since men had no communication among themselves nor any need for it, I fail to see either the necessity of this invention or its possibility, if it were not indispensable. I might well say, as do many others, that languages were born in the domestic intercourse among fathers, mothers, and children. But aside from the fact that this would not resolve the difficulties, it would make the mistake of those who, reasoning about the state of nature, intrude into it ideas taken from society. They

---

[38] [Étienne Bonnot de Condillac (1715–1780), *Essay on the Origins of Human Knowledge* (1746).]

always see the family gathered in one and the same dwelling, with its members maintaining among themselves a union as intimate and permanent as exists among us, where so many common interests unite them. But the fact of the matter is that in that primitive state, since nobody had houses or huts or property of any kind, each one bedded down in some random spot and often for only one night. Males and females came together fortuitously as a result of chance encounters, occasion, and desire, without there being any great need for words to express what they had to say to one another. They left one another with the same nonchalance.[xii] The mother at first nursed her children for her own need; then, with habit having endeared them to her, she later nourished them for their own need. Once they had the strength to look for their food, they did not hesitate to leave the mother herself. And since there was practically no other way of finding one another than not to lose sight of one another, they were soon at the point of not even recognizing one another. It should also be noted that, since the child had all his needs to explain and consequently more things to say to the mother than the mother to the child, it is the child who must make the greatest effort toward inventing a language, and that the language he uses should in large part be of his own making, which multiplies languages as many times as there are individuals to speak them. This tendency was abetted by a nomadic and vagabond life, which does not give any idiom time to gain a foothold. For claiming that the mother teaches her child the words he ought to use in asking her for this or that is a good way of showing how already-formed languages are taught, but it does not tell us how languages are formed.

Let us suppose this first difficulty has been overcome. Let us disregard for a moment the immense space that there must have been between the pure state of nature and the need for languages. And, on the supposition that they are necessary,[xiii] let us inquire how they might have begun to be established. Here we come to a new difficulty, worse still than the preceding one. For if men needed speech in order to learn to think, they had a still greater need for knowing how to think in order to discover the art of speaking. And even if it were understood how vocal sounds had been taken for the conventional expressions of our ideas, it would still remain for us to determine what could have been the conventional expressions for ideas that, not having a sensible object, could not be indicated either by gesture or by voice. Thus we are scarcely able to form tenable conjectures regarding the birth of this art of communicating thoughts and establishing intercourse between minds, a sublime art that is already quite far from its origin, but which the philosopher still sees at so prodigious a distance from its perfection that there is no man so foolhardy as to claim that it will ever achieve it, even if the sequences of change that time necessarily brings were suspended in its favor, even if prejudices were to be barred from the academies or be silent before them, and even if they were able to occupy themselves with that thorny problem for whole centuries without interruption.

Man's first language, the most universal, the most energetic, and the only language he needed before it was necessary to persuade men assembled together, is the cry of nature. Since this cry was elicited only by a kind of instinct in pressing circumstances, to beg for help in great dangers, or for relief of violent ills, it was not used very much in the ordinary course of life, where more moderate feelings prevail. When the ideas of men begin to spread and multiply, and closer communication was established among them, they sought more numerous signs and a more extensive language. They multiplied vocal inflections and combined them with gestures, which, by their nature, are more expressive, and whose meaning is less dependent on a prior determination. They therefore signified visible and mobile objects by means of gestures and audible ones by imitative sounds. But since a gesture indicates hardly anything more than present or easily described objects and visible actions; since its use is not universal, because darkness or the interposition of a body renders it useless; and since it requires rather than stimulates attention, men finally thought of replacing them with vocal articulations, which, while not having the same relationship to certain ideas, were better suited to represent all ideas as conventional signs. Such a substitution could only be made by a common consent and in a way rather difficult to practice for men whose crude organs had as yet no exercise, and still more difficult to conceive in itself, since that unanimous agreement had to have had a motive, and speech appears to have been necessary in order to establish the use of speech.

We must infer that the first words men used had a much broader meaning in their mind than do those used in languages that are already formed; and that, being ignorant of the division of discourse into its constitutive parts, at first they gave each word the meaning of a whole sentence. When they began to distinguish subject from attribute and verb from noun, which was no mean effort of genius, substantives were at first only so many proper nouns; the <present> infinitive was the only verb tense; and the notion of adjectives must have developed only with considerable difficulty, since every adjective is an abstract word, and abstractions are difficult and not particularly natural operations.

At first each object was given a particular name without regard to genus and species that those first founders were not in a position to distinguish; and all individual things presented themselves to their minds in isolation, as they are in the spectacle of nature. If one oak tree was called A, another was called B. <For the first idea one draws from two things is that they are not the same; and it often requires quite some time to observe what they have in common.> Thus the more limited the knowledge, the more extensive becomes the dictionary. The difficulty inherent in all this nomenclature could not easily be alleviated, for in order to group beings under various common and generic denominations, it was necessary to know their properties and their differences. What was needed were observations and definitions: that is to say, natural history and metaphysics, which went far beyond anything the men of those times could have accomplished.

Moreover, general ideas can be introduced into the mind only with the aid of words, and the understanding grasps them only through sentences. That is one reason why animals cannot form such ideas or even acquire the perfectibility that depends on them. When a monkey moves unhesitatingly from one nut to another, does anyone think the monkey has the general idea of that type of fruit and that he compares its archetype with these two individuals? Undoubtedly not; but the sight of one of these nuts recalls to his memory the sensations he received of the other; and his eyes, modified in a certain way, announce to his sense of taste the modification it is about to receive. Every general idea is purely intellectual; but the slightest involvement of the imagination with it at once makes it particular. Try to draw for yourself the image of a tree in general; you will never succeed in doing it. In spite of yourself, it must be seen as small or large, barren or leafy, light or dark; and if you were in a position to see in it nothing but what you see in every tree, this image would no longer resemble a tree. Purely abstract beings are perceived in the same way, or are conceived only through discourse. The definition of a triangle alone gives you the true idea of it. As soon as you behold one in your mind, it is a particular triangle and not some other one, and you cannot avoid making its lines to be perceptible or its plane to have color. It is therefore necessary to utter sentences, and thus to speak, in order to have general ideas. For as soon as the imagination stops, the mind proceeds no further without the aid of discourse. If, then, the first inventors of language could give names only to ideas they already had, it follows that the first substantives could not have been anything but proper nouns.

But when, by means I am unable to conceive, our new grammarians began to extend their ideas and to generalize their words, the ignorance of the inventors must have subjected this method to very strict limitations. And just as they had at first unduly multiplied the names of individual things, owing to their failure to know the genera and species, they later made too few species and genera, owing to their failure to have considered beings in all their differences. Pushing these divisions far enough would have required more experience and enlightenment than they could have had, and more investigations and work than they were willing to put into it. However, if even today new species are discovered every day that until now had escaped all our observations, just imagine how many species must have escaped the attention of men who judged things only on first appearance! As for primary classes and the most general notions, it is superfluous to add that they too must have escaped them. How, for example, would they have imagined or understood the words "matter," "mind," "substance," "mode," "figure," and "movement," when our philosophers, who for so long have been making use of them, have a great deal of difficulty understanding them themselves; and when, since the ideas attached to these words are purely metaphysical, they found no model of them in nature?

I stop with these first steps, and I implore my judges to suspend their reading here to consider, concerning the invention of physical substantives alone, that is to say, concerning the easiest part of the language to discover, how far language still had to go in order to express all the thoughts of men, assume a durable form, be capable of being spoken in public, and influence society. I implore them to reflect upon how much time and knowledge were needed to discover numbers,[xiv] abstract words, aorists and all the tenses of verbs, particles, syntax, the connecting of sentences, reasoning, and the forming of all the logic of discourse. As for myself, being shocked by the unending difficulties and convinced of the almost demonstrable impossibility that languages could have arisen and been established by merely human means, I leave to anyone who would undertake it the discussion of the following difficult problem: which was the more necessary, an already formed society for the invention of languages, or already invented languages for the establishment of society?

Whatever these origins may be, it is clear, from the little care taken by nature to bring men together through mutual needs and to facilitate their use of speech, how little it prepared them for becoming habituated to the ways of society, and how little it contributed to all that men have done to establish the bonds of society. In fact, it is impossible to imagine why, in that primitive state, one man would have a greater need for another man than a monkey or a wolf has for another of its respective species; or, assuming this need, what motive could induce the other man to satisfy it; or even, in this latter instance, how could they be in mutual agreement regarding the conditions. I know that we are repeatedly told that nothing would have been so miserable as man in that state; and if it is true, as I believe I have proved, that it is only after many centuries that men could have had the desire and the opportunity to leave that state, that would be a charge to bring against nature, not against those whom nature has thus constituted. But if we understand the word *miserable* properly, it is a word that is without meaning or that signifies merely a painful privation and suffering of the body or the soul. Now I would very much like someone to explain to me: what kind of misery can there be for a free being whose heart is at peace and whose body is in good health? I ask: which of the two, civil or natural life, is more likely to become insufferable to those who live it? We see about us practically no people who do not complain about their existence; many even deprive themselves of it to the extent they are able, and the combination of divine and human laws is hardly enough to stop this disorder. I ask: has anyone ever heard of a savage who was living in liberty ever dreaming of complaining about his life and of killing himself? Let the judgment therefore be made with less pride on which side real misery lies. On the other hand, nothing would have been so miserable as savage man, dazzled by enlightenment, tormented by passions, and reasoning about a state different from his own. It was by a very wise providence that the latent faculties he possessed should develop only as the occasion to exercise them presented itself, so that they would be neither superfluous nor troublesome to him beforehand, nor underdeveloped and useless in time of need. In instinct alone, man had everything he needed in order to live in the state of nature; in a cultivated reason, he has only what he needs to live in society.

At first it would seem that men in that state, having among themselves no type of moral relations or acknowledged duties, could be neither good nor evil, and had neither vices nor virtues, unless, if we take these words in a physical sense, we call those qualities that can harm an individual's preservation "vices" in him, and those that can contribute to it "virtues." In that case it would be necessary to call the one who least resists the simple impulses of nature the most virtuous. But without departing from the standard meaning of these words, it is appropriate to suspend the judgment we could make regarding such a situation and to be on our guard against our prejudices, until we have examined, with scales in hand, whether there are more virtues than vices among civilized men; or whether their virtues are more advantageous than their vices are lethal; or whether the progress of their knowledge is sufficient compensation for ills they inflict on one another as they learn of the good they ought to do; or whether, all things considered, they would not be in a happier set of circumstances if they had neither evil to fear nor good to hope for from anyone, rather than subjecting themselves to a universal dependence and obliging themselves to receive everything from those who do not oblige themselves to give them anything.

Above all, let us not conclude with Hobbes that because man has no idea of goodness he is naturally evil; that he is vicious because he does not know virtue; that he always refuses to perform services for his fellowmen he does not believe he owes them; or that, by virtue of the right, which he reasonably attributes to himself, to those things he needs, he foolishly imagines himself to be the sole proprietor of the entire universe. Hobbes has very clearly seen the defect of all modern definitions of natural right, but the consequences he draws from his own definition show that he takes it in a sense that is no less false. Were he to have reasoned on the basis of the principles he establishes, this author should have said that since the state of nature is the state in which the concern for our self-preservation is the least prejudicial to that of others, that state was consequently the most appropriate for peace and the best suited for the human race. He says precisely the opposite, because he had wrongly injected into the savage man's concern for self-preservation the need to satisfy a multitude of passions that are the product of society and have made laws necessary. The evil man, he says, is a robust child.[39] It remains to be seen whether savage man is a robust child. Were we to grant him this, what would we conclude from it? That if this man were as dependent on others when he is

---

[39] [Hobbes, *De Cive*, ch. 10, §1, and, here, *Praefatio ad lectores*.]

robust as he is when he is weak, there is no type of excess to which he would not tend: he would beat his mother, were she too slow in offering him her breast; he would strangle one of his younger brothers, should he find him annoying; he would bite someone's leg, should he be assaulted or aggravated by him. But being robust and being dependent are two contradictory suppositions in the state of nature. Man is weak when he is dependent, and he is emancipated from that dependence before he is robust. Hobbes did not see that the same cause that prevents savages from using their reason, despite what our jurists think, is what prevents them at the same time from abusing their physical capacities, despite what he himself thinks. Hence we could say that savages are not evil precisely because they do not know what it is to be good; for it is neither the development of enlightenment nor the restraint imposed by the law, but the calm of their passions and their ignorance of vice that prevents them from doing evil. "So much more profitable to these is the ignorance of vice than the knowledge of virtue is to those."[40] Moreover, there is another principle that Hobbes failed to notice, and that, having been given to man in order to mitigate, in certain circumstances, the ferocity of his egocentrism [amour propre] or the desire for self-preservation before this egocentrism of his came into being,[xv] tempers the ardor he has for his own well-being by an innate repugnance to seeing his fellowmen suffer. I do not believe I have any contradiction to fear in granting to man the only natural virtue that the most excessive detractor of human virtues was forced to recognize.[41] I am referring to pity, a disposition that is fitting for beings that are as weak and as subject to ills as we are; a virtue all the more universal and all the more useful to man in that it precedes in him any kind of reflection, and so natural that even animals sometimes show noticeable signs of it. Without speaking of the tenderness of mothers for their young and of the perils they have to brave in order to protect them, one daily observes the repugnance that horses have for trampling a living body with their hooves. An animal does not go undisturbed past a dead animal of its own species. There are even some animals that give them a kind of tomb; and the mournful lowing of cattle entering a slaughterhouse voices the impression they receive of the horrible spectacle that strikes them. One notes with pleasure the author of *The Fable of the Bees*, having been forced to acknowledge man as a compassionate and sensitive being, departing from his cold and subtle style in the example he gives, to offer us the pathetic image of an imprisoned man who sees outside his cell a ferocious animal tearing a child from its mother's breast, mashing its frail limbs with its murderous teeth, and ripping with its claws the child's quivering entrails. What horrible agitation must be felt by this witness of an event in which he has no personal interest! What anguish must he suffer

[40] [Justin, *Historiae*, bk. 2, ch. 2, §15, probably cited from Grotius, *Law of War and Peace*, bk. 2, ch. 2, §2.]
[41] [Bernard Mandeville (1670–1733), author of *The Fable of the Bees* (1714).]

at this sight, being unable to be of any help to the fainting mother or to the dying child?[42]

Such is the pure movement of nature prior to all reflection. Such is the force of natural pity, which the most depraved mores still have difficulty destroying, since every day one sees in our theaters someone affected and weeping at the ills of some unfortunate person, and who, were he in the tyrant's place, would intensify the torments of his enemy still more; <like the bloodthirsty Sulla, so sensitive to ills he had not caused, or like Alexander of Pherae, who did not dare attend the performance of any tragedy, for fear of being seen weeping with Andromache and Priam, and yet who listened impassively to the cries of so many citizens who were killed every day on his orders. "Nature, in giving men tears, bears witness that it gave the human race the softest hearts."[43]> Mandeville has a clear awareness that, with all their mores, men would never have been anything but monsters, if nature had not given them pity to aid their reason; but he has not seen that from this quality alone flow all the social virtues that he wants to deny in men. In fact, what are generosity, mercy, and humanity, if not pity applied to the weak, to the guilty, or to the human species in general? Benevolence and even friendship are, properly understood, the products of a constant pity fixed on a particular object; for is desiring that someone not suffer anything but desiring that he be happy? Were it true that commiseration were merely a sentiment that puts us in the position of the one who suffers, a sentiment that is obscure and powerful in savage man, developed but weak in man dwelling in civil society, what importance would this idea have to the truth of what I say, except to give it more force? In fact, commiseration will be all the more energetic as the witnessing animal identifies itself more intimately with the suffering animal. Now it is evident that this identification must have been infinitely closer in the state of nature than in the state of reasoning. Reason is what engenders egocentrism [*amour propre*], and reflection strengthens it. Reason is what turns man in upon himself. Reason is what separates him from all that troubles him and afflicts him. Philosophy is what isolates him and moves him to say in secret, at the sight of a suffering man, "Perish if you will; I am safe and sound." No longer can anything but danger to the entire society trouble the tranquil slumber of the philosopher and yank him from his bed. His fellowman can be killed with impunity underneath his window. He has merely to place his hands over his ears and argue with himself a little in order to prevent nature, which rebels within him, from identifying him with the man being assassinated.[44] Savage man does not have this admirable talent, and for lack of wisdom and reason he is always seen thoughtlessly giving in to the first sentiment of humanity. When there is a riot or a street brawl, the

---

[42] [Mandeville, *An Essay on Charity and Charity Schools*, added to *The Fable of the Bees* in 1723.]

[43] [Juvenal, *Satire 15*, lines 131–33.]

[44] [Rousseau later said that this passage was suggested to him by Diderot.]

populace gathers together; the prudent man withdraws from the scene. It is the rabble, the women of the marketplace, who separate the combatants and prevent decent people from killing one another.

It is therefore quite certain that pity is a natural sentiment, which, by moderating in each individual the activity of the love of oneself, contributes to the mutual preservation of the entire species. Pity is what carries us without reflection to the aid of those we see suffering. Pity is what, in the state of nature, takes the place of laws, mores, and virtue, with the advantage that no one is tempted to disobey its sweet voice. Pity is what will prevent every robust savage from robbing a weak child or an infirm old man of his hard-earned subsistence, if he himself expects to be able to find his own someplace else. Instead of the sublime maxim of reasoned justice, *Do unto others as you would have them do unto you*, pity inspires all men with another maxim of natural goodness, much less perfect but perhaps more useful than the preceding one: *Do what is good for you with as little harm as possible to others.* In a word, it is in this natural sentiment rather than in subtle arguments that one must search for the cause of the repugnance at doing evil that every man would experience, even independently of the maxims of education. Although it might be appropriate for Socrates and minds of his stature to acquire virtue through reason, the human race would long ago have ceased to exist, if its preservation had depended solely on the reasonings of its members.

With passions so minimally active and with such a salutary restraint, being more wild than evil, and more attentive to protecting themselves from the harm they could receive than tempted to do harm to others, men were not subject to very dangerous conflicts. Since they had no sort of intercourse among themselves; since, as a consequence, they knew neither vanity, nor deference, nor esteem, nor contempt; since they had not the slightest notion of mine and thine, nor any true idea of justice; since they regarded the acts of violence that could befall them as an easily redressed evil and not as an offense that must be punished; and since they did not even dream of vengeance except perhaps as a knee-jerk response right then and there, like the dog that bites the stone that is thrown at it, their disputes would rarely have had bloody consequences, if their subject had been no more sensitive than food. But I see a more dangerous matter that remains for me to discuss.

Among the passions that agitate the heart of man, there is an ardent, impetuous one that renders one sex necessary to the other; a terrible passion that braves all dangers, overcomes all obstacles, and that, in its fury, seems fitted to destroy the human race it is destined to preserve. What would become of men, victimized by this unrestrained and brutal rage, without modesty and self-control, fighting every day over the object of their passion at the price of their blood?

There must first be agreement that the more violent the passions are, the more necessary the laws are to contain them. But over and above the fact that the disorders and the crimes, caused daily in our midst by these passions, show quite well the insufficiency of the laws in this regard, it would still be good to examine whether these disorders did not come into being with the laws themselves; for then, even if they were capable of repressing them, still the least one would expect of them would be that they call a halt to an evil that would not exist without them.

Let us begin by distinguishing between the moral and the physical aspects of the sentiment of love. The physical aspect is that general desire that inclines one sex to unite with another. The moral aspect is what determines this desire and fixes it exclusively on one single object, or which at least gives it a greater degree of energy for this preferred object. Now it is easy to see that the moral aspect of love is an artificial sentiment born of social custom, and extolled by women with so much skill and care in order to establish their hegemony and make dominant the sex that ought to obey.[45] Since this feeling is founded on certain notions of merit or beauty that a savage is not in a position to have, and on comparisons he is incapable of making, it must be almost nonexistent for him. For since his mind could not form abstract ideas of regularity and proportion, his heart is not susceptible to sentiments of admiration and love, which, even without their being observed, come into being from the application of these ideas. He pays exclusive attention to the sexual appetite[46] he has received from nature, and none to the taste <The 1782 edition substitutes "aversion" for "taste"> he has been unable to acquire; any woman suits his purpose.

Limited merely to the physical aspect of love, and fortunate enough to be ignorant of those preferences that stir up the feeling and increase the difficulties in satisfying it, men must feel the ardors of their sexual appetite less frequently and less vividly, and consequently have fewer and less cruel conflicts among themselves. Imagination, which wreaks so much havoc among us, does not speak to savage hearts; each man peacefully awaits the impetus of nature, gives himself over to it without choice, and with more pleasure than frenzy; and once the need is satisfied, all desire is snuffed out.

Hence it is incontestable that love itself, like all the other passions, has acquired only in society that impetuous ardor that so often makes it lethal to men. And it is all the more ridiculous to represent savages as continually slaughtering each other in order to satisfy their brutality, since this opinion is directly contrary to experience; and since the Caribs, who, of all existing peoples, are the people that until now has wandered least from the state of nature, are precisely the people least subject to jealousy, even though they

---

[45] [Voltaire, who believed that men and women are equal, wrote in the margin of his copy one word: "why?"]

[46] [Rousseau's word is *tempérament*. The 1762 edition of the *Dictionnaire de l'Académie française* says, "On dit absolument, *Avoir du tempérament*, pour dire, Être fort porté à l'amour" (to have a very powerful sex drive).]

live in a hot climate, which always seems to make these passions all the more forceful.

As to any inferences that could be drawn, in the case of several species of animals, from the clashes between males that bloody our poultry yards throughout the year, and which make our forests resound in the spring with the cries of the males as they quarrel over a female, it is necessary to begin by excluding all species in which nature has manifestly established, in the relative power of the sexes, relations other than those that exist among us. Hence cockfights do not form the basis for an inference regarding the human species. In species where the difference between males and females is less marked, these fights can have for their cause only the scarcity of females in relation to the number of males, or the limited periods of time during which the female continually rejects the advances of the male, which amounts to the same thing. For if each female receives the male for only two months a year, in this respect it is as if the number of females were reduced by five-sixths. Now neither of these two cases is applicable to the human species, where the number of females generally surpasses the number of males, and where human females, unlike those of other species, have never been observed to have periods of heat and exclusion, even among savages. Moreover, among several of these animal species, where the entire species goes into heat simultane-ously, there comes a terrible moment of common ardor, tumult, disorder, and combat: a moment that does not happen in the human species, where love is never seasonal. Therefore one cannot conclude from the combats of certain animals for the possession of females that the same thing would happen to man in the state of nature. And even if one could draw that conclusion, given that these conflicts do not destroy the other species, one should conclude that they would not be any more lethal for ours. And it is quite apparent that they would wreak less havoc in the state of nature than in society, especially in countries where mores still count for something and where the jealousy of lovers and the vengeance of husbands every day give rise to duels, murders, and still worse things; where the duty of eternal fidelity serves merely to create adulterers; and where even the laws of continence and honor inevitably spread debauchery and multiply the number of abortions.

Let us conclude that, wandering in the forests, without skills, without speech, without dwelling, without war, without relationships, with no need for his fellowmen, and correspondingly with no desire to do them harm, perhaps never even recognizing any of them individually, savage man, subject to few passions and self-sufficient, had only the sentiments and enlightenment appropriate to that state; he felt only his true needs, took notice of only what he believed he had an interest in seeing; and his intelligence was no more developed than his vanity. If by chance he made some discovery, he was all the less able to communicate it to others because he did not even know his own children. Art perished with its inventor. There was neither education nor progress; generations were multiplied to no purpose. Since each one always began from the same point, centuries went by with all the crudeness of the first ages; the species was already old, and man remained ever a child.

If I have gone on at such length about this hypothetical primitive condition, it is because, having ancient errors and inveterate prejudices to destroy, I felt I should dig down to the root and show, through the depiction of the true state of nature, how far even natural inequality is from having as much reality and influence in that state as our writers claim.

In fact, it is easy to see that, among the differences that distinguish men, several of them pass for natural ones that are exclusively the work of habit and of the various sorts of life that men adopt in society. Thus a robust or delicate temperament, and the strength or weakness that depend on it, frequently derive more from the harsh or effeminate way in which one has been raised than from the primitive constitution of one's body. The same holds for mental powers; and not only does education make a difference between cultivated minds and those that are not, it also augments the difference among the former in proportion to their culture; for were a giant and a dwarf walking on the same road, each step they both took would give a fresh advantage to the giant. Now if one compares the prodigious diversity of educations and lifestyles to be found in the different orders of the civil state[47] with the simplicity and uniformity of animal and savage life, where all nourish themselves from the same foods, live in the same manner, and do exactly the same things, it will be understood how much less the difference between one man and another must be in the state of nature than in that of society, and how much natural inequality must increase in the human species through inequality occasioned by social institutions.

But even if nature were to display, in the distribution of its gifts, as many preferences as is claimed, what advantage would the most favored men derive from them, to the detriment of others, in a state of things that allowed practically no sort of relationships among them? Where there is no love, what use is beauty? What use is wit for people who do not speak, and cunning for those who have no dealing with others? I always hear it repeated that the stronger will oppress the weaker. But let me have an explanation of the meaning of the word "oppression." Some will dominate with violence; others will groan, enslaved to their every whim—well, that is precisely what I observe among us, but I do not see how this could be said of savage men, to whom it would be difficult even to explain what servitude and domination are. A man could well lay hold of the fruit another has gathered, the game he has killed, the cave that served as his shelter. But how will he ever succeed in making himself be obeyed? And what can be the chains of dependence among men who possess nothing? If someone chases me from one tree, I am free to go to another; if someone torments me in one place, who will prevent me from

[47] [Rousseau's phrase is *les différents ordres de l'état civil*. One might almost translate it as "the social classes of civilized society."]

going elsewhere? Is there a man with strength sufficiently superior to mine and who is, moreover, sufficiently depraved, sufficiently lazy, and sufficiently ferocious to force me to provide for his subsistence while he remains idle? He must resolve not to take his eyes off me for a single instant, to keep me carefully tied down while he sleeps, for fear that I may escape or that I would kill him. In other words, he is obliged to expose himself voluntarily to a much greater hardship than the one he wants to avoid and gives me. After all that, were his vigilance to relax for an instant, were an unforeseen noise to make him turn his head, I take twenty steps into the forest; my chains are broken, and he never sees me again for the rest of his life.

Without needlessly prolonging these details, anyone should see that, since the bonds of servitude are formed merely from the mutual dependence of men and the reciprocal needs that unite them, it is impossible to enslave a man without having first put him in the position of being incapable of doing without another. This being a situation that did not exist in the state of nature, it leaves each person free of the yoke, and renders pointless the law of the strongest.

After having proved that inequality is hardly observable in the state of nature, and that its influence there is almost nonexistent, it remains for me to show its origin and progress in the successive developments of the human mind. After having shown that *perfectibility*, social virtues, and the other faculties that natural man had received in a state of potentiality could never develop by themselves, that to achieve this development they required the chance coming together of several unconnected causes that might never have come into being and without which he would have remained eternally in his primitive condition <The 1782 edition substitutes "constitution" for "condition">, it remains for me to consider and to bring together the various chance happenings that were able to perfect human reason while deteriorating the species, make a being evil while rendering it habituated to the ways of society, and, from so distant a beginning, finally bring man and the world to the point where we see them now.

I admit that, since the events I have to describe could have taken place in several ways, I cannot make a determination among them except on the basis of conjecture. But over and above the fact that these conjectures become reasons when they are the most probable ones that a person can draw from the nature of things and the sole means that a person can have of discovering the truth, the consequences I wish to deduce from mine will not thereby be at all conjectural, since, on the basis of the principles I have just established, no other system is conceivable that would not furnish me with the same results, and from which I could not draw the same conclusions.

This will excuse me from expanding my reflections on the way in which the lapse of time compensates for the slight probability of events; on the surprising power that quite negligible causes may have when they act without interruption; on the impossibility, on the one hand, of our being able to disprove certain hypotheses, even though, on the other hand, we are in a position to accord them the level of certitude that would justify regarding them as facts. Note that in a situation in which two facts have been acknowledged as real, but need to be connected by a series of intermediate facts that are unknown or regarded as such, it belongs to history, where it exists, to provide the facts that connect them; but it belongs to philosophy, where history is unavailable, to determine what sort of facts could connect them. Finally, bear in mind that, with respect to events, similarity reduces the facts to a much smaller number of different classes than one might imagine. It is enough for me to submit these topics to the consideration of my judges; it is enough for me to have seen to it that ordinary readers should have no need to consider them.

PART TWO

The first person who, having enclosed a plot of land, took it into his head to say, "This is mine," and found people simple enough to believe him, was the true founder of civil society. What crimes, wars, murders, what miseries and horrors would the human race have been spared, had someone pulled up the stakes or filled in the ditch and cried out to his fellowmen, "Do not listen to this impostor. You are lost if you forget that the fruits of the earth belong to all and the earth to no one!"? But it is quite likely that by then things had already reached the point where they could no longer continue as they were. For this idea of property, depending on many prior ideas that could only have arisen successively, was not formed all at once in the human mind. It was necessary to make great progress, acquire many skills and much enlightenment, and transmit and augment them from one age to another before arriving at this final limit to the state of nature. Let us therefore go back to an earlier point and try to piece together from a single point of view that slow succession of events and advances in knowledge, taking them in their most natural order.

Man's first sentiment was that of his own existence; his first concern was that of his preservation. The products of the earth provided him with all the help he needed; instinct led him to make use of them. With hunger and other appetites making him experience by turns various ways of existing, there was one appetite that invited him to perpetuate his species; and this blind inclination, devoid of any sentiment of the heart, produced a purely animal act. Once this need had been satisfied, the two sexes would not recognize each other if they met again, and even the child no longer meant anything to the mother once it could do without her.

Such was the condition of man in his nascent stage; such was the life of an animal limited at first to pure sensations, and scarcely profiting from the gifts nature offered him, let alone dreaming of forcing her to hand over anything against her will. But difficulties soon presented themselves to him; it was necessary to learn to overcome them. The height of trees, which kept him from reaching their fruits, the competition of animals that sought to feed themselves on these same fruits, the ferocity of those animals that wanted to take his own life: everything obliged him to apply himself to bodily exercises. It was necessary to become agile, fleet-footed, and vigorous in combat. Natural weapons, which are tree branches and stones, were soon found ready at hand. He learned to surmount nature's obstacles, combat other animals when necessary, fight for his subsistence even with men, or compensate himself for what he had to yield to those stronger than him.

In proportion as the human race spread, difficulties multiplied with the men. Differences in soils, climates, and seasons could force them to introduce corresponding differences in their lifestyles. Barren years, long and hard winters, hot summers that consume everything required new resourcefulness from them. Along the seashore and the riverbanks they invented the fishing line and hook, and became fishermen and fish eaters. In the forests they made bows and arrows and became hunters and warriors. In cold countries they covered themselves with the skins of animals they had killed. Lightning, a volcano, or some lucky accident acquainted them with fire: a new resource against the rigors of winter. They learned to preserve this element, then to reproduce it, and finally to use it to prepare meats that previously they had devoured raw.

This repeated counterposition of the various creatures to himself, and of each species to the others, must naturally have engendered in man's mind a perception of certain relations. These relationships, which we express by the words *large, small, strong, weak, fast, slow, timorous, bold*, and other similar ideas, comparisons carried out when needed and almost without thinking about it, finally produced in him a kind of reflection, or rather a mechanical prudence that pointed out to him the precautions that were most necessary for his safety.

The new enlightenment that resulted from this development increased his superiority over the other animals by making him aware of it. He trained himself to set traps for them; he tricked them in a thousand different ways. And although several surpassed him in fighting strength or in swiftness in running, of those that could serve him or hurt him, he became in time the master of the former and the scourge of the latter. Thus the first glance he directed upon himself produced within him the first stirrings of pride; thus, as yet hardly knowing how to distinguish the ranks, and contemplating himself in the first rank by virtue of his species, he prepared himself from afar to lay claim to it in virtue of his individuality.

Although his fellowmen were not for him what they are for us, and although he had hardly anything more to do with them than with other animals, they were not forgotten in his observations. The conformities that over time he could perceive between them, his female, and himself, made him judge those he did not perceive. And seeing that they all acted as he would have done under similar circumstances, he concluded that their way of thinking and feeling was in complete conformity with his own. And this important truth, well established in his mind, made him follow, by a presentiment as sure as dialectic and more prompt, the best rules of conduct that it was appropriate to observe toward them for his advantage and safety.

Taught by experience that love of well-being is the sole motive of human actions, he found himself in a position to distinguish the rare occasions when common interest should make him count on the assistance of his fellowmen, and those even rarer occasions when competition ought to make him distrust them. In the first case, he united with them in a herd, or at most in some sort of free association, that obligated no one and that lasted only as long as the passing need that had formed it. In the second case, everyone sought to obtain his own advantage, either by overt force, if he believed he could, or by cleverness and cunning, if he felt himself to be the weaker.

This is how men could imperceptibly acquire some crude idea of mutual commitments and of the advantages to be had in fulfilling them, but only insofar as present and perceptible interests could require it, since foresight meant nothing to them, and far from concerning themselves about a distant future, they did not even give a thought to the next day. Were it a matter of catching a deer, everyone was quite aware that he must faithfully keep to his post in order to achieve this purpose; but if a hare happened to pass within reach of one of them, no doubt he would have pursued it without giving it a second thought, and that, having obtained his prey, he cared very little about causing his companions to miss theirs.

It is easy to understand that such intercourse did not require a language much more refined than that of crows or monkeys, which flock together in practically the same way. Inarticulate cries, many gestures, and some imitative noises must for a long time have made up the universal language. By joining to this in each country a few articulate and conventional sounds, whose institution, as I have already said, is not too easy to explain, there arose individual languages, but crude and imperfect ones, quite similar to those still spoken by various savage nations today. Constrained by the passing of time, the abundance of things I have to say, and the practically imperceptible progress of the beginnings, I am flying like an arrow over the multitudes of centuries. For the slower events were in succeeding one another, the quicker they can be described. These first advances enabled man to make more rapid ones. The more the mind was enlightened, the more skills were perfected. Soon they ceased to fall asleep under the first tree or to retreat into caves, and found various types of hatchets made of hard, sharp stones, which served to cut wood, dig up the soil, and make huts from branches they later found it useful to cover with clay and mud. This was the period of a first revolution, which formed the establishment of the distinction among families and which introduced a kind of property, whence perhaps there already arose many quarrels and fights. However, since the strongest were probably the first to make themselves lodgings they felt capable of defending, presumably the weak found it quicker and safer to imitate them than to try to dislodge them; and as for those who already had huts, each of them must have rarely sought to appropriate that of his neighbor, less because it did not belong to him than because it was of no use to him, and because he could not seize it without exposing himself to a fierce battle with the family that occupied it.

The first developments of the heart were the effect of a new situation that united the husbands and wives, fathers and children in one common habitation. The habit of living together gave rise to the sweetest sentiments known to men: conjugal love and parental love. Each family became a little society all the better united because mutual attachment and liberty were its only bonds; and it was then that the first difference was established in the lifestyle of the two sexes, which until then had had only one. Women became more sedentary and grew accustomed to watch over the hut and the children, while the man went to seek their common subsistence. With their slightly softer life, the two sexes also began to lose something of their ferocity and vigor. But while each one separately became less suited to combat savage beasts, on the other hand it was easier to assemble in order to jointly resist them.

In this new state, with a simple and solitary life, very limited needs, and the tools they had invented to provide for them, since men enjoyed a great deal of leisure time, they used it to procure for themselves many types of conveniences unknown to their fathers; and that was the first yoke they imposed on themselves without realizing it, and the first source of evils they prepared for their descendants. For in addition to their continuing thus to soften body and mind (those conveniences having through habit lost almost all their pleasure, and being at the same time degenerated into true needs), being deprived of them became much more cruel than possessing them was sweet; and they were unhappy about losing them without being happy about possessing them.

At this point we can see a little better how the use of speech was established or imperceptibly perfected itself in the bosom of each family; and one can further conjecture how various particular causes could have extended the language and accelerated its progress by making it more necessary. Great floods or earthquakes surrounded the inhabited areas with water or precipices. Upheavals of the globe detached parts of the mainland and broke them up into islands. Clearly among men thus brought together and forced to live together, a common idiom must have been formed sooner than among those who wandered freely about the forests of the mainland. Thus it is quite possible that after their first attempts at navigation, the islanders brought the use of speech to us; and it is at least quite probable that society and languages came into being on islands and were perfected there before they were known on the mainland.

Everything begins to take on a new appearance. Having previously wandered about the forests and having assumed a more fixed situation, men slowly came together and united into different bands, eventually forming in each country a particular nation, united by mores and characteristic features, not by regulations and laws, but by the same kind of life and foods and by the common influence of the climate. Eventually a permanent proximity cannot fail to engender some intercourse among different families. Young people of different sexes live in neighboring huts; the passing intercourse demanded by nature soon leads to another, through frequent contact with one another, no less sweet and more permanent. People become accustomed to consider different objects and to make comparisons. Imperceptibly they acquire the ideas of merit and beauty that produce feelings of preference. By dint of seeing one another, they can no longer get along without seeing one another again. A sweet and tender feeling insinuates itself into the soul and at the least opposition becomes an impetuous fury. Jealousy awakens with love; discord triumphs, and the sweetest passion receives sacrifices of human blood.

In proportion as ideas and sentiments succeed one another and as the mind and heart are trained, the human race continues to be tamed, relationships spread, and bonds are tightened. People grew accustomed to gather in front of their huts or around a large tree; song and dance, true children of love and leisure, became the amusement or rather the occupation of idle men and women who had flocked together. Each one began to look at the others and to want to be looked at himself, and public esteem had a value. The one who sang or danced the best, the handsomest, the strongest, the most adroit, or the most eloquent became the most highly regarded. And this was the first step toward inequality and, at the same time, toward vice. From these first preferences were born vanity and contempt on the one hand, and shame and envy on the other. And the fermentation caused by these new leavens eventually produced compounds fatal to happiness and innocence.

As soon as men had begun mutually to value one another, and the idea of esteem was formed in their minds, each one claimed to have a right to it, and it was no longer possible for anyone to be lacking it with impunity. From this came the first duties of civility, even among savages; and from this every voluntary wrong became an outrage, because along with the harm that resulted from the injury, the offended party saw in it contempt for his person, which often was more insufferable than the harm itself. Hence each man punished the contempt shown him in a manner proportionate to the esteem in which he held himself; acts of revenge became terrible, and men became bloodthirsty and cruel. This is precisely the stage reached by most of the savage people known to us; and it is for want of having made adequate distinctions among their ideas or of having noticed how far these peoples already were from the original state of nature that many have hastened to conclude that man is naturally cruel, and that he needs civilization in order to soften him. On the contrary, nothing is so gentle as man in his primitive state, when, placed by nature at an equal distance from the stupidity of brutes and the fatal enlightenment of civil man, and limited equally by instinct and reason to protecting himself from the harm that threatens him, he is restrained by natural pity from needlessly harming anyone himself, even if he has been harmed. For according to the axiom of the wise Locke, "where there is no property, there is no injury."[48]

But it must be noted that society in its beginning stages and the relations already established among men required in them qualities different from those they derived from their primitive constitution; that, with morality beginning to be introduced into human actions, and everyone, prior to the existence of laws, being sole judge and avenger of the offenses he had received, the goodness appropriate to the pure state of nature was no longer what was appropriate to an emerging society; that it was necessary for punishments to become more severe in proportion as the occasions for giving offense became more frequent; and that it was for the fear of vengeance to take the place of the deterrent character of laws. Hence although men had become less forbearing, and although natural pity had already undergone some alteration, this period of the development of human faculties, maintaining a middle position between the indolence of our primitive state and the petulant activity of our egocentrism [amour propre], must have been the happiest and most durable epoch. The more one reflects on it, the more one finds that this state was the least subject to upheavals and the best for man,[xvi] and that he must have left it only by virtue of some fatal chance happening that, for the common good, ought never have happened. The example of savages, almost all of whom have been found in this state, seems to confirm that the human race had been made to remain in it always; that this state is the veritable youth of the world; and that all the subsequent progress has been in appearance so many steps toward the perfection of the individual, and in fact toward the decay of the species.

As long as men were content with the rustic huts, as long as they were limited to making their clothing out of skins sewn together with thorns or fish bones, adorning themselves with feathers and shells, painting their bodies with various colors, perfecting or embellishing their bows and arrows, using sharp-edged stones to make some fishing canoes or some crude musical instruments; in a word, as long as they applied themselves exclusively to tasks that a single individual could do and to the arts that did not require the cooperation of several hands, they lived as free, healthy, good, and happy as they could in accordance with their nature; and they continued to enjoy among themselves the sweet rewards of independent intercourse. But as soon as one man needed the help of another, as soon as one man realized that it was useful for a single individual to have provisions for two, equality disappeared, property came into existence, labor became necessary. Vast forests

---

[48] [Essay Concerning Human Understanding, bk. 4, ch. 3, §18.]

were transformed into smiling fields that had to be watered with men's sweat, and in which slavery and misery were soon seen to germinate and grow with the crops.

Metallurgy and agriculture were the two arts whose invention produced this great revolution. For the poet, it is gold and silver; but for the philosopher, it is iron and wheat that have civilized men and sealed the fate of the human race. Thus they were both unknown to the savages of America, who for that reason have always remained savages. Other peoples even appear to have remained barbarous, as long as they practiced one of those arts without the other. And perhaps one of the best reasons why Europe has been, if not sooner, at least more constantly and better governed than the other parts of the world, is that it is at the same time the most abundant in iron and the most fertile in wheat.

It is very difficult to guess how men came to know and use iron, for one cannot believe that by themselves they thought of drawing the ore from the mine and performing the necessary preparations on it for smelting it before they knew what would result. From another point of view, it is even less plausible to attribute this discovery to some accidental fire, because mines are set up exclusively in arid places devoid of trees and plants, so that one would say that nature had taken precautions to conceal this deadly secret from us. Thus there remains only the extraordinary circumstance of some volcano that, in casting forth molten metal, would have given observers the idea of imitating this operation of nature. Even then we must suppose them to have had a great deal of courage and foresight to undertake such a difficult task and to have envisaged so far in advance the advantages they could derive from it. This is hardly suitable except for minds already better trained than theirs ought to have been.

As for agriculture, its principle was known long before its practice was established, and it is hardly possible that men, constantly preoccupied with deriving their subsistence from trees and plants, did not rather quickly get the idea of the methods used by nature to grow plant life. But their skills probably did not turn in that direction until very late either because trees, which, along with hunting and fishing, provided their nourishment, had no need of their care; or for want of knowing how to use wheat; or for want of tools with which to cultivate it; or for want of foresight regarding future needs; or, finally, for want of the means of preventing others from appropriating the fruits of their labors. Having become more skillful, it is credible that, with sharp stones and pointed sticks, they began by cultivating some vegetables or roots around their huts long before they knew how to prepare wheat and had the tools necessary for large-scale cultivation. Moreover, to devote oneself to that occupation and to sow the lands, one must be resolved to lose something at first in order to gain a great deal later: a precaution quite far removed from the mind of savage man, who, as I have said, finds it quite difficult to give thought in the morning to what he will need at night.

The invention of the other arts was therefore necessary to force the human race to apply itself to that of agriculture. Once men were needed in order to smelt and forge iron, other men were needed in order to feed them. The more the number of workers increased, the fewer hands there were to obtain food for the common subsistence, without there being fewer mouths to consume it; and since some needed foodstuffs in exchange for their iron, the others finally found the secret of using iron to multiply foodstuffs. From this there arose farming and agriculture, on the one hand, and the art of working metals and multiplying their uses, on the other.

From the cultivation of land, there necessarily followed the division of land; and from property once recognized, the first rules of justice. For in order to render everyone what is his, it is necessary that everyone can have something. Moreover, as men began to look toward the future and as they saw that they all had goods to lose, there was not one of them who did not have to fear reprisals against himself for wrongs he might do to another. This origin is all the more natural as it is impossible to conceive of the idea of property arising from anything but manual labor, for it is not clear what man can add, beyond his own labor, in order to appropriate things he has not made. It is labor alone that, in giving the cultivator a right to the product of the soil he has tilled, consequently gives him a right, at least until the harvest, and thus from year to year. With this possession continuing uninterrupted, it is easily transformed into property. When the ancients, says Grotius, gave Ceres the epithet of legislatrix, gave the name Thesmophoria to a festival celebrated in her honor, they thereby made it apparent that the division of lands has produced a new kind of right: namely, the right of property, different from that which results from the natural law.[49]

Things in this state could have remained equal, if talents had been equal, and if the use of iron and the consumption of foodstuffs had always been in precise balance. But this proportion was not maintained by anything, and was soon broken. The strongest did the most work; the most adroit turned theirs to better advantage; the most ingenious found ways to shorten their labor. The farmer had a greater need for iron, or the blacksmith had a greater need for wheat; and in laboring equally, the one earned a great deal while the other barely had enough to live. Thus it is that natural inequality imperceptibly manifests itself together with inequality occasioned by the socialization process. Thus it is that the differences among men, developed by those of circumstances, make themselves more noticeable, more permanent in their effects, and begin to influence the fate of private individuals in the same proportion.

With things having reached this point, it is easy to imagine the rest. I will not stop to describe the successive invention of the arts, the progress of languages, the testing and use of talents, the inequality of fortunes, the use

[49] [Grotius, *Law of War and Peace*, bk. 2, ch. 2, §2.]

or abuse of wealth, nor all the details that follow these and that everyone can easily supply. I will limit myself exclusively to taking a look at the human race placed in this new order of things.

Thus we find here all our faculties developed, memory and imagination in play, egocentrism [*amour propre*] looking out for its interests, reason rendered active, and the mind having nearly reached the limit of the perfection of which it is capable. We find here all the natural qualities put into action, the rank and fate of each man established not only on the basis of the quantity of goods and the power to serve or harm, but also on the basis of intelligence, beauty, strength, or skill, on the basis of merit or talents. And since these qualities were the only ones that could attract consideration, he was soon forced to have them or affect them. It was necessary, for his advantage, to show himself to be something other than what he in fact was. Being something and appearing to be something became two completely different things; and from this distinction there arose grandiose ostentation, deceptive cunning, and all the vices that follow in their wake. On the other hand, although man had previously been free and independent, we find him, so to speak, subject, by virtue of a multitude of fresh needs, to all of nature and particularly to his fellowmen, whose slave in a sense he becomes even in becoming their master: rich, he needs their services; poor, he needs their help; and being midway between wealth and poverty does not put him in a position to get along without them. It is therefore necessary for him to seek incessantly to interest them in his fate and to make them find their own profit, in fact or in appearance, in working for his. This makes him two-faced and crooked with some, imperious and harsh with others, and puts him in the position of having to abuse everyone he needs when he cannot make them fear him and does not find it in his interests to be of useful service to them. Finally, consuming ambition, the zeal for raising the relative level of his fortune, less out of real need than in order to put himself above others, inspires <inspire> in all men a wicked tendency to harm one another, a secret jealousy all the more dangerous because, in order to strike its blow in greater safety, it often wears the mask of benevolence; in short, competition and rivalry on the one hand, opposition of interest<s> on the other, and always the hidden desire to profit at the expense of someone else. All these ills are the first effect of property and the inseparable offshoot of incipient inequality.

Before signs to represent wealth had been invented, it could hardly have consisted of anything but lands and livestock, the only real goods men can possess. Now when inheritances had grown in number and size to the point of covering the entire landscape and of all bordering on one another, some could no longer be enlarged except at the expense of others; and the supernumeraries, whom weakness or indolence had prevented from acquiring an inheritance in their turn, became poor without having lost anything, because while everything changed around them, they alone had not changed at all. Thus they were forced to receive or steal their subsistence from the hands of

the rich. And from that there began to arise, according to the diverse characters of the rich and the poor, domination and servitude, or violence and thefts.
For their part, the wealthy had no sooner known the pleasure of domination,
than before long they disdained all others, and using their old slaves to subdue
new ones, they thought of nothing but the subjugation and enslavement of
their neighbors, like those ravenous wolves that, on having once tasted human
flesh, reject all other food and desire to devour only men.

Thus, when both the most powerful or the most miserable made of their
strength or their needs a sort of right to another's goods, equivalent, according to them, to the right of property, the destruction of equality was followed
by the most frightful disorder. Thus the usurpations of the rich, the acts of
brigandage by the poor, the unbridled passions of all, stifling natural pity and
the still weak voice of justice, made men greedy, ambitious, and wicked. There
arose between the right of the strongest and the right of the first occupant a
perpetual conflict that ended only in fights and murders.[xvii] Emerging society
gave way to the most horrible state of war; since the human race, debased and
distressed, was no longer able to retrace its steps or give up the unfortunate
acquisitions it had made, and since it labored only toward its shame by abusing
the faculties that honor it, it brought itself to the brink of its ruin. "Horrified
by the newness of the ill, both the poor man and the rich man hope to flee
from wealth, hating what they once had prayed for."[50]

It is not possible that men should not have eventually reflected upon so
miserable a situation and upon the calamities that overwhelm them. The rich
in particular must have soon felt how disadvantageous to them it was to have
a perpetual war in which they alone paid all the costs, and in which the risk
of losing one's life was common to all and the risk of losing one's goods was
personal. Moreover, regardless of the light in which they tried to place their
usurpations, they knew full well that they were established on nothing but a
precarious and abusive right, and that having been acquired merely by force,
force might take them away from them without their having any reason to
complain. Even those enriched exclusively by their skills could hardly base
their property on better claims. They could very well say: "I am the one who
built that wall; I have earned this land with my labor." In response to them
it could be said: "Who gave you the boundary lines? By what right do you
lay claim to exact payment at our expense for labor we did not impose upon
you? Are you unaware that a multitude of your brothers perish or suffer from
need of what you have in excess, and that you needed explicit and unanimous
consent from the human race for you to help yourself to anything from the
common subsistence that went beyond your own immediate needs?" Bereft
of valid reasons to justify himself and sufficient forces to defend himself;
easily crushing a private individual, but himself crushed by troops of bandits;
alone against all and unable on account of mutual jealousies to unite with his

---

[50] [Ovid, *Metamorphoses*, bk. 11, line 127.]

equals against enemies united by the common hope of plunder, a rich man, pressed by necessity, finally conceived the most thought-out project that ever entered the human mind. It was to use in his favor the very strength of those who attacked him, to turn his adversaries into his defenders, to instill in them other maxims, and to give them other institutions that were as favorable to him as natural right was unfavorable to him.

With this end in mind, after having shown his neighbors the horror of a situation that armed them all against each other and made their possessions as burdensome as their needs, and in which no one could find safety in either poverty or wealth, he easily invented specious reasons to lead them to his goal. "Let us unite," he says to them, "in order to protect the weak from oppression, restrain the ambitious, and assure everyone of possessing what belongs to him. Let us institute rules of justice and peace to which all will be obliged to conform, which will make special exceptions for no one, and which will in some way compensate for the caprices of fortune by subjecting the strong and the weak to mutual obligations. In short, instead of turning our forces against ourselves, let us gather them into one supreme power that governs us according to wise laws, that protects and defends all the members of the association, repulses common enemies, and maintains us in an eternal concord."

Considerably less than the equivalent of this discourse was needed to convince crude, easily seduced men who also had too many disputes to settle among themselves to be able to get along without arbiters, and too much greed and ambition to be able to get along without masters for long. They all ran to chain themselves, in the belief that they secured their liberty, for although they had enough sense to realize the advantages of a political establishment, they did not have enough experience to foresee its dangers. Those most capable of anticipating the abuses were precisely those who counted on profiting from them; and even the wise saw the need to be resolved to sacrifice one part of their liberty to preserve the other, just as a wounded man has his arm amputated to save the rest of his body.

Such was, or should have been, the origin of society and laws, which gave new fetters to the weak and new forces to the rich,[xviii] irretrievably destroyed natural liberty, established forever the law of property and of inequality, changed adroit usurpation into an irrevocable right, and for the profit of a few ambitious men henceforth subjected the entire human race to labor, servitude, and misery. It is readily apparent how the establishment of a single society rendered indispensable that of all the others, and how, to stand head to head against the united forces, it was necessary to unite in turn. Societies, multiplying or spreading rapidly, soon covered the entire surface of the earth; and it was no longer possible to find a single corner in the universe where someone could free himself from the yoke and withdraw his head from the often ill-guided sword that everyone saw perpetually hanging over his own head. With civil right thus having become the common rule of citizens, the law of nature no longer was operative except between the various societies, when, under the name of the law of nations, it was tempered by some tacit conventions in order to make intercourse possible and to serve as a substitute for natural compassion which, losing between one society and another nearly all the force it once had between one man and another, no longer resides anywhere but in a few great cosmopolitan souls, who overcome the imaginary barriers that separate peoples, and who, following the example of the sovereign being who has created them, embrace the entire human race in their benevolence. Remaining thus among themselves in the state of nature, the bodies politic soon experienced the inconveniences that had forced private individuals to leave it; and that state became even more deadly among these great bodies than it had been among the private individuals of whom they were composed. Whence came the national wars, battles, murders, and reprisals that make nature tremble and offend reason, and all those horrible prejudices that rank the honor of shedding human blood among the virtues. The most decent people learned to consider it one of their duties to kill their fellowmen. Finally, men were seen massacring one another by the thousands without knowing why. More murders were committed in a single day of combat and more horrors in the capture of a single city than were committed in the state of nature during entire centuries over the entire face of the earth. Such are the first effects one glimpses of the division of mankind into different societies. Let us return to the founding of these societies.

I know that many have ascribed other origins to political societies, such as conquests by the most powerful, or the union of the weak; and the choice among these causes is indifferent to what I want to establish. Nevertheless, the one I have just described seems to me the most natural, for the following reasons. 1. In the first case, the right of conquest, since it is not a right, could not have founded any other, because the conqueror and conquered peoples always remain in a state of war with one another, unless the nation, returned to full liberty, were to choose voluntarily its conqueror as its leader. Until then, whatever the capitulations that may have been made, since they have been founded on violence alone and are consequently null by this very fact, on this hypothesis there can be neither true society nor body politic, nor any other law than that of the strongest. 2. These words *strong* and *weak* are equivocal in the second case, because in the interval between the establishment of the right of property or of the first occupant and that of political governments, the meaning of these terms is better rendered by the words *poor* and *rich*, because, before the laws, man did not in fact have any other means of placing his equals in subjection except by attacking their goods or by giving them part of his. 3. Since the poor had nothing to lose but their liberty, it would have been utter folly for them to have voluntarily surrendered the only good remaining to them, gaining nothing in return. On the contrary, since the rich men were, so to speak, sensitive in all parts of their goods, it was much easier to do them harm, and consequently they had to take greater precautions to protect themselves. And finally it is reasonable to believe that a thing was invented by those to whom it is useful rather than by those to whom it is harmful.

Incipient government did not have a constant and regular form. The lack of philosophy and experience permitted only present inconveniences to be perceived, and there was thought of remedying the others only as they presented themselves. Despite all the labors of the wisest legislators, the political state always remained imperfect, because it was practically the work of chance and, because it had been badly begun, time, in discovering faults and suggesting remedies, could never repair the vices of the constitution. People were continually patching it up, whereas they should have begun by clearing the air and putting aside all the old materials, as Lycurgus did in Sparta, in order to raise a good edifice later on. At first, society consisted merely of some general conventions that all private individuals promised to observe, and concerning which the community became the guarantor for each of them. Experience had to demonstrate how weak such a constitution was, and how easy it was for lawbreakers to escape conviction or punishment for faults of which the public alone was to be witness and judge. The law had to be evaded in a thousand ways; inconveniences and disorders had to multiply continually in order to make them finally give some thought to confiding to private individuals the dangerous trust of public authority, and to make them entrust to magistrates the care of enforcing the observance of the deliberations of the people. For to say that the leaders were chosen before the confederation was brought about and that the ministers of the laws existed before the laws themselves is a supposition that does not allow of serious debate.

It would be no more reasonable to believe that initially the peoples threw themselves unconditionally and for all time into the arms of an absolute master, and that the first means of providing for the common security dreamed up by proud and unruly men was to rush headlong into slavery. In fact, why did they give themselves over to superiors, if not to defend themselves against oppression and to protect their goods, their liberties, and their lives, which are, as it were, the constitutive elements of their being? Now, since, in relations between men, the worst that can happen to someone is for him to see himself at the discretion of someone else, would it not have been contrary to good sense to begin by surrendering into the hands of a leader the only things for whose preservation they needed his help?[51] What equivalent could he have offered them for the concession of so fine a right? And if he had dared to demand it on the pretext of defending them, would he not have immediately received the reply given in the fable: "What more will the enemy do

---

[51] [In claiming that the worst that can happen is to be placed at the discretion of someone else, Rousseau is defending a classical conception of liberty against Hobbes, who had insisted that we are free unless we are prevented by force from doing as we wish.]

to us?"[52] It is therefore incontestable, and it is a fundamental maxim of all political right, that peoples have given themselves leaders in order to defend their liberty and not to enslave themselves. "If we have a prince," Pliny said to Trajan, "it is so that he may preserve us from having a master."[53]

<Our> political theorists produce the same sophisms about the love of liberty that <our> philosophers have produced about the state of nature. On the basis of the things they see they make judgments about very different things they have not seen; and they attribute to men a natural inclination to servitude owing to the patience with which those who are before their eyes endure their servitude, without giving a thought to the fact that it is the same for liberty as it is for innocence and virtue: their value is felt only as long as one has them oneself, and the taste for them is lost as soon as one has lost them. "I know the delights of your country," said Brasidas to a satrap who compared the life of Sparta to that of Persepolis, "but you cannot know the pleasures of mine."[54]

As an unbroken steed bristles his mane, paws the ground with his hoof, and struggles violently at the mere approach of the bit, while a trained horse patiently endures the whip and the spur, barbarous man does not bow his head for the yoke that civilized man wears without a murmur, and he prefers the most stormy liberty to tranquil subjection. Thus it is not by the degradation of enslaved peoples that man's natural dispositions for or against servitude are to be judged, but by the wonders that all free peoples have accomplished to safeguard themselves from oppression. I know that enslaved peoples do nothing but boast of the peace and tranquility they enjoy in their chains and that "they give the name 'peace' to the most miserable slavery."[55] But when I see free peoples sacrificing pleasures, tranquility, wealth, power, and life itself for the preservation of this sole good which is regarded so disdainfully by those who have lost it; when I see animals born free and abhorring captivity break their heads against the bars of their prison; when I see multitudes of utterly naked savages scorn European pleasures and brave hunger, fire, sword, and death, simply to preserve their independence, I sense that it is inappropriate for slaves to reason about liberty.

As for paternal authority, from which several have derived absolute government and all society, it is enough, without having recourse to the contrary proofs of Locke and Sidney, to note that nothing in the world is farther from the ferocious spirit of despotism than the gentleness of that authority which looks more to the advantage of the one who obeys than to the utility of the

---

[52] [La Fontaine, *Fables*, bk. 6, no. 8.]

[53] [Pliny, *Panegyric of Trajan* 55.]

[54] [Rousseau has misremembered an anecdote reported both by Herodotus (*Histories* 7.135) and Plutarch (*Spartan Sayings*, 235F).]

[55] [Tacitus, *Histories*, bk. 4, ch. 17; but Rousseau's source is Algernon Sidney, *Discourses Concerning Government* (1698), from which he made notes as he wrote the second Discourse.]

one who commands; that by the law of nature, the father is master of the child as long as his help is necessary for him; that beyond this point they become equals, and the son, completely independent of the father, then owes him merely respect and not obedience; for gratitude is clearly a duty that must be rendered, but not a right that can be demanded.[56] Instead of saying that civil society derives from paternal power, on the contrary it must be said that it is from civil society that this power draws its principal force. An individual was not recognized as the father of several children until the children remained gathered about him. The goods of the father, of which he is truly the master, are the goods that keep his children in a state of dependence toward him, and he can decide that any share they receive of his estate reflects the extent to which they will have merited it from him by continuous deference to his wishes. Now, far from having some similar favor to expect from their despot (since they belong to him as personal possessions—they and all they possess— or at least he claims this to be the case), subjects are reduced to receiving as a favor what he leaves them of their goods. He does what is just when he despoils them; he does them a favor when he allows them to live.

If we continued thus to examine the facts from the viewpoint of right, no more solidity than truth would be found in the belief that the establishment of tyranny was voluntary; and it would be difficult to show the validity of a contract that would obligate only one of the parties, where all the commitments would be placed on one side with none on the other, and that would turn exclusively to the disadvantage of the one making the commitments. This odious system is quite far removed from being, even today, that of wise and good monarchs, and especially of the kings of France, as may be seen in various places in their edicts, and particularly in the following passage of a famous writing published in 1667 in the name of and by order of Louis XIV: "Let it not be said therefore that the sovereign is not subject to the laws of his state, for the contrary statement is a truth of the law of nations, which flattery has on occasion attacked, but which good princes have always defended as a tutelary divinity of their states. How much more legitimate is it to say, with the wise Plato, that the perfect felicity of a kingdom is that a prince be obeyed by his subjects, that the prince obey the law, and that the law be right and always directed to the public good." I will not stop to investigate whether, with liberty being the most noble of man's faculties, he degrades his nature, places himself on the level of animals enslaved by instinct, offends even his maker, when he unreservedly renounces the most precious of all God's gifts, and allows himself to commit all the crimes He forbids us to commit, in order to please a ferocious or crazed master; nor whether this sublime workman should be more irritated at seeing His finest work destroyed rather than at seeing it dishonored. <I will disregard, if you will, the authority of Barbeyrac,

---

[56] [Both Locke and Sidney had written against the *Patriarcha* (1680) of Robert Filmer (1588–1653).]

who flatly declares, following Locke, that no one can sell his liberty to the point of submitting himself to an arbitrary power that treats him according to its fancy. For, he adds, "this would be selling his own life, of which he is not the master."[57]> I will merely ask by what right those who have not been afraid of debasing themselves to this degree have been able to subject their posterity to the same ignominy and to renounce for it goods that do not depend on their own liberality, and without which life itself is burdensome to all who are worthy of it.

Pufendorf says that just as one transfers one's goods to another by conventions and contracts, one can also divest oneself of one's liberty in favor of someone else.[58] That, it seems to me, is very bad reasoning; for, in the first place, the goods I give away become something utterly foreign to me, and it is a matter of indifference to me whether or not these goods are abused; but it is important to me that my liberty is not abused, and I cannot expose myself to becoming the instrument of crime without making myself guilty of the evil I will be forced to commit. Moreover, since the right of property is merely the result of convention and human institution, every man can dispose of what he possesses as he sees fit. But it is not the same for the essential gifts of nature such as life and liberty, which everyone is allowed to enjoy, and of which it is at least doubtful that one has the right to divest oneself. In giving up liberty one degrades one's being; in giving up life one annihilates that being insofar as one can. And because no temporal goods can compensate for the one or the other, it would offend at the same time both nature and reason to renounce them, regardless of the price. But even if one could give away one's liberty as one does one's goods, the difference would be very great for the children who enjoy the father's goods only by virtue of a transmission of his right; whereas, since liberty is a gift they receive from nature in virtue of being men, their parents had no right to divest them of it. Thus, just as violence had to be done to nature in order to establish slavery, nature had to be changed in order to perpetuate this right. And the jurists, who have gravely pronounced that the child of a slave woman is born a slave, have decided, in other words, that a man is not born a man.

Thus it appears certain to me not only that governments did not begin with arbitrary power, which is but their corruption and extreme limit, and which finally brings them back simply to the law of the strongest, for which they were initially to have been the remedy; but also that even if they had begun thus, this power, being illegitimate by its nature, could not have served as a foundation for the rights of society, nor, as a consequence, for the inequality occasioned by social institutions.

---

[57] [Rousseau is quoting a note in Barbeyrac's edition of Samuel Pufendorf, *Of the Law of Nature and Nations*. Jean Barbeyrac (1674–1744) translated and edited Pufendorf, Grotius, and Cumberland.]

[58] [Pufendorf, *Law of Nature and Nations*, bk. 8, ch. 3, §1.]

Without entering at present into the investigations that are yet to be made into the nature of the fundamental compact of all government,[59] I restrict myself, in following common opinion, to considering here the establishment of the body politic as a true contract between the populace and the leaders it chooses for itself: a contract by which the two parties obligate themselves to observe the laws that are stipulated in it and that form the bonds of their union. Since, with respect to social relations, the populace has united all its wills into a single one, all the articles in which this will is explicated become so many fundamental laws obligating all the members of the state without exception, and one of these regulates the choice and power of the magistrates charged with watching over the execution of the others. This power extends to everything that can maintain the constitution, without going so far as to change it. To it are joined honors that make the laws and their ministers worthy of respect, and, for the ministers personally, prerogatives that compensate them for the troublesome labors that a good administration requires. The magistrate, for his part, obligates himself to use the power entrusted to him only in accordance with the intention of the constituents, to maintain each one in the peaceful enjoyment of what belongs to him, and to prefer on every occasion the public utility to his own interest.

Before experience had shown or knowledge of the human heart had made men foresee the inevitable abuses of such a constitution, it must have seemed all the better because those who were charged with watching over its preservation were themselves the ones who had the greatest interest in it. For since the magistracy and its rights were established exclusively on fundamental laws, were they to be destroyed, the magistracy would immediately cease to be legitimate; the people would no longer be bound to obey them. And since it was not the magistrate but the law that had constituted the essence of the state, everyone would rightfully return to his natural liberty.

The slightest attentive reflection on this point would confirm this by new reasons, and by the nature of the contract it would be seen that it could not be irrevocable. For were there no superior power that could guarantee the fidelity of the contracting parties or force them to fulfill their reciprocal commitments, the parties would remain sole judges in their own case, and each of them would always have the right to renounce the contract as soon as he should find that the other party violated the conditions of the contract, or as soon as the conditions should cease to suit him. It is on this principle that it appears the right to abdicate can be founded. Now to consider, as we are doing, only what is of human institution, if the magistrate, who has all the power in his hands and who appropriates to himself all the advantages of the contract, nevertheless had the right to renounce his authority, a fortiori the populace, which pays for all the faults of the leaders, should have the right to renounce their dependence. But the horrible dissensions, the infinite

---

[59] [A clear indication that Rousseau already had in mind the argument of the *Social Contract*.]

disorders that this dangerous power would necessarily bring in its wake, demonstrate more than anything else how much need human governments had for a basis more solid than reason alone, and how necessary it was for public tranquility that the divine will intervened to give to sovereign authority a sacred and inviolable character which took from the subjects the fatal right to dispose of it. If religion had brought about this good for men, it would be enough to oblige them to cherish and adopt it, even with its abuses, since it spares even more blood than fanaticism causes to be shed. But let us follow the thread of our hypothesis.

The various forms of government take their origin from the greater or lesser differences that were found among private individuals at the moment of institution. If a man were eminent in power, virtue, wealth, or prestige, he alone was elected magistrate, and the state became monarchical. If several men, more or less equal among themselves, stood out over all the others, they were elected jointly, and there was an aristocracy. Those whose fortune or talents were less disproportionate, and who least departed from the state of nature, kept the supreme administration and formed a democracy. Time made evident which of these forms was the most advantageous to men. Some remained in subjection only to the laws; the others soon obeyed masters. Citizens wanted to keep their liberty; the subjects thought only of taking it away from their neighbors, since they could not endure others enjoying a good they themselves no longer enjoyed. In a word, on the one hand were riches and conquests, and on the other were happiness and virtue.

In these various forms of government all the magistratures were at first elective; and when wealth did not prevail, preference was given to merit, which gives a natural ascendancy, and to age, which gives experience in conducting business and cool-headedness in deliberation. The elders of the Hebrews, the gerontes of Sparta, the senate of Rome, and even the etymology of our word *seigneur* show how much age was respected in former times. The more elections fell upon men of advanced age, the more frequent elections became, and the more their difficulties were made to be felt. Intrigues were introduced; factions were formed; parties became embittered; civil wars flared up. Finally, the blood of citizens was sacrificed to the alleged happiness of the state, and people were on the verge of falling back into the anarchy of earlier times. The ambition of the leaders profited from these circumstances to perpetuate their offices within their families. The people, already accustomed to dependence, tranquility, and the conveniences of life, and already incapable of breaking their chains, consented to let their servitude increase in order to secure their tranquility. Thus it was that the leaders, having become hereditary, grew accustomed to regard their magistratures as family property, to regard themselves as the proprietors of the state (of which at first they were but the officers), to call their fellow citizens their slaves, to count them, like cattle, in the number of things that belonged to them, and to call themselves equals of the gods and kings of kings.

If we follow the progress of inequality in these various revolutions, we will find that the first stage was the establishment of the law and of the right of property, the second stage was the institution of the magistracy, and the third and final stage was the transformation of legitimate power into arbitrary power. Thus the condition of rich and poor was authorized by the first epoch, that of the strong and the weak by the second, and that of master and slave by the third: the ultimate degree of inequality and the limit to which all the others finally lead, until new revolutions completely dissolve the government or bring it nearer to a legitimate institution.

To grasp the necessity of this progression, we must consider less the motives for the establishment of the body politic than the form it takes in its implementation and the disadvantages that follow in its wake. For the vices that make social institutions necessary are the same ones that make their abuses inevitable. And with the sole exception of Sparta, where the law kept watch chiefly over the education of children, and where Lycurgus established mores that nearly dispensed with having to add laws to them, since laws are generally less strong than passions and restrain men without changing them, it would be easy to prove that any government that always operated in conformity with the purpose for which it was founded without being corrupted or altered, would have been needlessly instituted, and that a country where no one eluded the laws and abused the magistrature would need neither magistracy nor laws.

Political distinctions necessarily lend themselves to civil distinctions. The growing inequality between the people and its leaders soon makes itself felt among private individuals, and is modified by them in a thousand ways according to passions, talents, and events. The magistrate cannot usurp illegitimate power without surrounding himself with hangers-on to whom he is forced to yield some part of it. Moreover, citizens allow themselves to be oppressed only insofar as they are driven by blind ambition; and looking more below than above them, domination becomes more dear to them than independence, and they consent to wear chains in order to be able to give them in turn to others. It is very difficult to reduce to obedience someone who does not seek to command; and the most adroit politician would never succeed in subjecting men who wanted merely to be free. But inequality spreads easily among ambitious and cowardly souls always ready to run the risks of fortune and who scarcely care whether they dominate or serve, depending on whether fortune is with them or against them. Thus it is that there must have come a time when the eyes of the people were beguiled to such an extent that its leaders merely had to say to the humblest of men, "Be great, you and all your progeny," and he immediately appeared great to everyone as well as in his own eyes, and his descendants were elevated even more in proportion as they were at some remove from him. The more remote and uncertain the cause, the more the effect increased; the more loafers one could count in a family, the more illustrious it became.

If this were the place to go into detail, I would easily explain how <even without government involvement> the inequality of prestige and authority becomes inevitable among private individuals,[xix] as soon as they are united in one single society and are forced to make comparisons among themselves and to take into account the differences they discover in the continual use they have to make of one another. These differences are of several sorts, but in general, since wealth, nobility or rank, power, and personal merit are the principal distinctions by which someone is measured in society, I would prove that the agreement or conflict of these various forces is the surest indication of a well- or ill-constituted state. I would make it apparent that among these four types of inequality, personal qualities are the origin of all the others, but wealth is the last to which they are ultimately reduced, because, since it is the most immediately useful to well-being and the easiest to communicate, it readily serves to buy all the rest. This observation enables one to judge rather precisely the extent to which each people is removed from its primitive institution, and of the progress it has made toward the final stage of corruption. I would note how much that universal desire for reputation, honors, and privileges, which devours us all, develops and compares our talents and strengths; how much it excites and multiplies the passions; and, by making all men competitors, rivals, or rather enemies, how many setbacks, successes, and catastrophes of every sort it causes every day, by making so many contenders run the same race. I would show that it is to this ardor for making oneself the topic of conversation, to this frenzy to distinguish oneself which nearly always keeps us outside ourselves, that we owe what is best and worst among men, our virtues and vices, our sciences and our errors, our conquerors and our philosophers, that is to say, a multitude of bad things against a small number of good ones. Finally, I would prove that if one sees a handful of powerful and rich men at the height of greatness and fortune while the mob grovels in obscurity and misery, it is because the former prize the things they enjoy only to the extent that the others are deprived of them; and because, without changing their position, they would cease to be happy, if the people ceased to be miserable.

But these details alone would be the subject of a large work in which one would weigh the advantages and the disadvantages of every government relative to the rights of the state of nature, and where one would examine all the different faces under which inequality has appeared until now and may appear in <future> ages, according to the nature of these governments and the upheavals that time will necessarily bring in its wake. We would see the multitude oppressed from within as a consequence of the very precautions it had taken against what menaced it from without. We would see oppression continually increase, without the oppressed ever being able to know where it would end or what legitimate means would be left for them to stop it. We would see the rights of citizens and national liberties gradually die out, and the protests of the weak treated like seditious murmurs. We would see politics restrict the honor of defending the common cause to a mercenary portion of the people. We would see arising from this the necessity for taxes, the discouraged farmer leaving his field, even during peacetime, and leaving his plow in order to gird himself with a sword. We would see the rise of fatal and bizarre rules in the code of honor. We would see the defenders of the homeland sooner or later become its enemies, constantly holding a dagger over their fellow citizens, and there would come a time when we would hear them say to the oppressor of their country: "If you order me to plunge my sword into my brother's breast or my father's throat, and into my pregnant wife's entrails, I will do so, even though my right hand is unwilling."[60]

From the extreme inequality of conditions and fortunes, from the diversity of passions and talents, from useless arts, from pernicious arts, from frivolous sciences there would come a pack of prejudices equally contrary to reason, happiness, and virtue. One would see the leaders fomenting whatever can weaken men united together by disuniting them; whatever can give society an air of apparent concord while sowing the seeds of real division; whatever can inspire defiance and hatred in the various classes through the opposition of their rights and interests, and can as a consequence strengthen the power that contains them all.

It is from the bosom of this disorder and these upheavals that despotism, by gradually raising its hideous head and devouring everything it had seen to be good and healthy in every part of the state, would eventually succeed in trampling underfoot the laws and the people, and in establishing itself on the ruins of the republic. The times that would precede this last transformation would be times of troubles and calamities; but in the end everything would be swallowed up by the monster, and the peoples would no longer have leaders or laws, but only tyrants. Also, from that moment on, there would no longer be any question of mores and virtue, for wherever despotism, "in which decency affords no hope,"[61] reigns, it tolerates no other master. As soon as it speaks, there is neither probity nor duty to consult, and the blindest obedience is the only virtue remaining for slaves.

Here is the final stage of inequality, and the extreme point that closes the circle and touches the point from which we started. Here all private individuals become equals again, because they are nothing. And since subjects no longer have any law other than the master's will, nor the master any rule other than his passions, the notions of good and the principles of justice again vanish. Here everything is brought back to the law of the strongest, and to that alone, and consequently to a new state of nature different from the one with which we began, in that the one was the state of nature in its purity, and this last one is the fruit of an excess of corruption. Moreover, there is so little difference between these two states, and the governmental contract

---

[60] [Lucan, *Civil War* 1.376.]

[61] [Tacitus, quoted inaccurately by Algernon Sidney, *Discourses Concerning Government* §19.]

is so utterly dissolved by despotism, that the despot is master only as long as he is the strongest; and as soon as he can be ousted, he has no cause to protest against violence. The uprising that ends in the strangulation or the dethronement of a sultan is as lawful an act as those by which he disposed of the lives and goods of his subjects the day before. Force alone maintained him; force alone brings him down. Thus everything happens in accordance with the natural order, and whatever the outcome of these brief and frequent upheavals may be, no one can complain about someone else's injustice, but only of his own imprudence or his misfortune.

In discovering and following thus the forgotten and lost routes that must have led man from the natural state to the civil state; in reestablishing, along with the intermediate positions I have just outlined, those which pressure of time have made me suppress or that my imagination has not suggested to me, no attentive reader can fail to be struck by the immense space that separates these two states. It is in this slow succession of things that he will see the solution to an infinity of moral and political problems that the philosophers are unable to resolve. He will realize that, since the human race of one age is not the human race of another age, the reason why Diogenes did not find his man is because he searched among his contemporaries for a man who no longer existed.[62] Cato, he will say, perished with Rome and liberty because he was out of place in his age; and this greatest of men merely astonished a world that five hundred years earlier he would have governed. In short, he will explain how the soul and human passions are imperceptibly altered and, as it were, change their nature; why, in the long run, our needs and our pleasures change their objects; why, with original man gradually disappearing, society no longer offers to the eyes of the wise man anything but an assemblage of artificial men and factitious passions which are the work of all these new relations and have no true foundation in nature. What reflection teaches us on this subject is perfectly confirmed by observation: savage man and civilized man differ so greatly in the depths of their hearts and in their inclinations, that what constitutes the supreme happiness of the one would reduce the other to despair. Savage man breathes only tranquility and liberty; he wants simply to live and rest easy; and not even the unperturbed tranquility of the Stoic approaches his profound indifference for any other objects. On the other hand, the citizen is always active and in a sweat, always agitated, and unceasingly tormenting himself in order to seek still more laborious occupations. He works until he dies; he even runs to his death in order to be in a position to live, or renounces life in order to acquire immortality. He pays court to the great whom he hates and to the rich whom he scorns. He stops at nothing to obtain the honor of serving

---

[62] [Diogenes went around in broad daylight with a lighted lamp. When asked what he was doing, he would say that he was searching for a human being; his complaint was that he could find no human beings, only rascals and scoundrels.]

them. He proudly crows about his own baseness and their protection; and proud of his slavery, he speaks with disdain about those who do not have the honor of taking part in it. What a spectacle for a Carib[63] would be the difficult and envied labors of a European minister! How many cruel deaths would that indolent savage not prefer to the horror of such a life, which often is not mollified even by the pleasure of doing good. But in order to see the purpose of so many cares, the words *power* and *reputation* would have to have a meaning in his mind; he would have to learn that there is a type of men who place some value on the regard the rest of the world has for them, and who know how to be happy and content with themselves on the testimony of others rather than on their own. Such, in fact, is the true cause of all these differences; the savage lives in himself; the man accustomed to the ways of society is always outside himself and knows how to live only in the opinion of others. And it is, as it were, from their judgment alone that he draws the sentiment of his own existence. It is not pertinent to my subject to show how, from such a disposition, so much indifference toward good and evil arises, along with such fine discourse on morality; how, with everything reduced to appearances, everything becomes factitious and bogus: honor, friendship, virtue, and often even our vices, about which we eventually find the secret of boasting; how, in a word, we, who are always asking others what we are and never daring to question ourselves on this matter, who are in the midst of so much philosophy, humanity, politeness, and so many sublime maxims, we have merely a deceitful and frivolous exterior: honor without virtue, reason without wisdom, and pleasure without happiness. It is enough for me to have proved that this is not the original state of man, and that it is only the spirit of society and the inequality that society engenders that thus change and alter all our natural inclinations.

I have tried to set forth the origin and progress of inequality, the establishment and abuse of political societies, to the extent that these things can be deduced from the nature of man by the light of reason alone, and independently of the sacred dogmas that give to sovereign authority the sanction of divine right. It follows from this presentation that, since inequality is practically nonexistent in the state of nature, it derives its force and growth from the development of our faculties and the progress of the human mind, and eventually becomes stable and legitimate through the establishment of property and laws. Moreover, it follows that inequality in status,[64] authorized by positive right alone, is contrary to natural right whenever it is not combined in the same proportion with physical inequality: a distinction that is sufficient to determine what one should think in this regard about the sort of inequality that reigns among all civilized people, for it is obviously contrary to the law of nature, however it may be defined, for a child to command an old man, for an

---

[63] [An inhabitant of the Caribbean.]

[64] [Here again Rousseau's phrase is *inégalité morale* (inequality with regard to mores).]

imbecile to lead a wise man, and for a handful of people to gorge themselves on superfluities while the starving multitude lacks necessities.[65]

---

[65] [Cf. Montaigne, *Essays*, bk. 1, ch. 30, "Of Cannibals."]

Rousseau's Notes to

Discourse on the Origin and Foundations of Inequality among Men

Note i *(page 32, "at his discretion")* Herodotus relates that after the murder of the false Smerdis, the seven liberators of Persia being assembled to deliberate on the form of government they would give the state, Otanes was fervently in support of a republic—an opinion all the more extraordinary in the mouth of a satrap since, over and above the claim he could have to the empire, a grandee fears more than death a type of government that forces him to respect men.[66] Otanes, as may readily be believed, was not listened to; and seeing that things were progressing toward the election of a monarch, he, who wanted neither to obey nor command, voluntarily yielded to the other rivals his right to the crown, asking as his sole compensation that he and his descendants be free and independent. This was granted to him. If Herodotus did not inform us of the restriction that was placed on this privilege, it would be necessary to suppose it; otherwise Otanes, not acknowledging any sort of law and not being accountable to anyone, would have been all powerful in the state and more powerful than the king himself. But there was hardly any likelihood that a man capable of contenting himself, in similar circumstances, with such a privilege was capable of abusing it. In fact, there is no evidence that this right ever caused the least trouble in the kingdom, either from wise Otanes or from any of his descendants.

Note ii *(page 39, "that of man")* From the start I rely with confidence on one of those authorities that are respectable for philosophers, because their authority derives from a solid and sublime reason, which philosophers alone know how to find and perceive.

"Whatever interest we may have in knowing ourselves, I do not know whether we do not have a better knowledge of everything that is not us. Provided by nature with organs uniquely destined for our preservation, we use them merely to receive impressions of external things; we seek merely to extend ourselves outward and to exist outside ourselves. Too much taken with multiplying the functions of our senses and with increasing the external range of our being, we rarely make use of that internal sense that reduces us to our true dimensions and that separates us from all that is not us. Nevertheless, this is the sense we must use if we wish to know ourselves. It is the only one by which we can judge ourselves. But how can this sense be activated and given its full range? How can our soul, in which it resides, be rid of all the illusions of our mind? We have lost the habit of using it; it has remained unexercised in the midst of the tumult of our bodily sensations; it has been dried out by the

[66] [Herodotus, *Histories* 3.67–84.]

fire of our passions; the heart, the mind, the senses, everything has worked against it." *Hist. Nat.*, Vol. IV: *de la Nat. de l'homme*, p. 151.[67]

Note iii *(page 47, "on all fours")* The changes that a long-established habit of walking on two feet could have brought about in the conformation of man, the relationships that are still to be observed between his arms and the forelegs of quadrupeds, and the conclusion that may be drawn from their manner of walking could have given rise to doubts about the manner of locomotion that must have been the most natural to us. All children begin by walking on all fours and need our example and our lessons to learn to stand upright. There are even savage nations, such as the Hottentots, who, greatly neglecting their children, allow them to walk on their hands for so long that they then have a great deal of trouble getting them to straighten up. The children of the Caribs of the Antilles do the same thing. There are various examples of quadruped men, and I could cite among others that of the child who was found in 1344 near Hesse, where he had been raised by wolves, and who said afterward at the court of Prince Henry that had the decision been left exclusively to him, he would have preferred to return to the wolves rather than to live among men. He had embraced to such an extent the habit of walking like those animals that wooden boards had to be attached to him to force him to stand upright and maintain his balance on two feet. It was the same with the child who was found in 1694 in the forests of Lithuania and who lived among bears. He did not give, says Mr. Condillac, any sign of reason, walked on his hands and feet, had no language, and formed sounds that bore no resemblance whatever to those of a man. The little savage of Hanover, who was brought to the court of England several years ago, had all sorts of trouble getting himself to walk on two feet. And in 1719, two other savages, who were found in the Pyrenees, ran about the mountains in the manner of quadrupeds. As for the objection one might make that this deprives one of the use of one's hands from which we derive so many advantages, over and above the fact that the example of monkeys shows that the hand can be used quite well in both ways, this would prove only that man can give his limbs a purpose more useful than the one they have been given by nature, and not that nature has destined man to walk otherwise than it teaches him.

But there are, it seems to me, much better reasons to state in support of the claim that man is a biped. First, if it were shown that he could have originally been formed otherwise than we see him and yet finally become what he is, this would not suffice to conclude that this is how it happened; for, after having shown the possibility of these changes, it would still be necessary, prior to granting them, to demonstrate at least their probability. Moreover, if it seems man's arms could have served as legs when needed, that is the sole observation

---

[67] [Rousseau's Discourse draws extensively on the work of Georges-Louis Leclerc, Count of Buffon (1707–1788). By 1754 Buffon had published the first four volumes of his *Natural History*.]

favorable to that theory out of a great number of others that are contrary to it. The chief ones are that the manner in which man's head is attached to his body, instead of directing his view horizontally (as is the case for all other animals and for man himself when he walks upright), would have kept him, while walking on all fours, with his eyes fixed directly on the ground, a situation hardly conducive to the preservation of the individual; that the tail he is lacking, and for which he has no use when walking on two feet, is useful to quadrupeds, and none of them is deprived of one; that the breast of a woman, very well located for a biped who holds her child in her arms, is so poorly located for a quadruped that none has it located in that way; that, since the hind part is of an excessive height in proportion to the forelegs (which causes us to crawl on our knees when walking on all fours), the whole would have made an animal that was poorly proportioned and that walked uncomfortably; that if he had placed his foot as well as his hand down flat, he would have had one less articulation in the hind leg than do other animals, namely, the one that joins the cannon[68] to the tibia; and that by setting down only the tip of the foot, as doubtlessly he would have been forced to do, the tarsus (not to mention the plurality of bones that make it up) appears too large to take the place of the cannon, and its articulations with the metatarsus and the tibia too close together to give the human leg in this situation the same flexibility as those of quadrupeds. Since the example of children is taken from an age when natural forces are not yet developed nor the members strengthened, it proves nothing whatever. I might just as well say that dogs are not destined to walk because several weeks after their birth they merely crawl. Particular facts also have little force against the universal practice of all men, even of nations that have had no communication with others and so could not have imitated anything about them. A child abandoned in a forest before he is able to walk and nourished by some beast will have followed the example of his nurse in training himself to walk like her. Habit could have given him capabilities he did not have from nature, and just as one-armed men are successful, by dint of exercise, at doing with their feet whatever we do with our hands, he will finally have succeeded in using his hands as feet.

Note iv *(page 47, "its natural fertility")* Should there be found among my readers a scientist bad enough to try to cause me difficulties regarding this supposition of the natural fertility of the earth, I am going to answer him with the following passage:

"As plants derive for their sustenance much more substance from air and water than they do from the earth, it happens that when they rot they return to the earth more than they have derived from it.[69] Moreover, a forest captures rainwater by stopping evaporation. Thus, in a wooded area that was

---

[68] [The cannon is a bone in the rear leg of a horse that joins the hock to the pastern.]

[69] [Since photosynthesis was not understood in the eighteenth century, theories of plant growth were necessarily very different from ours.]

preserved for a long time without being touched, the bed of earth that serves for vegetation would increase considerably. But since animals return to the soil less than they derive from it, and since men consume huge quantities of wood and plants for fire and other uses, it follows that the bed of vegetative earth of an inhabited country must always diminish and finally become like the terrain of Arabia Petraea[70] and like that of so many other provinces of the Orient (which in fact is the region that has been inhabited from the most ancient times), where only salt and sand are found. For the fixed salt of plants and animals remains, while all the other parts are volatilized." Mr. Buffon, *Hist. Nat.*

Moreover the evidence corresponds to the theory, witness the quantity of trees and plants of every sort that filled almost all the uninhabited islands that have been discovered in the last few centuries, and what history teaches us about the immense forests all over the earth that had to be cut down as each region in turn became populated or civilized. On this I will also make the following three remarks. First, if there is a kind of vegetation that can make up for the loss of vegetative matter that was occasioned by animals, according to Mr. Buffon's reasoning, it is above all the wooded areas, where the treetops and the leaves gather and appropriate more water and vapors than do other plants. Second, the destruction of the soil, that is, the loss of the substance that is appropriate for vegetation, should accelerate in proportion as the earth is more cultivated and as more skillful inhabitants consume in greater abundance its products of every sort. My third and most important remark is that the fruits of trees supply animals with more abundant nourishment than other forms of vegetation are capable of—an experiment I made myself by comparing the products of two landmasses of equal size and quality, the one covered with chestnut trees and the other sown with wheat.

Note v (*page 48, "various foods"*) Among the quadrupeds, the two most universal distinguishing traits of carnivorous species are derived, on the one hand, from the shape of the teeth and, on the other, from the structure of the intestines. Animals that live solely on vegetation all have flat teeth like the horse, ox, sheep, and hare, but carnivorous animals have pointed teeth like the cat, dog, wolf, and fox. And as for the intestines, the frugivorous ones have some, such as the colon, which are not found in carnivorous animals. It appears therefore that man, having teeth and intestines like frugivorous animals, should naturally be placed in that class. And not only do anatomical observations confirm this opinion, but the monuments of antiquity are also very favorable to it. "Dicaearchus," says St. Jerome, "relates in his books on Greek antiquities that under the reign of Saturn, when the earth was still fertile by itself, no man ate flesh, but that all lived on fruits and vegetables that

---

[70] [Arabia Petraea is a region of Arabia whose capital is the city of Petra.]

grew naturally." (*Adv. Jovinian.*, Bk. II)[71] <This opinion can also be supported by the reports of several modern travelers. François Corréal,[72] among others, testifies that the majority of inhabitants of the Bahamas, whom the Spaniards transported to the islands of Cuba, Santo Domingo, and elsewhere, died from having eaten flesh.> From this one can see that I am neglecting several advantageous considerations that I could turn to account. For since prey is nearly the exclusive subject of fighting among carnivorous animals, and since frugivorous animals live among themselves in continual peace, if the human species were of this latter genus, it is clear that it would have had a much easier time subsisting in the state of nature and much less need and occasion to leave it.

Note vi (*page 48, "as it were, with one"*) All the kinds of knowledge that demand reflection, all those acquired only by the concatenation of ideas and that are perfected only over time, appear to be utterly beyond the grasp of savage man, owing to the lack of communication with his fellowmen, that is to say, owing to the lack of the instrument that is used for that communication and to the lack of the needs that make it necessary. His understanding and his skills are limited to jumping, running, fighting, throwing a stone, climbing a tree. But if he knows only those things, in return he knows them much better than we, who do not have the same need for them as he. And since they depend exclusively on bodily exercise and are not capable of any communication or progress from one individual to another, the first man could have been just as adept at them as his last descendants.

The reports of travelers are full of examples of the force and vigor of men of barbarous and savage nations. They praise scarcely less their adroitness and nimbleness. And since eyes alone are needed to observe these things, nothing hinders us from giving credence to what eyewitnesses certify on the matter. I draw some random examples from the first books that fall into my hands.

"The Hottentots," says Kolben,[73] "understand fishing better than the Europeans at the Cape. Their skill is equal when it comes to the net, the hook, and the spear, in coves as well as in rivers. They catch fish by hand no less skillfully. They are incomparably good at swimming. Their style of swimming has something surprising about it, something entirely unique to them. They swim with their body upright and their hands stretched out of the water, so that they appear to be walking on land. In the greatest agitation of the sea, when the waves form so many mountains, they somehow dance on the top of the waves, rising and falling like a piece of cork.

[71] [Dicaearchus (c. 350–c. 285 BC) was a Greek historian. Rousseau's information comes secondhand from Jean Barbeyrac, whose editions of Pufendorf and Grotius provided Rousseau with an education in political philosophy.]

[72] [Francisco (François) Coreal. Rousseau misspells his name.]

[73] [Peter Kolbe (1675–1726), whom Rousseau had read in *Histoire générale des voyages* (1746–), edited by Abbot Prévost; twelve volumes had appeared by 1754.]

"The Hottentots," says the same author further, "are surprisingly good at hunting, and the nimbleness of their running surpasses the imagination." He is amazed that they did not put their agility to ill use more often, which, however, sometimes happens, as can be judged from the example he gives. "A Dutch sailor," he says, "on disembarking at the Cape, charged a Hottentot to follow him to the city with a roll of tobacco that weighed about twenty pounds. When they were both some distance from the crew, the Hottentot asked the sailor if he knew how to run. 'Run!' answered the Dutchman, 'yes, very well.' 'Let us see,' answered the African. And fleeing with the tobacco, he disappeared almost immediately. The sailor, confounded by such marvelous quickness, did not think of following him, and he never again saw either his tobacco or his porter.

"They have such quick sight and such a sure hand that Europeans cannot compete with them. At a hundred paces they will hit with a stone a mark the size of a halfpenny. And what is more amazing, instead of fixing their eyes on the target as we do, they make continuous movements and contortions. It appears that their stone is carried by an invisible hand."

Father Du Tertre[74] says about the savages of the Antilles nearly the same things that you have just read about the Hottentots of the Cape of Good Hope. He praises, above all, their accuracy in shooting with their arrows birds in flight and swimming fish, which they then catch by diving for them. The savages of North America are no less famous for their strength and adroitness, and here is an example that will lead us to form a judgment about those qualities in the Indians of South America.

In the year 1746, an Indian from Buenos Aires, having been condemned to the galleys of Cadiz, proposed to the governor that he buy back his liberty by risking his life at a public festival. He promised that by himself he would attack the fiercest bull with no other weapon in his hand but a rope; that he would bring him to the ground, seize him with his rope by whatever part they would indicate, saddle him, bridle him, mount him, and so mounted he would fight two other of the fiercest bulls to be released from the Torillo; and that he would put all of them to death, one after the other, the moment they would command him to do so and without anyone's help. This was granted to him. The Indian kept his word and succeeded in everything he had promised. On the way in which he did it and on the details of the fight, one can consult Mr. Gautier, *Observations sur l'Histoire Naturelle*, Vol. I (in-12°), p. 262, whence this report is taken.

Note vii *(page 50, "equal in this respect")* "The life span of horses," says Mr. Buffon, "is, as in all other species of animals, proportionate to the length of their growth period. Man, who takes fourteen years to grow, can live six or seven times as long, that is to say, ninety or a hundred years. The horse, whose

[74] [Jean Baptiste Du Tertre (1610–1687).]

growth period is four years, can live six or seven times as long, that is to say, twenty-five or thirty years. The examples that could be contrary to this rule are so rare that they should not even be regarded as an exception from which conclusions can be drawn. And just as large horses achieve their growth in less time than slender horses, they also have a shorter life span and are old from the age of fifteen."

Note viii *(page 50, "number of young")* I believe I see another difference between carnivorous and frugivorous animals still more general than the one I have remarked upon in **Note v,** since this one extends to birds. This difference consists in the number of young, which never exceeds two in each litter for the species that lives exclusively on plant life and ordinarily exceeds this number for carnivorous animals. It is easy to know nature's plan in this regard by the number of teats, which is only two in each female of the first species, like the mare, the cow, the goat, the doe, the ewe, etc., and which is always six or eight in the other females, such as the dog, the cat, the wolf, the tigress, etc. The hen, the goose, the duck, which are all omnivorous[75] birds (as are the eagle, the sparrow hawk, the screech owl), also lay and hatch a large number of eggs, which never happens to the pigeon, the turtledove, or to birds that eat nothing but grain, which lay and hatch scarcely more than two eggs at a time. The reason that can be given for this difference is that the animals that live exclusively on grass and plants, remaining nearly the entire day grazing and being forced to spend considerable time feeding themselves, could not be up to the task of nursing several young; whereas the carnivorous animals, taking their meal almost in an instant, can more easily and more often return to their young and to their hunting and can compensate for the loss of so large a quantity of milk. There would be many particular observations and reflections to make on all this, but this is not the place to make them, and it is enough for me to have shown in this part the most general system of nature, a system that furnishes a new reason to remove man from the class of carnivorous animals and to place him among the frugivorous species.

Note ix *(page 53, "himself and nature")* A famous author, on calculating the goods and evils of human life and comparing the two sums, has found that the latter greatly exceeded the former and that, all things considered, life was a rather poor present for man.[76] I am not surprised by his conclusion; he has drawn all of his arguments from the constitution of civil man. Had he gone back as far as natural man, the judgment can be made that he would have found very different results, that he would have realized that man has

---

[75] [Rousseau's word *vorax* here and below appears to mean "omnivorous," but it is a little difficult to see what hens and hawks have in common.]

[76] [Pierre-Louis Moreau de Maupertuis (1698–1759), *Essai de philosophie morale* (1749).]

scarcely any evils other than those he has given himself, and that nature would have been vindicated. It is not without trouble that we have managed to make ourselves so unhappy. When, on the one hand, one considers the immense labors of men, so many sciences searched into, so many arts invented, and so many forces employed, abysses filled up, mountains razed, rocks broken, rivers made navigable, lands cleared, lakes dug, marshes drained, enormous buildings raised upon the earth, the sea covered with ships and sailors, and when, on the other hand, one searches with a little meditation for the true advantages that have resulted from all this for the happiness of the human species, one cannot help being struck by the astonishing disproportion that exists between these things and to deploring man's blindness, which, to feed his foolish pride and who knows what vain sense of self-importance, makes him run ardently after all the miseries to which he is susceptible, and which beneficent nature has taken pains to keep from him.

Men are wicked; a sad and continual experience dispenses us from having to prove it. Nevertheless, man is naturally good; I believe I have demonstrated it. What therefore can have depraved him to this degree, if not the changes that have befallen his constitution, the progress he has made, and the sorts of knowledge he has acquired? Let human society be admired as much as one wants; it will be no less true that it necessarily brings men to hate one another to the extent that their interests are at cross-purposes with one another, to render mutually to one another apparent services and in fact do every evil imaginable to one another. What is one to think of an interaction where the reason of each private individual dictates to him maxims directly contrary to those that public reason preaches to the body of society, and where each finds his profit in the misfortune of another? Perhaps there is not a wealthy man whose death is not secretly hoped for by greedy heirs and often by his own children; not a ship at sea whose wreck would not be good news to some merchant; not a firm that a defaulting debtor would not wish to see burn with all the papers it contains; not a people that does not rejoice at the disasters of its neighbors. Thus it is that we find our advantage in the setbacks of our fellowmen and that one person's loss almost always brings about another's prosperity. But what is even more dangerous is that public calamities are anticipated and hoped for by a multitude of private individuals. Some want diseases, others death, others war, others famine. I have seen ghastly men weep with sadness at the prospect of a fertile year. And the great and deadly fire of London,[77] which cost the lives or the goods of so many unfortunates, made the fortunes of perhaps more than ten thousand people. I know that Montaigne blames the Athenian Demades for having had a worker punished who, by selling coffins at a high price, made a great deal from the death of the citizens.[78] However, according to the reason Montaigne proposes, namely

[77] [The great fire of 1666, which destroyed much of the City of London.]
[78] [*Essays*, bk. 1, ch. 22.]

that everyone would have to be punished, it is evident that this reason confirms my own. Let us therefore penetrate, behind our frivolous expressions of goodwill, to what happens at the bottom of our hearts; and let us reflect on what the state of things must be where all men are forced to caress and destroy one another and where they are born enemies by duty and crooks by interest. If someone answers me by claiming that society is constituted in such a manner that each man gains by serving others, I will reply that this would be very well and good, provided he did not gain still more by harming them. There is no profit, however legitimate, that is not surpassed by one that can be made illegitimately, and wrong done to a neighbor is always more lucrative than services. It is therefore no longer a question of anything but finding the means of being assured of impunity. And this is what the powerful spend all their strength on, and the weak all their clever machinations.

Savage man, when he has eaten, is at peace with all nature and the friend of all his fellowmen. Is it sometimes a question of his disputing over his meal? He never comes to blows without having first compared the difficulty of winning with that of finding his sustenance elsewhere. And since pride is not involved in the fight, it is ended by a few swings of the fist. The victor eats, the vanquished is on his way to seek his fortune, and the quarrel is over. But for man in society, it is a quite different business. It is first of all a question of providing for the necessary and then for the superfluous; next come delights, and then immense riches, and then subjects, and then slaves. He has not a moment's respite. What is most singular is that the less natural and pressing the needs, the more the passions increase and, what is worse, the power to satisfy them; so that after long periods of prosperity, after having swallowed up many treasures and ruined many men, my hero will end by butchering everything until he is the sole master of the universe. This, in brief, is a faithful representation of our mores—if not of human life, then at least of the secret pretensions in the heart of every civilized man.

Compare, without prejudices, the state of civil man with that of savage man and seek, if you can, how many new doors to suffering and death (without even mentioning his wickedness, his needs, and his miseries) the former has opened. If you consider the emotional turmoil that consumes us, the violent passions that exhaust and desolate us, the excessive labors with which the poor are overburdened, the still more dangerous softness to which the rich abandon themselves and that cause the former to die of their needs and the latter of their excesses; if you call to mind the monstrous combinations of foods, their pernicious seasonings, the corrupted foodstuffs, tainted drugs, the knavery of those who sell them, the errors of those who administer them, the poison of the vessels in which they are prepared; if you pay attention to the epidemic diseases engendered by the bad air among the multitudes of men gathered together, to the illnesses occasioned by the effeminacy of our lifestyle, by the coming and going from the inside of our houses to the open air, the use of garments put on or taken off with too little precaution, and all the cares that our excessive sensuality has turned into necessary habits, the neglect or privation of which then costs us our life or our health; if you take into account fires and earthquakes, which, in consuming or turning upside down whole cities, cause their inhabitants to die by the thousands; in a word, if you unite the dangers that all these causes continually gather over our heads, you will realize how dearly nature makes us pay for the scorn we have shown for her lessons.

I will not repeat here what I have said elsewhere about war, but I wish that informed men would, for once, want or dare to give the public the detail of the horrors that are committed in armies by those who contract to provide food or medical care. One would see that their not too secret maneuvers, on account of which the most brilliant armies dissolve into less than nothing, cause more soldiers to perish than are cut down by enemy swords. Moreover, no less surprising is the calculation of the number of men swallowed up by the sea every year, by either hunger, or scurvy, or pirates, or fire, or ship-wrecks. It is clear that we must also put to the account of established property, and consequently to that of society, the assassinations, the poisonings, the highway robberies, and even the punishments of these crimes, punishments necessary to prevent greater ills, but that, costing the lives of two or more for the murder of one man, do not fail really to double the loss to the human species. How many are the shameful ways to prevent the birth of men or to fool nature: either by those brutal and depraved tastes that insult its most charming work, tastes that neither savages nor animals ever knew, and that have arisen in civilized countries only as the result of a corrupt imagination; or by those secret abortions, worthy fruits of debauchery and vicious honor; or by the exposure or the murder of a multitude of infants, victims of the misery of their parents or of the barbarous shame of their mothers; or, finally, by the mutilation of those unfortunates, part of whose existence and all of whose posterity are sacrificed to vain songs or, what is worse still, to the brutal jealousy of a few men—a mutilation that, in this last case, doubly outrages nature, both by the treatment received by those who suffer it and by the use to which they are destined.[79]

<But are there not a thousand more frequent and even more dangerous cases in which paternal rights overtly offend humanity? How many talents are buried and inclinations are forced by the imprudent constraint of fathers! How many men would have distinguished themselves in a suitable station who die unhappy and dishonored in another station for which they have no taste! How many happy but unequal marriages have been broken or disturbed, and how many chaste wives dishonored by this order of conditions always in contradiction with that of nature! How many other bizarre unions formed by interests and disavowed by love and by reason! How many even honest and

---

[79] [Rousseau has in mind castration. *Castrati* sang in Italian choirs, and eunuchs were entrusted with the care of female slaves in the Ottoman empire.]

virtuous couples cause themselves torment because they were ill matched! How many young and unhappy victims of their parents' greed plunge into vice or pass their sorrowful days in tears and moan in indissoluble chains that the heart rejects and that gold alone has formed! Happy sometimes are those whose courage and even virtue tear them from life before a barbarous violence forces them into crime or despair. Forgive me, father and mother, who are forever pitiable. I regrettably worsen your sorrows; but may they serve as an eternal and terrible example to whoever dares, in the name of nature, to violate the most sacred of its rights!

If I have spoken only of those ill-formed relationships that are the result of our civil order, is one to think that those where love and sympathy have presided are themselves exempt from drawbacks?>

What would happen if I were to undertake to show the human species attacked in its very source, and even in the most holy of all bonds, where one no longer dares to listen to nature until one has taken into account one's financial interests, and where, with civil disorder confounding virtues and vices, continence becomes a criminal precaution, and the refusal to give life to one's fellowman an act of humanity? But without tearing away the veil that covers so many horrors, let us content ourselves with pointing out the evil, for which others must supply the remedy.

Let us add to all this that quantity of unwholesome trades that shorten lives or destroy one's health, such as work in mines, various jobs involving the processing of metals, minerals, and especially lead, copper, mercury, cobalt, arsenic, realgar; those other perilous trades that every day cost the lives of a number of workers, some of them roofers, others carpenters, others masons, others working in quarries; let us bring all of these objects together, I say, and we will be able to see in the establishment and the perfection of societies the reasons for the diminution of the species, observed by more than one philosopher.

Luxury, impossible to prevent among men who are greedy for their own conveniences and for the esteem of others, soon completes the evil that societies have begun; and on the pretext of keeping the poor alive (but of course they should not have been reduced to poverty in the first place), luxury impoverishes everyone else and sooner or later depopulates the state.

Luxury is a remedy far worse than the evil it means to cure; or rather it is itself the worst of all evils in any state, however large or small it may be, and which, in order to feed the hordes of lackeys and wretches it has produced, crushes and ruins the laborer and the citizen—like those scorching south winds that, by covering grass and greenery with devouring insects, take sustenance away from useful animals and bring scarcity and death to all the places where they make themselves felt.

From society and the luxury it engenders, arise the liberal and mechanical arts, commerce, letters, and all those useless things that make skills flourish, enriching and ruining states. The reason for this decay is quite simple. It is easy to see that agriculture, by its nature, must be the least lucrative of all the arts, because, with its product being of the most indispensable use to all men, its price must be proportionate to the abilities of the poorest. From the same principle can be drawn this rule: that, in general, the arts are lucrative in inverse proportion to their usefulness and that the most necessary must finally become the most neglected. From this it is clear what must be thought of the true advantages of skills and of the real effect that results from their progress.

Such are the discernible causes of all the miseries into which opulence finally brings down the most admired nations. To the degree that skills and the arts expand and flourish, the scorned farmer, burdened with taxes necessary to maintain luxury and condemned to spend his life between toil and hunger, abandons his fields to go to the cities in search of the bread he ought to be carrying there. The more the capital cities strike the stupid eyes of the people as wonderful, the more it will be necessary to groan at the sight of countrysides abandoned, fields fallow, and main roads jammed with unhappy citizens who have become beggars or thieves, destined to end their misery one day on the rack or on a dung heap. Thus it is that the state, enriching itself on the one hand, weakens and depopulates itself on the other and that the most powerful monarchies, after much labor to become opulent and deserted, end by becoming the prey of poor nations that succumb to the deadly temptation to invade them and that enrich and enfeeble themselves in their turn, until they are themselves invaded and destroyed by others.

Let someone deign to explain to us for once what could have produced those hordes of barbarians that for so many centuries have overrun Europe, Asia, and Africa. Was it to the skills of their arts, the wisdom of their laws, the excellence of their civil order that they owed that prodigious population? Would our learned ones be so kind as to tell us why, far from multiplying to that degree, those ferocious and brutal men, without enlightenment, without restraint, without education, did not all kill one another at every moment in the course of arguing with one another over their fodder or their game? Let them explain to us how these wretches even had the gall to look right in the eye such capable people as we were, with such fine military discipline, such fine codes, and such wise laws, and why, finally, after society was perfected in the countries of the north and so many pains were taken there to teach men their mutual duties and the art of living together agreeably and peaceably, we no longer see come out of them anything like those multitudes of men they produced formerly. I am very much afraid that someone might finally get it into his head to reply to me that all these great things, namely, the arts, sciences, and laws, have been very wisely invented by men as a salutary plague to prevent the excessive multiplication of the species, out of fear that this world, which is destined for us, might finally become too small for its inhabitants.

What then! Must we destroy societies, annihilate thine and mine, and return to live in the forests with bears?—a conclusion in the style of my adversaries, which I prefer to anticipate, rather than leave to them the shame of drawing it. Oh you, to whom the heavenly voice has not made itself heard and who recognize for your species no other destination except to end this brief life in peace! You who can leave in the midst of the cities your deadly acquisitions, your troubled minds, your corrupt hearts, and your unbridled desires! Since it depends on you, retake your ancient and first innocence; go into the woods to lose sight and memory of the crimes of your contemporaries, and have no fear of bringing your species into disgrace by renouncing its enlightenment in order to renounce its vices. As for men like me, whose passions have forever destroyed their original simplicity, who can no longer feed on grass and acorn[s], nor get by without laws and chiefs; those who were honored in their first father with supernatural lessons; those who will see, in the intention of giving human actions from the beginning a morality they would not have acquired for a long time, the reason for a precept indifferent in itself and inexplicable in any other system; those, in a word, who are convinced that the divine voice called the entire human race to the enlightenment and the happiness of the celestial intelligences; all those latter ones will attempt, through the exercise of virtues they oblige themselves to practice while learning to know them, to merit the eternal reward that they ought to expect for them. They will respect the sacred bonds of the societies of which they are members; they will love their fellowmen and will serve them with all their power; they will scrupulously obey the laws and the men who are their authors and their ministers; they will honor above all the good and wise princes who will know how to prevent, cure, or palliate that pack of abuses and evils always ready to overpower us; they will animate the zeal of these worthy chiefs by showing them without fear or flattery the greatness of their task and the rigor of their duty. Nevertheless they will scorn a constitution that can be maintained only with the help of so many respectable people, who are desired more often than they are obtained, and from which, despite all their care, always arise more real calamities than apparent advantages.[80]

Note x *(page 54, "purely animal functions")* Among the men we know, whether by ourselves, or from historians, or from travelers, some are black, others white, others red. Some wear their hair long; others have merely curly wool. Some are almost entirely covered with hair; others do not even have a beard. There have been and perhaps there still are nations of men of gigantic size; and apart from the fable of the Pygmies (which may well be merely an

---

[80] [This passage is notoriously difficult to interpret. Rousseau appears to be attributing to his adversaries his own view, that human beings would be better off without modern civilization, and claiming for himself the view that religion (symbolized by God's command to Adam and Eve not to eat of the tree of knowledge) requires the preservation of the existing social order, even though he concludes by insisting that he will continue to despise it. The obvious explanation is that Rousseau is trying to placate the censor.]

exaggeration), we know that the Laplanders and above all the Greenlanders are considerably below the average size of man. It is even maintained that there are entire peoples who have tails like quadrupeds. And without putting blind faith in the accounts of Herodotus and Ctesias,[81] we can at least draw from them the very likely opinion that had one been able to make good observations in those ancient times when various peoples followed lifestyles differing more greatly among themselves than do those of today, one would have also noted much more striking variations in the shape and posture of the body. All these facts, for which it is easy to furnish incontestable proofs, are capable of surprising only those who are accustomed to look solely at the objects that surround them and who are ignorant of the powerful effects of the diversity of climates, air, foods, lifestyle, habits in general, and especially the astonishing force of the same causes when they act continually for long successions of generations. Today, when commerce, voyages, and conquests reunite various peoples further, and their lifestyles are constantly approximating one another through frequent communication, it is evident that certain national differences have diminished; and, for example, everyone can take note of the fact that today's Frenchmen are no longer those large, white, and blond-haired bodies described by Latin historians, although time, together with the mixture of the Franks and the Normans, themselves white and blond-haired, should have reestablished what commerce with the Romans could have removed from the influence of the climate in the natural constitution and complexion of the inhabitants. All of these observations on the varieties that a thousand causes can produce and have in fact produced in the human species cause me to wonder whether the various animals similar to men, taken without much scrutiny by travelers for beasts, either because of some differences they noticed in their outward structure or simply because these animals did not speak, would not in fact be veritable savage men, whose race, dispersed in the woods during olden times, had not had an occasion to develop any of its virtual faculties, had not acquired any degree of perfection, and was still found in the primitive state of nature. Let us give an example of what I mean.

"There are found in the kingdom of the Congo," says the translator of the *Histoire des Voyages*, "many of those large animals called *orangutans* in the East Indies, which occupy a middle ground between the human species and the baboons. Battel[82] relates that in the forests of Mayomba, in the kingdom of Loango,[83] one sees two kinds of monsters, the larger of which are called *pongos* and the others *enjocos*.[84] The former bear an exact resemblance to man, except they are much larger and very tall. With a human face, they have very

---

[81] [Herodotus and Ctesias were ancient Greek historians of Persia.]

[82] [Andrew Battel (c. 1565–c. 1640), an English traveler and trader.]

[83] [In Ethiopia.]

[84] [Gorillas, orangutans, and chimpanzees were not reliably distinguished in Rousseau's day. Buffon thought *pongo*, *jocko*, and *enjoko* were other names for orangutan.]

deep-set eyes. Their hands, cheeks, and ears are without hair, except for their eyebrows, which are very long. Although the rest of their body is quite hairy, the hair is not very thick. The color of the hair is brown. Finally, the only part that distinguishes them from men is their leg, which has no calf. They walk upright, grasping the hair of their neck with their hand. Their retreat is in the woods. They sleep in the trees, and there they make a kind of roof that offers them shelter from the rain. Their foods are fruits or wild nuts; they never eat flesh. The custom of the Negroes who cross the forests is to light fires during the night. They note that in the morning, at their departure, the pongos take their place around the fire and do not withdraw until it is out; because, for all their cleverness, they do not have enough sense to lay wood on the fire to keep it going.

"They occasionally walk in groups and kill the Negroes who cross the forests. They even fall upon elephants who come to graze in the places they inhabit, and they irritate the elephants so much with punches or with whacks of a stick that they force them howling to take flight. Pongos are never taken alive, because they are so strong that ten men would not be enough to stop them. But the Negroes take a good many young ones after having killed the mother, to whose body the young stick very closely. When one of these animals dies, the others cover its body with a pile of branches or leaves. Purchass[85] adds that, in the conversations he has had with Battel, he had learned that a pongo abducted a little Negro from him who passed an entire month in the society of these animals, for they do not harm men they take by surprise, at least when these men do not pay any attention to them, as the little Negro had observed. Battel had not described the second species of monster.

"Dapper[86] confirms that the kingdom of the Congo is filled with those animals that in the Indies bear the name orangutans, that is to say, inhabitants of the woods, and that the Africans call *quojas-morros*. This beast, he says, is so similar to man, that it has occurred to some travelers that it could have issued from a woman and a monkey—a myth that even the Negroes reject. One of these animals was transported from the Congo to Holland and presented to the Prince of Orange, Frederick Henry. It was the height of a three-year-old child, moderately stocky, but square and well proportioned, very agile and lively; its legs fleshy and robust; the entire front of the body naked, but the rear covered with black hairs. At first sight, its face resembled that of a man, but it had a flat and turned-up nose; its ears were also those of the human species, its breast (for it was a female) was plump, its navel sunken, its shoulders very well joined, its hands divided into fingers and thumbs, its calves and heels fat and fleshy. It often walked upright on its legs. It was capable of lifting and

[85] [Samuel Purchas (c. 1575–1626), who published histories of voyages.]

[86] [Olfert Dapper (d. 1690), a Dutch geographer who wrote a description of Africa, translated into French in 1668.]

carrying heavy burdens. When it wanted to drink, it took the cover of the pot in one hand, and held the base with the other; afterward it graciously wiped its lips. It lay down to sleep with its head on a cushion, covering itself with such skill that it would have been taken for a man in bed. The Negroes tell strange stories about this animal. They assert not only that it takes women and girls by force but that it dares to attack armed men. In a word, there is great likelihood that it is the satyr of the ancients. Perhaps Merolla[87] is speaking only of these animals when he relates that Negroes sometimes lay hold of savage men and women in their hunts."

These species of anthropomorphic animals are again discussed in the third volume of the same *Histoire des Voyages* under the name of *beggos* and *mandrills*. But sticking to the preceding accounts, we find in the description of these alleged monsters striking points of conformity with the human species and lesser differences than those that would be assigned between one man and another. From these pages it is not clear what the reasons are that the authors have for refusing to give the animals in question the name "savage men"; but it is easy to conjecture that it is on account of their stupidity and also because they did not speak—feeble reasons for those who know that although the organ of speech is natural to man, nevertheless speech itself is not natural to him, and who know to what point his perfectibility can have elevated civil man above his original state. The small number of lines these descriptions contain can enable us to judge how badly these animals have been observed and with what prejudices they have been viewed. For example, they are categorized as monsters, and yet there is agreement that they reproduce. In one place, Battel says that the pongos kill the Negroes who cross the forests; in another place, Purchass adds that they do not do any harm, even when they surprise them, at least when the Negroes do not fix their gaze upon them. The pongos gather around fires lit by the Negroes upon the Negroes' withdrawal and withdraw in their turn when the fire is out. There is the fact. Here now is the commentary of the observer: *because, for all their cleverness, they do not have enough sense to lay wood on the fire to keep it going.* I would like to hazard a guess how Battel, or Purchass, his compiler, could have known that the withdrawal of the pongos was an effect of their stupidity rather than their will. In a climate such as Loango, fire is not something particularly necessary for the animals; and if the Negroes light a fire, it is less against the cold than to frighten ferocious beasts. It is therefore a very simple matter that, after having been for some time delighted with the flame or being well warmed, the pongos grow tired of always remaining in the same place and go off to graze, which requires more time than if they ate flesh. Moreover, we know that most animals, man not excluded, are naturally lazy and that they refuse all sorts of efforts that are not absolutely necessary. Finally, it seems very strange that pongos, whose adroitness and strength are praised, the pongos who know how to bury

[87] [Girolamo Merolla, who published an account of the Congo in 1692.]

their dead and to make themselves roofs out of branches, should not know how to push wood into the fire. I recall having seen a monkey perform the same maneuver that people deny the pongos can do. It is true that since my ideas were not oriented in this direction, I myself committed the mistake for which I reproach our travelers: I neglected to examine whether the intention of the monkey was actually to sustain the fire or simply, as I believe is the case, to imitate the actions of a man. Whatever the case may be, it is well demonstrated that the monkey is not a variety of man: not only because he is deprived of the faculty of speech, but above all because it is certain that his species does not have the faculty of perfecting itself, which is the specific characteristic of the human species: experiments that do not seem to have been made on the pongos and the orangutan with sufficient care to enable one to draw the same conclusion in their case. However, there would be a means by which, if the orangutan or others were of the human species, even the least sophisticated observers could assure themselves of it in a definitive fashion. But beyond the fact that a single generation would not be sufficient for this experiment, it should be regarded as unworkable, since it would be necessary that what is merely a supposition be demonstrated to be true and demonstrated before the test that should establish the fact of the matter could be innocently performed.[88]

Judgments that are hasty, and that are not the fruit of an enlightened reason, are prone to be extreme. Without any fuss, our travelers made into beasts, under the names *pongos, mandrills, orangutans,* the same beings that the ancients, under the names *satyrs, fauns, sylvans,* made into divinities. Perhaps, after more precise investigations it will be found that they are <neither beasts nor gods but> men. Meanwhile, it would seem to me that there is as much reason to defer on this point to Merolla, an educated monk, an eyewitness, and one who, with all his naïveté, did not fail to be a man of intelligence, as to the merchant Battel, Dapper, Purchass, and the other compilers.

What judgment do we think such observers would have made regarding the child found in 1694, of whom I have spoken before, who gave no indication of reason, walked on his feet and hands, had no language, and made sounds that bore no resemblance whatever to those of a man? It took a long time, continues the same philosopher who provided me with this fact, before he could utter a few words, and then he did it in a barbarous manner. Once he could speak, he was questioned about his first state, but he did not recall it any more than we recall what happened to us in the cradle. If, unhappily[89] for him, this child had fallen into the hands of our travelers, there can be no

---

[88] [The experiment Rousseau has in mind is to breed between humans and orangutans on the assumption that, if they belong to different species, any offspring will be sterile, as mules are.]

[89] [In the copy of the Discourse sent to Richard Davenport, Rousseau inserts here "or perhaps happily."]

doubt that after having observed his silence and stupidity, they would have resolved to send him back to the woods or lock him up in a menagerie, after which they would have spoken eruditely about him in their fine accounts as a very curious beast who looked rather like a man.

For the past three or four hundred years the inhabitants of Europe have inundated the other parts of the world and continually published new collections of travels and stories; yet I am convinced that we know no other men but the Europeans alone. Moreover, it would appear, from the ridiculous prejudices that have not been extinguished even among men of letters, that everybody does hardly anything under the pompous name of "the study of man" except study the men of his country. Individuals may well come and go. It seems that philosophy travels nowhere; moreover, the philosophy of one people is little suited to another. The reason for this is manifest, at least for distant countries. There are hardly more than four sorts of men who make long voyages: sailors, merchants, soldiers, and missionaries. Now we can hardly expect the first three classes to provide good observers; and as for those in the fourth, occupied by the sublime vocation that calls them, even if they were not subject to the prejudices of social position as are all the rest, we must believe that they would not voluntarily commit themselves to investigations that would appear to be sheer curiosity and that would sidetrack them from the more important works to which they are destined. Besides, to preach the Gospel in a useful manner, zeal alone is needed, and God gives the rest. But to study men, talents are needed that God is not required to give anyone and that are not always the portion of saints. One cannot open a book of voyages in which one does not find descriptions of characters and mores. But one is utterly astonished to see that these people who have described so many things have said merely what everyone already knew; that, at the other end of the world, they only knew how to recognize behavior that they could have discovered without leaving their own street; and that those true qualities that characterize nations and strike eyes made to see have almost always escaped theirs. Whence this fine moral slogan, so bandied about by the philosophizing rabble: that men are everywhere the same; that, since everywhere they have the same passions and the same vices, it is rather pointless to seek to characterize different peoples—which is about as well reasoned as it would be for someone to say that Peter and James cannot be distinguished from one another because they both have a nose, a mouth, and eyes.

Will we never see those happy days reborn when the people did not dabble in philosophizing, but when a Plato, a Thales, a Pythagoras, taken with an ardent desire to know, undertook the greatest voyages merely to inform themselves and went far away to shake off the yoke of national prejudices in order to learn to know men by their similarities and their differences and to acquire those sorts of universal knowledge that are not exclusively those of a single century or country, but that, since they are of all times and all places, are, as it were, the common science of the wise?

We admire the splendor of some curious men who, at great expense, made or caused to be made voyages to the Orient with learned men and painters in order to sketch hovels and to decipher or copy inscriptions. But I have trouble conceiving how, in a century where people take pride in fine sorts of knowledge, there are not to be found two men linked closely together—rich, one in money, the other in genius, both loving glory and aspiring for immortality—one of whom sacrifices twenty thousand crowns of his goods and the other ten years of his life for a famous voyage around the world in order to study, not always rocks and plants but, for once, men and mores, and who, after so many centuries used to measure and examine the house, would finally be of a mind to want to know its inhabitants.

The academicians who have traveled through the northern parts of Europe and the southern parts of America had for their object to visit them more as geometers than as philosophers. Nevertheless, since they were both simultaneously, we cannot regard as utterly unknown the regions that have been seen and described by La Condamine and Maupertuis.[90] The jeweler Chardin, who has traveled like Plato, has left nothing to be said about Persia. China seemed to have been well observed by the Jesuits. Kempfer[91] gives a passable idea of what little he has seen in Japan. Except for these reports, we know nothing about the peoples of the East Indies, who have been visited exclusively by Europeans interested more in filling their purses than their heads. All of Africa and its numerous inhabitants, as unique in character as in color, are yet to be examined. The entire earth is covered with nations of which we know only the names, and we dabble in judging the human race! Let us suppose a Montesquieu, a Buffon, a Diderot, a Duclos, a d'Alembert, a Condillac, or men of that ilk traveling in order to inform their compatriots, observing and describing as they know how to do Turkey, Egypt, Barbary, the empire of Morocco, Guinea, the land of the Bantus, the interior of Africa and its eastern coastlines, the Malabars, Mogul, the banks of the Ganges, the kingdoms of Siam, Pegu, and Ava, China, Tartary, and especially Japan; then in the other hemisphere, Mexico, Peru, Chile, the straits of Magellan, not to forget the Patagonias true or false,[92] Tucuman, Paraguay (if possible), Brazil; finally the Caribbean Islands, Florida, and all the savage countries—the most important voyage of all and the one that should be embarked upon with the greatest care. Let us suppose that these new Hercules, back from these memorable treks, then wrote at leisure the natural, moral, and political history of what

[90] [In 1736 Charles-Marie de La Condamine (1701–1774) had measured three degrees of the earth's circumference in Ecuador, while at the same time Maupertuis measured one degree in Lapland. These measurements helped confirm Newtonianism by showing that the earth was not spherical.]

[91] [Engelbrecht Kaempfer (1651–1716), whose account of Japan appears in Kolbe's *Histoire générale des voyages*.]

[92] [The Patagonians were supposed to be giants, but many doubted the reliability of these reports.]

they would have seen; we ourselves would see a new world traced out by their pen, and we would thus learn to know our own. I say that when such observers will affirm of an animal that it is a man and of another that it is a beast, we will have to believe them. But it would be terribly simpleminded to defer in this to unsophisticated travelers, concerning whom we will sometimes be tempted to put the same question that they dabble at resolving concerning other animals.[93]

Note xi (*page 54, "his physical needs"*) That appears utterly evident to me, and I am unable to conceive whence our philosophers can derive all the passions they ascribe to natural man. With the single exception of the physically necessary that nature itself demands, all our other needs are such merely out of habit (previous to which they were not needs) or by our own desires; and we do not desire what we are not in a position to know. Whence it follows that since savage man desires only the things he knows and knows only those things whose possession is in his power or easily acquired, nothing should be so tranquil as his soul and nothing so limited as his mind.

Note xii (*page 57, "same nonchalance"*) I find in Locke's *Civil Government* an objection that seems to me too specious for me to be permitted to hide it.

"For the end of conjunction, between male and female," says this philosopher, "being not barely procreation, but the continuation of the species; this conjunction betwixt male and female ought to last, even after procreation, so long as is necessary to the nourishment and support of the young ones, who are to be sustained by those that got them, till they are able to shift and provide for themselves. This rule, which the infinite wise maker hath set to the works of his hands, we find the inferior creatures steadily obey. In those viviparous animals which feed on grass, the conjunction between male and female lasts no longer than the very act of copulation; because the teat of the dam being sufficient to nourish the young, till it be able to feed on grass, the male only begets, but concerns not himself for the female or young, to whose sustenance he can contribute nothing. But in beasts of prey the conjunction lasts longer: because the dam not being able well to subsist herself, and nourish her numerous off-spring by her own prey alone, a more laborious, as well as more dangerous way of living, than by feeding on grass, the assistance of the male is necessary to the maintenance of their common family, which cannot subsist till they are able to prey for themselves, but by the joint care of male and female. The same is to be observed in all birds, (except some domestic ones, where plenty of food excuses the cock from feeding, and taking care of the young brood) whose young needing food in the nest, the cock and hen continue mates, till the young are able to use their wing, and provide for themselves.

---

[93] [I.e., we may doubt whether they are intelligent enough to be properly human.]

"And herein I think lies the chief, if not the only, reason, why the male and female in mankind are tied to a longer conjunction than other creatures, viz. because the female is capable of conceiving, and de facto is commonly with child again, and brings forth too a new birth, long before the former is out of a dependency for support on his parents' help, and able to shift for himself, and has all the assistance is due to him from his parents: whereby the father, who is bound to take care for those he hath begot, is under an obligation to continue in conjugal society with the same woman longer than other creatures, whose young being able to subsist of themselves, before the time of procreation returns again, the conjugal bond dissolves of itself, and they are at liberty, till Hymen at his usual anniversary season summons them again to choose new mates. Wherein one cannot but admire the wisdom of the great Creator, who having given to man an ability to lay up for the future, as well as to supply the present necessity, hath made it necessary, that society of man and wife should be more lasting, than of male and female amongst other creatures; that so their industry might be encouraged, and their interest better united, to make provision and lay up goods for their common issue, which uncertain mixture, or easy and frequent solutions of conjugal society would mightily disturb."[94]

The same love of truth that has made me to set forth sincerely this objection moves me to accompany it with some remarks, if not to resolve it, at least to clarify it.

1. I will observe first that moral proofs[95] do not have great force in the natural sciences[96] and that they serve more to explain existing facts than to establish the real existence of those facts. Now such is the type of proof that Mr. Locke employs in the passage I have just quoted; for although it may be advantageous to the human species for the union between man and woman to be permanent, it does not follow that it has been thus established by nature. Otherwise it would be necessary to say that nature also instituted civil society, the arts, commerce, and all that is asserted to be useful to men.

2. I do not know where Mr. Locke has found that among animals of prey, the society of the male and female lasts longer than does the society of those that live on grass and that the former assists the latter to feed the young; for it is not manifest that the dog, the cat, the bear, or the wolf recognize their female better than the horse, the ram, the bull, the stag, or all the other

[94] [The excerpted passage is from the original English text of Locke's *Two Treatises*, 2, ch. 7, §79–80.]

[95] [Rousseau's phrase is *preuves morales*. According to the language of the day, a "moral proof" is the sort of certainty we express when we say, "Tom would never do that" because we know his character and what he is capable of.]

[96] [Rousseau's phrase is *matière de physique*, but according to eighteenth-century dictionaries, *physique* includes all aspects of the study of nature. According to scholastic and Cartesian philosophy, proofs in the natural sciences should be demonstrations from first principles, as in geometry.]

quadruped animals do theirs. On the contrary, it seems that if the assistance of the male were necessary to the female to preserve her young, it would be particularly in the species that live only on grass, because a long period of time is needed by the mother to graze and during that entire interval she is forced to neglect her brood, whereas the prey of a female bear or wolf is devoured in an instant, and, without suffering hunger, she has more time to nurse her young. This line of reasoning is confirmed by an observation upon the relative number of teats and young, which distinguishes carnivorous from frugivorous species, and of which I have spoken in **Note viii.** If this observation is accurate and general, since a woman has only two teats and rarely has more than one child at a time, this is one more strong reason for doubting that the human species is naturally carnivorous. Thus, it seems that, in order to draw Locke's conclusion, it would be necessary to reverse completely his reasoning. There is no more solidity in the same distinction when it is applied to birds. For who could be persuaded that the union of the male and female is more durable among vultures and crows than among turtledoves? We have two species of domestic birds, the duck and the pigeon, that furnish us with examples directly contrary to the system of this author. The pigeon, which lives solely on grain, remains united to its female, and they feed their young in common. The duck, which is known to be carnivorous, recognizes neither its female nor its young and provides no help in their sustenance. And among hens, a species hardly less carnivorous, we do not observe that the rooster bothers itself in the least with the brood. And if in the other species the male shares with the female the care of feeding the young, it is because birds, which at first cannot fly and which the female cannot suckle, are much less in a position to get along without the help of the father than are quadrupeds, for which the mother's teat is sufficient, at least for a time.

3. There is much uncertainty about the principal fact that serves as a basis for all of Mr. Locke's reasoning; for in order to know whether, as he asserts, in the pure state of nature the female ordinarily is pregnant again and has a new child long before the preceding one could see to its needs by itself, it would be necessary to perform experiments that Mr. Locke surely did not perform and that no one is in a position to perform. The continual cohabitation of husband and wife is so likely to tempt them into risking a new pregnancy that it is very difficult to believe that the chance encounter or the mere impulsion of temperament produced such frequent effects in the pure state of nature as in that of conjugal society—a delay that would contribute perhaps toward making the children more robust and that, moreover, might be compensated by the power to conceive being prolonged to a greater age in women who would have abused it less in their youth. As for children, there are several reasons for believing that their capacities and their organs develop much later among us than they did in the primitive state of which I am speaking. The original weakness that they derive from the constitution of the parents, the cares taken to envelop and constrain all of their members, the softness in

which they are raised, perhaps the use of milk other than that of their mother, everything contradicts and slows down in them the initial progress of nature. The heed they are forced to pay to a thousand things on which their attention is continually fixed, while no exercise is given to their bodily forces, can also bring about considerable deflection from their growth. Thus, if, instead of first overworking and exhausting their minds in a thousand ways, their bodies were allowed to be exercised by the continual movements that nature seems to demand of them, it is to be believed that they would be in a much better position to walk and to provide for their needs by themselves.

4. Finally, Mr. Locke at most proves that there could well be in a man a motive for remaining attached to a woman when she has a child, but in no way does he prove that the man must have been attached to her before the childbirth and during the nine months of pregnancy. If a particular woman is indifferent to the man during those nine months, if she even becomes unknown to him, why will he help her after childbirth? Why will he help her to raise a child that he does not know belongs to him alone and whose birth he has neither decided upon nor foreseen? Evidently Mr. Locke presumes what is in question; for it is not a matter of knowing why the man will remain attached to the woman after childbirth but why he will be attached to her after conception. Once his appetite is satisfied, the man has no further need for a particular woman, nor the woman for a particular man. The man does not have the least care or perhaps the least idea of the consequences of his action. The one goes off in one direction, the other in another, and there is no likelihood that at the end of nine months they have the memory of having known one another. For this type of memory, by which one individual gives preference to another for the act of generation, requires, as I prove in the text, more progress or corruption in human understanding than may be supposed in man in the state of animality we are dealing with here. Another woman can therefore satisfy the new desires of the man as congenially as the one he has already known, and another man in the same manner satisfy the woman, supposing she is impelled by the same appetite during the time of pregnancy, about which one can reasonably be in doubt. And if in the state of nature the woman no longer feels the passion of love after the conception of the child, the obstacle to her society with the man thus becomes much greater still, since she then has no further need either for the man who has made her pregnant or for anyone else. There is not, therefore, in the man any reason to seek the same woman or in the woman any reason to seek the same man. Thus Locke's reasoning falls in ruin, and all the dialectic of this philosopher has not shielded him from the mistake committed by Hobbes and others. They had to explain a fact of the state of nature, that is to say, of a state where men lived in isolation and where a particular man did not have any motive for living in proximity to another particular man, nor perhaps did a particular group of men have a motive for living in proximity to another particular group of men, which is much worse. And they gave no thought

to transporting themselves beyond the centuries of society, that is to say, of those times when men always have a reason for living in proximity to one another and when a particular man often has a reason for living in proximity to a particular man or woman.

Note xiii *(page 57, "they are necessary")* I will hold back from embarking on the philosophical reflections that one could make concerning the advantages and disadvantages of this institution of languages. There are people who have permission to attack vulgar errors, but I am not one of them; and educated people respect their prejudices too much to abide patiently my alleged paradoxes. So let us allow those men to speak who have not been branded as criminals for occasionally daring to take the side of reason against the opinion of the multitude. "Nor would anything be deducted from the happiness of the human race if, when the disaster and confusion of so many languages has been cast out, mortals should cultivate one art and if it should be allowed to explain anything by means of signs, movements, and gestures. But now it has been so established that the condition of animals commonly believed to be brutes is considerably better than ours in this respect, inasmuch as they articulate their feelings and their thoughts without an interpreter more readily and perhaps more felicitously than any mortals can, especially if they are speaking a foreign language."[97] Is. Vossius[98] *de Poëmat. Cant. et Viribus Rythmi*, p. 66.

Note xiv *(page 60, "to discover numbers")* In showing how ideas of discrete quantity and its relationships are necessary in the humblest of the arts, Plato mocks with good reason the authors of his time who alleged that Palamedes[99] had invented numbers at the siege of Troy, as if, says this philosopher, Agamemnon could have been ignorant until then of how many legs he had. In fact, one senses the impossibility that society and the arts should have arrived at the point where they already were at the time of the siege of Troy unless men had the use of numbers and arithmetic. But the necessity for knowing numbers, before acquiring other types of knowledge, does not make their invention easier to imagine. Once the names of the numbers are known, it is easy to explain their meaning and to elicit the ideas that these names represent; but in order to invent them, it was necessary, prior to conceiving of these same ideas, to be, as it were, on familiar terms with philosophical meditations, to be trained to consider beings by their essence alone and independently of all other perception—a very difficult, very metaphysical, hardly natural abstraction, and yet one without which these ideas could never have been

---

[97] [Rousseau here quotes the Latin text.]

[98] [Isaac Vossius (1618–1689), a Dutch scholar, worked briefly for Queen Christina of Sweden and then settled in England.]

[99] [Palamedes, in Greek mythology, was responsible for involving Odysseus in the Trojan War. He was believed to have invented dice, backgammon, and numbers.]

transported from one species or genus to another, nor could numbers have become universal. A savage could consider separately his right leg and his left leg or look at them together under the indivisible idea of a pair without ever thinking that he had two of them; for the representative idea that portrays for us an object is one thing, and the numerical idea that determines it is another. Even less was he able to count to five. And although, by placing his hands one on top of the other, he could have noticed that the fingers corresponded exactly, he was far from thinking of their numerical equality. He did not know the sum of his fingers any more than that of his hairs. And if, after having made him understand what numbers are, someone had said to him that he had as many fingers as toes, he perhaps would have been quite surprised, in comparing them, to find that this was true.

Note xv (*page 62, "egocentrism of his came into being"*) We must not confuse egocentrism [*amour propre*] with love of oneself [*amour de soi-même*], two passions very different by virtue of both their nature and their effects. Love of oneself is a natural sentiment that moves every animal to be vigilant in its own preservation and that, directed in man by reason and modified by pity, produces humanity and virtue. Egocentrism is merely a sentiment that is relative, artificial, and born in society that moves each individual to value himself more than anyone else, that inspires in men all the evils they cause one another, and that is the true source of honor.

   With this well understood, I say that in our primitive state, in the veritable state of nature, egocentrism does not exist; for since each particular man regards himself as the only spectator who observes him, as the only being in the universe that takes an interest in him, as the only judge of his own merit, it is impossible that a sentiment that has its source in comparisons that he is not in a position to make could germinate in his soul. For the same reason, this man could not have either hatred or desire for revenge, passions that can arise only from the belief that offense has been received. And since what constitutes the offense is scorn or the intention to harm and not the harm itself, men who know neither how to appraise nor to compare themselves can do considerable violence to one another when it returns them some advantage for doing it, without ever offending one another. In a word, on seeing his fellowmen hardly otherwise than he would see animals of another species, each man can carry away the prey of the weaker or yield his own to the stronger, viewing these lootings as merely natural events, without the least stirring of insolence or resentment and without any other passion but the sadness or the joy of a good or bad venture.

Note xvi (*page 74, "the best for man"*) It is something extremely remarkable that, for all the many years that the Europeans torment themselves in order to acclimate the savages of various countries to their lifestyle, they have not yet been able to win over a single one of them, not even by means of Christianity;

for our missionaries sometimes turn them into Christians, but never into civilized men. Nothing can overcome the invincible repugnance they have against appropriating our mores and living in our way. If these poor savages are as unhappy as is alleged, by what inconceivable depravity of judgment do they constantly refuse to civilize themselves in imitation of us or to learn to live happily among us; whereas one reads in a thousand places that the French and other Europeans have voluntarily taken refuge among those nations and have spent their entire lives there, no longer able to leave so strange a lifestyle; and whereas we even see level-headed missionaries regret with tenderness the calm and innocent days they have spent among those much scorned peoples? If one replies that they do not have enough enlightenment to make a sound judgment about their state and ours, I will reply that the reckoning of happiness is less an affair of reason than of sentiment. Moreover, this reply can be turned against us with still greater force; for there is a greater distance between our ideas and the frame of mind one would need to be in, in order to conceive the satisfaction that the savages find in their lifestyle than between the ideas of savages and those that can make them conceive our lifestyle. In fact, after a few observations it is easy for them to see that all our labors are directed toward but two objects, namely, the conveniences of life for oneself and esteem among others. But what are the means by which we are to imagine the sort of pleasure a savage takes in spending his life alone amid the woods, or fishing, or blowing into a sorry-looking flute without ever knowing how to get it to elicit a single note and without bothering himself to learn?

Savages have frequently been brought to Paris, London, and other cities; people have been eager to display our luxury, our wealth, and all our most useful and curious arts. None of this has ever excited in them anything but a stupid admiration, without the least stirring of covetousness. I recall, among others, the story of a chief of some North Americans who was brought to the court of England about thirty years ago. A thousand things were made to pass before his eye in an attempt to give him some present that could please him, but nothing was found about which he seemed to care. Our weapons seemed heavy and cumbersome to him, our shoes hurt his feet, our clothes restricted him; he rejected everything. Finally, it was noticed that, having taken a wool blanket, he seemed to take some pleasure in wrapping it around his shoulders. You will agree at least, someone immediately said to him, on the usefulness of this furnishing? Yes, he replies, this seems to me to be nearly as good as an animal skin. However, he would not have said that had he worn them both in the rain.

Perhaps someone will say to me that it is habit that, in attaching everyone to his lifestyle, prevents savages from realizing what is good in ours. In which case, it must at least appear quite extraordinary that habit has more force in maintaining savages in their preference for their misery than Europeans in their enjoyment of their felicity. But to give to this last objection a response to which there is not a word that can be said in reply, without adducing all the young savages that people have tried in vain to civilize, without speaking of the Greenlanders and the inhabitants of Iceland, whom people have tried to raise and feed in Denmark, and all of whom sadness and despair caused to perish, whether from languor or in the sea when they attempted to regain their homeland by swimming back to it, I will be content to cite a single, well-documented example, which I give to the admirers of European civilization to examine.

"All the efforts of the Dutch missionaries at the Cape of Good Hope have never been able to convert a single Hottentot. Van der Stel, governor of the Cape, having taken one from infancy, had raised him in the principles of the Christian religion and in the practice of the customs of Europe. He was richly clothed; he was taught several languages and his progress corresponded very closely to the care that was taken for his education. Having great hopes for his wit, the governor sent him to the Indies with a commissioner general who employed him usefully in the affairs of the company. He returned to the Cape after the death of the commissioner. A few days after his return, on a visit he made to some of his Hottentot relatives, he made the decision to strip himself of his European dress in order to clothe himself with a sheepskin. He returned to the fort in this new outfit, carrying a bundle containing his old clothes, and, on presenting them to the governor, he made the following speech to him: 'Please, sir, be so kind as to pay heed to the fact that I forever renounce this clothing. I also renounce the Christian religion for the rest of my life. My resolution is to live and die in the religion, ways, and customs of my ancestors. The only favor I ask of you is that you let me keep the necklace and cutlass I am wearing. I will keep them for love of you.' Thereupon, without waiting for Van der Stel's reply, he escaped by taking flight and was never seen again at the Cape." *Histoire des Voyages*, vol. V, p. 175.

Note xvii *(page 78, "fights and murders")* One could raise against me the objection that, in such a disorder, men, instead of willfully murdering one another, would have dispersed, had there been no limits to their dispersion. But first, these limits would at least have been those of the world. And if one thinks about the excessive population that results from the state of nature, one will judge that the earth in that state would not have taken long to be covered with men thus forced to keep together. Besides, they would have dispersed, had the evil been rapid and had it been an overnight change. But they were born under the yoke; they were in the habit of carrying it by the time they felt its weight, and they were content to wait for the opportunity to shake it off. Finally, since they were already accustomed to a thousand conveniences that forced them to keep together, dispersion was no longer as easy as in the first ages, when, since no one had need for anyone but himself, everyone made his decision without waiting for someone else's consent.

Note xviii *(page 79, "new forces to the rich")* Marshal de V***[100] related that, on one of his campaigns, when the excessive knavery of a provisions supplier had made the army suffer and complain, he gave him a severe dressing down and threatened to have him hanged. "This threat has no effect on me," the knave boldly replied to him, "and I am quite pleased to tell you that nobody hangs a man with a hundred thousand crowns at his disposal." I do not know how it happened, the Marshal added naïvely, but in fact he was not hanged, even though he deserved to be a hundred times over.

Note xix *(page 88, "inevitable among private individuals")* Distributive justice would still be opposed to this rigorous equality of the state of nature, even if it were workable in civil society. And since all the members of the state owe it services proportionate to their talents and forces, the citizens for their part should be distinguished and favored in proportion to their services. It is in this sense that one must understand a passage of Isocrates[101] in which he praises the first Athenians for having known well how to distinguish that of the two sorts of equality was the more advantageous, one of which consists in portioning out indifferently to all citizens the same advantages, and the other in distributing them according to each one's merit. These able politicians, adds the orator, in banishing that unjust equality that makes no differentiation between wicked and good men, adhered inviolably to that equality that rewards and punishes each according to his merit. But first, no society has ever existed, regardless of the degree of corruption they may have achieved, in which no differentiation between wicked and good men was made. And in the matter of mores, where the law cannot set a sufficiently precise measurement to serve as a rule for the magistrate, the law very wisely prohibits him from the judgment of persons, leaving him merely the judgment of actions in order not to leave the fate or the rank of citizens to his discretion. Only mores as pure as those of the ancient Romans could withstand censors; such tribunals would soon have overturned everything among us. It is for public esteem to differentiate between wicked and good men. The magistrate is judge only of strict entitlement; but the populace is the true judge of mores—an upright and even enlightened judge on this point, occasionally deceived but never corrupted. The ranks of citizens ought therefore to be regulated not on the basis of their personal merit, which would be to leave to the magistrate the freedom to make an almost arbitrary application of the law, but upon the real services that they render to the state and that lend themselves to a more precise reckoning.

---

[100] [Louis-Hector, Duke of Villars (1653–1734).]
[101] [Isocrates (436–338 BC) was a leading Athenian rhetorician.]

Discourse on Political Economy

Rousseau's essay "Political Economy" was first published in the fifth volume of the Encyclopédie, *which appeared in November 1755. It acquired the title by which it is generally known,* Discourse on Political Economy, *when it was reprinted as a pamphlet in Geneva in 1758. Rousseau himself adopted the new title in authorized editions of his works. When he composed the essay, Rousseau was writing for his still close friend Denis Diderot; the two only began to disagree in 1757. The general view is that the text was written after Rousseau's return to Paris from Geneva in October 1754. If it fails to repeat some of the radical arguments of the second Discourse, for example in its account of the origins of property, this is presumably because Rousseau thought an encyclopedia article should be based on generally accepted assumptions. Accounts of Rousseau's political theory often fail to take account of the terms in which Rousseau presents* amour propre *and the general will in this essay, which is crucial for an understanding of the development of his political theory.*

D.W.

DISCOURSE ON POLITICAL ECONOMY[1]

ECONOMY or OECONOMY *(Morals and Politics)*.[2] This word is derived from οἶκος, *house*, and νόμος, *law*, and originally signified merely the wise and legitimate government of the household for the common good of the entire family. The meaning of this term was later extended to the government of the large family, that is, the state. To distinguish these two usages, in the latter case it is called *general* or *political economy*, and in the former case it is called *domestic* or *private economy*. Only the first of these is the subject of this article. Regarding *domestic economy*, see FATHER OF THE FAMILY.

Even if there were as much similarity between the state and the family as many authors would have us believe, it would not follow as a consequence that the rules of conduct proper to one of these societies would be suitable to the other. They differ too much in size to be capable of being administered in the same fashion. Moreover, there will always be an extreme difference between domestic government, where the father can see everything for himself, and civil government, where the leader sees hardly anything unless through someone else's eyes. For things to become equal in this regard, the talents, force, and all the faculties of the father would have to increase in proportion to the size of his family, and the soul of a powerful monarch would have to be, in comparison with that of an ordinary man, what the size of his empire is to that of the private individual's patrimony.

But how could the government of the state be similar to that of the family, whose basis is so different? With the father being physically stronger than his children, paternal power is reasonably said to be established by nature for as long as his help is needed by them. In the large family, all of whose members are naturally equal, political authority, purely arbitrary as far as its establishment is conceived, can be founded only upon conventions, and the magistrate can command others only by virtue of the laws. The duties of the father are dictated to him by natural feelings and in a manner that seldom allows him to be disobedient. Leaders have no such similar rule and are not really bound to the people except in regard to what they have promised to do for them, promises that the people can rightfully demand they carry out.

---

[1] [As will become evident, by the term *political economy*, Rousseau does not mean "economics" in the modern sense (which appears in both French and English only in the nineteenth century).]

[2] ["Morals" *(la morale)* and "Politics" refer to the broader entries within the *Encyclopédie* that cover the fields of which "Economics" forms part. In the same way, Rousseau's article "Allegro" falls within the larger field of "Music." "Morals" here means the theory of mores; it refers both to what we would call "morality" and what we would call "sociology"—the study of people's behavior.]

Another even more important difference is that, since everything children have they receive from their father, it is obvious that all property rights belong to or emanate from him. It is quite the contrary in the case of the large family, where the general administration is established merely to ensure private property, which is antecedent to it. The chief purpose of the entire household's labors is to maintain and increase the father's patrimony so that he can someday disperse it among his children without reducing them to poverty. On the other hand, the wealth of the public treasury is merely a means—often very much misunderstood—of maintaining private individuals in peace and prosperity. In a word, the small family is destined to die off and be dissolved someday into many other families; on the other hand, the large family is made to last forever in the same condition, so that the first must grow in order to reproduce, whereas not only is it enough that the large family maintains itself, it is easily proved that any increase does it more harm than good.

For several reasons derived from the nature of things, in the family it is the father who should command. First, the authority of the father and mother ought not to be equal; on the contrary, there must be a single government, and when there are differences of opinion there must be one dominant voice that decides. Second, however slight we regard the handicaps that are peculiar to a wife, since they always occasion a period of inactivity for her, this is a sufficient reason for excluding her from this primacy. For when the balance is perfectly equal, a straw is enough to tip the scales. Moreover, a husband should oversee his wife's conduct, for it is important to him to be assured that the children he is forced to recognize and nurture belong to no one but himself. The wife, who has nothing like this to fear, does not have the same right over her husband. Third, children ought to obey their father—initially out of necessity, later out of gratitude. After having their needs met by him for half their lives, they ought to devote the other half to seeing to his needs. Fourth, as far as domestic servants are concerned, they too owe him their services in exchange for the livelihood he provides them, unless they cancel their arrangement once it ceases to be to their advantage. I say nothing here of slavery, since it is contrary to nature and no right can authorize it.

None of this is to be found in political society. Far from the leader's having a natural interest in the happiness of private individuals, it is not uncommon for him to seek his own happiness in the misery of others. If the magistracy is hereditary, often it is a child that is in command of men. If it is elective, a thousand inconveniences make themselves to be felt in the elections. In either case, one loses all the advantages of paternity. Were you to have but one leader, you are at the discretion of a master who has no reason to love you. Were you to have several, you must endure both their tyranny and their disagreements. In short, abuses are inevitable and their consequences devastating in every society where the public interest and the laws have no natural force and are constantly attacked by the personal interest and passions of the leader and his followers.

Although the functions of the father of a family and those of a chief magistrate ought to tend toward the same goal, their paths are so different, their duty and rights so unlike, that one cannot confound them without forming false ideas about the fundamental laws of society and without falling into errors that are fatal to the human race. In effect, although nature's voice is the best advice a good father could listen to in the fulfillment of his duty, for the magistrate it is merely a false guide that works constantly to divert him from his duties and that sooner or later leads to his downfall or to that of the state, unless he is restrained by the most sublime virtue. The only precaution necessary to the father of a family is that he protect himself from depravity and prevent his natural inclinations from becoming corrupt, whereas it is these very inclinations that corrupt the magistrate. To act properly, the former need only consult his heart; the latter becomes a traitor as soon as he listens to his. Even his own reason ought to be suspect to him, and the only rule he should follow is the public reason, which is the law. Thus, nature has made a multitude of good fathers of families, but it is doubtful that, since the beginning of the world, human wisdom has ever produced ten men capable of governing their peers.

It follows from all I have just put forward that one has good reason to distinguish *public* from *private economy* and that, since the state has nothing in common with the family except the obligation their respective leaders bear to render each of them happy, the same rules of conduct could not be suitable to both. I thought these few lines would suffice to overturn the odious system that Sir Filmer attempted to establish in a work titled *Patriarcha*, to which two famous men have already done too much honor by writing books to refute it.[3] Besides, this error is very old, since Aristotle himself saw fit to combat it with arguments that can be found in Book One of his *Politics*.

I ask my readers also to distinguish carefully between the *public economy* about which I will be speaking and that I call *government*, and the supreme authority that I call *sovereignty*. This distinction consists in the one having the right of legislation and, in certain cases, in placing an obligation on the very body of the nation, while the other has only executive power and can place an obligation only upon private individuals. See POLITICS and SOVEREIGNTY.

Permit me to use for a moment a common comparison, inaccurate in many respects, but useful for making myself better understood.

The body politic, taken individually, can be considered to be like a body that is organized, living, and similar to that of a man. The sovereign power represents the head; the laws and customs are the brain, source of the nerves, and seat of the understanding, the will, and the senses, of which the judges

---

[3] [Robert Filmer's posthumous *Patriarcha* was published in 1680 and was promptly refuted by John Locke and Algernon Sidney (though Locke's *Two Treatises of Government* were not published until 1689 and Sidney's *Discourses Concerning Government* until 1698).]

and magistrates are the organs; the commerce, industry, and agriculture are the mouth and stomach that prepare the common subsistence; the public finances are the blood that is discharged by a wise *economy*, performing the functions of the heart in order to distribute nourishment and life throughout the body; the citizens are the body and limbs that make the machine move, live, and work and that cannot be harmed in any part without a painful impression immediately being transmitted to the brain, if the animal is in a state of good health.

The life of both [the human body and the state] is the *self* common to the whole, the reciprocal sensibility, and the internal coordination of all the parts. What if this communication were to cease, if the formal unity were to disappear, and if contiguous parts were to be related to one another solely by their juxtaposition? The man is dead or the state is dissolved.

The body politic, therefore, is also a moral being that possesses a will; and this general will, which always tends toward the conservation and well-being of the whole and of each part and which is the source of the laws, is for all the members of the state, in their relations both to one another and to the state, the rule of what is just and what is unjust. This, by the way, is a truth that shows how absurd many writers have been for regarding as theft the cunning prescribed to the children of Sparta for obtaining their frugal meal, as if anything prescribed by law could fail to be lawful.[4] See the word RIGHT for the source of this great and luminous principle, of which this article is an elucidation.[5]

It is important to observe that this rule of justice, which is entirely reliable when dealing with citizens, can be defective with regard to foreigners; and the reason for this is obvious. For the will of the state, however general it may be in relation to its members, is no longer so in relation to other states and to their members, but becomes for them a private and individual will that has its rule of justice in the law of nature, which brings us right back to the principle we have established. For then the great city of the world becomes the political body whose law of nature is always the general will and whose states and diverse peoples are merely private individuals.[6]

From these same distinctions, applied to each political society and to its members, are derived the most universal and most secure rules on whose basis one could judge a government to be good or bad, and in general of the morality of all human actions.

---

[4] [Spartan children were encouraged to steal food, provided they were not caught; if they were caught, they were punished. Rousseau is here following Hobbes, *De Cive*, ch. 6, §16.]

[5] [Diderot's article "Natural Right" in the *Encyclopédie* does indeed seem to be the source of Rousseau's theory of the general will.]

[6] [This account of the law of nature as a universal general will is taken straight from Diderot's article "Natural Right."]

Every political society is composed of other smaller societies, of differing natures, each of which has its interests and maxims. But these societies, which everyone perceives (since they have an external and authorized form), are not the only ones really existing in the state. All the private individuals who are united by a common interest make up as many others, permanent or transitory, whose force is no less real for being less apparent, and the proper observation of whose various relationships is the true knowledge of mores. It is all these tacit or formal associations that modify in so many ways the appearances of the public will by the influence of their will. The will of these particular societies always has two relations: for the members of the association it is a general will; for the large society it is a particular will, which is quite often found to be upright in the first respect and vice-ridden in the second. Someone could be a devout priest or a brave soldier or a zealous man of action but a bad citizen. A deliberation can be advantageous to the small community and quite pernicious to the large community. It is true that, since particular societies are always subordinated to those that contain them, one should obey the latter rather than the former; the duties of the citizen take precedence over those of the senator, and those of the man over those of the citizen. But unfortunately, private interest is always found in inverse proportion to duty, and it increases to the extent that the association becomes narrower and the commitment less sacred. This is irrefutable proof that the most general will is also always the most just and that the voice of the populace is, in effect, the voice of God.[7]

It does not thence follow that public deliberations are always equitable; they could fail to be so when it is a question of matters involving foreigners. I have stated the reason for this. Thus, it is not impossible for a well-governed republic to wage an unjust war. Nor is it any less impossible for the council of a democracy to pass bad decrees and to condemn the innocent. But this will never happen unless the populace is seduced by private interests that certain clever men have managed to substitute for those of the state by means of personal trust and eloquence. Then the public resolution will be one thing and the general will another. So please do not offer me the democracy of Athens as a counterinstance, because Athens was not really a democracy but a highly tyrannical aristocracy, governed by learned men and orators.[8] Examine carefully what goes on in any deliberation and you will see that the general will is always for the common good; however, quite often there is a secret schism, a tacit confederation, which causes the natural disposition of the assembly to be lost sight of for the sake of private purposes. Then the social body really is divided into other bodies whose members take on a general will that is good

[7] [*Vox populi, vox dei* (the voice of the people is the voice of God) is a traditional saying first recorded in a letter of Alcuin, AD 798.]

[8] [Athens provides the classic example of a public deliberation resulting in the condemnation of an innocent man in the trial of Socrates.]

and just as regards these new bodies, and bad as regards the whole from which each of them has cut itself off.

We see how easy it is to explain by means of these principles the apparent contradictions one notices in the conduct of many men who are filled with scruple and honor in some respects, while deceitful and unprincipled in others. They trample underfoot the most sacred duties and are faithful to the death to commitments that are often illegitimate. Thus, the most corrupt of men always pay some sort of homage to the public faith. Thus (as is noted in the article titled RIGHT) even bandits, who are the enemies of virtue in the large society, worship something like virtue in their lairs.

In establishing the general will as the first principle of public *economy* and as the fundamental rule of government, I did not believe it necessary to examine seriously whether the magistrates belong to the populace or the populace to the magistrates and whether in public affairs one should keep in mind the good of the state or that of the leaders. This question was decided long ago in one way in practice and in another in theory; and in general it would be great folly to hope that those who are in fact masters would prefer some interest other than their own. It would therefore be appropriate to divide public *economy* once again into popular and tyrannical. The former is that of every state where there reigns a unity of interest and will between the populace and the leaders. The latter necessarily exists wherever the government and the populace have different interests and, consequently, opposing wills. The maxims of the latter are inscribed at some length in the archives of history and in the satires of Machiavelli.[9] The maxims of the former are found only in the writings of philosophers who dare to reclaim the rights of humanity.

1. The first and most important maxim of legitimate or popular government, that is to say, of a government that has the good of the populace for its object, is therefore, as I have said, to follow the general will in all things. But to follow the general will one must know it and, above all, properly distinguish it from the private will, beginning with oneself; a distinction that is always most difficult to make and only the most sublime virtue is capable of shedding enough light on it. Since one must be free in order to will, another no less formidable difficulty is how to secure both the public liberty and the authority of the government. Examine the motives that have brought men, united by their mutual needs in the large society,[10] to unite themselves more closely by means of civil societies. You will find no other motive than that of securing the goods, life, and liberty of each member through the protection of all. For how can men be forced to defend the liberty of one of their number without infringing on the liberty of others? And how can the public needs be attended to without altering the private property of those who are forced

[9] [Rousseau held that Machiavelli's *Prince* is a satirical text, designed to encourage hatred of tyranny, not a handbook for tyrants.]

[10] [The community of all human beings.]

to contribute to it? Whatever sophisms one uses to whitewash all this, it is certain that I am no longer free if someone can constrain my will and that I am no longer master of my estate if someone else can get his hands on it. This difficulty, which must have seemed insurmountable, was removed with the first inspiration that taught man to imitate here below the immutable decrees of the divinity. By what inconceivable art could one have found the means to place men in subjection in order to make them free? To use the goods, the manual labor, even the very life of all its members in the service of the state without forcing them and without consulting them? To bind their will by their own consent? To force them to punish themselves when they do what they did not want to do? How is it possible that they obey and no one commands, that they serve and have no master, and yet are actually more free because, under what appears to be subjection, no one loses any of his liberty except what can be harmful to the liberty of another? These wonders are the work of the law. It is to the law alone that men owe justice and liberty. It is this healthy tool of the will of all that reestablishes as a civil right the natural equality among men. This is the heavenly way that dictates to each citizen the precepts of public reason and teaches him to act in accordance with the maxims of his own judgment and not to be at odds with himself. It is also with this voice alone that leaders should speak when they command; for no sooner does a man claim, independently of the laws, to subject another to his private will than he at once leaves the civil state and, in relation to the other man, places himself in the pure state of nature, where obedience is never prescribed except out of necessity.

The leader's most pressing concern, as well as his most indispensable duty, is therefore to keep watch over the observance of the laws of which he is the minister and upon which all his authority is based. If he must make others observe them, then a fortiori he ought to observe them himself, since he enjoys all their favor. For his example is so powerful that even if the populace were willing to allow him to free himself from the yoke of the law, he ought to avoid taking advantage of such a dangerous prerogative—a prerogative others would in turn try to usurp, and often to his disadvantage. At bottom, since all the commitments of society are reciprocal in nature, it is impossible to put oneself outside the law without renouncing its advantages, and no one owes anything to someone who claims to owe nothing to anyone. For the same reason, no exception from the law will ever be accorded for any reason whatever in a well-policed government. Even the citizens who are most deserving of recognition by the homeland should be rewarded with honors but never with privileges. For the republic is on the verge of its ruin at the very moment someone can think it is a fine thing not to obey the laws. But if the nobility or the military or some other order within the state were ever to adopt such a maxim, everything would be irretrievably lost.

The power of the laws depends far more on the wisdom of the laws than on their severity, and the public will draws its greatest weight from the reason that dictated it. It is for this reason that Plato regards it as a very important precaution always to place at the beginning of an edict a well-reasoned preamble that shows its justice and usefulness.[11] In effect, the first of the laws is to respect the laws. Harshness of punishments is merely a vain expedient dreamed up by small minds to substitute terror for the respect they cannot obtain. It has always been remarked that the countries where punishments are the most severe are also those where they are the most frequent, so that the cruelty of punishments is indicative of nothing but the multitude of lawbreakers, and when every criminal is punished with equal severity, the guilty are forced to commit crimes to escape punishment for their faults.[12]

But although the government is not the master of the law, it is not an insignificant thing to be its guarantor and to have a thousand ways of making people love it. The talent for reigning consists of nothing else but this. When one has force at hand, there is no art to making everyone tremble and not even very much to winning over people's hearts, for experience has long taught the populace to be deeply grateful to its leaders for all the evils they do not do to it and to worship its leaders when it is not despised by them. An imbecile can, like anyone else, punish crimes; the real statesman knows how to prevent them. He extends his venerable rule over wills even more than over actions. If he could bring it about that everyone behaved correctly, he himself would have nothing left to do, and the masterpiece of his works would be to remain at his ease. At least it is certain that the greatest talent of leaders is to disguise their power in order to render it less odious and to manage the state so peacefully that it seems to have no need of managers.

I conclude therefore that just as the legislator's first duty is to conform the laws to the general will, the first rule of the public *economy* is that the administration should be in conformity with the laws. This alone will be sufficient to keep the state from being poorly governed, if the legislator has paid the attention he should to everything that is required by the locale, climate, soil, mores, and surrounding areas, and all the particular relationships between the people that he had to institute. This is not to say that there does not still remain an infinity of administrative and *economic* details that are left to the wisdom of the government. But it always has two infallible rules for behaving correctly in these matters. The one is the spirit of the law that should help decide cases the law could not have foreseen. The other is the general will, source and supplement of all the laws and that ought always be consulted where there is no law. How, I will be asked, does one go about knowing the general will in the situation where it is not expressed? Must the whole nation be assembled at each unforeseen event? It will be all the more mistaken to assemble it, because it is not sure its decision would be the expression of the general will; because this means is unworkable for a large populace; because

---

[11] [Plato, *Laws*, bk. 4, 723c.]
[12] [Cf. Montesquieu, *The Spirit of the Laws*, bk. 6, chs. 9, 12, 14.]

it is rarely necessary when the government is well intentioned. For the leaders know very well that the general will is always on the side most favorable to the public interest, that is, the most equitable, so that it is necessary simply to be just to be assured of following the general will. Often, when this is flouted too openly, it makes its presence known despite the terrifying repression by the public authority. I look as close to home as I can for examples to follow in such a case. In China,[13] the prince has as an unwavering maxim that he should side against his officials in every dispute that rises between them and the populace. Is bread expensive in one province? The intendant of that province is thrown in prison. Is there a civil disturbance in another? The governor is dismissed and each mandarin answers with his life for all the unpleasantness that takes place in his department. This is not to say that there is no subsequent examination of the affair in a regular trial. But on the basis of long experience, they anticipate the final judgment. There is rarely any injustice to rectify as a result of this; and the emperor, convinced that public clamor never arises without cause, always discerns among the seditious cries he punishes some just grievances that he remedies.

It is no mean feat to have made peace and order reign in all parts of the republic; it is no small matter that the state is tranquil and the law is respected. But if one did nothing more, then there would be more appearance than reality in all that, and the government would have a difficult time making itself obeyed if it limited itself to obedience. If it is good to know how to use men as they are, it is better still to turn them into what one needs them to be. The most absolute authority is that which penetrates to the inner part of a man and is exerted no less on his will than on his actions. It is certain that in the long run people are what the government makes them: warriors, citizens, men when it so wishes; rabble and riffraff when it so pleases. And every prince who belittles his subjects dishonors himself by showing that he did not know how to turn them into something worthy of respect. Therefore, train men if you want to command them. If you want the laws obeyed, make them beloved, so that to get men to do what they should, they need only consider that they ought to do it. That was the great art of governments of old, in those remote times when philosophers gave laws to the peoples and merely used their authority to make them wise and happy. From this came the many sumptuary laws, the many regulations concerning mores, the many public maxims accepted or rejected with the greatest of care. Even the tyrants did not forget this important part of administration, and they took as many pains in corrupting the mores of their slaves as did the magistrates in correcting the mores of their fellow citizens. But our modern governments, which are under the impression they have done all there is to do when they have raised money, never imagine it to be either necessary or possible to go that far.

---

[13] [In other words, Rousseau can find no examples of good government in contemporary French political life and has to go to far distant China for his examples.]

2. The second essential rule of public *economy* is no less important than the first. Do you want the general will to be accomplished? Make all private wills be in conformity with it. And since virtue is merely this conformity of the private to the general will, in a word, make virtue reign.

If politicians were less blinded by their ambition, they would see how impossible it is for any establishment whatever to function according to the principles on which it was instituted, if it is not directed in accordance with the law of duty. They would be aware of the fact that the greatest support for public authority lies in the hearts of the citizens, and that nothing can take the place of mores in the maintenance of the government. Not only is it only men of good character who know how to administer the laws, but it is essentially only upright men who know how to obey them. Anyone who gets the upper hand on remorse will not put off defying punishments that are less severe, less continuous forms of chastisement and that there is at least some hope of evading. And whatever precautions one takes, those who are on the lookout for impunity in order to do wrong hardly lack the means of eluding the law or escaping a penalty. Then, since all private interests are joined together against the general interest (which is no longer that of any individual), public vices have greater power to enervate the laws than the laws have to repress vices. And the corruption of the populace and the leaders at length extends to the government, however wise it may be. The worst of all abuses is to obey the laws in appearance only in order to transgress them in reality with security. Eventually the best laws become the most baneful. It would have been a hundred times better had they never existed. Then the laws would be one final resource that would be available when everything else had been tried. In such a situation it is pointless to add edicts upon edicts, regulations upon regulations. All that merely introduces additional abuses without correcting the abuses with which one began. The more you multiply laws, the more contemptible you make them. All the overseers you put in place are merely the latest crop of lawbreakers, who are destined either to join in with the veteran lawbreakers or to do their pillaging on their own. Before long the rewards of virtue become just like the rewards of highway robbery. Men of the vilest character are the ones held in the highest regard, whereas the more distinguished they are, the more they are held in contempt. Their infamy is manifest in their dignities, and they are dishonored by their honors. If they buy off the votes of leaders or the protection of women, it is so that they in their turn can sell justice, duty, and the state. And the populace, which fails to see that its own vices are the primary cause of its troubles, mutters and cries, groaning, "All my troubles come from no one but those I pay to protect me."

At times like this, in place of the voice of duty that no longer speaks in men's hearts, the leaders are forced to substitute the cry of terror or the lure of an apparent interest with which they deceive their dependents. At times like this, one must have recourse to all the disgusting little tricks they call "state maxims" and "cabinet mysteries." Whatever vigor there remains to the government is used by its members to bring down and to replace one another, while day-to-day business continues to be neglected or is dealt with only to the extent that personal interest demands it and in accordance with its dictates. Finally, the entire skill of these great politicians consists in so mesmerizing the eyes of those whose help they need, that each individual believes he is working for his own interest while he is working for theirs. I say "theirs," if indeed it actually is the real interest of the leaders to annihilate the populace in order to place it in subjection and to destroy their own estate in order to secure its possession.

But when the citizens love their duty, and when those entrusted with public authority sincerely apply themselves to nurturing this love through their example and efforts, all difficulties vanish and administration takes on an easiness that enables it to dispense with that shady art whose murkiness constitutes its entire mystery. Those ambitious minds, so dangerous and so admired, all the great ministers whose glory is mingled with the people's troubles, are not missed anymore. Public mores stand in for the genius of the leaders; and the more virtue reigns the less talents are needed. Ambition itself is better served by duty rather than by usurpation. Convinced that its leaders work exclusively for its happiness, the populace exempts them by its deference from working to strengthen their power. And history shows us in a thousand ways that the authority the populace accords to those it loves and by whom it is loved is a hundred times more absolute than all the tyranny of usurpers. This does not mean that the government should fear using its power, but that it should use it only in a legitimate manner. There are a thousand examples in history of ambitious or pusillanimous leaders who were ruined either by softness or pride, but there are no examples of someone for whom things went badly simply because he was equitable. But negligence should not be confused with moderation, nor mildness with weakness. To be just one must be severe. Putting up with wickedness when one has the right and the power to repress it is being wicked oneself.

It is not enough to say to the citizens: be good. They must be taught to be so; and example itself, which is in this respect the first lesson, is not the only means to be used. Love of country is the most effective, for as I have already said, every man is virtuous when his private will is in conformity with the general will in all things, and we willingly want what is wanted by the people we love.

It seems that the sentiment of humanity evaporates and weakens in being extended over the entire world and that we cannot be affected by the calamities in Tartary or Japan the way we are by those of a European people. Interest and commiseration must somehow be limited and restrained to be active. For since this inclination in us can be useful only to those with whom we have to live, it is a good thing that the humanity concentrated among fellow citizens takes on a new force through the habit of seeing each other and through the common interest that unites them. It is certain that the greatest miracles of virtue have been produced by the love of country. In joining together the force of self-love [*amour propre*] and all the beauty of virtue, this sweet and lively sentiment takes on an energy that, without disfiguring it, makes it the most heroic of all the passions. This is the passion that produced so many immortal actions whose radiance dazzles our feeble eyes, and so many great men whose ancient virtues were thought to be fables once the love of country became the object of derision. We should not find this surprising. The ecstasies of tender hearts appear utterly fanciful to anyone who has not felt them. And the love of country, a hundred times more ardent and delightful than that of a mistress, likewise cannot be conceived except by being felt. But it is easy to observe, in all the hearts it inflames and in all the actions it inspires, that fiery and sublime ardor that the purest virtue is lacking when it is separated from the love of country. Let us dare to compare Socrates himself to Cato. The one was more a philosopher, the other more a citizen. Athens was already lost, and Socrates had no other country but the whole world. Cato always carried his country in the bottom of his heart. He lived only for it and could not outlive it. The virtue of Socrates is that of the wisest of men. But compared with Caesar and Pompey, Cato seems like a god among mortals. One teaches a few individuals, combats the sophists, and dies for the truth. The other defends the state, liberty, and the laws against the conquerors of the world, and finally leaves the earth when he no longer sees a country to serve. A worthy student of Socrates would be the most virtuous of his contemporaries. A worthy imitator of Cato would be the greatest. The virtue of the first would constitute his happiness; the second would seek his happiness in that of others. We ought to be taught by the one and led by the other, and that alone would decide our preference. For a people consisting of wise men has never been produced; however, it is not impossible to make a people happy.

Do we want people to be virtuous? Let us begin then by making them love their country. But how can they love it, if their country means nothing more to them than it does to foreigners and if it allots to them only what it cannot refuse to anyone? It would be worse still if they did not enjoy even civil welfare, and if their goods, their life, or their liberty were at the discretion of powerful men, without it being possible or permitted for them to dare to invoke the laws. In such circumstances, subjected to the duties of the civil state without enjoying even the rights of the state of nature and without being able to use their strength to defend themselves, they would as a result be in the worst condition in which free men can find themselves, and the word *country* could have only an odious or ridiculous meaning for them. There is no point to believing that one can strike or cut off an arm without pain being transmitted to the head. And it is no more believable that the general will would permit a member of the state, whoever he might be, to injure or destroy another member than that the fingers of a man in his right mind would put out his eyes. Individual welfare is so closely linked to the public confederation that, were it not for the fact that one must take account of human frailty, this convention would be dissolved by right if just one citizen within the state were to perish who could have been saved, if just one citizen were wrongly held in prison, and if a single court case were to be lost because of an obvious injustice. For when these fundamental conventions are violated, it is no longer apparent what right or what interest could maintain the populace in the social union, unless it is restrained by force alone, which brings about the dissolution of the civil state.

In effect, is it not the commitment of the body of the nation to provide for the maintenance of the humblest of its members with as much care as for that of all others? And is the welfare of a citizen any less the common cause than the welfare of the entire state? If someone were to tell us that it is good that one person should perish for all, I would admire this saying were it to come from the lips of a worthy and virtuous patriot who dedicates himself willingly and out of duty to die for the welfare of his country. But if this means that the government is permitted to sacrifice an innocent person for the welfare of the multitude, I hold this maxim to be one of the most despicable that tyranny has ever invented, the most false that one might propose, the most dangerous that one might accept, and the most directly opposed to the fundamental laws of society. For far from it being the case that one individual should die for all, all have committed their goods and their lives in defense of each of them, so that individual weakness would always be protected by public force, and each member by the entire state. After conjuring up an image of the attrition of the people, one after another, press the partisans of this maxim to explain better what they mean by *the body of the state*, and you will see that eventually they will reduce it to a small number of men who are not the people but the officers of the people, and who, having obliged themselves by a personal oath to perish for its welfare, maintain they prove by this that it is the people's place to die for them.

Does anyone want to find examples of the protection that the state owes its members and of the respect it owes their persons? These examples are to be found only among the world's most illustrious and courageous nations, and it is almost exclusively among free peoples where one knows what a man is worth. It is commonly known how great was the perplexity in which the whole republic of Sparta found itself, when there arose the question of punishing a guilty citizen. In Macedonia, a human life was such an important matter that, in all his grandeur, Alexander, that powerful monarch, would not have dared to put to death in cold blood a Macedonian criminal unless the accused had appeared to defend himself before his fellow citizens and had been condemned by them. But the Romans were preeminent among all the peoples of the earth for the government's deference toward private individuals and for its scrupulous attention to respecting the inviolable rights of all the members of the state. Nothing was as sacred as the life of the simple citizens. There needed to be no less than the assembly of the entire people in order to condemn one of them. Neither the senate itself nor the consuls, in all their majesty, had the right to do this. And among the most powerful people in the world the crime and punishment of a citizen was a public affliction. It also appeared so harsh to shed blood for any crime whatever, that by the *Lex Porcia* the death penalty was converted to exile for all those who wished to outlive the loss of so sweet a country. Everything in Rome and in the armies betokened that love of fellow citizens for one another and that respect for the Roman name that stirred up the courage and animated the virtue of whoever had the honor to bear it. The hat of a citizen freed from slavery, the civic crown of him who had saved the life of another, these were things that were viewed with the greatest pleasure in the midst of the celebrations of their military triumphs. And it is worth noting that of the crowns with which in time of war one honors noble actions, only the civic crown and that of the victors were made of grass and leaves, all the rest being made of gold. Thus it was that Rome was virtuous and became the mistress of the world. Ambitious leaders! A shepherd governs his dogs and his flocks, and he is but the humblest of men. If it is a fine thing to command, it is when those who obey us can honor us. Therefore respect your fellow citizens and you will make yourselves respectable. Respect liberty and your power will increase daily. Never go beyond your rights, and eventually they will be limitless.

Let the homeland, therefore, show itself as the common mother of all citizens. Let the advantages they enjoy in their homeland endear it to them. Let the government leave them a large enough part of the public administration so that they can feel that they are at home. And let the laws be in their eyes nothing but the guarantors of the common liberty. These rights, fine as they all are, belong to all men. But without appearing to attack them directly, the bad will of the leaders easily reduces their effect to nothing. The law that is abused at the same time serves the powerful as an offensive weapon and as a shield against the weak, and the pretext of the public good is always the most dangerous scourge of the people. What is most necessary and perhaps most difficult in government is rigorous integrity in dispensing justice to all and especially in protecting the poor against the tyranny of the rich. The greatest evil is already done when there are poor people to defend and rich ones to keep in check. It is only at intermediate levels of wealth that the full force of the laws is exerted. Laws are equally powerless against the wealth of the rich and against the wretched state of the poor. The first eludes them; the second escapes them. The one breaks through the net and the other slips through.

Consequently, one of the most important items of business for government is to prevent extreme inequality of fortunes, not by appropriating wealth from its owners but by denying everyone the means of acquiring it, and not by building hospitals for the poor but by protecting citizens from becoming poor. Men unequally distributed over the territory and crowded into one place while other areas are underpopulated; arts of pleasure and pure skill favored over useful and demanding crafts; agriculture sacrificed to commerce; the tax farmer[14] made necessary by the bad administration of state funds; finally, venality pushed to such excess that esteem is measured in gold coins and the virtues themselves are sold for money—such are the most readily apparent causes of opulence and destitution, of the substitution of private interest for the public interest, of the mutual hatred of citizens, of their indifference to the common cause, of the corruption of the people, and of the enfeebling of all of governmental power. Such, as a consequence, are the ills that are difficult to treat once they make themselves felt but that a wise administration ought to prevent in order to maintain, along with good mores, respect for the laws, love of country, and the vitality of the general will.

But all these precautions will be insufficient without going further still. I end this part of the public *economy* where I ought to have started it. A home-land cannot subsist without liberty, nor can liberty without virtue, nor can virtue without citizens. You will have everything if you train citizens; without this you will merely have wicked slaves, beginning with the leaders of the state. But training citizens is not to be accomplished in one day, and turn-ing them into men requires that they be taught as children. Somebody will say to me that anyone who has men to govern should not seek outside their nature a perfection of which they are incapable, that he should not desire to destroy their passions, and that the execution of such a project would be no more desirable than it is possible. I will agree more strongly with all of this because a man who had no passion would certainly be a very bad citizen. But one must agree that even though men cannot be taught to love nothing, it is not impossible for them to learn to love one object rather than another and what is truly beautiful rather than what is deformed. If, for example, they are trained early enough never to consider their own persons except in terms of being related to the body of the state, and, if I may put it like this, not to perceive their own existence except as part of the state's existence, they will eventually come to identify themselves in some way with this larger whole, to feel themselves to be members of the country, to love it with that exquisite sentiment that every isolated man feels only for himself, to elevate their soul perpetually toward this great object, and thus to transform into a sublime virtue this dangerous disposition from which arises all our vices. Not only does philosophy demonstrate the possibility of these new instructions,[15] but history furnishes us with a thousand striking examples. If they are so rare

---

[14] [Rousseau's word is *publicain* (as in the King James Bible's "publicans and sinners") meaning "tax collector." In France the right to collect a tax was generally sold—a system that provided money up front for the government. So most tax collectors were also tax farmers—people who had bought the right to "farm" the tax, i.e., to put money into it with a view to maximizing their return.]

[15] [Rousseau's word is *directions*. According to an eighteenth-century dictionary, this is normally found in the plural only as a translation of the English word "directions" meaning "instruc-tions" (in the singular it means "management," a word that also rarely occurs in the plural).

among us, it is because no one is concerned about whether there are any citizens, and still less does anyone give any thought to take steps early enough to train them. It is too late to alter our natural inclinations when they have taken their course and habit has been joined with self-love [*amour propre*]. It is too late to draw us out of ourselves, once the *human self* concentrated in our hearts has acquired that disreputable activity that absorbs all virtue and constitutes the life of mean-spirited people. How could love of homeland develop in the midst of so many other passions that choke it? And what is left for fellow citizens of a heart already dividing its affections among greed, a mistress, and vanity?

It is from the first moment of life that one must learn to deserve to live; and since at birth one shares the rights of citizens, the moment of our own birth should be the beginning of the exercise of our duties. If there are laws for those of mature age, there should also be some for the very young that teach them to obey others. And just as each man's reason is not allowed to be the sole arbiter of his duties, so all the more the education of children should not be abandoned to the lights and prejudices of their fathers, since it is of even more importance to the state than it is to their fathers.[16] For, according to the natural course of things, the death of the father often deprives him of the ultimate benefits of this education, but sooner or later the country feels its effects. The state endures; the family breaks up. Now if the public authority, in taking the fathers' place and charging itself with this important function, acquires their rights by fulfilling their duties, the fathers have that much less reason to complain, because strictly speaking, in this regard, they are merely changing a name and will have in common, under the name "citizens," the same authority over their children they exercised separately under the name "fathers," and will be obeyed no less well when they speak in the name of the law than they were when they spoke in the name of nature. Public education, under the rules prescribed by the government and under the authorities put in place by the sovereign, is therefore one of the fundamental maxims of popular or legitimate government. If children are raised in common and in the bosom of equality, if they are imbued with the laws of the state and the maxims of the general will, if they are instructed to respect them above all things, if they are surrounded by examples and objects that constantly speak to them of the tender mother[17] who nourishes them, of the love she bears for them, of the inestimable benefits they receive from her, and in turn of the debt they owe her, undoubtedly they thus will learn to cherish one another as brothers, never to want anything but what the society wants, to substitute the actions of men and of citizens for the sterile and vain babbling of sophists,

---

Rousseau had hesitated, and in the manuscript he tried out three alternatives before he settled on *directions:* "transformations," "changes," "metamorphoses."]

[16] [Cf. Montaigne, *Essays*, bk. 2, ch. 25, and Plato, *Republic* and *Laws*.]

[17] [The mother here is *la patrie,* "the homeland."]

and to become one day the defenders and the fathers of the country whose children they will have been for so long.

I will not discuss the authorities destined to preside over this education, which certainly is the state's most important business. Clearly, if such marks of public confidence were lightly granted, if this sublime function were not, for those who had honorably fulfilled all the others, the reward for their labors, the honorable and sweet repose of their old age and the high point of all their honors, the entire undertaking would be useless and the education unsuccessful. For wherever the lesson is unsupported by authority, or the precept by example, instruction remains fruitless, and even virtue loses its influence in the mouth of him who does not practice it. But let illustrious warriors who are bent under the weight of their laurels preach courage; let upright judges, whose hair has turned white in the wearing of the purple[18] and in service in the courts, teach justice. Both of these groups will thus train virtuous successors and will transmit from age to age to the generations that follow the experience and talents of leaders, the courage and virtue of citizens, and the aspiration[19] common to all of living and dying for one's country.

I know of but three peoples who in an earlier era practiced public education, namely, the Cretans, the Lacedaemonians, and the ancient Persians. Among all three it was the greatest success and brought about marvels among the latter two. Since the world was divided into nations too large to be governed well, this method has not been practicable. And other reasons the reader can easily see have also prevented it from being tried by any modern people. It is quite remarkable that the Romans were able to do without it. But Rome was for five hundred years a continual miracle that the world cannot hope to see again. The virtue of the Romans, engendered by the horror of tyranny and the crimes of tyrants and by an inborn love of country, made all their homes into as many schools for citizens. And the unlimited power of fathers over their children placed so much severity in private enforcement that the father, more feared than the magistrates, was the censor of mores and the avenger of laws in his domestic tribunal.

In this way an attentive and well-intentioned government, constantly vigilant to maintain or restore love of country and good mores among the people, anticipates far in advance the evils that sooner or later result from citizens' indifference to the fate of the republic and restricts within narrow limits that personal interest that so isolates private individuals that the state is weakened by their power and has nothing to hope for from their good will. Anywhere

[18] [The color purple signified authority in ancient Greece and Rome; French judges did not wear purple, but the term was used figuratively of anyone exercising authority, particularly royal authority.]

[19] [In eighteenth-century French, Rousseau's word *emulation* refers to competition that is to be encouraged; competition to be discouraged is rivalry. In English "emulation" can have negative as well as positive connotations, whereas "aspiration" (a word unavailable to Rousseau since in eighteenth-century French it was used only in a religious context) is always positive.]

the populace loves its country, respects its laws, and lives simply, little else remains to do to make it happy. And in public administration, where fortune plays less of a role than it does in the fate of private individuals, wisdom is so close to happiness that these two objects are blended together.

3. It is not enough to have citizens and to protect them; it is also necessary to give some thought to their subsistence. And seeing to the public needs is an obvious consequence of the general will and the third essential duty of the government. This duty is not, as should be apparent, to fill the granaries of private individuals and to exempt these people from working, but rather to maintain abundance so within their reach that, to acquire it, labor is always necessary and never useless. It also extends to all the operations regarding the preservation of the public treasury and the expenditures of the public administration. Thus, after having discussed the general *economy* in relation to the government of persons, it remains for us to consider it in relation to the administration of goods.

This section offers no fewer difficulties to resolve or contradictions to overcome than the preceding one. Certainly the right to property is the most sacred of all the citizens' rights and more important in certain respects than liberty itself, either because it is more intimately linked with the preservation of life or because, possessions being easier to usurp and more difficult to defend than one's person, more respect needs to be given to what can more easily be seized, or finally because property is the true foundation of civil society and the true guarantee of the citizens' commitments.[20] For if goods were not answerable for persons, nothing would be so easy as eluding one's duties and scoffing at the laws. On the other hand, it is no less certain that the maintenance of the state and of the government demands costs and expenditures. And since anyone agreeing to the end cannot refuse the means, it follows that the members of the society should contribute their goods toward its preservation. In addition, it is difficult to protect the security of the property of private individuals in one respect without undermining it in another. And it is impossible for all the regulations bearing on inheritance, wills, and contracts not to restrict the citizens in certain respects regarding the disposition of their estate, and consequently regarding their right to property.

But besides what I have already said about the unanimity that reigns between the authority of the law and the liberty of the citizen, there is, in relation to the disposition of goods, an important point to be made that eliminates several difficulties. It is, as Pufendorf has shown, that by the nature of the right to property, it does not extend beyond the life of the property owner, and the moment a man dies his estate no longer belongs to him.[21] Thus,

---

[20] [The statement that property is the true foundation of civil society hardly fits with the argument of the *Discourse on the Origin of Inequality* or the *Social Contract*; but it is the sort of Lockean argument a reader of the *Encyclopédie* might expect.]

[21] [Pufendorf, *Of the Law of Nature and Nations* (1672), bk. 4, ch. 10, §4.]

prescribing to him the conditions under which he can dispose of it is actually less an apparent alteration of his right than it is a real extension of it.

In general, although the institution of the laws that govern the power of private individuals in the disposition of their own estate belongs only to the sovereign, the spirit of the laws that the government must follow in carrying them out is that, from father to son and from relative to relative, the family's goods should leave the family and be alienated as little as possible. There is good reason for this in favor of children, to whom the right to property would be quite useless, were the father to leave them nothing and who, more-over, having often contributed by their labor to the acquisition of the father's goods, are associated in their own right with his right. But another reason, more remote and no less important, is that nothing is more baneful to mores and to the republic than continual changes of status and fortune among the citizens, changes that are the proof and the source of a thousand disorders that overturn and confuse everything, and because of which those who were raised for one thing and find themselves destined for another—neither those who rise nor those who fall—cannot acquire the maxims or the knowledge suitable to their new status, and much less fulfill its duties. I turn now to the matter of public finances.

If the populace were to govern itself and there were nothing interposed between the administration of the state and the citizens, they would only have to tax themselves when circumstances made it necessary, in proportion to the public needs and the abilities of private individuals. And since no one would ever lose sight either of the collection or the use of funds, neither fraud nor abuse could slip into the management of them. The state would never be weighed down with debts, nor would the populace be crushed by taxes; or at least the assurance of how it would be used would console the people for the burden of the tax. But things cannot happen this way; and however limited a state may be, the civil society is always too populous to be capable of being governed by all its members. Public funds must necessarily pass through the hands of the leaders, who all have, over and above the interest of the state, their own private interest, which is not the last to be heard. The populace, for its part, perceiving the leaders' greed and ridiculous expenditures more than the public needs, grumbles about seeing itself despoiled of essentials to furnish someone else with superfluities. And when once these maneuvers have embittered it to a certain degree, the most honorable administration would utterly fail to reestablish confidence. In such circumstances, if contributions are voluntary, they produce nothing. If they are forced, they are illegitimate. And the difficulty of a just and wise *economy* lies in the cruel alternatives of allowing the state to perish or attacking the sacred right to property that is its underpinning.

The first thing to be done by the founder of a republic, after the estab-lishment of the laws, is to find a sufficient fund for the maintenance of the judges and other officers and for all public expenditures. This fund is called *aerarium*, or fisc, if it consists of money and *public domain* if it consists of lands. And the latter is far preferable to the former for reasons that are not hard to see. Anyone who has reflected enough on this matter could hardly be of any other opinion than that of Bodin, who views the public domain as the most upright and the most secure of all the means of providing for the needs of the state.[22] It is worth noting that Romulus' first concern in the division of lands was to set aside a third of the land for this use. I confess that it is not impossible for the proceeds of a badly administered public domain to be reduced to nothing. But it is not of the essence of the domain to be administered poorly.

Prior to any use of this fund, it ought to be *assigned*, or accepted by the assembly of the people or the estates of the country, which should then determine its use. After this solemnity, which renders this fund inalienable, it changes its nature, as it were, and its revenues become so sacred that diverting the least amount to the detriment of its destination is not only the most infamous of all thefts but a crime of high treason. It is a great dishonor for Rome that the integrity of the quaestor Cato was felt worthy of remark and that an emperor, on rewarding a singer's talent with a few crowns, needed to add that the money came from his family's property and not from the state's. But if there are not many like Galba, where will we find Catos? And once vice is no longer a cause for dishonor, what leaders will be scrupulous enough to refrain from getting their hands on the public funds left to their discretion and not eventually fool themselves by pretending to confuse their vain and scandalous dissipations with the glory of the state and the means of extending their own authority with those of increasing the state's power? It is above all in this delicate part of the administration that virtue is the only effective instrument and that the integrity of the official is the only restraint capable of containing his greed. Account books and all the ledgers of financial managers seem less to reveal their infidelities than to cover them up. And prudence is never as prompt at imagining new precautions as knaves are at eluding them. Therefore forget about the ledgers and papers, and place the finances in faithful hands; this is the only way to have them faithfully administered.

Once the public fund is established, the leaders of the state are rightfully its administrators, for this administration constitutes a part of the government, always an essential part, though not always equally so. Its influence increases in proportion to the decrease of the influence of the other parts of the government. One could say that a government has reached its final degree of corruption when the only source of strength it has left is money. And since every government constantly tends to grow weaker, this reason alone shows why no state can subsist if its revenues do not constantly increase.

The first experience of the force of this argument is also the first sign of the interior disorder of the state. And the wise administrator, in giving

---

[22] [Jean Bodin, *The Six Books of the Republic* (1576), bk. 6, ch. 2.]

thought to finding money in order to see to present need, does not neglect to seek the distant cause of this new need, just as a sailor, on seeing water flood his vessel, does not forget, while working the pumps, to take steps to find and plug the leak.

From this rule flows the most important maxim of the administration of finances, which is to work with much greater care to prevent needs than to augment revenues. However diligent one might be, help that comes only after the misfortune took place, and more slowly, always leaves the state in distress. While one gives thought to the remedy for one problem, another problem is already making itself felt, and the resources themselves produce new difficulties. Thus in the end the nation is thrown into debt, the populace is downtrodden, the government loses all its vigor and it spends a great deal of money doing not much of anything. I believe it was from this great and well-established maxim that the marvels of ancient governments flowed, which did more with their parsimony than ours do with all their resources. And it is perhaps from this that the commonest meaning of the word *economy* is derived, which denotes more the wise management of what one has than the means of acquiring what one does not have.

Independently of the public domain, which supplies funds to the state in proportion to the probity of those who supervise it, were one to have sufficient knowledge of the whole force of the general administration, especially when it confines itself to legitimate means, one would be astonished at the resources leaders have available for anticipating all the public needs without touching the goods of private individuals. Since they are the masters of the state's entire commerce, nothing is easier for them than to direct it in a manner that provides for everything, often without them appearing to have been involved. The distribution of commodities, money, and merchandise in just proportions according to time and place is the true secret of the government's finances and the source of their riches, provided those who administer them know how to be farsighted enough and on occasion to take an apparent present loss to really obtain immense profits at some time in the distant future. When one sees a government paying duties instead of receiving them for the export of grain in years of plenty and for its import in years of scarcity, one needs to have such facts right before one's eyes to believe them true; and they would have merited being classed as fantastical fictions if they had happened long ago. Suppose that, to prevent scarcity in bad years, one were to propose the establishment of public warehouses. In many countries, would not the maintenance of so useful an establishment serve as a pretext for new taxes? In Geneva, such granaries, established and maintained by a wise administration, are a public resource in bad years and the state's chief revenue at all times. "It nourishes and enriches"[23] is the fine and just inscription one reads on the facade of the building. To show here the economic system of a good government, I have

---

[23] [Rousseau gives the Latin: "Alit et ditat."]

often turned my eyes toward that of this republic, delighted to find in my homeland an example of the wisdom and happiness I would like to see reign in every country.

If one examines how the needs of a state grow, one will find that this often arises in the same way as do those of private individuals—less by a true necessity than by an increase in useless desires—and that expenditures are often increased simply in order to have a pretext for increasing income. Thus, the state would sometimes gain if it gave up on being rich, and such apparent wealth is essentially more burdensome than poverty itself. It is true one can hope to hold peoples in a stricter subordination by giving them with one hand what one has taken away from them with the other, and this was the style of politics Joseph used with the Egyptians. But this vain sophism is all the more fatal to the state in that the money does not return to the same hands it left. Such maxims only serve to enrich the idle with spoils taken from useful men.

The taste for conquests is one of the most obvious and dangerous causes of this increase. This taste, often engendered by another sort of ambition than the one it seems to proclaim, is not always what it appears to be, and its true motive is not the seeming desire to expand the nation but rather the hidden desire to increase the authority of the leaders at home, with the help of the increase in the army and under the cover of the diversion created in the minds of citizens by wartime objectives.

What is at least very certain is that no one is as oppressed or as miserable as a conquering people, and even their successes serve only to increase their miseries. Even if history did not teach us this, reason would suffice to show us that the larger a state is, the heavier and more burdensome will its expenditures become. For all the provinces are required to furnish their share of the expenses of the general administration, and, in addition, each province is required to spend the same amount for its own particular administration as it would if it were independent. Add to this the fact that all fortunes are made in one place and consumed in another. This eventually upsets the equilibrium of production and consumption, impoverishing a great deal of the country to enrich a single city.

Another source of the increase in public needs is linked to the preceding one. There may come a time when the citizens, no longer considering themselves interested in the common cause, would cease to be the defenders of the homeland, and when the magistrates would prefer to command mercenaries rather than free men, if only to use the former at a suitable time and place to subjugate the latter more effectively. Such was the state of Rome at the end of the Republic and under the emperors. For all the victories of the first Romans, just like those of Alexander, had been won by brave citizens who knew how to give their blood to their country in time of need, but never sold it. Marius was the first who, in the Jugurthine War, dishonored the legions by introducing free men, vagabonds, and other mercenaries. Having become enemies of the peoples whom they were assigned to make happy, the tyrants established regular standing armies, in appearance to contain foreigners and in fact to oppress the inhabitants. To raise these troops, farmers had to be taken away from their land; the lack of their services decreased the quality of the provisions, and maintaining these troops required the imposition of taxes, which in turn increased food prices. This first disorder caused the people to murmur. Repressing them required the troops to be multiplied and, consequently, the misery to be augmented. And the more despair increased, the more one was constrained to increase it again to prevent its effects. Nevertheless, these mercenaries, whose value could be determined on the basis of the price at which they sold themselves, were proud of their debasement, held in contempt the laws by which they were protected, as well as their fellow citizens whose bread they ate, and believed it a greater honor to be Caesar's henchmen than Rome's defenders. And sworn as they were to blind obedience, their task was to have their swords raised against their fellow citizens, ready to slaughter them all at the first signal. It would not be difficult to show that this was one of the principal causes of the ruin of the Roman Empire.

The invention of artillery and fortifications has in our times forced the sovereigns of Europe to reestablish the use of regular standing troops to guard their fortresses. Yet however legitimate the motives, there is reason to fear that the effect will be no less fatal. It will be no less necessary to depopulate the rural areas in order to raise armies and garrisons. To maintain them it will be no less necessary to oppress the peoples. And these dangerous establishments have in recent times been growing so rapidly in all of our part of the world that no one can foresee anything but the imminent depopulation of Europe and, sooner or later, the ruin of the people who inhabit it.

Be that as it may, it should be noted that such institutions necessarily subvert the true economic system, which draws the principle revenue of the state from the public domain, leaving only the troublesome expedient of subsidies and taxes, which remain for me to discuss.

It should be remembered here that the foundation of the social compact is property and its first stipulation is that each person should be maintained in the peaceful enjoyment of what belongs to him.[24] It is true that by the same treaty each person at least tacitly obliges himself to pay taxes to meet public needs. But since this commitment cannot undo the fundamental law and since it presumes that the taxpayers acknowledge the evidence of need, it is clear that to be legitimate, this taxation should be voluntary. I do not mean that it should be based on the wills of individual citizens, as if it were necessary to have the consent of each citizen, who should pay only as much as he pleases. This would be directly contrary to the spirit of the confederation. Rather,

[24] [Locke, *Two Treatises*, Second Treatise, ch. 11, §134.]

it should be through the general will, by majority vote, and on the basis of proportional rates that leave no room for an arbitrary assessment.[25]

This truth (that taxes can be legitimately established only by the consent of the people or its representatives) has generally been recognized by all the philosophers and jurists who have acquired any reputation in matters of political right, including even Bodin.[26] While some of them have established maxims that appear contrary, it is easy to see the private motives that moved them to do so. In any case, they stipulate so many conditions and restrictions that it all boils down to exactly the same thing. For whether the people can refuse it or whether the sovereign should not demand it is a matter of indifference as far as right is concerned. And if it is only a question of force, it is utterly pointless to inquire what is or is not legitimate.

The contributions levied on the people are of two kinds: real taxes (levied on things) and personal taxes (paid by the head). Both are called *taxes* or *subsidies*. When the people set the overall amount it pays, it is called a *subsidy*; when it grants the entire proceeds of a duty, it is a *tax*. In *The Spirit of the Laws*, we find that a head tax is more in keeping with servitude, while a real tax is more suited to liberty.[27] This would be incontestable, were each person's share of a head tax equal. For nothing would be more disproportionate than such a tax. It is especially in an exacting observance of proportions that the spirit of liberty consists. But if a head tax is exactly proportioned to the means of private individuals (as the tax in France known as the *capitation* could be) and is thus at once both real and personal, it is the most equitable and, as a result, the one best suited to free men. At first these proportions appear quite easy to observe because, being relative to each person's position in the world, the evidence is always public. But besides the fact that greed, influence peddling, and fraud know how to leave no evidence behind, it is rare that an account is taken of all the elements that should enter into these calculations. First, one ought to consider the relationship of quantities according to which, all things being equal, someone who has ten times more goods than someone else should pay ten times more. Second, one ought to consider the relationship of use, that is, the distinction between what is necessary and what is superfluous. Someone who has only the bare necessities of life should not pay anything at all. The tax on someone who has superfluities can, in time of need, be extended to everything over and above the necessities of life. To this he will declare that, given his rank, what would be superfluous for a man of inferior standing is a necessity for him. But that is a lie. For a man of superior standing has two legs, just like a cowherd and, like the cowherd, has only one stomach. Moreover, this alleged necessity of life is so little necessary to his standing that, if he knew how to renounce these things for some worthy cause, he could only be

---

[25] [In his draft Rousseau wrote in the margin here "See Locke."]

[26] [Locke, *Two Treatises*, 2, ch. 11, §140; Bodin, *Six Books of the Republic*, bk. 6, ch. 2.]

[27] [Montesquieu, *Spirit of the Laws*, bk. 13, ch. 14.]

respected more. The people would prostrate themselves before a minister who would go on foot to the council because he had sold his carriages when the state had a pressing need. Finally, the law does not demand magnificence of anyone, and propriety is never a reason to go against right.

A third relationship that is never taken into account, although it always ought to be reckoned the chief concern, is that of the utility each person derives from the social confederation that provides powerful protection for the immense possessions of the rich and hardly allows a poor wretch to enjoy the cottage he built with his own hands. Are not all the advantages of society for the powerful and the rich? Are not all the lucrative posts filled by them alone? Are not all the privileges and exemptions reserved for them alone? And is not the public authority entirely in their favor? When a man of high standing steals from his creditors or commits other acts of knavery, is he not always certain of impunity? Are not the assaults, the acts of violence he commits, even the murders and assassinations he is guilty of, are not these things hushed up and after six months not given a thought? If this same man is robbed, the entire police force is immediately put in motion, and woe to the innocent persons he suspects. Does he have to pass through a dangerous area? Security guards are mobilized to protect him. Has the axle of his carriage broken? Everyone flies to his aid. Is there a noisy disturbance outside his door? He says one word and everyone is silent. Does a crowd get in his way? He makes a gesture and everyone steps aside for him. Does a wagon driver block his route? His servants are ready to beat him up. And fifty honest pedestrians going about their business will be crushed rather than that some lazy scoundrel's coach should be delayed. All this respect costs him not a penny; it is the right of a rich man, not the price of riches. How different a picture is to be painted of the poor man! The more humanity owes him, the more society refuses him. All doors are closed to him, even when he has a right to open them. And if sometimes he obtains justice, it is with greater difficulty than the rich man would have obtaining a pardon. If there is an unpleasant job to do or troops to be raised, he is the first to be called on. Besides his own burden, he always bears the one from which his more wealthy neighbor has the influence to get himself exempted. At the least accident that happens to him, everyone avoids him. If his humble cart tips over, far from being helped by anyone, I count him lucky if he avoids the insults of the smart-aleck servants of some young duke who is passing by. In short, any free assistance escapes him when he needs it, precisely because he has nothing with which to pay for it. But I take him for a lost man, if he has the misfortune of having an honest soul, a beautiful daughter, and a powerful neighbor.

Another no less important point to make is that the losses of poor men are much more difficult to recoup than those of the rich and that the difficulty of acquiring always grows in proportion to need. Nothing comes from nothing; it is just as true in business as it is in physics. Money breeds money, and the first *pistole* is sometimes harder to earn than the second million. But there is still more. All the money the poor man hands over is forever lost to him; it remains in or returns to the hands of the rich. And since the proceeds of the taxes sooner or later pass only to those men who take part in the government or who are closely connected with it, they have, even in paying their share, a clear interest in increasing taxes.

Let us summarize in a few words the social contract between the two estates. "You need me, for I am rich and you are poor. Let us come to an agreement between ourselves. I will permit you to have the honor of serving me, provided you give me what little you have left in return for the trouble I will be taking to command you."

If all these things are carefully combined, we will find that in order to levy taxes in an equitable and truly proportionate way, the imposition should not be made merely in proportion to the goods belonging to the contributors but in a proportion consisting in the difference of their conditions and in the superfluity of their goods. This terribly important and difficult operation is accomplished every day by multitudes of honest clerks who know their arithmetic; but a Plato or a Montesquieu would not have dared to undertake such a task without trembling and imploring heaven for enlightenment and integrity.

Another disadvantage of the personal tax is that it makes itself felt too much and is levied with too much severity. This does not prevent its being subject to many instances of nonpayment, since it is much easier to hide one's head than one's possessions from the tax rolls and from prosecution.

Of all the other kinds of tax assessment, the land tax or real tax has always passed for the most advantageous in countries where more thought is given to both the quantity of the proceeds and the certainty of raising the required funds than to causing the least annoyance to the people. Some people have even dared to say that the peasant must be burdened in order to rouse him from his idleness and that he would do nothing if he did not have to pay anything. But among all the peoples of the world experience contradicts this ridiculous maxim. It is in Holland and England, where the farmer pays very little, and above all in China, where he pays nothing, that the land is best cultivated. On the other hand, wherever the worker finds himself taxed in proportion to the product of his fields, he lets them lie fallow or else harvests just as much from them as he needs in order to live. For to him who loses the fruit of his labors, doing nothing pays well. Imposing a fine on work is a rather unusual method of abolishing idleness.

Taxes on land or on grain, especially when they are excessive, result in two disadvantages that are so terrible that they cannot in the long run avoid depopulating and ruining every country where they are established.

The first comes from the lack of circulation of currency, for commerce and industry draw all the money from the rural areas into the capitals; and because the tax destroys the proportion that might otherwise obtain between the needs of the farmer and the price of his grain, money constantly arrives and never returns. The richer the city, the more miserable the rural areas. The proceeds from the tax pass from the hands of the prince or the financier into those of artists and merchants. And the farmer, who never receives anything more than the smallest part of the proceeds, is eventually exhausted by always paying the same amount and always receiving less. How could a man live if he had veins and no arteries, or if the arteries carried blood only to within four inches of his heart? Chardin says that in Persia the king's duties on commodities are also paid in commodities. This custom, which, Herodotus tells us, was practiced previously in the same country as far back as Darius, could prevent the evil of which I have been speaking. But unless the intendants, directors, commissioners, and warehouse security guards in Persia are a breed apart from what they are everywhere else, I am hard pressed to believe that the smallest part of all these products reaches the king, that the grain does not rot in the granaries, and that fire does not consume the greater part of the warehouses.[28]

The second disadvantage comes from an apparent advantage, which lets the problems become aggravated before they are noticed, namely that grain is a commodity whose price is not increased by taxes in the countries where it is produced, so that despite its absolute necessity, the quantity is diminished without the price being increased. This is what causes many people to die of hunger, even though grain remains cheap, and the farmer is the only one to bear the burden of the tax, which he has been unable to recoup in his selling price. It must be noted that one should not reason about a real tax the way one would about duties on all merchandise that in turn raise the price on all these goods and that are paid not so much by the sellers as by the buyers. For these duties, however heavy they may be, are still voluntary and are paid by the shopkeeper only in proportion to the quantity he buys. And since he buys only in proportion to his sales, he applies the law to private individuals.[29] But the farmer, who is required to pay at a fixed rate for the land he cultivates, whether he sells or not, is not in a position to wait until he gets the price he wants for his produce. And even if he were not to sell it to support himself, he would be forced to sell it to be able to pay the tax, so that sometimes it is the enormity of the assessment that keeps the produce at a low price.

Note too that the resources of commerce and industry, far from making the tax more endurable through an abundance of money, only make it more burdensome. I will not dwell upon a very obvious point, namely that, although a greater or lesser quantity of money in a state can give it more or less credit outside the state, it in no way alters the real fortune of the citizens and does not make them any more or less prosperous. But I must make two important remarks. First, unless the state has more commodities than it can use and the

---

[28] [I don't think that Rousseau means that the grain literally rots or the warehouses literally burn down, rather losses are written off to rot and fire when what is really going on is theft.]

[29] [He passes on the tax to the consumer.]

abundance of money comes from an export trade, only the commercial towns are aware of this abundance, and the peasant only becomes relatively poorer. Second, since the price of everything increases with the increase in money, taxes must be increased proportionately, so that the farmer finds himself under a greater burden without having greater resources.

It should be noted that the tax on lands is actually a tax on its product. While everyone agrees that nothing is so dangerous as a tax on grain paid by the buyer, how is it we do not see that it is a hundred times worse if this tax is paid by the farmer himself? Is this not an attack on the very source of the state's subsistence? Is it not the most direct method possible of depopulating the homeland and thus in the long run of ruining it? For there is no worse scarcity for a nation than that of men.

Only the true statesman can raise his sights when it comes to taxes above the financial objective of increasing revenue. Only he can transform onerous burdens into useful regulations of public administration. Only he can make the people wonder whether such laws have for their purpose the good of the nation rather than the revenue raised by taxes.

Duties on the importation of foreign merchandise that the local people are eager to have but that the homeland does not need; on the exportation of agricultural produce of which the homeland has none to spare and that foreigners cannot do without; on the product of useless and excessively lucrative arts; on the importation into towns of pure luxuries; and in general on all luxury items, these will all achieve this twofold purpose. It is by means of such taxes, which ease the burden of poverty and place the onus on wealth, that one must prevent the continual increase in the inequality of fortunes, the subjection of a multitude of workers and useless servants to the rich, the multiplication of idle people in the cities, and the depopulation of rural areas.

It is important to place a proportion between the price of things and the duties imposed on them such that the greediness of private individuals is not too strongly tempted to commit fraud by the size of the profits. Moreover, smuggling must be made difficult by singling out merchandise that is more difficult to conceal. Finally, it is appropriate for the tax to be paid by the one who consumes the thing taxed rather than the one who sells it, for the quantity of the duties with which he would be charged would provide him with greater temptations and means of committing fraud. This is the usual practice in China, the country where the taxes are the heaviest and the best paid in the world. The merchant pays nothing. Only the buyer pays the duty, without any murmuring or sedition resulting, for since the provisions necessary for life, such as rice and grain, are completely exempt, the people are not oppressed and the tax falls only on the wealthy. Moreover, all these precautions ought to be dictated not so much by the fear of smuggling as by the attention the government ought to pay to protecting private individuals from the seduction of illegitimate profits, which, after having turned them into bad citizens, would waste no time turning them into dishonest people.

Let heavy taxes be levied on livery servants, on carriages, on mirrors, chandeliers, and furnishings, on fabrics and gilding, on the courtyards and gardens of large homes, on public entertainment of all kinds, on the idle professions, such as those of buffoons, singers, and actors, and, in short, on that population of objects of luxury, amusement, and idleness that catch everyone's eye and that can scarcely be hidden, since their whole purpose is to be on display and they would be useless if they should fail to be seen.

There is no cause for fear that the proceeds of such taxes would be unpredictable, because they are imposed only on things that are not absolutely necessary. It shows a poor knowledge of men to believe that men who have once been seduced by luxury can ever renounce it. They would a hundred times rather renounce necessities, preferring to die of hunger rather than of shame. The increase in their expenditure is only a new reason for sustaining it, since the vanity of displaying oneself as wealthy will take advantage both of the price of the thing and of the expense of the tax. As long as there are rich people, they will want to distinguish themselves from poor people, and the state cannot contrive a revenue less onerous and more secure than one based on this distinction.

For the same reason, industry would have nothing to suffer from an economic order that enriched the public finances, revitalized agriculture by relieving the farmer, and imperceptibly brought all fortunes closer to that intermediate level of wealth that constitutes the true strength of a state. I confess it could happen that these taxes might contribute to making some fashions come and go more quickly, but it would never happen without substituting others on which the worker would earn a profit without the public treasury taking a loss. In short, suppose the spirit of the government were constantly to levy all taxes on the superfluities of the rich; one of two things must happen. Either the rich would renounce their superfluous expenditures and instead spend their money usefully, which would redound to the profit of the state, in which case, the imposition of taxes would have produced the effect of the best sumptuary laws. The expenses of the state will of necessity have diminished along with those of private individuals; and any fall in government revenue would be more than offset by a reduction in prices. Or, if the rich do not cut back on any of their extravagances, the public treasury would have, in tax proceeds on these extravagances, the resources it was seeking in order to provide for the real needs of the state. In the first case, the public treasury is enriched by the reduction in its expenditures. In the second case, it is enriched by the useless expenditures of private individuals.

Let us add to all this an important distinction in the matter of political right and to which governments, eager to do everything by themselves, should pay great attention. I have said that since personal taxes and taxes on absolute necessities attack the right to property and consequently the true foundation of public society, they are always subject to dangerous consequences if they are not established with the express consent of the people or its representatives. It is not the same for duties on things whose use one can decide to give up. For then, since the private individual is not at all absolutely constrained to pay, his contribution can be reckoned as voluntary. Thus the individual consent of each of the contributors takes the place of the general consent and even presupposes it in a certain way. For why would the people be opposed to any tax that falls only on whoever wants to pay it?[30] It would appear to me evident that if something is neither proscribed by the laws nor contrary to mores but is something that the government can forbid, it can then permit it on payment of a duty. If, for example, the government can forbid the use of carriages, a fortiori it can impose a tax on carriages, a wise and useful way to condemn their use without terminating it. Then one can view the tax as a type of fine whose proceeds compensate for the abuse it punishes.

Someone may perhaps object that since those whom Bodin calls *impostors*,[31] that is, those who impose or invent the taxes, are in the class of the rich, they will not take care to spare others at their own expense and to burden themselves in order to relieve the poor. But such ideas must be rejected. If in each nation those to whom the sovereign commits the government of the people were, in virtue of their position, the enemies of the people, it would not be worth the trouble to inquire what they should do to make the people happy.[32]

---

[30] [It follows from this argument that the American colonists were not entitled to object to the Tea Act of 1773.]

[31] [Bodin, *Six Books of the Republic*, bk. 6, ch. 2.]

[32] [Rousseau is of course being ironic here, i.e., he thinks most governments are the enemies of the people and have no interest in making them happy.]

On the Social Contract

Rousseau described his Social Contract *as an extract from a larger work,* Political Institutions, *which he had begun in 1751 (and the idea of which, he says, dated back to his time in Venice).*[1] *An incomplete first draft ("the Geneva manuscript") exists and was first published in 1887. This, in all likelihood, is a surviving remnant of the draft Rousseau sent to his publisher, Marc-Michel Rey, on December 23, 1760. On August 9, 1761, Rousseau declared that his book was finished and ready to be published. In 1758 Rousseau was still working on his* Political Institutions, *and it seems likely that* On the Social Contract *took on its present form only after he abandoned that undertaking, although in the published texts Rousseau occasionally repeats entire passages from the* Discourse on Political Economy *of 1755. In any event, a crucial source for his argument was Diderot's article "Natural Right," published in November 1755. The argument of the* Social Contract *can only have taken on its final form after Rousseau read this article (presumably only shortly prior to its publication in the* Encyclopédie). *Conceived in 1743, begun in 1751, rethought in 1755, reconstructed in 1758, largely completed by the end of 1760, the* Social Contract *was published alongside* Émile. *Rousseau was even afraid that in France it would be thought of as an appendix to his treatise on education.*[2] *But the two books were intended to have different audiences:* Émile *was to be published in France for a French audience; the* Social Contract *was to be published in Holland and, Rousseau said, "was certainly not intended for the French."*[3] *Rey received the manuscript on December 4, 1761 and had copies on sale by the middle of April 1762. In the space of a few months he printed 5,000 copies in two editions—the first an octavo and the second a duodecimo, which appeared a month after the first. These were swiftly followed by pirated editions. But in France the book was banned immediately upon being submitted for approval. There was no prospect of its being approved, it was made clear, even if revised. Pirated copies were soon being smuggled in, but they found few readers. In Geneva, however, the book was widely distributed in the fortnight before it was banned. Rousseau claimed in 1764 that "everybody" had a copy. The book had found its intended audience; its banning provoked a crisis in Geneva while it passed virtually unremarked in France.*

D.W.

---

[1] [Letter to Moultou, January 18, 1762.]

[2] [Letter to Duchesne, May 23, 1762.]

[3] ["Ce livre n'étant point fait pour la France," letter to Duchesne, May 23, 1762.]

ON THE
SOCIAL CONTRACT,

OR

PRINCIPLES
OF
POLITICAL RIGHT

By J.-J. Rousseau,
Citizen of Geneva

"Let us propose fair terms for the peace settlement."
—*Aeneid*, XI[4]

---

[4] [Rousseau gives the Latin: "foederis aequas / Dicamus leges" (bk. 11, line 302).]

FOREWORD

This little treatise is part of a longer work I undertook some time ago without taking stock of my abilities, and have long since abandoned. Of the various selections that could have been drawn from what had been completed, this is the most considerable, and, it appears to me, the one least unworthy of being offered to the public. The rest no longer exists.

BOOK I

I want to inquire whether there can be some legitimate and sure rule of administration in the civil order,[5] taking men as they are and laws as they might be. I will always try in this inquiry to bring together what right permits with what interest prescribes, so that justice and utility do not find themselves at odds with one another.

I begin without demonstrating the importance of my subject. It will be asked if I am a prince or a legislator that I should be writing about politics. I answer that I am neither, and that is why I write about politics. Were I a prince or a legislator, I would not waste my time saying what ought to be done. I would do it or keep quiet.

Since I was born a citizen of a free state and a member of the sovereign,[6] the right to vote is enough to impose upon me the duty to instruct myself in public affairs, however little influence my voice may have in them. Happy am I, for every time I meditate on governments, I always find new reasons in my inquiries for loving that of my country.

Chapter 1
Subject of the First Book

Man is born free, and everywhere he is in chains. He who believes himself the master of others does not escape being more of a slave than they. How did this change take place? I do not know. What can render it legitimate? I believe I can answer this question.

Were I to consider only force and the effect that flows from it, I would say that as long as a people is constrained to obey and does obey, it does well. As soon as it can shake off the yoke and does shake it off, it does even better. For by recovering its liberty by means of the same right that stole it, either

---

[5] [Rousseau has only one word, *civil*, where we have two, "civil" and "civic." This translation generally translates *civil* as "civil," but it should be remembered that "civic" may also be right.]

[6] [The free state is the Republic of Geneva; Rousseau held that the sovereign authority in Geneva was the general council, an assembly of all the citizens.]

the populace is justified in getting it back or else those who took it away were not justified in their actions. But the social order is a sacred right that serves as a foundation for all other rights. Nevertheless, this right does not come from nature. It is therefore founded upon agreement.[7] The real question is: what is this agreement? Before coming to that, I ought to substantiate what I just claimed.

Chapter 2
Of the First Societies

The most ancient of all societies, and the only natural one, is that of the family. Even so, children remain bound to their father only as long as they need him to take care of them. As soon as the need ceases, the natural bond is dissolved. Once the children are freed from the obedience they owed the father and their father is freed from the care he owed his children, all return equally to independence. If they continue to remain united, this no longer takes place naturally but voluntarily, and the family itself is maintained only by means of agreement.[8]

This common liberty is one consequence of the nature of man. Its first law is to see to his preservation; its first concerns are those he owes himself; and, as soon as he reaches the age of reason, since he alone is the judge of the proper means of taking care of himself, he thereby becomes his own master.

The family therefore is, so to speak, the prototype of political societies; the leader is the image of the father, the populace is the image of the children, and, since all are born equal and free, none give up their liberty except for their utility. The entire difference consists in the fact that in the family the love of the father for his children repays him for the care he takes for them, while in the state, where the leader does not have love for his peoples, the pleasure of commanding takes the place of this feeling.

---

[7] [Rousseau uses three words with related meanings: *contrat* (contract), *pacte* (compact), and *convention* (agreement). In Rousseau's day *convention* means "agreement" (*accord* or *pacte*); it does not mean the same thing as modern English "convention"—Oxford English Dictionary (OED), senses 9 and 10: "a rule or practice based upon general consent"; it acquired this meaning in French only in the nineteenth century. The same is true in English: Hume, in his *Treatise of Human Nature* and *Enquiry Concerning the Principles of Morals*, when he argues that justice is established by convention, uses "agreement" as a synonym for "convention" (carefully distinguishing his usage of the word from what he recognizes to be "the usual sense of the word" in which "convention" is used as a synonym for "promise," since he is writing about a tacit not an explicit agreement), though Hume's argument points directly to the more modern sense of the word (which the OED [accessed April 24, 2011] dates to 1778) and this modern sense may indeed derive from Hume.]

[8] [Here Rousseau follows Locke, *Two Treatises of Government*, Second Treatise, ch. 5.]

Grotius denies that all human authority is established for the benefit of the governed, citing slavery as an example.[9] His characteristic method of reasoning is always to present fact as a proof of right.[10] A more logical method could be used, but not one more favorable to tyrants.

According to Grotius, it is therefore doubtful whether the human race belongs to a hundred men, or whether these hundred men belong to the human race. And throughout his book he appears to lean toward the former view. This is Hobbes' position as well. On this account, the human race is divided into herds of cattle, each one having its own leader who guards it in order to devour it.

Just as a herdsman possesses a nature superior to that of his herd, the herdsmen of men, who are their leaders, also have a nature superior to that of their peoples. According to Philo,[11] the emperor Caligula reasoned thus, concluding quite properly from this analogy that kings were gods, or that the peoples were beasts.

Caligula's reasoning coincides with that of Hobbes and Grotius. Aristotle, before these three, had also said that men are by no means equal by nature, but that some are born for slavery and others for domination.[12]

Aristotle was right, but he took the effect for the cause. Every man born in slavery is born for slavery; nothing is more certain. In their chains, slaves lose everything, even the desire to escape. They love their servitude the way the companions of Ulysses loved being turned into beasts.[13] If there are slaves by nature, it is because there have been slaves contrary to nature. Force has produced the first slaves; their cowardice has perpetuated them.

I have said nothing about King Adam or Emperor Noah, father of three great monarchs who partitioned the universe, as did the children of Saturn, whom some have believed they recognize in them.[14] I hope I will be appreciated for this moderation, for since I am a direct descendant of one of these princes, and perhaps of the eldest branch, how am I to know whether, after the verification of titles, I might not find myself the legitimate king of the human species? Be that as it may, we cannot deny that Adam was the sovereign of the

---

[9] [Hugo Grotius, *On the Law of War and Peace*, bk. 1, ch. 3, §8.]

[10] "Learned research on public right is often nothing more than the history of ancient abuses, and taking a lot of trouble to study them too closely gets one nowhere." *Treatise on the Interests of France along with Her Neighbors*, by the Marquis d'Argenson. This is just what Grotius has done.

[11] [Philo of Alexandria (20 BC–AD 50), best known as author of *Antiquities of the Jews*. The text referred to here is the *Embassy to Gaius*.]

[12] [Aristotle, *Politics*, bk. 1, ch. 2, 1252a.]

[13] See a short treatise of Plutarch titled "That Animals Reason." [Ulysses' companions were turned into beasts by Circe.]

[14] [Rousseau is referring to the *Patriarcha* of Robert Filmer, published posthumously in 1680 and refuted by John Locke, Algernon Sidney, and James Tyrrell.]

world, just as Robinson Crusoe was sovereign of his island, as long as he was its sole inhabitant. And the advantage this empire had was that the monarch, securely on his throne, had no rebellions, wars, or conspirators to fear.

Chapter 3
On the Right of the Strongest

The strongest is never strong enough to be master all the time, unless he transforms force into right and obedience into duty—hence the right of the strongest, a right that seems like something intended ironically and is actually presented as a basic principle.[15] But will no one explain this word [strongest] to me? Force is a physical power; I fail to see what morality can result from its effects. To give in to force is an act of necessity, not of will. At most, it is an act of prudence. In what sense could it be a duty?

Let us suppose for a moment that there is such a thing as this alleged right. I maintain that all that results from it is an inexplicable mishmash. For once force produces right, the effect changes places with the cause. Every force that is superior to the first succeeds to its right. As soon as one can disobey with impunity, one can do so legitimately; and since the strongest is always right, the only thing to do is to make oneself the strongest. But what kind of right is it that perishes when the force on which it is based ceases? If one must obey because of force, one need not do so out of duty; and if one is no longer forced to obey, one is no longer obliged. Clearly then, this word "right" adds nothing to force. It is utterly meaningless here.

Obey the powers that be. If that means giving in to force, the precept is sound, but superfluous. I reply it will never be violated. All power comes from God[16]—I admit it—but so does every disease. Does this mean that calling in a physician is prohibited? If a brigand takes me by surprise at the edge of a wooded area, is it not only the case that I must surrender my purse, but even that I am in good conscience bound to surrender it, if I were able to withhold it? After all, the pistol he holds is also a power.

Let us then agree that force does not bring about right and that one is obliged to obey only legitimate powers. Thus my original question keeps returning.

Chapter 4
On Slavery

Since no man has a natural authority over his fellowman, and since force does not give rise to any right, agreements alone therefore remain as the basis of all legitimate authority among men.

---

[15] [Rousseau's target here is Hobbes.]
[16] [Romans 13:1.]

If, says Grotius, a private individual can alienate his liberty and turn himself into the slave of a master, why could not an entire people alienate its liberty and turn itself into the subject of a king?[17] There are many equivocal words here that need explanation, but let us confine ourselves to the word *alienate*. To alienate is to give or to sell. A man who makes himself the slave of someone else does not give himself; he sells himself, at least for his subsistence. But why does a people sell itself? Far from furnishing his subjects with their subsistence, a king derives his own from them alone, and, according to Rabelais, a king does not live cheaply. Do subjects then give their persons on the condition that their possessions will also be taken? I fail to see what remains for them to preserve.

It will be said that the despot assures his subjects of civil tranquility.[18] Very well. But what do they gain, if the wars his ambition drags them into, if his insatiable greed, if the oppressive demands caused by his ministers, occasion more grief for his subjects than their own dissensions would have done? What do they gain, if this very tranquility is one of their miseries? A tranquil life is also had in dungeons; is that enough to make them desirable? The Greeks who were locked up in the Cyclops' cave lived a tranquil existence as they awaited their turn to be devoured.[19]

To say that a man gives himself gratuitously is to say something absurd and inconceivable. Such an act is illegitimate and null, if only for the fact that he who commits it does not have his wits about him. To say the same thing of an entire populace is to suppose a populace composed of madmen. Madness does not make right.

Even if each person can alienate himself, he cannot alienate his children. They are born men and free. Their liberty belongs to them; they alone have the right to dispose of it. Before they have reached the age of reason, their father can, in their name, stipulate conditions for their preservation and for their well-being. But he cannot give them irrevocably and unconditionally, for such a gift is contrary to the ends of nature and goes beyond the rights of paternity. For an arbitrary government to be legitimate, it would therefore be necessary in each generation for the people to be master of its acceptance or rejection. But in that event, this government would no longer be arbitrary.

Renouncing one's liberty is renouncing one's dignity as a man, the rights of humanity, and even its duties. There is no possible compensation for anyone who renounces everything. Such a renunciation is incompatible with the nature of man. Taking away all liberty from his will is tantamount to removing all morality from his actions. Finally, it is a vain and contradictory agreement that stipulates absolute authority on one side and a limitless obedience on the other. Is it not clear that no commitments are made to a

---

[17] [Grotius, *Law of War and Peace*, bk. 1, ch. 3, §12.]

[18] [This is what Hobbes would say.]

[19] [Cf. Locke, *Two Treatises*, Second Treatise §228.]

person from whom one has the right to demand everything? And does this condition alone not bring with it, since there is no equivalent or exchange, the nullity of the act? For what right would my slave have against me, given that all he has belongs to me, and that, since his right is my right, my having a right against myself makes no sense?

Grotius and others[20] derive from war another origin for the alleged right of slavery. Since, according to them, the victor has the right to kill the vanquished, these latter can ransom their lives at the price of their liberty—a contract all the more legitimate since it turns a profit for both of them.

But clearly, this alleged right to kill the vanquished does not in any way derive from the state of war.[21] Men are not naturally enemies, for the simple reason that men living in their original state of independence do not have sufficiently constant relationships among themselves to bring about either a state of peace or a state of war. It is the relationship between things and not that between men that brings about war. And since this state of war cannot come into existence from simple personal relations, but only from real relations,[22] a private war between one man and another can exist neither in the state of nature, where there is no constant property, nor in the social state, where everything is under the authority of the laws.

Fights between private individuals, duels, and brawls are not acts that produce a state. And with regard to private wars, authorized by the ordinances of King Louis IX of France and suspended by The Peace of God, they are abuses peculiar to feudal government, an absurd system if there ever was one, contrary to the principles of natural right and to all sound polity.

War is not, therefore, a relationship between one man and another, but a relationship between one state and another. In war private individuals are enemies only incidentally—not as men or even as citizens[23] but as soldiers; not as members of the homeland but as its defenders. Finally, each state can

[20] [Hobbes, *De Cive*, ch. 8, and Samuel Pufendorf, *Of the Law of Nature and Nations*, bk. 6, ch. 3.]

[21] [See Rousseau's essay "The State of War" in this volume.]

[22] ["Real" is used here in the same way that we talk about "real estate," i.e., real relations are proprietary relations.]

[23] [At this point the following passage was added to the 1782 edition: "The Romans, who had a better understanding of and a greater respect for the right of war than any other nation, carried their scruples so far in this regard that a citizen was not allowed to serve as a volunteer unless he had expressly committed himself against the enemy and against a specifically named enemy. When a legion in which Cato the son first served had been reorganized, Cato the Elder wrote Popilius that if he wanted his son to continue to serve under him, he would have to make him swear the military oath afresh, since, with the first one having been annulled, he could no longer take up arms against the enemy. And this very same Cato wrote to his son to take care to avoid going into battle without swearing this military oath afresh. I know the siege of Clusium and other specific cases can be raised as counterexamples to this, but for my part I cite laws and customs. The Romans were the ones who transgressed their laws least often and are the only ones to have such noble laws."]

have as enemies only other states and not men, since there can be no real relationship between things of disparate natures.

This principle is even in conformity with the established maxims of all times and with the constant practice of all civilized peoples. Declarations of war are warnings not so much to powers as to their subjects. The foreigner (be he king, private individual, or a people) who robs, kills, or detains subjects of another prince without declaring war on the prince, is not an enemy but a brigand. Even in the midst of war, a just prince rightly appropriates to himself everything in an enemy country belonging to the public, but respects the person and goods of private individuals. He respects the rights upon which his own rights are founded. Since the purpose of war is the destruction of the enemy state, one has the right to kill the defenders of that state as long as they bear arms. But as soon as they lay down their arms and surrender, they cease to be enemies or instruments of the enemy. They return to being simply men; and one no longer has a right to their lives. Sometimes a state can be killed without a single one of its members being killed. For war does not grant a right that is unnecessary to its purpose.[24] These principles are not those of Grotius; they are not based on the authority of poets.[25] Rather they are derived from the nature of things; they are based on reason.

As to the right of conquest, the only basis it has is the law of the strongest. If war does not give the victor the right to massacre the vanquished peoples, this right (which he does not have) cannot be the basis for the right to enslave them. One has the right to kill the enemy only when one cannot enslave him. The right to enslave him does not therefore derive from the right to kill him. Hence, it is an iniquitous exchange to make him buy his life, to which no one has any right, at the price of his liberty. In establishing the right of life and death on the right of slavery, and the right of slavery on the right of life and death, is it not clear that one falls into a vicious circle?

Even if we were to suppose that there were this terrible right to kill everyone, I maintain that neither a person enslaved during wartime nor a conquered people bears any obligation whatever toward its master, except to obey him for as long as it is forced to do so. In taking the equivalent of his life, the victor has done him no favor. Instead of killing him unprofitably, he kills him usefully. Hence, far from the victor having acquired any authority over him beyond force, the state of war subsists between them just as before. Their relationship itself is the effect of war, and the usage of the right to war does not suppose any peace treaty. They have made a contract. Fine. But this contract, far from destroying the state of war, presupposes its continuation.

Thus, from every point of view, the right of slavery is null, not simply because it is illegitimate, but because it is absurd and meaningless. These words, *slavery* and *right*, are contradictory. They are mutually exclusive.

---

[24] [Cf. Montesquieu, *The Spirit of the Laws*, bk. 10, ch. 3.]

[25] [An attack on Grotius, who cites poets in the course of his argument.]

Whether it is the statement of one man to another man, or of one man to a people, the following sort of talk will always be equally nonsensical. "*I* make an agreement with you that is wholly at your expense and wholly to my advantage; and, for as long as it pleases me, I will observe it and so will you."

Chapter 5
That It Is Always Necessary to Return to a First Agreement

Even if I were to grant all that I have thus far refuted, the supporters of despotism would not be any better off. There will always be a great difference between subduing a multitude and ruling a society. If scattered men were successively enslaved by a single individual, I see nothing there—however many they may be—but a master and slaves; I do not see a people and its leader. It is, if you will, an aggregation, but not an association. There is neither a public good nor a body politic there. Even if that man had enslaved half the world, he is always just a private individual. His interest, separated from that of others, is never anything but a private interest. If this same man happens to die, after his passing his empire remains scattered and disunited, just as an oak tree disintegrates and falls into a pile of ashes after fire has consumed it.

A people, says Grotius, can give itself to a king. According to Grotius, therefore, a people is a people before it gives itself to a king. This gift itself is a civil act; it presupposes a public deliberation. Thus, before examining the act whereby a people chooses a king, it would be well to examine the act whereby a people is a people. For since this act is necessarily prior to the other, it is the true foundation of society.

In fact, if there were no prior agreement, then, unless the vote were unanimous, what would be the basis of the minority's obligation to submit to the majority's choice, and where do one hundred who want a master get the right to vote on behalf of ten who do not? The law of majority rule is itself established by agreement and presupposes unanimity on at least one occasion.

Chapter 6
On the Social Compact

I suppose that men have reached the point where obstacles that are harmful to their maintenance in the state of nature gain the upper hand by their resistance to the forces that each individual can bring to bear to maintain himself in that state. Such being the case, that original state cannot subsist any longer, and the human race would perish if it did not alter its mode of existence.

For since men cannot engender new forces, but merely unite and direct existing ones, they have no other means of maintaining themselves but to form by aggregation a sum of forces that could gain the upper hand over the resistance, so that their forces are directed by means of a single moving power and made to act in concert.

This sum of forces cannot come into being without the cooperation of many. But since each man's force and liberty are the primary instruments of his maintenance, how is he going to entrust them to others without hurting himself and without neglecting the care that he owes himself? This difficulty, seen in terms of my subject, can be stated in the following terms:

"Find a form of association that defends and protects with all common forces the person and goods of each associate, and, by means of which, each one, while uniting with all, nevertheless obeys only himself and remains as free as before." This is the fundamental problem for which the social contract provides the solution.

The clauses of this contract are so determined by the nature of the act that the least modification renders them vain and ineffectual, that, although perhaps they have never been formally promulgated, they are everywhere the same, everywhere tacitly accepted and acknowledged. The result is that once the social compact is violated, each person then regains his first rights and resumes his natural liberty, while losing the contractual liberty[26] for which he renounced it.

These clauses, properly understood, are all reducible to a single one, namely, the total alienation of each associate together with all of his rights to the entire community. For first of all, since each person gives himself whole and entire, the condition is equal for everyone; and since the condition is equal for everyone, no one has an interest in making it burdensome for the others.

Moreover, since the alienation is made without reservation, the union is as perfect as possible, and no associate has anything further to demand. For if some rights remained with private individuals, in the absence of any common superior who could decide between them and the public, each person would eventually claim to be his own judge in all things, since he is on some particular point his own judge. The state of nature would subsist and the association would necessarily become tyrannical or hollow.

Finally, in giving himself to all, each person gives himself to no one. And since there is no associate over whom he does not acquire the same right that he would grant others over himself, he gains the equivalent of everything he loses, along with a greater amount of force to preserve what he has.

If, therefore, one eliminates from the social compact whatever is not essential to it, one will find that it is reducible to the following terms. *Each of us places his person and all his power in common under the supreme direction of the general will; and as one, we receive each member as an indivisible part of the whole.*

At once, in place of the individual person of each contracting party, this act of association produces a moral[27] and collective body composed of as many

---

[26] [Rousseau's phrase is *la liberté conventionelle*.]

[27] [When Rousseau writes about a moral person, being, or body, he is using *moral* in a technical sense. In law a moral person is an entity capable of being legally responsible; corporations are

members as there are voices in the assembly, which receives from this same act its unity, its common *self*, its life, and its will. This public person, formed thus by union of all the others, formerly took the name *city*,[28] and at present takes the name *republic* or *body politic*, which is called *state* by its members when it is passive, *sovereign* when it is active, *power* when compared to others like itself. As for the associates, they collectively take the name *people*; individually they are called *citizens*, insofar as they are participants in the sovereign authority, and *subjects*, insofar as they are subjected to the laws of the state. But these terms are often confused and mistaken for one another. It is enough to know how to distinguish them when they are used with absolute precision.

Chapter 7
On the Sovereign

This formula shows that the act of association includes a reciprocal commitment between the public and private individuals, and that each individual, contracting, as it were, with himself, finds himself under a twofold commitment, namely, as a member of the sovereign toward private individuals, and as a member of the state toward the sovereign. But the maxim of civil law that no one is held to commitments made to himself cannot be applied here, for there is a considerable difference between being obligated to oneself or to a whole of which one is a part.

It must be further noted that the public deliberation that can obligate all the subjects to the sovereign, owing to the two different relationships in which each of them is viewed, cannot, for the opposite reason, obligate the sovereign to itself and that consequently it is contrary to the nature of the

---

therefore moral persons. This translation reproduces Rousseau's terminology, but one could often simply substitute "artificial" in order to grasp his sense.]

[28] The true meaning of this word is almost entirely lost on modern men. Most of them mistake a town for a city and a townsman for a citizen. They do not know that houses make a town but citizens make a city. Once this mistake cost the Carthaginians dearly. I have not found in my reading that the title of *citizen* has ever been given to the subjects of a prince, not even in ancient times to the Macedonians or in our own time to the English, although they are closer to liberty than all the others. Only the French adopt this name *citizen* with complete familiarity, since they have no true idea of its meaning, as can be seen from their dictionaries. If this were not the case, they would become guilty of treason for using it. For them, this name expresses a virtue and not a right. When Bodin wanted to speak about our citizens and townsmen, he committed a terrible blunder, for he mistook the one group for the other. Mr. d'Alembert was not in error, and in his article titled "Geneva" he has carefully distinguished the four orders of men (even five, counting ordinary foreigners) who are in our town [i.e., Geneva], and of whom only two make up the republic. No other French author I am aware of has grasped the true meaning of the word *citizen*. [Cf. Jean Bodin, *The Six Books of the Republic*, bk. 1, ch. 6.]

body politic that the sovereign impose upon itself a law it could not break. Since the sovereign can be considered under but one single relationship, it is then in the position of a private individual contracting with himself. Whence it is apparent that there neither is nor can be any type of fundamental law that is obligatory for the people as a body, not even the social contract.[29] This does not mean that the whole body cannot perfectly well commit itself to another body with respect to things that do not infringe on this contract. For in regard to the foreigner, it becomes a simple being, an individual.

However, since the body politic or the sovereign derives its being exclusively from the sanctity of the contract, it can never obligate itself, not even to another power, to do anything that derogates from the original act, such as alienating some portion of itself or submitting to another sovereign. Violation of the act whereby it exists would be self-annihilation, and whatever is nothing produces nothing.

As soon as this multitude is thus united in a body, one cannot harm one of the members without attacking the whole body. It is even less possible that the body can be harmed without the members feeling it. Thus duty and interest equally obligate the two contracting parties to come to one another's aid, and the same men should seek to combine in this twofold relationship all the advantages that result from it.

For since the sovereign is formed entirely from the private individuals who make it up, it neither has nor could have an interest contrary to theirs. Hence, the sovereign power has no need to offer a guarantee to its subjects, since it is impossible for a body to want to harm all of its members, and, as we will see later, it cannot harm any one of them in particular. The sovereign, by the mere fact that it exists, is always all that it should be.

But the same thing cannot be said of the subjects in relation to the sovereign, for whom, despite their common interest, their commitments would be without substance if it did not find ways of being assured of their fidelity.

In fact, each individual can, as a man, have a private will contrary to or different from the general will that he has as a citizen. His private interest can speak to him in an entirely different manner than the common interest. His absolute and naturally independent existence can cause him to envisage what he owes the common cause as a gratuitous contribution, the loss of which will be less harmful to others than its payment is burdensome to him. And in viewing the moral person that constitutes the state as a theoretical entity[30] because it is not a man, he would enjoy the rights of a citizen without wanting

---

[29] [It is this argument, which undermines the notion of a constitution that must be preserved and respected, that led to Rousseau's book being condemned by the government of Geneva as destructive of all systems of government.]

[30] [Rousseau's term is *être de raison*, which corresponds to the scholastic *ens rationis*. Eighteenth-century dictionaries distinguish *êtres de raison* from *êtres réels*. This particular person—Tom Smith—or this particular dog—Fido—is real; humankind or the domesticated dog is an abstraction or *être de raison*.]

to fulfill the duties of a subject, an injustice whose growth would bring about the ruin of the body politic.

Thus, in order for the social compact to avoid being an empty formula, it tacitly entails the commitment—which alone can give force to the others—that whoever refuses to obey the general will, will be forced to do so by the entire body. This means merely that he will be forced to be free. For it is this condition that, by giving each citizen to the homeland, guarantees him against all personal dependence, this condition that produces the skill and the performance of the political machine and that alone bestows legitimacy upon civil commitments. Without it, such commitments would be absurd, tyrannical, and subject to the worst abuses.

Chapter 8
On the Civil State

This passage from the state of nature to the civil state produces quite a remarkable change in man, for it substitutes justice for instinct in his behavior and gives his actions a moral quality they previously lacked. Only then, when the voice of duty replaces physical impulse and right replaces appetite, does man, who had hitherto taken only himself into account, find himself forced to act upon other principles and consult his reason before listening to his inclinations. Although in this state he deprives himself of several of the advantages belonging to him in the state of nature, he gains equally great ones in return. His faculties are exercised and developed, his ideas are broadened, his feelings are ennobled, his entire soul is elevated to such a height that, if the abuse of this new condition did not often lower his condition to beneath the level he left, he ought constantly to bless the happy moment that tore him away from it forever and that transformed him from a stupid, limited animal into an intelligent being and a man.

Let us summarize this entire balance sheet so that the credits and debits are easily compared. What man loses through the social contract is his natural liberty and an unlimited right to everything that tempts him and that he can acquire. What he gains is civil liberty and the proprietary ownership of all he possesses. So as not to be in error with regard to the value of these exchanges, it is necessary to draw a careful distinction between natural liberty (which is limited solely by the force of the individual involved) and civil liberty (which is limited by the general will), and between possession (which is merely the effect of the force or the right of the first occupant) and proprietary ownership (which can only be based on a positive title).

To the preceding could be added the acquisition in the civil state of moral liberty, which alone makes man truly the master of himself. For to be driven by appetite alone is slavery, and obedience to the law one has prescribed for oneself is liberty. But I have already said too much on this subject, and the philosophical meaning of the word *liberty* is not part of my subject here.

Chapter 9
On Real Property[31]

Each member of the community gives himself to it at the instant of its constitution, just as he actually is, himself and all his forces, including all the goods in his possession. This is not to say that by this act alone possession changes its nature as it changes hands and becomes property in the hands of the sovereign. Rather, since the forces of the city are incomparably greater than those of a private individual, public possession is by that very fact stronger and more irrevocable, without being more legitimate, at least to strangers. For with regard to its members, the state is master of all their goods in virtue of the social contract, which serves in the state as the basis of all rights. But with regard to other powers, the state is master only in virtue of the right of the first occupant, which it derives from private individuals.

The right of first occupant, though more real than the right of the strongest, does not become a true right until after the establishment of the right of property. Every man by nature has a right to everything he needs; however, the positive act whereby he becomes a proprietor of some goods excludes him from all the rest. Once his lot has been determined, he should limit himself thereto, no longer having any right against the community. This is why the right of the first occupant, so weak in the state of nature, is able to command the respect of every man living in the civil state. In this right, one respects not so much what belongs to others as what does not belong to oneself.

In general, the following rules are necessary in order to authorize the right of the first occupant on any land. First, this land may not already be occupied by anyone. Second, no one may occupy more than the amount needed to subsist. Third, one is to take possession of it not by an empty ceremony, but by working and cultivating it—the only sign of property that ought, in the absence of legal titles, to be respected by others.[32]

In fact, by according the right of the first occupant only to those who need and who work, have we not extended it as far as it can go? Is it possible to avoid setting limits to this right? Will setting one's foot on a piece of common land be sufficient to claim it at once as one's own? Will having the force for a moment to drive off other men be sufficient to deny them the right ever to return? How can a man or a people seize a vast amount of territory and deprive the entire human race of it except by a punishable usurpation, since this seizure deprives all other men of the shelter and sustenance that nature gives them in common? When Nuñez Balboa stood on the shoreline and took possession of the South Sea and all of South America in the name of

---

[31] [Rousseau's title is *Du domaine réel*. "Real" refers to property in land (as in "real estate"), whereas *domaine* is a somewhat old-fashioned synonym for "property" but is used particularly for property in land.]

[32] [Rousseau here follows the chapter on property in Locke's *Two Treatises*, Second Treatise.]

the crown of Castille, was this enough to dispossess all the inhabitants and to exclude all the princes of the world? On that basis, those ceremonies would be multiplied quite in vain. All the Catholic king had to do was take possession of the universe all at once from his study, excepting afterward from his empire only what already belonged to other princes.

One can imagine how the combined and contiguous lands of private individuals become public territory and how the right of sovereignty, extending from subjects to the land they occupy, becomes at once real and personal. This places its owners in a greater dependence, turning their very own forces into guarantees of their loyalty. This advantage does not seem to have been fully appreciated by the ancient monarchs, who, calling themselves merely kings of the Persians, the Scythians, and the Macedonians, appeared to regard themselves merely as the leaders of men rather than the masters of the country. Today's monarchs more shrewdly call themselves kings of France, Spain, England, and so on. In holding the land thus, they are quite sure of holding the inhabitants.

What is remarkable about this alienation is that, in accepting the goods of private individuals, the community is far from despoiling them; rather, in so doing, it merely assures them of legitimate possession, changing usurpation into a true right, and enjoyment into proprietary ownership. So, since owners are considered trustees of the public good, and since their rights are respected by all members of the state and maintained with all its force against foreigners, through a surrender that is advantageous to the public and still more so to themselves, they have, so to speak, acquired all they have given. This paradox is easily explained by the distinction between the rights the sovereign and the proprietor have to the same land,[33] as will be seen later.

It can also happen that men begin to unite before possessing anything and later appropriate a piece of land sufficient for everyone, so that they enjoy it in common or divide it among themselves either in equal shares or according to proportions laid down by the sovereign. In whatever way this acquisition is accomplished, each private individual's right to his own land is always subordinate to the community's right to all, without which there could be neither solidity in the social fabric nor real force in the exercise of sovereignty.[34]

I will end this chapter and this book with a remark that should serve as a basis for every social system. It is that instead of destroying natural equality, the fundamental compact, on the contrary, substitutes a moral and legitimate equality to whatever physical inequality nature may have been able to impose

[33] [Here and below, Rousseau writes *fond* but must mean *fonds*. The mistake seems to have been fairly common, but, as Jean-François Féraud points out in his *Dictionnaire critique de la langue française* of 1787–1788, *fond* means "bottom" (as in the bottom of a cup) whereas *fonds* means "land." They are two quite different words.]

[34] [Cf. Hobbes, *De Cive*, ch. 12, §7.]

upon men, and that, however unequal in force or intelligence they may be, men all become equal by agreement and by right.[35]

End of the First Book

BOOK II

Chapter 1
That Sovereignty Is Inalienable

The first and most important consequence of the principles established above is that only the general will can direct the forces of the state according to the purpose for which it was instituted, which is the common good. For if the opposition of private interests made necessary the establishment of societies, it is the accord of these same interests that made it possible. It is what these different interests have in common that forms the social bond, and, were there no point of agreement among all these interests, no society could exist. For it is utterly on the basis of this common interest that society ought to be governed.

I therefore maintain that since sovereignty is merely the exercise of the general will, it can never be alienated, and that the sovereign, which is only a collective being, cannot be represented by anything but itself. Power can perfectly well be transferred, but not the will.

In fact, while it is not impossible for a private will to be in accord on some point with the general will, it is impossible at least for this accord to be durable and constant. For by its nature the private will tends toward giving advantages to some and not to others, and the general will tends toward equality. It is even more impossible for there to be a guarantee of this accord even if it ought always to exist. This accord is not the result of art but of chance. The sovereign may well say, "Right now I want what a certain man wants or at least what he says he wants." But it cannot say, "What this man will want tomorrow I too will want," since it is absurd for the will to tie its hands for the future and since it is not within the capacity of any will to consent to anything contrary to the good of the being that wills. If, therefore, the populace promises simply to obey, it dissolves itself by this act; it loses its standing as a people. The very moment there is a master, there no longer is a sovereign, and thenceforward the body politic is destroyed.

---

[35] Under bad governments this equality is only apparent and illusory. It serves merely to maintain the poor man in his misery and the rich man in his usurpation. In actuality, laws are always useful to those who have possessions and harmful to those who have nothing. Whence it follows that the social state is advantageous to men only insofar as they all have something and none of them has too much.

This is not to say that the commands of the leaders could not pass for manifestations of the general will, as long as the sovereign, who is free to oppose them, does not do so. In such a case, the consent of the people ought to be presumed on the basis of universal silence. This will be explained at greater length.

Chapter 2
That Sovereignty Is Indivisible

Sovereignty is indivisible for the same reason that it is inalienable. For either the will is general[36] or it is not. It is the will of either the people as a whole or of only a part. In the first case, this will once declared is an act of sovereignty and constitutes law. In the second case, it is merely a private will, or an act of magistracy. At most it is a decree.

However, our political theorists, unable to divide sovereignty in its principle, divide it in its object. They divide it into force and will; into legislative and executive power; into rights of imposing taxes, of justice, and of war; into internal administration and power to negotiate with foreigners. Occasionally they mix all these parts together and sometimes they separate them. They turn the sovereign into a fantastic being made of bits and pieces. It is as if they built a man out of several bodies, one of which had eyes, another had arms, another feet, and nothing more. Japanese sleight-of-hand artists are said to dismember a child before the eyes of spectators, then, throwing all the parts in the air one after the other, they make the child fall back down alive and all in one piece. These conjuring acts of our political theorists are more or less like these performances. After having taken apart the social body by means of a sleight of hand worthy of a carnival, they put the pieces back together who knows how.

This error comes from not having formed precise notions of sovereign authority, and from having taken for parts of that authority what were merely emanations from it. Thus, for example, the acts of declaring war and making peace have been viewed as acts of sovereignty, which they are not, since each of these acts is not a law but merely an application of the law, a particular act determining the legal circumstances, as will be clearly seen when the idea attached to the word *law* comes to be defined.

In reviewing the other divisions in the same way, one would find that one is mistaken every time one believes one sees sovereignty divided, and that the rights one takes to be the parts of this sovereignty are all subordinated to it and always presuppose supreme wills that these rights merely put into effect.

---

[36] For a will to be general, it need not always be unanimous; however, it is necessary for all the votes to be counted. Any formal exclusion is a breach of generality.

It would be impossible to say how much this lack of precision has obscured the decisions of authors who have written about political right when they wanted to judge the respective rights of kings and peoples on the basis of the principles they had established. Anyone can see, in Chapters III and IV of Book I of Grotius, how this learned man and his translator, Barbeyrac, become entangled and caught up in their sophisms, for fear of either saying too much or too little according to their perspectives, and of offending the interests they needed to reconcile. Grotius, having taken refuge in France, unhappy with his homeland, and desirous of paying court to Louis XIII (to whom his book is dedicated) spares no pain to rob the people of all their rights and to invest kings with them by every possible artifice. This would also have been the wish of Barbeyrac, who dedicated his translation to King George I of England. But unfortunately, the expulsion of James II (which he calls an abdication) forced him to be evasive and on his guard and to beat around the bush, in order to avoid making William out to be a usurper.[37] If these two writers had adopted the true principles, all their difficulties would have been alleviated and they would always have been consistent. However, they would have reluctantly told the truth and found themselves paying court only to the people. For truth does not lead to success, and the populace grants neither ambassadorships, nor university chairs, nor pensions.

Chapter 3
Whether the General Will Can Err

It follows from what has preceded that the general will is always right and always tends toward the public utility. However, it does not follow that the deliberations of the people always have the same degree of rectitude. We always want what is good for us, but we do not always see what it is. The populace is never corrupted, but it is often tricked, and only then does it appear to want what is bad.

There is often a great deal of difference between the will of all and the general will. The latter considers only the general interest, whereas the former considers private interest and is merely the sum of private wills. But remove from these same wills the pluses and minuses that cancel each other out,[38] and what remains as the sum of the differences is the general will.

---

[37] [The Catholic James II was expelled from Britain in the revolution of 1688 and replaced by William and Mary. Rousseau is right to regard the word "abdication" as fundamental; it implies that no revolution had taken place and therefore implicitly denies a right of revolution. However, Jean Barbeyrac was more sympathetic to the arguments of Locke than Rousseau perhaps recognizes.]

[38] "Each interest," says the Marquis d'Argenson [in *Considerations on the Former and Present Government of France*], "has different principles. The accord of two private interests is formed in opposition to that of a third." He could have added that the accord of all the interests is found in the opposition to that of each. If there were no different interests,

If, when a sufficiently informed populace deliberates, the citizens were to have no communication among themselves, the general will would always result from the large number of small differences, and the deliberation would always be good. But when intrigues and partial associations come into being at the expense of the large association, the will of each of these associations becomes general in relation to its members and particular in relation to the state. It can be said, then, that there are no longer as many voters as there are men, but merely as many as there are associations. The differences become less numerous and yield a result that is less general. Finally, when one of these associations is so large that it dominates all the others, the result is no longer a sum of minor differences, but a single difference. Then there is no longer a general will, and the opinion that dominates is merely a private opinion.

For the general will to be well articulated, it is therefore important that there should be no partial society in the state and that each citizen make up his own mind.[39] Such was the unique and sublime institution of the great Lycurgus. If there are partial societies, their number must be multiplied and inequality among them prevented, as was done by Solon, Numa, and Servius.[40] These precautions are the only effective way of bringing it about that the general will is always enlightened and that the populace does not deceive itself.

Chapter 4
On the Limits of Sovereign Power

If the state or the city is merely a moral person whose life consists in the union of its members, and if the most important of its concerns is that of its own conservation, it ought to have a universal compulsory force to move and arrange each part in the manner best suited to the whole. Just as nature gives each man an absolute power over all his members, the social compact gives the body politic an absolute power over all its members, and it is the same power that, as I have said, is directed by the general will and bears the name *sovereignty*.

---

the common interest, which would never encounter any obstacle, would scarcely be felt. Everything would proceed on its own and politics would cease being an art.

[39] "It is true," says Machiavelli, "that some divisions are harmful to the republic while others are helpful to it. Those that are accompanied by sects and partisan factions are harmful while those are beneficial that maintain themselves without sects and partisan factions. Since, therefore, a ruler of a republic cannot prevent enmities from arising within it, he at least ought to prevent them from becoming sects," *The History of Florence*, Book VII. [Rousseau here quotes the Italian.]

[40] [Lycurgus was the author of the constitution of Sparta, Solon the key figure in the construction of Athenian democracy. Numa and Servius (the second and sixth kings of Rome) played crucial roles in the construction of Roman institutions; on Servius, see Book IV, Chapter 4.]

But over and above the public person, we need to consider the private persons who make it up and whose life and liberty are naturally independent of it. It is, therefore, a question of making a rigorous distinction between the respective rights of the citizens and the sovereign,[41] and between the duties the former have to fulfill as subjects and the natural right they should enjoy as men.

We grant that each person alienates, by the social compact, only that portion of his power, his goods, and liberty whose use is of consequence to the community;[42] but we must also grant that only the sovereign is the judge of what is of consequence.

A citizen should render to the state all the services he can as soon as the sovereign demands them. However, for its part, the sovereign cannot impose on the subjects any fetters that are of no use to the community. It cannot even will to do so, for under the law of reason nothing takes place without a cause, any more than under the law of nature.

The commitments that bind us to the body politic are obligatory only because they are mutual, and their nature is such that in fulfilling them one cannot work for someone else without also working for oneself. Why is the general will always right, and why do all constantly want the happiness of each of them, if not because everyone applies the word *each* to himself and thinks of himself as he votes for all? This proves that the equality of right and the notion of justice it produces are derived from the preference each person gives himself, and thus from the nature of man; that the general will, to be really such, must be general in its object as well as in its essence; that it must derive from all in order to be applied to all; and that it loses its natural rectitude when it tends toward any individual, determinate object. For then, judging what is foreign to us, we have no true principle of equity to guide us.

In effect, once it is a question of a state of affairs or a particular right concerning a point that has not been regulated by a prior, general agreement, the issue becomes contentious. It is a suit in which the interested private individuals are one of the parties and the public the other, but in which I fail to see either what law should be followed or what judge should render the decision. In these circumstances it would be ridiculous to want to appeal to an express decision of the general will, which can only be the conclusion reached by one of its parts, and which, for the other part, therefore, is merely an alien, particular will, inclined on this occasion to injustice and subject to error. Thus, just as a private will cannot represent the general will, the general will, for its part, alters its nature when it has a particular object; and, as general, it is unable to render a decision on either a man or a state of

---

[41] Attentive readers, please do not rush to accuse me of contradiction here. I have been unable to avoid it in my choice of words, given the poverty of the language. But wait.

[42] [Rousseau agrees with Locke, *Two Treatises*, Second Treatise, ch. 8.]

affairs. When, for example, the populace of Athens appointed or dismissed its leaders, decreed that honors be bestowed on one or inflicted penalties on another, and by a multitude of particular decrees indiscriminately exercised all the acts of government, the people in this case no longer had a general will in the strict sense. It no longer functioned as sovereign but as magistrate.[43] This will appear contrary to commonly held opinions, but I must be given time to present my own.

It should be seen from this that what makes the will general is not so much the number of votes as the common interest that unites them, for in this institution each person necessarily submits himself to the conditions he imposes on others, an admirable accord between interest and justice that bestows on common deliberations a quality of equity that disappears when any particular matter is discussed, for lack of a common interest uniting and identifying the reference point of the judge with that of the party.

From whatever viewpoint one approaches this principle, one always arrives at the same conclusion, namely that the social compact establishes among the citizens an equality of such a kind that they all commit themselves under the same conditions and should all enjoy the same rights. Thus by the very nature of the compact, every act of sovereignty (that is, every authentic act of the general will) obligates or favors all citizens equally, so that the sovereign knows only the nation as a body and does not draw distinctions between any of those members that make it up. Strictly speaking, then, what is an act of sovereignty? It is not an agreement between a superior and an inferior, but an agreement of the body with each of its members. This agreement is legitimate, because it has the social contract as a basis; equitable, because it is common to all; useful, because it can have only the general good for its object; and solid, because it has the public force and the supreme power as a guarantee. As long as the subjects are subordinated only to such agreement, they obey no one, but only obey their own will. And asking how far the respective rights of the sovereign and the citizens extend is asking how far the latter can commit themselves to one another, each to all and all to each.

We can see from this that the sovereign power, wholly absolute, sacred, and inviolable as it is, does not and cannot exceed the limits of general agreements, and that every man can completely dispose of such goods and freedom

---

[43] [Rousseau's word is *magistrat*; but in eighteenth-century French, a "magistrate" can be someone who exercises justice (as with the English word) or someone responsible for what the French call *police*—a term that covers all measures to order a society—in other words, any member of the executive. Rousseau's examples cover both senses of the word. In modern French, one can say that the president of France is the first magistrate, which is to say only that he is the highest officer of the state. Thus Rousseau works with a bipartite classification—sovereign and magistrate—where we work with a tripartite classification—legislature (which represents the people, who are sovereign), executive, and judiciary. Since modern English terminology tends to draw a clear distinction between the executive and the judiciary, there is no convenient term in English that covers the range of the French term.]

as has been left to him by these agreements. This results in the fact that the sovereign never has the right to lay more charges on one subject than on another, because in that case the matter becomes particular, and no longer within the range of the sovereign's competence.

Once these distinctions are granted, it is so false that there is, in the social contract, any genuine renunciation on the part of private individuals that their situation, as a result of this contract, is really preferable to what it was beforehand; and, instead of an alienation, they have merely made an advantageous exchange of an uncertain and precarious mode of existence for another that is better and surer. Natural independence is exchanged for liberty; the power to harm others is exchanged for their own security; and their force, which others could overcome, for a right that the social union renders invincible. Their life itself, which they have devoted to the state, is continually protected by it; and when they risk their lives for its defense, what are they then doing but returning to the state what they have received from it? What are they doing, that they did not do more frequently and with greater danger in the state of nature, when they would inevitably have to fight battles, defending at the peril of their lives the means of their preservation? It is true that everyone has to fight, if necessary, for the homeland; but it also is the case that no one ever has to fight on his own behalf. Do we not still gain by running, for something that brings about our security, a portion of the risks we would have to run for ourselves once our security was taken away?

Chapter 5
On the Right of Life or Death

The question arises how private individuals who have no right to dispose of their own lives can transfer to the sovereign this very same right that they do not have. This question seems difficult to resolve only because it is poorly stated. Every man has the right to risk his own life in order to preserve it. Has it ever been said that a person who jumps out a window to escape a fire is guilty of committing suicide? Has this crime ever been imputed to someone who perishes in a storm, even though he was aware of the danger when he embarked?

The social treaty has as its purpose the conservation of the contracting parties. Whoever wills the end also wills the means, and these means are inseparable from some risks, even from some losses. Whoever wishes to preserve his life at the expense of others should also give it up for them when necessary. For the citizen is no longer judge of the peril to which the law wishes him to expose himself, and when the prince[44] has said to him, "It is expedient for the state that you should die," he should die. Because it is under this condition

---

[44] [Rousseau explains the meaning he gives to the word "prince" in Book III, Chapter 1.]

alone that he has lived in security up to then, and because his life is no longer only a kindness of nature, but a conditional gift of the state.

The death penalty inflicted on criminals can be viewed from more or less the same point of view. It is in order to avoid being the victim of an assassin that a person consents to die if he were to become one. In making this treaty, far from disposing of one's own life, one thinks only of guaranteeing it. And it cannot be presumed that any of the contracting parties is then planning to get himself hanged.

Moreover, every malefactor who attacks the social right becomes through his transgressions a rebel and a traitor to the homeland; in violating its laws, he ceases to be a member, and he even wages war against it. In that case the preservation of the state is incompatible with his own. Thus one of the two must perish; and when the guilty party is put to death, it is less as a citizen than as an enemy. The legal proceeding and the judgment are the proofs and the declaration that he has broken the social treaty, and consequently that he is no longer a member of the state. For since he has acknowledged himself to be such, at least by his living there, he ought to be removed from it by exile as a violator of the compact, or by death as a public enemy. For such an enemy is not a moral person,[45] but a man, and in this situation the right of war is to kill the vanquished.[46]

But it will be said that the condemnation of a criminal is a particular act. Fine. So this condemnation is not a function of the sovereign. It is a right the sovereign can confer without itself being able to exercise it. All of my opinions are consistent, but I cannot present them all at once.

In addition, frequency of corporal punishment[47] is always a sign of weakness or of torpor in the government. There is no wicked man who could not be made good for something. One has the right to put to death, even as an example to others, only someone who cannot be preserved without danger.

With regard to the right of pardon, or of exempting a guilty party from the penalty decreed by the law and pronounced by the judge, this belongs only to one who is above the judge and the law, that is, to the sovereign. Still its right in this regard is not clearly defined, and the cases in which it is rightly

---

[45] [Rousseau's term is *personne morale*, which we consistently translate as "moral person." But in normal usage the claim that a corporate entity is a moral person means that a corporate entity is *like* an individual human being (who is also a moral person) in that it can be held responsible for its actions. Here Rousseau uses *personne morale* to refer to a corporate entity *as opposed to* an individual human being. He is thus using *personne morale* as a technical term to refer to a corporate entity or an *artificial* being.]

[46] [This is hard, even impossible, to reconcile with Rousseau's argument in Book I, Chapter 4.]

[47] [Rousseau's term is *supplices*, which means corporal punishment. In *ancien régime* France, the standard punishments for crime were corporal—whipping, branding, breaking on the wheel, etc.—and so Rousseau does not intend to distinguish between corporal punishment and non-corporal punishment (prison, for example) but to refer to judicial punishments in general.]

used are truly rare. In a well-governed state, there are few punishments, not because many pardons are granted but because there are few criminals. When a state is in decline, the sheer number of crimes ensures impunity. Under the Roman Republic, neither the senate nor the consuls ever tried to grant pardons. The people itself did not do so, although it sometimes revoked its own judgment. Frequent pardons indicate that transgressions will eventually have no need of them, and everyone sees where that leads. But I feel that my heart murmurs and holds back my pen. Let us leave these questions to be discussed by a just man who has not done wrong and who himself never needed pardon.

Chapter 6
On Law

Through the social compact, we have given existence and life to the body politic. It is now a matter of giving it movement and will through legislation. For the primitive act whereby this body is formed and united in no way determines what it should do to preserve itself.

Whatever is good and in conformity with order is such by the nature of things and independently of human agreements. All justice comes from God; he alone is its source. But if we knew how to receive it from so exalted a source, we would have no need for government or laws. Undoubtedly there is a universal justice emanating from reason alone; but this justice, to be admitted among us, ought to be reciprocal. Considering things from a human standpoint, the lack of a natural sanction causes the laws of justice to be without teeth among men. They do nothing but good to the wicked and evil to the just, when the latter observes them in his dealings with everyone while no one observes them in their dealings with him. There must therefore be agreements and laws to unite rights and duties and refer justice back to its object. In the state of nature where everything is commonly held, I owe nothing to those to whom I have promised nothing. I recognize as belonging to someone else only what is not useful to me. It is not this way in the civil state where all rights are fixed by law.

But what then, to get to the point, is a law? As long as we continue to be satisfied with attaching only metaphysical ideas to this word,[48] we will continue to reason without understanding each other. And when we have declared what a law of nature is, we will not thereby have a better grasp of what a law of the state is.

I have already stated that there is no general will concerning a particular object. In effect, this particular object is either within or outside of the state. If it is outside of the state, a will that is foreign to it is not general in relation to it. And if this object is within the state, that object is part of it; in that

---

[48] [Rousseau is attacking Montesquieu, *Spirit of the Laws*, bk. 1, ch. 1.]

case, a relationship is formed between the whole and its parts that makes two separate beings, one of which is the part, and the other is the whole less that same part. But the whole less a part is not the whole, and as long as this relationship is the case, there is no longer a whole but rather two unequal parts. Whence it follows that the will of the one is certainly not general in relation to the other.

But when the entire populace enacts a statute concerning the entire populace, it considers only itself, and if in that case a relationship is formed, it is between the entire object seen from one perspective and the entire object seen from another, without any division of the whole. Then the subject matter about which a statute is enacted is general like the will that enacts it. It is this act that I call a law.

When I say that the object of the laws is always general, I have in mind that the law considers subjects as a body and actions in the abstract, never a man as an individual or a particular action. Thus the law can perfectly well enact a statute to the effect that there be privileges, but it cannot bestow them by name on anyone. The law can create several classes of citizens, and even stipulate the qualifications that determine membership in these classes, but it cannot name specific persons to be admitted to them. It can establish a royal government and a hereditary line of succession, but it cannot elect a king or name a royal family. In a word, any function that relates to an individual does not belong to the legislative power.

On this view, it is immediately obvious that it is no longer necessary to ask who is to make the laws, since they are the acts of the general will; nor whether the prince is above the laws, since he is a member of the state; nor whether the law can be unjust, since no one is unjust to himself; nor how one is both free and subject to the laws, since they are merely the record of our own wills.

Moreover, it is apparent that since the law combines the universality of the will and that of the object, what a man, whoever he may be, decrees on his own authority is not a law. What even the sovereign decrees concerning a particular object is no closer to being a law; rather, it is a decree. Nor is it an act of sovereignty but of magistracy.

I therefore call every state ruled by laws a republic, regardless of the form its administration may take.[49] For only then does the public interest govern, and only then is the "public thing" [in Latin: *res publica*] something real.

---

[49] [As Rousseau goes on to explain, by his definition a monarchy can be a republic. Rousseau's definition of "republic" as any legitimate government was becoming unusual (in Montesquieu, for example, republic is an antonym of monarchy), but it had been until recently the standard definition—thus Bodin's *Six Books of the Republic* is about legitimate government in general and not about "republics" in the modern, Montesquieuean sense—and it corresponds to classical usage.]

Every legitimate government is republican.[50] I will explain later on what government is.

Strictly speaking, laws are merely the conditions of civil association. The populace that is subjected to the laws ought to be their author. The regulating of the conditions of a society belongs to no one but those who are in association with one another. But how will they regulate these conditions? Will it be by a common accord, by a sudden inspiration? Does the body politic have an organ for making known its will? Who will give it the necessary foresight to formulate acts and to promulgate them in advance, or how will it announce them in time of need? How will a blind multitude, which often does not know what it wants (since it rarely knows what is good for it), carry out on its own an enterprise as great and as difficult as a system of legislation? By itself the populace always wants the good, but by itself it does not always see it. The general will is always right, but the judgment that guides it is not always enlightened. It must be made to see objects as they are, and sometimes as they ought to appear to it. The good path it seeks must be pointed out to it. It must be made safe from the seduction of private wills. It must be given a sense of time and place. It must weigh present, tangible advantages against the danger of distant, hidden evils. Private individuals see the good they reject. The public wills the good that it does not see. Everyone is equally in need of guides. The former must be obligated to conform their wills to their reason; the latter must learn to know what it wants. Then public enlightenment results in the union of the understanding and the will in the social body—hence, the full cooperation of the parts and finally the greatest force of the whole. Whence there arises the necessity of having a legislator.

Chapter 7
On the Legislator

Discovering the rules of society best suited to nations would require a superior intelligence that beheld all the passions of men without feeling any of them; who had no affinity with our nature, yet knew it through and through; whose happiness was independent of us, yet who nevertheless was willing to concern itself with ours; finally, who, in the passage of time, procures for himself a distant glory, being able to labor in one age and obtain his reward in another.[51] Gods would be needed to give men laws.

---

[50] By this word I do not have in mind merely an aristocracy or a democracy, but in general every government guided by the general will, which is the law. To be legitimate, the government need not be made indistinguishable from the sovereign, but it must be its servant. Then the monarchy itself is a republic. This will become clear in the next Book.

[51] A people never becomes famous except when its legislation begins to decline. It is not known for how many centuries the constitution established by Lycurgus caused the happiness of the Spartans before the rest of Greece took note of it.

The same reasoning used by Caligula[52] in practice was used by Plato when dealing with questions of principle in order to define the civil[53] or royal man he looks for in his dialogue *The Statesman*. But if it is true that a great prince is a rare man, what about a great legislator? The former merely has to follow the model the latter should propose to him. The latter is the engineer who invents the machine; the former is merely the workman who constructs it and makes it run. "At the birth of societies," says Montesquieu, "it is the leaders of republics who bring about the institution, and thereafter it is the institution that forms the leaders of republics."[54]

He who dares to undertake the establishment of a people should feel that he is, so to speak, in a position to change human nature, to transform each individual (who by himself is a perfect and solitary whole) into a part of a larger whole from which this individual receives, in a sense, his life and his being; to alter man's constitution in order to strengthen it; to substitute a partial and moral existence for the physical and independent existence we have all received from nature. In a word, he must deny man his own forces in order to give him forces that are alien to him and that he cannot make use of without the help of others. The more these natural forces are dead and obliterated, and the greater and more durable are the acquired forces, the more too is the constitution solid and perfect. Thus if each citizen is nothing and can do nothing except in concert with all the others, and if the force acquired by the whole is equal or superior to the sum of the natural forces of all the individuals, one can say that the legislation has achieved the highest possible point of perfection.

The legislator is in every respect an extraordinary man in the state.[55] If he ought to be so by his genius, he is no less so by his office, which is neither magistracy nor sovereignty. This office, which constitutes the republic, does not enter into its constitution. It is a particular and superior function having nothing in common with the dominion over men. For if he who has command over men must not have command over laws, he who has command over the laws must no longer have any authority over men. Otherwise, his laws, ministers of his passions, would often only serve to perpetuate his injustices, and he could never avoid specific judgments altering the sanctity of his work.

When Lycurgus gave laws to his homeland, he began by abdicating the throne. It was the custom of most Greek cities to entrust the establishment of their laws to foreigners. The modern republics of Italy often imitated this

---

[52] [That kings are gods.]

[53] [Rousseau is using *civil* here to mean "fit to be a citizen." In Latin *civilis* is the adjective from *civis*, "citizen."]

[54] [The quotation comes from Montesquieu's *Considerations on the Causes of the Greatness of the Romans and Their Decline*, ch. 1.]

[55] [See Machiavelli, *Discourses*, bk. 1, chs. 9–10.]

custom. The Republic of Geneva did the same and things worked out well.[56] In its finest age Rome saw the revival within its midst of all the crimes of tyranny and saw itself on the verge of perishing as a result of having united the legislative authority and the sovereign power in the same hands.

Nevertheless, the decemvirs[57] themselves never claimed the right to have any law passed on their authority alone. "Nothing we propose," they would tell the people, "can become law without your consent. Romans, be yourselves the authors of the laws that should bring about your happiness."

He who drafts the laws, therefore, does not or should not have any legislative right. And the populace itself cannot, even if it wanted to, deprive itself of this incommunicable right, because, according to the fundamental compact, only the general will obligates private individuals, and there can never be any assurance that a private will is in conformity with the general will until it has been submitted to the free vote of the people. I have already said this, but it is not a waste of time to repeat it.

Thus we find together in the work of legislation two things that seem incompatible: an undertaking that transcends human capacities and, to execute it, an authority that is nil.

Another difficulty deserves attention. The wise men who want to speak to the common masses in the former's own language rather than in the common vernacular cannot be understood by the masses. For there are a thousand kinds of ideas that are impossible to translate into the language of the populace. Overly general perspectives and overly distant objects are equally beyond its grasp. Each individual, in having no appreciation for any other plan of government but the one that relates to his own private interest, finds it difficult to realize the advantages he ought to draw from the continual privations that good laws impose. For an emerging people to be capable of appreciating the sound maxims of politics and of following the fundamental rules of statecraft, the effect would have to become the cause. The social spirit that ought to be the work of that constitution would have to preside over the writing of the constitution itself. And men would be, prior to the advent of laws, what they ought to become by means of laws. Since, therefore, the legislator is incapable of using either force or reasoning, he must of necessity have recourse to an authority of a different order, which can compel without violence and persuade without convincing.

---

[56] Those who view Calvin simply as a theologian fail to grasp the extent of his genius. The codification of our wise edicts, in which he had a large role, does him as much honor as his *Institutes*. Whatever revolution time may bring out in our religious worship, as long as the love of homeland and of liberty is not extinguished among us, the memory of this great man will never cease to be held sacred.

[57] [A committee of ten established in the Roman Republic for the first time in 451 BC to reform the laws.]

This is what has always forced the fathers of nations to have recourse to the intervention of heaven and to credit the gods with their own wisdom, so that the peoples, subjected to the laws of the state as to those of nature and recognizing the same power in the formation of man and of the city, might obey with liberty and bear with docility the yoke of public felicity.

It is this sublime reason, which transcends the grasp of ordinary men, whose decisions the legislator puts in the mouth of the immortals in order to compel by divine authority those whom human prudence could not move.[58] But not everybody is capable of making the gods speak or of being believed when he proclaims himself their interpreter. The great soul of the legislator is the true miracle that should prove his mission. Any man can engrave stone tablets, buy an oracle, or feign secret intercourse with some divinity, or train a bird to talk in his ear, or find other crude methods of imposing his beliefs on the people. He who knows no more than this may perchance assemble a troupe of lunatics, but he will never found an empire and his extravagant work will soon die with him. Pointless sleights of hand form a fleeting connection; only wisdom can make it lasting. The Judaic law, which still exists, and that of the child of Ishmael, which has ruled half the world for ten centuries, still proclaim today the great men who enunciated them. And while pride-ridden philosophy or the blind spirit of factionalism sees in them nothing but lucky impostors, the true political theoretician admires in their institutions that great and powerful genius which presides over establishments that endure.

We should not, with Warburton,[59] conclude from this that politics and religion have a common object among us, but that in the beginning stages of nations the one serves as an instrument of the other.

Chapter 8
On the People

Just as an architect, before putting up a large building, surveys and tests the ground to see if it can bear the weight, the wise teacher does not begin by laying down laws that are good in themselves. Rather he first examines whether the people for whom they are destined are fitted to bear them. For this reason, Plato refused to give laws to the Arcadians and to the Cyrenians, knowing that these two peoples were rich and could not abide equality. For

---

[58] "And in truth," says Machiavelli, "there has never been among a people a single legislator who, in proposing extraordinary laws, did not have recourse to God, for otherwise they would not be accepted, since there are many benefits known to a prudent man that do not have in themselves evident reasons enabling them to persuade others." *Discourses on Titus Livy*, Book I, Ch. XI. [Rousseau here quotes the Italian.]

[59] [Bishop William Warburton (1698–1779), author of *The Alliance between Church and State* (1736, translated into French in 1742) and *The Divine Legation of Moses* (1737–1741).]

this reason, one finds good laws and evil men in Crete, because Minos had disciplined nothing but a vice-ridden people.

A thousand nations have achieved brilliant earthly success that could never have abided good laws; and even those that could have would have been able to have done so for a very short period of their entire existence. Peoples,[60] like men, are docile only in their youth. As they grow older they become incorrigible. Once customs are established and prejudices have become deeply rooted, it is a dangerous and vain undertaking to want to reform them. The people cannot abide having even their evils touched in order to eliminate them, just like those stupid and cowardly patients who quiver at the sight of a physician.

This is not to say that, just as certain maladies unhinge men's minds and remove from them the memory of the past, one does not likewise sometimes find in the period during which states have existed violent epochs when revolutions do to peoples what certain crises do to individuals, when the horror of the past takes the place of forgetfulness, and when the state, set afire by civil wars, is reborn, as it were, from its ashes and takes on again the vigor of youth as it escapes death's embrace. Such was Sparta at the time of Lycurgus; such was Rome after the Tarquins; and such in our time have been Holland and Switzerland after the expulsion of the tyrants.

But these events are rare. They are exceptions whose cause is always to be found in the particular constitution of the states in question. They cannot take place even twice to the same people, for it can make itself free as long as it is merely barbarous; but it can no longer do so when civil strength is exhausted. At that point internal conflicts can destroy it with revolutions being unable to reestablish it. And as soon as its chains are broken, it falls apart and exists no longer. Henceforward a master is needed, not a liberator. Free peoples, remember this axiom: liberty can be acquired, but it can never be recovered.

For nations, as for men, there is a time of maturity that must be awaited before subjecting them to the laws.[61] But the maturity of a people is not always easily recognized; and if it is anticipated, the work is ruined. One people lends itself to discipline at its inception; another, not even after ten centuries. The Russians will never be truly civilized, since they have been civilized too early. Peter had a genius for imitation.[62] He did not have true genius, the kind that creates and makes everything out of nothing. Some of the things he did were good; most of them were out of place. He saw that his people was barbarous; he did not see that it was not ready for civilization. He

---

[60] [In the 1782 edition, this sentence was revised to read, "Most peoples, like men. . . ."]

[61] [In the 1782 edition, this sentence was revised to read, "Youth is not childhood. For nations, as for men, maturity must be awaited. . . ."]

[62] [Peter the Great (1672–1725), who had been praised by Voltaire in his *History of the Russian Empire under Peter the Great* (1759–1763).]

wanted to civilize it when all it needed was toughening. He wanted to begin by making Germans and Englishmen, when he should have started by making Russians. He prevented his subjects from ever becoming what they could have been by persuading them that they were something they are not. This is exactly how a French tutor trains his pupil to shine for a short time in his childhood, and afterward never to amount to a thing. The Russian Empire would like to subjugate Europe and will itself be subjugated. The Tartars, its subjects or its neighbors, will become its masters and ours. This revolution appears inevitable to me. All the kings of Europe are working in concert to hasten its occurrence.

Chapter 9
The People (continued)

Just as nature has set limits to the stature of a well-formed man, beyond which there are but giants or dwarfs, so too, with regard to the best constitution of a state, there are limits to the size it can have, so as not to be too large to be capable of being well governed, nor too small to be capable of preserving itself on its own. In every body politic there is a *maximum* force that it cannot exceed and that it often falls short of by increasing in size. The more the social bond extends the looser it becomes, and in general a small state is proportionately stronger than a large one.

A thousand reasons prove this maxim. First, administration becomes more difficult over great distances, just as a weight becomes heavier at the end of a longer lever. It also becomes more onerous as the number of administrative levels multiplies, because first each city has its own administration that the populace pays for; each district has its own, again paid for by the people; next each province has one and then the great governments, the satrapies, and vice royalties, requiring a greater cost the higher you go and always at the expense of the unfortunate people. Finally, there is the supreme administration that crushes everyone. All these surcharges continually exhaust the subjects. Far from being better governed by these different orders, they are worse governed than if there were but one administration over them. Meanwhile, hardly any resources remain for meeting emergencies; and when recourse must be made to them, the state is always on the verge of its ruin.

This is not all. Not only does the government have less vigor and quickness in enforcing the observance of the laws, preventing nuisances, correcting abuses, and foreseeing the seditious undertakings that can occur in distant places, but also the populace has less affection for its leaders when it never sees them, for the homeland, which, to its eyes, is like the world, and for its fellow citizens, the majority of whom are foreigners to it. The same laws cannot be suitable to so many diverse provinces that have different customs, live in contrasting climates, and are incapable of enduring the same form of government. Different laws create only trouble and confusion among peoples who live under the same rulers and are in continuous communication. They intermingle and intermarry and, being under the sway of other customs, never know whether their patrimony is actually their own. Talents are hidden; virtues are unknown; vices are unpunished in this multitude of men who are unknown to one another and who are brought together in once place by the seat of supreme administration. The leaders, overwhelmed with work, see nothing for themselves; clerks govern the state. Finally, the measures that need to be taken to maintain the general authority, which so many distant officials want to avoid or mislead, absorb all the public attention. Nothing more remains for the people's happiness, and there remains barely enough for its defense in time of need. And thus a body that is too big for its constitution collapses and perishes, crushed by its own weight.

On the other hand, the state ought to provide itself with a firm foundation to give it solidity, to resist the shocks it is bound to experience, as well as the efforts it will have to make to sustain itself. For all the peoples have a kind of centrifugal force, by which they continually act one against the other and tend to expand at the expense of their neighbors, like Descartes' vortices. Thus the weak risk being soon swallowed up; scarcely any people can preserve itself except by putting itself in a kind of equilibrium with all, which nearly equalizes the pressure on all sides.

It is clear from this that there are reasons for expanding and reasons for contracting, and it is not the least of the statesman's talents to find, between the arguments on the one side and the arguments on the other, the proportion most advantageous to the preservation of the state. In general, it can be said that the former reasons, being merely external and relative, should be subordinated to the latter reasons, which are internal and absolute. A strong, healthy constitution is the first thing one needs to look for, and one should count more on the vigor born of a good government than on the resources furnished by a large territory.

Moreover, there have been states so constituted that the necessity for conquests entered into their very constitution and that, to maintain themselves, they were forced to expand endlessly. Perhaps they congratulated themselves greatly on account of this happy necessity, which nevertheless showed them, together with the limit of their size, the inevitable moment of their fall.

Chapter 10
The People (continued)

A body politic can be measured in two ways, namely, by the size of its territory and by the number of its people. And between these measurements, there is a relationship suitable for giving the state its true greatness. Men are what make up the state, and land is what feeds men. This relationship therefore consists in there being enough land for the maintenance of its inhabitants and as many inhabitants as the land can feed. It is in this proportion that the *maximum* force of a given population size is found. For if there is too much land, its defense is onerous, its cultivation inadequate, and its yield overabundant. This is the proximate cause of defensive wars. If there is not enough land, the state finds itself at the discretion of its neighbors for what it needs as a supplement. This is the proximate cause of offensive wars. Any people whose position provides it no alternative other than between commerce and war is inherently weak. It depends on its neighbors; it depends on events. It never has anything but an uncertain and brief existence. Either it conquers and changes the situation or it is conquered and obliterated. It can keep itself free only by shrinking or expanding.

No one can provide in mathematical terms a fixed relationship between the size of land and the population size that are sufficient for one another, as much because of the differences in the characteristics of the terrain, its degrees of fertility, the nature of its crops, the influence of its climates, as because of the differences to be noted in the temperaments of the men who inhabit the different countries, some of whom consume little in a fertile country, while others consume a great deal on a barren soil. Again, attention must be given to the greater or lesser fertility of women, to what the country can offer that is more or less favorable to the population, to the number of people that the legislator can hope to bring together there through what he establishes. Thus, the legislator should not base his judgment on what he sees but on what he foresees. And he should dwell less upon the present state of the population as upon the state it should naturally attain. Finally, there are a thousand situations where the idiosyncrasies of a place require or permit the acquisition of more land than appears necessary. Thus, there needs to be considerable expansion in mountainous country, where the natural crops—namely, woods and pastures—demand less work; where experience shows that women are more fertile than on the plains; and where a large amount of sloping soil provides only a very small amount of flat land, the only thing that can be counted on for crops. On the other hand, people can draw closer to one another at the seashore, even on rocks and nearly barren sand, since fishing can make up to a great degree for the lack of land crops, since men should be more closely gathered together in order to repulse pirates, and since in addition it is easier to unburden the country of surplus inhabitants by means of colonies.

To these conditions for instituting a people must be added one that cannot be a substitute for any other, but without which all the rest are useless: the enjoyment of prosperity and of peace. For the time when a state is being organized, like the time when a battalion is being formed, is the instant when the body is the least capable of resisting and the easiest to destroy. There would be better resistance at a time of absolute disorder than at a moment of fermentation, when each man is occupied with establishing his own position rather than with the danger. Were a war, famine, or sedition to arise in this time of crisis, the state inevitably is overthrown.

This is not to say that many governments are not established during such storms; but in these instances it is these governments themselves that destroy the state. Usurpers always bring about or choose these times of conflict to use public terror to pass destructive laws that the people would never adopt if they had their composure. The choice of the moment at which a government is to be instituted is one of the surest signs by which the work of a legislator can be distinguished from that of a tyrant.

What people, therefore, are suited for legislation? One that, finding itself bound by some union of origin, interest, or agreement, has not yet felt the true yoke of laws. One that has no customs or superstitions that are deeply rooted. One that does not fear being overpowered by sudden invasion. One that can, without entering into the squabbles of its neighbors, resist each of them single-handed or use the help of one to repel another. One where each member can be known to all, and where there is no need to impose a greater burden on a man than a man can bear. One that can get along without other peoples and without which every other people can get along.[63] One that is neither rich nor poor and can be sufficient unto itself; finally, one that brings together the stability of an ancient people and the docility of a new people. What makes the work of legislation trying is not so much what must be established as what must be destroyed. And what makes success so rare is the impossibility of finding the simplicity of nature together with the needs of society. All these conditions, it is true, are hard to find in combination. Hence few well-constituted states are to be seen.

In Europe there is still one country capable of receiving legislation. It is the island of Corsica. The valor and constancy with which this brave people has regained and defended its liberty would well merit having some wise man teach them how to preserve it. I have a feeling that some day that little island will astonish Europe.

Chapter 11
On the Various Systems of Legislation

If one enquires into precisely wherein the greatest good of all consists, which should be the purpose of every system of legislation, one will find that it boils down to these two principal objects, *liberty* and *equality*. Liberty, because all

---

[63] If there were two neighboring peoples, one being unable to get along without the other, it would be a very tough situation for the former and very dangerous for the latter. In such a case, every wise nation will work very quickly to free the other of its dependency. The Republic of Tlaxcala, enclosed within the Mexican Empire, preferred to do without salt rather than buy it from the Mexicans or even be given it by them without charge. The wise Tlaxcalans saw the trap hidden beneath this generosity. They kept themselves free, and this small state, enclosed within this great empire, was finally the instrument of its ruin.

personal dependence is that much force taken from the body of the state; equality, because liberty cannot subsist without it.

I have already said what civil liberty is. Regarding equality, we need not mean by this word that degrees of power and of wealth are to be absolutely the same, but rather that, with regard to power, it should fall short of any violence and never be exercised except by virtue of rank and laws; and, with regard to wealth, no citizen should be so rich as to be capable of buying another citizen, and none so poor that he is forced to sell himself. This presupposes moderation in goods and power on the part of the great, and moderation in avarice and covetousness[64] on the part of the lowly.

This equality is said to be a speculative fiction that cannot exist in practice. But if abuse is inevitable, does it follow that it should not at least be regulated? It is precisely because the force of things tends always to destroy equality that the force of legislation should always tend to maintain it.

But these general objectives of every good institution should be modified in each country in accordance with the relationships that arise as much from the local situation as from the temperament of the inhabitants. And it is on the basis of these relationships that each people must be assigned a particular institutional system that is the best, not perhaps in itself, but for the state for which it is destined. For example, is the soil barren and unproductive, or the country too confining for its inhabitants? Turn to industry and arts,[65] whose products you will exchange for the foodstuffs you lack. On the contrary, do you live in rich plains and fertile slopes? Do you have a good terrain, but lack inhabitants? Put all your effort into agriculture, which increases the number of men, and chase out the arts that would only bring about the depopulation of the countryside by causing the few inhabitants that there are to flock together around a few points within the whole territory.[66] Do you occupy extensive, convenient coastlines? Cover the sea with vessels; cultivate commerce and navigation. You will have a brilliant and brief existence. Does the sea wash against nothing on your coasts but virtually inaccessible rocks? Remain barbarous and fish eating. You will live in greater tranquility, better perhaps

---

[64] Do you therefore want to give stability to the state? Bring the extremes as close together as possible. Tolerate neither rich men nor beggars. These two estates, which are naturally inseparable, are equally fatal to the common good. From one come the supporters of tyranny, and from the other the tyrants. It is always between them that public liberty becomes a matter of commerce. The one buys it and the other sells it.

[65] [Rousseau's word *arts* means "crafts" here but is translated as "arts" throughout for consistency.]

[66] Any branch of foreign trade, says the Marquis d'Argenson, creates hardly anything more than a false utility for a kingdom in general. It can enrich some private individuals, even some towns, but the nation as a whole gains nothing and the populace is none the better for it.

and certainly happily. In a word, aside from the maxims common to all, each people has within itself some cause that organizes them in a particular way and renders its legislation proper for it alone. Thus it was that long ago the Hebrews and recently the Arabs have had religion as their main objective; the Athenians had letters; Carthage and Tyre, commerce; Rhodes, seafaring; Sparta, war; and Rome, virtue. The author of *The Spirit of the Laws*[67] has shown with a large array of examples the art by which the legislator directs the institution toward each of its objectives.

What makes the constitution of a state truly solid and lasting is that proprieties are observed with such fidelity that the natural relations and the laws are always in agreement on the same points and that the latter serve only to assure, accompany, and rectify the former. But if the legislator is mistaken about his object and takes a principle different from the one arising from the nature of things (whether the one tends toward servitude and the other toward liberty; the one toward riches, the other toward increased population; the one toward peace, the other toward conquests), the laws will weaken imperceptibly, the constitution will be altered, and the state will not cease being agitated until it is destroyed or changed, and invincible nature has regained her empire.

Chapter 12
Classification of the Laws

To set the whole in order or to give the commonwealth the best possible form, there are various relations to consider. First, the action of the entire body acting upon itself, that is, the relationship of the whole to the whole or of the sovereign to the state, and this relationship, as we shall see later, is composed of relationships of intermediate terms.

The laws regulating this relationship bear the name *political laws* and are also called *fundamental laws*, not without reason if these laws are wise. For if there is only one good way of organizing each state, the people who have found it should stand by it. But if the established order is evil, why should one accept as fundamental laws that prevent it from being good? Besides, a people is in any case always in a position to change its laws, even the best laws. For if it wishes to do itself harm, who has the right to prevent it from doing so?

The second relation is that of the members to each other or to the entire body. And this relationship should be as small as possible in regard to the former and as large as possible in regard to the latter, so that each citizen would be perfectly independent of all the others and excessively dependent upon the city. This always takes place by the same means, for only the force of the state brings about the liberty of its members. It is from this second relationship that civil laws arise.

---

[67] [Montesquieu, in *Spirit of the Laws*, bk. 11, ch. 5.]

We may consider a third sort of relation between man and law, namely, that of disobedience and penalty. And this gives rise to the establishment of criminal laws, which basically are not so much a particular kind of law as the sanction for all the others.

To these three sorts of law is added a fourth, the most important of all. It is not engraved on marble or bronze, but in the hearts of citizens. It is the true constitution of the state. Every day it takes on new forces. When other laws grow old and die away, it revives and replaces them, preserves a people in the spirit of its institution, and imperceptibly substitutes the force of habit for that of authority. I am speaking of mores, customs, and especially of opinion, a part of the law unknown to our statesmen but one on which depends the success of all the others:[68] a part with which the great legislator secretly occupies himself, though he seems to confine himself to the particular regulations that are merely the arching of the vault, whereas mores, slower to arise, form in the end its immovable keystone.

Among these various classes, only political laws, which constitute the form of government, are relevant to my subject.

END OF THE SECOND BOOK

BOOK III

Before speaking of the various forms of government, let us try to determine the precise meaning of this word, which has not as yet been explained very well.

Chapter 1
On Government in General

I am warning the reader that this chapter should be read carefully and that I do not know the art of being clear to those who do not want to be attentive.

Every free action has two causes that come together to produce it. The one is moral, namely, the will that determines the act; the other is physical, namely, the power that executes it. When I walk toward an object, I must first want to go there. Second, my feet must take me there. A paralyzed man who wants to walk or an agile man who does not want to walk will both remain where they are. The body politic has the same moving causes. The same distinction can be made between force and will, the one under the name

---

[68] [The word translated here as "statesmen" is *politiques*, which refers ambiguously to political leaders and political theorists. Among political theorists, Pierre Bayle had been the first to stress the importance of the law of opinion in maintaining social order in his *Diverse Thoughts on the Comet* (1682).]

legislative power and the other under the name *executive power*. Nothing is done or at least ought to be done without their concurrence.

We have seen that legislative power belongs to the people and can belong to it alone. On the contrary, it is easy to see by the principles established above that executive power cannot belong to the people at large in its role as legislator or sovereign, since this power consists solely of particular acts that are not within the province of the law, nor consequently of the sovereign, none of whose acts can avoid being laws.

Therefore the public force must have an agent of its own that unifies it and gets it working in accordance with the directions of the general will, that serves as a means of communication between the state and the sovereign, and that accomplishes in the public person just about what the union of soul and body accomplishes in man. This is the reason for having government in the state, something often badly confused with the sovereign, of which it is merely the servant.

What then is the government? An intermediate body established between the subjects and the sovereign for their mutual communication and charged with the execution of the laws and the preservation of liberty, both civil and political.

The members of this body are called magistrates or *kings*, that is to say, *governors*, and the entire body bears the name *prince*.[69] Therefore, those who claim that the act by which a people submits itself to leaders is not a contract are quite correct. It is absolutely nothing but a commission, an employment in which the leaders, as simple officials of the sovereign, exercise in its own name the power with which it has entrusted them. The sovereign can limit, modify, or reappropriate this power as it pleases, since the alienation of such a right is incompatible with the nature of the social body and contrary to the purpose of the association.

Therefore, I call *government* or supreme administration the legitimate exercise of executive power; I call *prince* or *magistrate* the man or the body charged with that administration.

In government one finds the intermediate forces whose relationships make up that of the whole to the whole or of the sovereign to the state. This last relationship can be represented as one between the extremes of a continuous proportion, whose proportional mean is the government.[70] The government receives from the sovereign the orders it gives the people, and for the state to be in good equilibrium, there must, all things considered, be an equality

---

[69] Thus in Venice the college is given the name *Most Serene Prince* even when the doge is not present.

[70] [In the language of eighteenth-century mathematics, a continuous proportion is one in which there are two ratios, but the second term of the first is identical to the first term of the second. Thus, if we have sovereign government and government state, we have a continuous proportion whose proportional mean is the government and whose extremes are sovereign and state.]

between the output or the power of the government, taken by itself, and the output or power of the citizens, who are sovereigns on the one hand and subjects on the other.

Moreover, none of these three terms could be altered without the simultaneous destruction of the proportion. If the sovereign wishes to govern, or if the magistrate wishes to give laws, or if the subjects refuse to obey, disorder replaces rule, force and will no longer act in concert, and thus the state dissolves and falls into despotism or anarchy. Finally, since there is only one proportional mean between each relationship, there is only one good government possible for a state. But since a thousand events can change the relationships of a people, different governments can be good not only for different peoples but also for the same people at different times.

In trying to provide an idea of the various relationships that can obtain between these two extremes, I will take as an example the number of people, since it is a more easily expressed relationship.

Suppose the state is composed of ten thousand citizens. The sovereign can only be considered collectively and as a body. But each private individual in his position as a subject is regarded as an individual. Thus the sovereign is to the subject as ten thousand is to one. In other words, each member of the state has as his share only one ten-thousandth of the sovereign authority, even though he is totally in subjection to it. If the populace is made up of a hundred thousand men, the condition of the subjects does not change, and each bears equally the entire dominion of the laws, while his vote, reduced to one hundred-thousandth, has ten times less influence in the drafting of them. In that case, since the subject always remains one, the ratio of the sovereign to the subject increases in proportion to the number of citizens. Whence it follows that the larger the state becomes, the less liberty there is.

When I say that the ratio increases, I mean that it diverges from equality. Thus the greater the ratio is in the sense employed by geometricians, the less relationship there is in the everyday sense of the word. In the former sense, the ratio, seen in terms of quantity, is measured by the quotient;[71] in the latter sense, ratio, seen in terms of identity, is reckoned by similarity.

Now the less relationship there is between private wills and the general will, that is, between mores and the laws, the more repressive force ought to increase. Therefore, in order to be good, the government must be relatively stronger in proportion as the populace is more numerous.

On the other hand, as the growth of the state gives the trustees of the public authority more temptations and the means of abusing their power, the more the force the government must have in order to contain the people, the more the force the sovereign must have in its turn in order to contain the

[71] [The quotient here is the second term of a ratio divided by the first. Thus in the ratio 2 : 8, the quotient is 4.]

government. I am speaking here not of an absolute force but of the relative force of the various parts of the state.

It follows from this twofold relationship that the continuous proportion between the sovereign, the prince, and the people is in no way an arbitrary idea, but a necessary consequence of the nature of the body politic. It also follows that since one of the extremes, namely, the people as subject, is fixed and represented by unity, whenever the doubled ratio increases or decreases, the simple ratio increases or decreases in like fashion, and that as a consequence the middle term is changed.[72] This makes it clear that there is no unique and absolute constitution of government but that there can be as many governments of differing natures as there are states of differing sizes.

If, in ridiculing this system, someone were to say that in order to find this proportional mean and to form the body of the government, it is necessary merely, in my opinion, to derive the square root of the number of people, I would reply that here I am taking this number only as an example; that the relationships I am speaking of are not measured solely by the number of men but in general by the quantity of action, which is the combination of a multitude of causes; and that, in addition, if to express myself in fewer words I borrow for the moment the terminology of geometry, I nevertheless am not unaware of the fact that geometrical precision has no place in moral quantities.

The government is on a small scale what the body politic that contains it is on a large scale. It is a moral person endowed with certain faculties, active like the sovereign and passive like the state, and capable of being broken down into other similar relationships whence there arises as a consequence a new proportion and yet again another within this one according to the order of tribunals, until an indivisible middle term is reached, that is, a single leader or supreme magistrate, who can be represented in the midst of this progression as the unity between the series of fractions and that of whole numbers.

Without involving ourselves in this multiplication of terms, let us content ourselves with considering the government as a new body in the state, distinct from the people and sovereign and intermediate between them.

The essential difference between these two bodies is that the state exists by itself while the government exists only through the sovereign. Thus the dominant will of the prince is not or should not be anything other than the general will or the law. His force is merely the public force concentrated in him. As soon as he wants to derive from himself some absolute and independent act, the bond that links everything together begins to come loose. If it should finally happen that the prince had a private will more active than that

[72] [Take the continuous proportion 8 : 2 and 2 : 4. The doubled ratio, in the language of the time, is (8×2) divided by (2×4). If the ratios were 4 : 2 and 2 : 1, the doubled ratio would be (4×2) divided by 2, i.e., 4; that is, it would be the same as the first term. Moreover, the first term would be the square of the middle terms.]

of the sovereign and that he had made use of some of the public force that is available to him in order to obey this private will, so that there would be, so to speak, two sovereigns—one de jure and the other de facto—at that moment the social union would vanish and the body politic would be dissolved.

However, for the body of the government to have an existence, a real life that distinguishes it from the body of the state, and for all its members to be able to act in concert and to fulfill the purpose for which it is instituted, there must be a particular *self*, a sensibility common to all its members, a force or will of its own that tends toward its preservation.

This particular existence presupposes assemblies, councils, a power to deliberate and decide, rights, titles, and privileges that belong exclusively to the prince and that render the condition of the magistrate more honorable in proportion as it is more onerous. The difficulties lie in the manner in which this subordinate whole is so organized within the whole that it in no way alters the general constitution by strengthening its own, that it always distinguishes its particular force, which is intended for its own preservation, from the public force intended for the preservation of the state, and that, in a word, it is always ready to sacrifice the government to the people and not the people to the government.

In addition, although the artificial body of the government is the work of another artificial body and has, in a sense, only a borrowed and subordinate life, this does not prevent it from being capable of acting with more or less vigor or speed or from enjoying, so to speak, more or less robust health. Finally, without departing directly from the purpose of its institution, it can deviate more or less from it, according to the manner in which it is constituted.

From all these differences arise the diverse relationships that the government should have with the body of the state, according to the accidental and particular relationships by which the state itself is modified. For often the government that is best in itself will become the most vicious if its relationships are not altered according to the defects of the body politic to which it belongs.

Chapter 2
On the Principle That Constitutes the Various Forms of Government

In order to lay out the general cause of these differences, a distinction must be made here between the prince and the government, just as I distinguished earlier between the state and the sovereign.

The body of the magistrates can be made up of a larger or smaller number of members. We have said that the ratio of the sovereign to the subjects was greater in proportion as the populace was more numerous, and by a manifest analogy we can say the same thing about the government in relation to the magistrates.

Since the total force of the government is always that of the state, it does not vary. Whence it follows that the more of this force it uses on its own members, the less that is left to it for acting on the whole populace.

Therefore, the more numerous the magistrates, the weaker the government. Since this maxim is fundamental, let us attempt to explain it more clearly.

We can distinguish in the person of the magistrate three essentially different wills. First, the individual's own will, which tends only to its own advantage. Second, the common will of the magistrates, which is uniquely related to the advantage of the prince. This latter can be called the corporate will and is general in relation to the government and particular in relation to the state, of which the government forms a part. Third, the will of the people or the sovereign will, which is general both in relation to the state considered as the whole and in relation to the government considered as a part of the whole.

In a perfect act of legislation, the private or individual will should be nonexistent; the corporate will proper to the government should be very subordinate; and consequently the general or sovereign will should always be dominant and the unique rule of all the others.

According to the natural order, on the contrary, these various wills become more active in proportion as they are the more concentrated. Thus the general will is always the weakest, the corporate will has second place, and the private will is first of all, so that in the government each member is first himself, then a magistrate, and then a citizen—a gradation directly opposite to the one required by the social order.

Granting this, let us suppose the entire government is in the hands of one single man. In that case the private will and the corporate will are perfectly united, and consequently the latter is at the highest degree of intensity it can reach. But since the use of force is dependent upon the degree of will, and since the absolute force of the government does not vary one bit, it follows that the most active of governments is that of one single man.

On the contrary, let us suppose we are uniting the government to the legislative authority. Let us make the sovereign the prince and all the citizens that many magistrates. Then the corporate will, confused with the general will, will have no more activity than the latter, and will leave the private will all its force. Thus the government, always with the same absolute force, will have its *minimum* relative force or activity.

These relationships are incontestable, and there are still other considerations that serve to confirm them. We see, for example, that each magistrate is more active in his body than each citizen is in his and consequently, that the private will has much more influence on the acts of the government than on those of the sovereign. For each magistrate is nearly always charged with the responsibility for some function of government whereas each citizen, taken by himself, exercises no function of sovereignty. Moreover, the more the state is extended, the more its real force increases, although it does not increase in proportion to its size. But if the state remains the same, the magistrates may be multiplied as much as one likes without the government acquiring any greater real force, since this force is that of the state, whose dimensions [as we have just stipulated] remain the same. Thus the relative force or activity of the government diminishes without its absolute or real force being able to increase.

It is also certain that the execution of public business becomes slower in proportion as more people are charged with the responsibility for it, that in attaching too much importance to prudence, too little importance is attached to fortune, opportunities are missed, and the fruits of deliberation are often lost by dint of deliberation.

I have just proved that the government becomes slack in proportion as the magistrates are multiplied; and I have previously proved that the more numerous the people, the greater should be the increase of repressive force. Whence it follows that the ratio of the magistrate to the government should be the inverse of the ratio of the subjects to the sovereign; that is to say, the more the state increases in size, the more the government should shrink, so that the number of leaders decreases in proportion to the increase in the number of people.

I should add that I am speaking here only about the relative force of the government and not about its rectitude. For, on the contrary, the more numerous the magistrates, the more closely the corporate will approaches the general will, whereas under a single magistrate, the same corporate will is, as I have said, merely a particular will. Thus what can be gained on the one hand is lost on the other, and the art of the legislator is to know how to determine the point at which the government's will and force, always in a reciprocal proportion, are combined in the relationship that is most advantageous to the state.

Chapter 3
Classification of Governments

We have seen in the previous chapter why the various kinds or forms of government are distinguished by the number of members that compose them. It remains to be seen in this chapter how this classification is made.

In the first place, the sovereign can entrust the government to the entire people or to the majority of the people, so that there are more citizens who are magistrates than who are ordinary private citizens. This form of government is given the name *democracy*.

Or else it can restrict the government to the hands of a small number, so that there are more ordinary citizens than magistrates, and this form is called *aristocracy*.

Finally, it can concentrate the entire government in the hands of a single magistrate from whom all the others derive their power. This third form is the most common and is called *monarchy* or royal government.

It should be noted that all these forms, or at least the first two, can be had in greater or lesser degrees and even have a rather wide range. For democracy can include the entire populace or be restricted to half. Aristocracy, for its part, can be indeterminately restricted from half the people down to the smallest number. Even royalty can be had in varying levels of distribution. Sparta always had two kings, as required by its constitution; and the Roman Empire is known to have had up to eight emperors at a time, without it being possible to say that the empire was divided. Thus there is a point at which each form of government is indistinguishable from the next, and it is apparent that, under just three names, government can take on as many diverse forms as the state has citizens.

Moreover, since this same government can, in certain respects, be subdivided into other parts, one administered in one way, another in another, there can result from the combination of these three forms a multitude of mixed forms, each of which can be multiplied by all the simple forms.

There has always been a great deal of argument over the best form of government without considering that each one of them is best in certain cases and the worst in others.

If the number of supreme magistrates in the different states ought to be in inverse ratio to that of the citizens, it follows that in general democratic government is suited to small states, aristocratic government to states of intermediate size, and monarchical government to large ones. This rule is derived immediately from the principle; but how is one to count the multitude of circumstances that can furnish exceptions?

Chapter 4
On Democracy

He who makes the law knows better than anyone else how it should be executed and interpreted. It seems therefore to be impossible to have a better constitution than one in which the executive power is united to the legislative power. But this is precisely what renders such a government inadequate in certain respects, since things that should be distinguished are not, and the prince and sovereign, being merely the same person, form, as it were, only a government without a government.

It is not good for the one who makes the laws to execute them, nor for the body of the people to turn its attention away from general perspectives in order to give it[73] to particular objects. Nothing is more dangerous than the

---

[73] [Following most modern editions in assuming that Rousseau's *les donner* is a mistake for *la donner*.]

influence of private interests on public affairs; and the abuse of the laws by the government is a lesser evil than the corruption of the legislator, which is the inevitable outcome of particular perspectives. In such a situation, since the state has been altered in its essence, all reform becomes impossible. A people that would never misuse the government would never misuse independence. A people that would always govern well would not need to be governed.

Taking the term in the strict sense, a true democracy has never existed and never will. It is contrary to the natural order that the majority governs and the minority is governed. It is unimaginable that the people would remain constantly assembled to handle public affairs, and it is readily apparent that it could not establish commissions for this purpose without changing the form of administration.

In fact, I believe I can lay down as a principle that when the functions of the government are shared among several tribunals, those with the fewest members sooner or later acquire the greatest authority, if only because of the facility in expediting public business that brings this about naturally.

Besides, how many things that are difficult to unite are presupposed by this government? First, a very small state where it is easy for the people to gather together and where each citizen can easily know all the others. Second, a great simplicity of mores, which is an obstacle to the proliferation of public business and thorny discussions. Next, a high degree of equality in ranks and fortunes, without which equality in rights and authority cannot subsist for long. Finally, little or no luxury, for luxury either is the effect of wealth or makes wealth necessary. It simultaneously corrupts both the rich and the poor, the one by possession, the other by covetousness. It sells the homeland to softness and vanity. It takes all its citizens from the state in order to make them slaves to one another, and all of them to opinion.

This is why a famous author[74] has made virtue the principle of the republic. For all these conditions could not subsist without virtue. But owing to his failure to have made the necessary distinctions, this great genius often lacked precision and sometimes clarity. And he did not realize that since the sovereign authority is everywhere the same, the same principle should have a place in every well-constituted state, though in a greater or lesser degree, it is true, according to the form of government.

Let us add that no government is so subject to civil wars and internal agitations as a democratic or popular one, since there is none that tends so forcefully and continuously to change its form or that demands greater vigilance and courage if it is to be maintained in its own form. Above all, it is under this constitution that the citizen ought to arm himself with force and constancy and to say each day of his life from the bottom of his heart what

---

[74] [Montesquieu, in *Spirit of the Laws*, bk. 3, ch. 3.]

a virtuous Palatine[75] said in the Diet of Poland: *Better to have liberty fraught with danger than servitude in peace.*

Were there a people of gods, it would govern itself democratically. So perfect a government is not suited to men.

Chapter 5
On Aristocracy

We have here two very distinct moral persons, namely, the government and the sovereign, and consequently two general wills, one in relation to all the citizens, the other only for the members of the administration.

Thus, although the government can regulate its internal administration as it chooses, it can never speak to the people except in the name of the sovereign, that is to say, in the name of the populace itself. This is something never to be forgotten.

The first societies governed themselves aristocratically. The leaders of families deliberated among themselves about public affairs. Young people deferred without difficulty to the authority of experience. This is the origin of the words *priests, ancients, senate,* and *elders.* The savages of North America still govern themselves that way to this day and are very well governed.

But to the extent that inequality occasioned by social institutions came to prevail over natural inequality, wealth or power[76] was preferred to age, and aristocracy became elective. Finally, the transmission of the father's power, together with his goods, to his children created patrician families; the government was made hereditary, and we find senators who are only twenty years old.

There are therefore three sorts of aristocracy: natural, elective, and hereditary. The first is suited only to simple people; the third is the worst of any government. The second is the best; it is aristocracy properly so called.

In addition to the advantage of the distinction between the two powers, aristocracy has that of the choice of its members. For in popular government all the citizens are born magistrates; however, this type of government limits them to a small number, and they become magistrates only through election,[77] a means by which probity, enlightenment, experience, and all the

---

[75] The Palatine of Posen, father of the King of Poland, Duke of Lorraine. [Rousseau quotes in Latin the maxim that follows.]

[76] It is clear that among the ancients the word *optimates* does not mean the best but the most powerful.

[77] It is of great importance that laws should regulate the form of the election of magistrates, for if it is left to the will of the prince, it is impossible to avoid falling into a hereditary aristocracy, as has taken place in the republics of Venice and Berne. Thus the former has long been a state in dissolution, while the latter maintains itself

other reasons for public preference and esteem are so many new guarantees of being well governed.

Furthermore, assemblies are more conveniently held, public business better discussed and carried out with more orderliness and diligence, the reputation of the state is better sustained abroad by venerable senators than by a multitude that is unknown or despised.

In a word, it is the best and most natural order for the wisest to govern the multitude, provided it is certain that they will govern for its profit and not for their own. There is no need for multiplying devices uselessly or for doing with twenty thousand men what one hundred handpicked men can do even better. But it must be noted here that the corporate interest begins to direct the public force in less strict a conformity with the rule of the general will and that another inevitable tendency removes from the laws a part of the executive power.

With regard to the circumstances that are specifically suitable, a state must not be so small nor its people so simple and upright that the execution of the laws follows immediately from the public will, as is the case in a good democracy. Nor must a nation be so large that the leaders, scattered about in order to govern it, can each play the sovereign in his own department and begin by making themselves independent in order finally to become the masters.

But if aristocracy requires somewhat fewer virtues than popular government, it also demands others that are proper to it, such as moderation among the wealthy and contentment among the poor. For it appears that rigorous equality would be out of place here. It was not observed even in Sparta.

Moreover, if this form of government carries with it a certain inequality of wealth, this is simply in order that in general the administration of public business may be entrusted to those who are best able to give all their time to it, but not, as Aristotle claims,[78] in order that the rich may always be given preference. On the contrary, it is important that an opposite choice should occasionally teach the people that more important reasons for preference are to be found in a man's merit than in his wealth.

Chapter 6
On Monarchy

So far, we have considered the prince as a moral and collective person, united by the force of laws, and as the trustee of the executive power in the state. We have now to consider this power when it is joined together in the hands

---

through the extreme wisdom of its senate. It is a very honorable and very dangerous exception.

[78] [This is a misrepresentation of Aristotle, who holds that the rich are given preference in an oligarchy.]

of a natural person, of a real man, who alone has the right to dispose of it in accordance with the laws. Such a person is called a monarch or a king.

In utter contrast to the other forms of administration where a collective entity represents an individual, in this form of administration an individual represents a collective entity, so that the moral unity constituting the prince is at the same time a physical unity in which all the faculties that are combined by the law in the other forms of administration with such difficulty are found naturally combined.

Thus the will of the people, the will of the prince, the public force of the state, and the particular force of the government all respond to the same moving agent; all the controls of the machine are in the same hand; everything moves toward the same end; there are no opposing movements that are at cross-purposes with one another; and no constitution is imaginable in which a lesser effort produces a more considerable action. Archimedes sitting serenely on the shore and effortlessly pulling a huge vessel through the waves is what comes to mind when I think of a capable monarch governing his vast states from his private study and making everything move while appearing himself to be immovable.

But if there is no government that has more vigor, there is none where the private will has greater sway and more easily dominates the others. Everything moves toward the same end, it is true; but this end is not that of public felicity, and the very force of the administration unceasingly operates to the detriment of the state.[79]

Kings want to be absolute, and from a distance one cries out to them that the best way to be so is to make themselves loved by their peoples. This maxim is very noble and even very true in certain respects. Unfortunately, it will always be an object of derision in courts. The power that comes from the peoples' love is undoubtedly the greatest, but it is precarious and conditional. Princes will never be satisfied with it. The best kings want to be able to be wicked if it pleases them, without ceasing to be the masters. A political sermonizer might well say to them that since the people's force is their force, their greatest interest is that the people should be flourishing, numerous, and formidable. They know perfectly well that this is not true. Their personal interest is first of all that the people should be weak and miserable and incapable of ever resisting them. I admit that, assuming the subjects were always in perfect submission, the interest of the prince would then be for the people to be powerful, so that this power, being his own, would render him formidable in the eyes of his neighbors. But since this interest is merely secondary and subordinate, and since the two assumptions are incompatible, it is natural that the princes should always give preference to the maxim that

[79] [Although Rousseau recognized monarchy as being, in principle, a legitimate form of government, this and the next paragraph make clear his profound opposition to it. One may conclude that Rousseau was, in some measure, following Machiavelli's example and hiding his love of liberty.]

is the most immediately useful to them. This is the point that Samuel made so forcefully to the Hebrews and that Machiavelli has made apparent. Under the pretext of teaching kings, he has taught important lessons to the peoples. Machiavelli's *The Prince* is the book for republicans.[80]

We have found, through general relationships, that the monarchy is suited only to large states, and we find this again in examining the monarchy itself. The more numerous the public administration, the more the ratio of the prince to subjects diminishes and approaches equality, so that this ratio is one or equality itself in a democracy. This same ratio increases in proportion as the government is restricted, and is at its *maximum* when the government is in the hands of a single man. Then there is too great a distance between the prince and the people, and the state lacks cohesiveness. In order to bring about this cohesiveness, there must therefore be intermediate orders;[81] there must be princes, grandees, and a nobility to fill them. Now none of this is suited to a small state, which is ruined by all these social levels.

But if it is difficult for a large state to be well governed, it is much harder still for it to be well governed by just one man, and everyone knows what happens when the king appoints substitutes.

An essential and inevitable defect, which will always place the monarchical form of government below the republican form, is that in the latter form the public voice hardly ever raises to the highest positions men who are not enlightened and capable and who would not fill their positions with honor.[82] On the contrary, those who attain these positions in monarchies are most often petty bunglers, petty swindlers, petty intriguers, whose petty talents, which cause them to attain high positions at court, serve only to display their incompetence to the public as soon as they reach these positions. The populace is much less often in error in its choice than the prince, and a man of real merit in the ministry is almost as rare as a fool at the head of a republican government. Thus, when by some happy chance one of these men who are born to govern takes the helm of public business in a monarchy that has nearly been sunk by this crowd of fine managers, there is utter amazement at the resources he finds, and his arrival marks an era in the history of the country.[83]

---

[80] [The following was inserted in the 1782 edition: "Machiavelli was a decent man and a good citizen. But since he was attached to the house of Medici, he was forced during the oppression of his homeland to disguise his love of liberty. The very choice of his execrable hero makes clear enough his hidden intention. And the contrast between the maxims of his book *The Prince* and those of his *Discourses on Titus Livy* and of his *History of Florence* shows that this profound political theorist has until now had only superficial or corrupt readers. The court of Rome has sternly prohibited his book. I can well believe it; it is the court he most clearly depicts."]

[81] [Cf. Montesquieu, *Spirit of the Laws*, bk. 2, ch. 4.]

[82] [Cf. Montesquieu, *Spirit of the Laws*, bk. 2, ch. 2; the same point is made by Machiavelli.]

[83] [This sentence was added as the book went through the press (letter to Rey, January 6, 1762) and was intended as praise of the leading minister of the day, Choiseul. Rousseau (mistakenly) hoped it would encourage him to oppose any move to ban the *Social Contract* in France.]

For a monarchical state to be capable of being well governed, its size or extent must be proportionate to the faculties of the one who governs. It is easier to conquer than to rule. With a long enough lever it is possible for a single finger to make the world shake; but holding it in place requires the shoulders of Hercules. However small a state may be, the prince is nearly always too small for it. When, on the contrary, it happens that the state is too small for its leader, which is quite rare, it is still poorly governed, since the leader, always pursuing his grand schemes, forgets the interests of the peoples, making them no less wretched through the abuse of talents he has too much of than does a leader who is limited for want of what he lacks. A kingdom must, so to speak, expand or contract with each reign, depending on the ability of the prince. Nevertheless, since the talents of a senate have a greater degree of stability, the state can have permanent boundaries without the administration working any less well.

The most obvious disadvantage of the government of just one man is the lack of that continuous line of succession that forms an unbroken bond of unity in the other two forms of government. When one king dies, another is needed. Elections leave dangerous intervals and are stormy. And unless the citizens have a disinterestedness and integrity that seldom accompany this form of government, intrigue and corruption enter the picture. It is difficult for one to whom the state has sold itself not to sell it in turn and reimburse himself at the expense of the weak for the money extorted from him by the powerful. Sooner or later everything becomes venal under such an administration, and then the peace enjoyed under kings is worse than the disorders of the interregna.

What has been done to prevent these ills? Crowns have been made hereditary within certain families, and an order of succession has been established that prevents all dispute when kings die. That is to say, by substituting the disadvantage of regencies for that of elections, an apparent tranquility has been preferred to a wise administration, the risk of having children, monsters, or imbeciles for leaders has been preferred to having to argue over the choice of good kings. No consideration has been given to the fact that in being thus exposed to the risk of the alternative, nearly all the odds are against them. There was a lot of sense in what Dionysius the Younger said in reply to his father, who, while reproaching his son for some shameful action, said, "Have I given you such an example?" "Ah," replied the son, "but your father was not king."

When a man has been elevated to command others, everything conspires to deprive him of justice and reason. A great deal of effort is made, it is said, to teach young princes the art of ruling. It does not appear that this education does them any good. It would be better to begin by teaching them the art of obeying. The greatest kings whom history celebrates were not brought up to reign. It is a science that one is never less in possession of than after one has learned it too much, and that one acquires better by obeying than by commanding. "For the most useful as well as the shortest method of finding out what is good and what is bad is to consider what you would have wished or not wished to have happened under another prince."[84]

One result of this lack of coherence is the instability of the royal form of government, which, now regulated by one plan now by another according to the character of the ruling prince or of those who rule for him, cannot have a fixed objective for very long or a consistent policy. This variation always causes the state to drift from maxim to maxim, from project to project, and does not take place in the other forms of government, where the prince is always the same. It is also apparent that in general, if there is more cunning in a royal court, there is more wisdom in a senate and that republics proceed toward their objectives by means of policies that are more consistent and better followed. However, each revolution in the ministry produces a revolution in the state, since the maxim common to all ministers and nearly all kings is to do the reverse of their predecessor in everything.

From this same incoherence we derive the solution to a sophism that is very familiar to royalist political theorists. Not only is civil government compared to domestic government and the prince to the father of the family (an error already refuted), but this magistrate is also liberally given all the virtues he might need, and it is always presupposed that the prince is what he ought to be. With the help of this presupposition, the royal form of government is obviously preferable to any other, since it is unquestionably the strongest; and it lacks only a corporate will that is more in conformity with the general will in order to be the best as well.

But if, according to Plato,[85] a king by nature is such a rare person, how many times will nature and fortune converge to crown him; and if a royal education necessarily corrupts those who receive it, what is to be hoped from a series of men who have been brought up to reign? Surely then it is deliberate self-deception to confuse the royal form of government with that of a good king. To see what this form of government is in itself, we need to consider it under princes who are incompetent or wicked, for either they come to the throne wicked or incompetent or else the throne makes them so.

These difficulties have not escaped the attention of our authors, but they have not been troubled by them. The remedy, they say, is to obey without a murmur. God in his anger gives us bad kings, and they must be endured as punishments from heaven. No doubt this sort of talk is edifying; however, I do not know but that it belongs more in a pulpit than in a book on political theory. What is to be said of a physician who promises miracles and whose art consists entirely of exhorting his sick patient to practice patience? It is quite obvious that we must put up with a bad government when that is what we have. The question would be how to find a good one.

---

[84] Tacitus, *Histories*, Book I. [Rousseau here quotes the Latin.]

[85] *The Statesman.*

Chapter 7
On Mixed Government

Strictly speaking, there is no such thing as a simple form of government. A single leader must have subordinate magistrates; a popular government must have a leader. Thus in the distribution of the executive power there is always a gradation from the greater to the lesser number, with the difference that sometimes the greater number depends on the few, and sometimes the few depend on the greater number.

At times the distribution is equal, either when the constitutive parts are in a state of mutual dependence, as in the government of England, or when the authority of each part is independent but imperfect, as in Poland.[86] This latter form is bad, since there is no unity in the government and the state lacks a bond of unity.

Which one is better, a simple or a mixed form of government? A question much debated among political theorists, to which the same reply must be given that I gave above regarding every form of government.

In itself the simple form of government is the best, precisely because it is simple. But when the executive power is not sufficiently dependent upon the legislative power, that is to say, when there is a closer relationship between the prince and the sovereign than there is between the people and the prince, this defect in the proportion must be remedied by dividing the government; for then all of its parts have no less authority over the subjects, and their division makes all of them together less forceful against the sovereign.

The same disadvantage can also be prevented through the establishment of intermediate magistrates, who, by being utterly separate from the government, serve merely to balance the two powers and to maintain their respective rights. In that case, the government is not mixed; it is tempered.

The opposite difficulty can be remedied by similar means. Thus when the government is too slack, tribunals can be set up to give it a concentrated focus. This is done in all democracies. In the first case the government is divided in order to weaken it, and in the second to strengthen it. For the *maximum* of force and weakness are both found in the simple forms of government, while the mixed forms of government provide an intermediate amount of strength.

---

[86] [Rousseau has in mind Montesquieu's account of the English constitution; in Poland (or at least so Rousseau believed) ministers were in effect unaccountable and could do as they pleased.]

Chapter 8
That Not All Forms of Government Are Suited to All Countries

Since liberty is not a fruit of every climate, it is not within the reach of all peoples. The more one meditates on this principle established by Montesquieu,[87] the more one is aware of its truth. The more one contests it, the more occasions there are for establishing it by means of new proofs.

In all the governments in the world, the public person consumes but produces nothing. Whence therefore does it get the substance it consumes? It is from the labor of its members. It is the surplus of private individuals that produces what is needed by the public. Whence it follows that the civil state can subsist only as long as men's labor produces more than they need.

Now this surplus is not the same in every country in the world. In many countries it is considerable; in others it is moderate; in others it is nil; in still others it is negative.

This ratio depends on the fertility of the climate, the sort of labor the land requires, the nature of its products, the force of its inhabitants, the greater or lesser consumption they need, and many other similar ratios of which it is composed.

On the other hand, not all governments are of the same nature. They are more or less voracious; and the differences are founded on this added principle that the greater the distance the public contributions have to travel from their source, the more onerous they are. It is not on the basis of the amount of the taxes that this burden is to be measured, but on the basis of the path they have to travel in order to return to the hands from which they came. When this circulation is prompt and well established, it is unimportant whether one pays little or a great deal. The populace is always rich and the finances are always in good shape. On the contrary, however little the populace gives, when this small amount does not return, it is soon wiped out by continual giving. The state is never rich and the populace is always destitute.

It follows from this that the greater the distance between the people and the government, the more onerous the taxes become. Thus in a democracy the populace is the least burdened; in an aristocracy it is more so; in a monarchy it bears the heaviest weight. Monarchy, therefore, is suited only to wealthy nations; aristocracy to states of moderate wealth and size; democracy to states that are small and poor.

In fact, the more one reflects on it, the more one finds in this the difference between free and monarchical states. In the former, everything is used for the common utility. In the latter, the public and private forces are reciprocal, the one being augmented by the weakening of the other. Finally, instead of governing subjects in order to make them happy, despotism makes them miserable in order to govern them.

---

[87] [Montesquieu, *Spirit of the Laws*, especially bk. 17.]

Thus in each climate there are natural causes on the basis of which one can assign the form of government that the force of the climate requires and can even say what kind of inhabitants it should have. Barren and unproductive lands, where the product is not worth the labor, ought to remain uncultivated and deserted or peopled only by savages. Places where men's labor yields only what is necessary ought to be inhabited by barbarous peoples; in places such as these, all polity[88] would be impossible. Places where the surplus of products over labor is moderate are suited to free peoples. Those where an abundant and fertile soil produces a great deal in return for a small amount of labor require a monarchical form of government, in order that the subject's excess of surplus may be consumed by the prince's luxurious living. For it is better for this excess to be absorbed by the government than dissipated by private individuals. I realize that there are exceptions; but these exceptions themselves prove the rule, in that sooner or later they produce revolutions that restore things to the order of nature.

General laws should always be distinguished from the particular causes that can modify their effect. Even if the entire south were covered with republics and the entire north with despotic states, it would still be no less true that the effect of climate makes despotism suited to hot countries, barbarism to cold countries, and good polity to intermediate regions. I also realize that, while granting the principle, disputes may arise over its application. It could be said that there are cold countries that are very fertile and southern ones that are quite barren. But this poses a difficulty only for those who have not examined the thing in all its relationships. As I have said, it is necessary to take into account those of labor, force, consumption, and so on.

Let us suppose that there are two parcels of land of equal size, one of which yields five units and the other ten. If the inhabitants of the first parcel consume four units and the inhabitants of the second consume nine, the excess of the first will be one-fifth and that of the other will be one-tenth. Since the ratio of these two excesses is therefore the inverse of that of the products, the parcel of land that produces only five units will yield a surplus that is double that of the parcel of land that produces ten.

But it is not a question of a doubled product, and I do not believe that anyone dares, as a general rule, to place the fertility of a cold country even on an equal footing with that of hot countries. Nevertheless, let us assume that this equality is the case. Let us, if you will, reckon England to be the equal of Sicily, and Poland the equal of Egypt. Further south we have Africa and the Indies; further north we have nothing at all. To achieve this equality of product, what difference must there be in agricultural techniques? In Sicily one needs merely to scratch the soil; in England what efforts it demands to

---

[88] [Rousseau's word is *politie*, which does not appear in eighteenth-century French dictionaries and would therefore have been more unusual than "polity." He means "political community."]

work it! Now where more hands are needed to obtain the same product, the surplus must necessarily be less.

Consider too that the same number of men consumes much less in hot countries. The climate demands that a person keep sober in order to be in good health. Europeans wanting to live there just as they do at home would all die of dysentery and indigestion. "We are," says Chardin, "carnivorous beasts, wolves, in comparison with the Asians. Some attribute the sobriety of the Persians to the fact that their land is less cultivated. On the contrary, I believe that this country is less abundant in commodities because the inhabitants need less. If their frugality," he continues, "were an effect of the country's scarcity, only the poor would eat little; however, it is generally the case that everyone does so. And more or less would be eaten in each province according to the fertility of the country; however, the same sobriety is found throughout the kingdom. They take great pride in their lifestyle, saying that one has only to look at their complexions to recognize how far it excels that of the Christians. In fact, the complexion of the Persians is clear. They have fair skin, fine and polished, whereas the complexion of their Armenian subjects, who live in the European style, is coarse and blotchy, and their bodies are fat and heavy."[89]

The closer you come to the equator, the less people live on. They rarely eat meat; rice, maize, couscous, millet, and cassava are their usual diet. In the Indies there are millions of men whose sustenance costs less than a penny a day. In Europe itself we see noticeable differences in appetite between the peoples of the north and the south. A Spaniard will live for eight days on a German's dinner. In countries where men are the most voracious, luxury too turns toward things edible. In England, luxury is shown in a table loaded with meats; in Italy you are regaled with sugar and flowers.

Luxury in clothing also offers similar differences. In the climate where the seasonal changes are sudden and violent, people have better and simpler clothing. In climates where people clothe themselves merely for ornamental purposes, flashiness is more sought after than utility. The clothes themselves are a luxury there. In Naples you see men strolling every day along the Posilippo decked out in gold-embroidered coats and bare legged. It is the same with buildings; magnificence is the sole consideration when there is nothing to fear from the weather. In Paris or London, people want to be housed warmly and comfortably. In Madrid, there are superb salons, but no windows that close, and people sleep in rat holes.

In hot countries foodstuffs are considerably more substantial and succulent. This is a third difference that cannot help but influence the second. Why do people eat so many vegetables in Italy? Because there they are good, nourishing, and have an excellent flavor. In France, where vegetables are fed nothing but water, they are not nourishing at all and are nearly counted for

---

[89] [Jean Chardin (1643–1713), *Voyages en Perse* (4 vols., Amsterdam, 1735), vol. 3, 76, 83–84. The first edition is 1711.]

nothing at table. Be that as it may, they occupy no less land and cost at least as much effort to cultivate. It is a known fact that the wheats of Barbary, in other respects inferior to those of France, yield far more flour, and that those of France, for their part, yield more flour than those of the north. It can be inferred from this that a similar gradation in the same direction is generally observed from the equator to the pole. Now is it not a distinct disadvantage to have a smaller quantity of nourishment from equal amounts of produce?

To all these different considerations, I can add one that depends on and strengthens them. It is that hot countries have less of a need for inhabitants than do cold countries and yet could feed more of them. This produces a double surplus, always to the advantage of despotism. The greater the area occupied by the same number of inhabitants, the more difficult it becomes to revolt, since concerted action cannot be taken promptly and secretly; and it is always easy for the government to discover plots and cut off communications. But the closer together a numerous people is drawn, the less the government can usurp from the sovereign. The leaders deliberate as safely in their rooms as the prince does in his council, and the crowd assembles as quickly in public squares as do troops in their barracks. In this regard, it is to the advantage of a tyrannical government, therefore, to act over great distances. With the help of the points of support it establishes, its force increases with distance like that of levers.[90] On the contrary, the strength of the people acts only when concentrated; it evaporates and is lost as it spreads, like the effect of gunpowder scattered on the ground, which catches fire only one grain at a time. The least populated countries are thus the best suited for tyranny. Ferocious animals reign only in deserts.

Chapter 9
On the Signs[91] of a Good Government

When the question arises which one is absolutely the best government, an insoluble question is being raised because it is indeterminate. Or, if you wish,

---

[90] This does not contradict what I said earlier in Book II, Chapter 9, regarding the disadvantages of large states, for there it was a question of the authority of the government over its members, and here it is a question of its force against the subjects. Its scattered members serve it as points of support for acting from a distance upon the people, but it has no support for acting directly on these members themselves. Thus in the one case the length of the lever causes its weakness, and in the other case its force. [This note was added as the *Social Contract* was on its way through the press: letter to Rey, February 18, 1762.]

[91] [The word *signe* (sign) is used in early modern French to refer to something that is an indication of something else; thus, a high temperature indicates a fever, and the tracks left by a wolf indicate its presence nearby. Rousseau would also have had available the words *symptome* and *indice*. The French language still lacks a word equivalent to "evidence" (in the sense that we describe a legal case as being based on "evidence." They speak of testimony, proofs, and

it has as many good answers as there are possible combinations in the absolute and relative positions of peoples.

But if it is asked by what sign it is possible to know that a given people is well or poorly governed, this is another matter, and the question of fact could be resolved.

However, there is no answer forthcoming, since each wants to answer it in his own way. The subjects praise public tranquility; the citizens praise the liberty of private individuals. The former prefers the security of possessions; the latter that of persons. The former has it that the best government is the one that is most severe; the latter maintains that the best government is the one that is mildest. This one wants crimes to be punished, and that one wants them prevented. The former think it a good thing to be feared by their neighbors; the latter prefer to be ignored by them. The one is content as long as money circulates; the other demands that the people have bread. Even if agreement were had on these and similar points, would we be any closer to an answer? Since moral quantities do not allow of precise measurement, even if there were agreement regarding the index, how could there be agreement regarding the evaluation?

For my part, I am always astonished that a sign that is straightforward is overlooked or that people are of such bad faith as not to agree on it. What is the goal of the political association? It is the preservation and prosperity of its members. And what is the surest sign that they are preserved and prospering? It is their number and their population. Therefore, do not go looking elsewhere for this much disputed sign. All other things being equal, the government under which, without external means, without naturalizations, without colonies, the citizens become populous and multiply the most is infallibly the best government. That government under which a populace diminishes and dies out is the worst. Statisticians, it is now up to you. Count, measure, compare.[92]

---

indications [*indices*] where we have one word that covers all three). Rousseau's word *signe* thus means something close to "evidence," but the term "evidence" carries with it the values and procedures of modern science, and it would, arguably, be anachronistic to ascribe these to Rousseau.]

[92] [This note was added while the *Social Contract* was on its way through the press: letter to Rey, February 18, 1762.] We should judge on this same principle the centuries that merit preference with respect to the prosperity of the human race. Those in which letters and arts are known to have flourished have been admired too much, without penetrating the secret object of their cultivation and without considering its devastating effect, "and this was called humanity by the inexperienced, when it was a part of servitude." [Rousseau here quotes Tacitus, *Agricola*, ch. 21, in Latin.] Will we never see in the maxims of books the crude interest that causes the authors to speak? No. Whatever they may say, when a country is depopulated, it is not true, despite its brilliance, that all goes well; and the fact that a poet has an income of a hundred thousand livres is not sufficient to make his century the best of all. The apparent calm and the tranquility

Chapter 10
On the Abuse of Government and Its Tendency to Degenerate

Just as the private will acts constantly against the general will, so the government makes a continual effort against sovereignty. The more this effort increases, the more the constitution is altered. And since there is here no other corporate will that, by resisting the will of the prince, would create an equilibrium with it, sooner or later the prince must finally oppress the sovereign and break the social treaty. That is the inherent and inevitable vice that, from the birth of the body politic, tends unceasingly to destroy it, just as old age and death destroy the human body.

There are two general ways in which a government degenerates, namely when it shrinks or when the state dissolves.

The government shrinks when it passes from a large to a small number, that is to say, from democracy to aristocracy and from aristocracy to royalty. That is its natural inclination.[93] If it were to go backward from a small

---

of the leader ought to be less of an object of consideration than the well-being of whole nations and especially of the most populous states. A hailstorm may devastate a few cantons, but it rarely causes famine. Riots and civil wars may greatly disturb the leaders, but they are not the true misfortunes of the people, who may even have a reprieve while people argue over who will tyrannize them. It is their permanent condition that causes real periods of prosperity or calamity. It is when everything remains crushed under the yoke that everything decays. It is then that the leaders destroy them at will, "where they bring about solitude they call it peace." [Rousseau here quotes Tacitus, *Agricola*, ch. 30, in Latin.] When the quarrels of the great disturbed the kingdom of France, and the coadjutor of Paris brought with him to the *parlement* a dagger in his pocket, this did not keep the French people from living happily and in great numbers in a free and decent ease. Long ago, Greece flourished in the midst of the cruelest wars. Blood flowed in waves, and the whole country was covered with men. It seemed, says Machiavelli [Rousseau paraphrases a passage in Machiavelli's *History of Florence*], that in the midst of murders, proscriptions, and civil wars, our republic became more powerful; the virtue of its citizens, their mores, and their independence did more to reinforce it than all its dissensions did to weaken it. A little agitation gives strength to souls, and what truly brings about prosperity for the species is not so much peace as liberty. [In "quarrels of the great disturbed the kingdom of France," Rousseau is referring to the civil war known as the second Fronde, or the Fronde of the nobles, 1650–1653. Rousseau's source is the *Mémoires* of the Cardinal de Retz. De Retz tells this story about himself—with some sense of shame because the clergy (coadjutor, assistant to a bishop) are not meant to carry weapons or shed blood.]

93 The slow formation and the progress of the Republic of Venice in its lagoons offers a notable example of this succession. And it is rather astonishing that after more than twelve hundred years the Venetians seem to be no further than the second stage, which began with the *Serrar di Consiglio* in 1198. As for the ancient dukes, for whom the Venetians are reproached, whatever the *Squitinio della libertà veneta* [an anonymous

number to a large number, it could be said to slacken, but this backward movement is impossible.

In fact, the government never changes its form except when its exhausted energy leaves it too enfeebled to be capable of preserving what belongs to it. Now if it were to become still more slack while it expanded, its force would become entirely null; it would be still less likely to subsist. It must therefore be wound up and tightened in proportion as it gives way; otherwise the state it sustains would fall into ruin.

The dissolution of the state can come about in two ways.

First, when the prince no longer administers the state in accordance with the laws and usurps the sovereign power. In that case a remarkable change takes place, namely that it is not the government but the state that shrinks. I mean that the state as a whole is dissolved, and another is formed inside it, composed exclusively of the members of the government, and that is no longer anything for the rest of the populace but its master and tyrant. As a result,

---

attack on Venice published in 1612] may say about them, it has been proven that they were not their sovereigns.

The Roman Republic does not fail to be brought forward as an objection against me, which, it will be said, followed a completely opposite course, passing from monarchy to aristocracy to democracy. That is not how I see it at all.

The first establishment of Romulus was a mixed government that promptly degenerated into despotism. For some particular reasons, the state perished before its time, just as one sees a newborn die before reaching manhood. The expulsion of the Tarquins was the true epoch of the birth of the republic. But it did not at first take on a constant form, because in failing to abolish the patriciate, only half the work was completed. For in this way, since hereditary aristocracy, which is the worst of all forms of legitimate administration, remained in conflict with democracy, the form of government remained uncertain and adrift and was not fixed, as Machiavelli has proven [*Discourses*, bk. 1, chs. 2–3], until the establishment of the tribunes. It was only then that there was a true government and a veritable democracy. In fact, the populace then was not merely sovereign but also magistrate and judge. The senate was merely a subordinate tribunal whose purpose was to temper and concentrate the government; and the consuls themselves, though they were patricians, the first magistrates, and absolute generals in war, in Rome were merely presiding officers of the people.

From that point on, the government was also seen to follow its natural inclination and to tend strongly toward aristocracy. With the patriciate having abolished itself, as it were, the aristocracy was no longer in the body of patricians, as it is in Venice and Genoa, but in the body of the senate, which was composed of patricians and plebeians, and even in the body of the tribunes when they began to usurp an active power. For words do not affect things, and when the populace has leaders who govern for it, it is always an aristocracy, regardless of the name these leaders bear.

The abuse of aristocracy gave birth to civil wars and the triumvirate. Sulla, Julius Caesar, and Augustus became in fact veritable monarchs, and finally, under the despotism of Tiberius, the state was dissolved. Roman history therefore does not invalidate my principle; it confirms it.

the instant that the government usurps sovereignty, the social compact is broken, and all ordinary citizens, on recovering by right their natural liberty, are forced but not obliged to obey.

The same thing happens also when the members of the government separately usurp the power they should only exercise as a body. This is no less an infraction of the laws and produces even greater disorder. Under these circumstances, there are, so to speak, as many princes as magistrates, and the state, no less divided than the government, perishes or changes its form.

When the state dissolves, the abuse of government, whatever it is, takes the common name *anarchy*. To distinguish, democracy degenerates into *ochlocracy*, aristocracy into *oligarchy*. I would add that royalty degenerates into *tyranny*; however, this latter term is equivocal and requires an explanation.

In the ordinary sense, a tyrant is a king who governs with violence and without regard for justice and the laws. In the strict sense, a tyrant is a private individual who arrogates to himself royal authority without having any right to it. This is how the Greeks understood the word tyrant. They gave the name indifferently to good and bad princes whose authority was not legitimate.[94] Thus *tyrant* and *usurper* are two perfectly synonymous words.

To give different names to different things, I call the usurper of royal authority a *tyrant*, and the usurper of sovereign power a *despot*. The tyrant is someone who intrudes himself, contrary to the laws, in order to govern according to the laws. The despot is someone who places himself above the laws themselves. Thus the tyrant need not be a despot, but the despot is always a tyrant.

Chapter 11
On the Death of the Body Politic

Such is the natural and inevitable tendency of the best-constituted governments. If Sparta and Rome perished, what state can hope to last forever? If we wish to form a durable establishment, let us then not dream of making it eternal. To succeed, one must not attempt the impossible or flatter oneself with giving to the work of men a solidity that things human do not allow.

The body politic, like the human body, begins to die from the very moment of its birth and carries within itself the causes of its destruction. But both can have a constitution that is more or less robust and suited to preserve them

---

[94] "For all are considered and are called tyrants who use perpetual power in a city accustomed to liberty." [Rousseau here quotes the Latin.] Cornelius Nepos, *Life of Miltiades*. It is true that Aristotle, *Nicomachean Ethics*, Book XVIII, Chapter 10, distinguishes between a tyrant and a king, in that the former governs for his own utility and the latter governs only for the utility of his subjects. But besides the fact that generally all the Greek authors used the word *tyrant* in another sense, as appears most clearly in Xenophon's *Hiero*, it would follow from Aristotle's distinction that there has not yet been a single king since the beginning of the world.

for a longer or shorter time. The constitution of man is the work of nature; the constitution of the state is the work of art. It is not within men's power to prolong their lives; it is within their power to prolong the life of the state as far as possible by giving it the best constitution it can have. The best-constituted state will come to an end, but later than another, if no unforeseen accident brings about its premature fall.

The principle of political life is in the sovereign authority. Legislative power is the heart of the state; the executive power is the brain, which gives movement to all the parts. The brain can fall into paralysis and yet the individual may still live. A man may remain an imbecile and live. But once the heart has ceased its functions, the animal is dead.

It is not through laws that the state subsists; it is through legislative power. Yesterday's law does not obligate today, but tacit consent is presumed from silence, and the sovereign is taken to be giving incessant confirmation to the laws it does not abrogate while having the power to do so. Whatever it has once declared it wants it still wants unless it revokes its declaration.

Why then is so much respect paid to ancient laws? For just this very reason. We must believe that nothing but the excellence of the ancient wills could have preserved them for so long. If the sovereign had not constantly recognized them to be salutary, it would have revoked them a thousand times. This is why, far from growing weak, the laws continually acquire new force in every well-constituted state. The prejudice in favor of antiquity each day renders them more venerable. However, wherever the laws weaken as they grow old, this proves that there is no longer a legislative power and that the state is no longer alive.

Chapter 12
How the Sovereign Authority Is Maintained

The sovereign, having no other force than legislative power, acts only through the laws. And since the laws are only authentic acts of the general will, the sovereign can act only when the populace is assembled. With the populace assembled, it will be said, what a chimera! It is a chimera today, but two thousand years ago it was not. Have men changed their nature?

The boundaries of what is possible in moral matters are less narrow than we think. It is our weaknesses, our vices, and our prejudices that shrink them. Base souls do not believe in great men; vile slaves smile with an air of mockery at this word *liberty*.

Let us consider what can be done in the light of what has been done. I will not speak of the ancient republics of Greece; however, the Roman Republic was, to my mind, a great state, and the town of Rome was a great town. The last census in Rome gave four hundred thousand citizens bearing arms, and the last census count of the empire gave four million citizens, not counting subjects, foreigners, women, children, and slaves.

What difficulty might not be imagined in frequently calling assemblies of the immense populace of that capital and its environs? Nevertheless, few weeks passed by without the Roman people being assembled, and even several times in one week. It exercised not only the rights of sovereignty but also a part of those of the government. It took care of certain matters of public business, it tried certain cases, and this entire populace was in the public meeting place hardly less often as magistrate than as citizen.

In looking back to the earliest history of nations, one would find that most of the ancient governments, even the monarchical ones such as those of the Macedonians and the Franks, had similar councils. Be that as it may, this lone uncontestable fact answers every difficulty: arguing from the actual to the possible seems like good logic to me.

Chapter 13
Continuation

It is not enough for an assembled people to have once determined the constitution of the state by sanctioning a body of laws. It is not enough for it to have established a perpetual government or to have provided once and for all for the election of magistrates. In addition to the extraordinary assemblies that unforeseen situations can necessitate, there must be some fixed, periodic assemblies that nothing can abolish or prorogue, so that on a specified day the populace is rightfully convened by law, without the need for any other formal convocation.[95]

But apart from these assemblies that are lawful by their date alone, any assembly of the people that has not been convened by the magistrates appointed for that task and in accordance with the prescribed forms should be regarded as illegitimate, and all that takes place there should be regarded as null, since the order itself to assemble ought to emanate from the law.

As to the question of the greater or lesser frequency of legitimate assemblies, this depends on so many considerations that no precise rules can be given about it. All that can be said is that in general the more force a government has, the more frequently the sovereign ought to show itself.

I will be told that this may be fine for a single town, but what is to be done when the state includes several? Will the sovereign authority be divided, or will it be concentrated in a single town with all the rest made subject to it?

I answer that neither should be done. In the first place, the sovereign authority is simple and one; it cannot be divided without being destroyed. In the second place, a town cannot legitimately be in subjection to another town, any more than a nation can be in subjection to another nation, since the

[95] [In Rousseau's view the absence of such assemblies of the general council was a major weakness of the Genevan constitution, allowing the oligarchical little council to usurp powers that properly belonged to the people as a whole.]

essence of the body politic consists in the harmony of obedience and liberty; and the words *subject* and *sovereign* are identical correlatives, whose meaning is combined in the single word *citizen*.

I answer further that it is always an evil to unite several towns in a single city,[96] and that anyone wanting to bring about this union should not expect to avoid its natural disadvantages. The abuses of large states should not be raised as an objection against someone who wants only small ones. But how are small states to be given enough force to resist the large ones? Just as the Greek cities long ago resisted a great king, and more recently Holland and Switzerland have resisted the house of Austria.

Nevertheless, if the state cannot be reduced to appropriate boundaries, one expedient still remains: not to allow a fixed capital, to make the seat of government move from one town to another, and to assemble the estates of the country in each of them in their turn.

Populate the territory uniformly, extend the same rights everywhere, spread abundance and life all over. In this way the state will become simultaneously as strong and as well governed as possible. Recall that town walls are built completely with materials from the wreckage of rural houses. With each palace I see being erected in the capital, I believe I see an entire countryside reduced to ruins.

Chapter 14
Continuation

Once the populace is legitimately assembled as a sovereign body, all jurisdiction of the government ceases, the executive power is suspended, and the person of the humblest citizen is as sacred and inviolable as that of the first magistrate; for where those who are represented are found, there is no longer any representative. Most of the tumults that arose in the comitia in Rome were due to ignorance or neglect of this rule. On such occasions the consuls were merely the presiding officers of the people; the tribunes, ordinary speakers;[97] the senate, nothing at all.

These intervals of suspension, during which the prince recognizes or ought to recognize an actual superior, have always been disturbing to him. And these assemblies of the people, which are the shield of the body politic and the curb on the government, have at all times been the horror of leaders.

[96] [Rousseau's word is *cité*. See note 28 for his understanding of the meaning of the word as referring to any political community where there is a common citizenship. Since he took such care to define the word, this translation sticks to it, but his sense might be more easily rendered by "political community" or "polity."]

[97] In nearly the same sense as is given this word in the English Parliament. [The speaker presides over debates in the British House of Commons, as in the U.S. House of Representatives.] The similarity between these activities would have put the consuls and the tribunes in conflict, even if all jurisdiction had been suspended.

Thus they never spare efforts, objections, difficulties, or promises to keep the citizens from having them. When the citizens are greedy, cowardly, and pusillanimous, more enamored of repose than of liberty, they do not hold out very long against the redoubled efforts of the government. Thus it is that, as the resisting force constantly grows, the sovereign authority finally vanishes, and the majority of political communities fall and perish prematurely.

But between the sovereign authority and arbitrary government, there sometimes is introduced an intermediate power about which we must speak.

Chapter 15
On Deputies or Representatives

Once public service ceases to be the chief business of the citizens, and they prefer to serve with their wallet rather than with their person, the state is already near its ruin. Is it necessary to march off to battle? They pay mercenary troops and stay at home. Is it necessary to go to the council? They name deputies and stay at home. By dint of laziness and money, they finally have soldiers to enslave the country and representatives to sell it.

The hustle and bustle of commerce and the arts, the avid interest in profits, softness, and the love of amenities: these are what change personal services into money. A person gives up part of his profit in order to increase it at his convenience. Give money and soon you will be in chains. The word *finance* is a slave's word. It is unknown in the city. In a truly free state the citizens do everything with their own hands and nothing with money. Far from paying to be exempted from their duties, they would pay to fulfill them themselves. Far be it from me to be sharing commonly held ideas; I believe that forced labor is less opposed to liberty than are taxes.

The better a state is constituted, the more public business takes precedence over private business in the minds of the citizens. There even is far less private business since, with the sum of common happiness providing a more considerable portion of each individual's happiness, less remains for him to look for through private efforts. In a well-run city everyone flies to the assemblies; under a bad government no one wants to take a step to get to them, since no one takes an interest in what happens there, for it is predictable that the general will won't predominate and that in the end domestic concerns absorb everything. Good laws lead to making better laws; bad laws bring about worse ones. Once someone says, "What do I care?" about the affairs of state, the state should be considered lost.

The cooling off of patriotism, the flurry of activity in the pursuit of private interest, the largeness of states, conquests, the abuse of government: these have suggested the route of using deputies or representatives of the people in the nation's assemblies. It is what in certain countries people dare call the third estate.[98] Thus the private interest of two orders is given first and second place; the public interest is given merely third place.

Sovereignty cannot be represented for the same reason that it cannot be alienated. It consists essentially in the general will, and the will does not allow of being represented. It is either itself or something else; there is nothing in between. The deputies of the people, therefore, neither are nor can be its representatives; they are merely its agents. They cannot conclude anything definitively. Any law that the populace has not ratified in person is null; it is not a law at all. The English people believes itself to be free. It is greatly mistaken; it is free only during the election of the members of parliament. Once they are elected, the populace is enslaved; it is nothing. The use the English people makes of that freedom in the brief moments of its liberty certainly warrants their losing it.

The idea of representatives is modern. It comes to us from feudal government, that iniquitous and absurd government in which the human race is degraded and the name of man is in dishonor. In the ancient republics and even in monarchies, the people never had representatives. The word itself was unknown. It is quite remarkable that in Rome where the tribunes were so sacred, no one even imagined that they could usurp the functions of the people, and that in the midst of such a great multitude, they never tried to pass a single plebiscite on their own authority. However, we can size up the difficulties that were sometimes caused by the crowd by what took place in the time of the Gracchi, when part of the citizenry voted from the rooftops.

Where right and liberty are everything, inconveniences are nothing. In the care of this wise people, everything was handled correctly. It allowed its lictors to do what its tribunes would not have dared to do. It had no fear that its lictors would want to represent it.

However, to explain how the tribunes sometimes represented it, it is enough to understand how the government represents the sovereign. Since the law is merely the declaration of the general will, it is clear that the people cannot be represented in the legislative power. But it can and should be represented in the executive power, which is merely force applied to the law. This demonstrates that, on close examination, very few nations would be found to have laws. Be that as it may, it is certain that, since they have no share in the executive power, the tribunes could never represent the Roman people by the rights of their office, but only by usurping those of the senate.

Among the Greeks, whatever the populace had to do, it did by itself. It was constantly assembled at the public square; it inhabited a mild climate; it was not greedy; its slaves did the work; its chief item of business was its liberty. No

---

[98] [Rousseau is thinking of France in particular. There in the Estates General (which did not meet between 1614 and the Revolution of 1789), the first estate was the clergy, the second the nobility, and the third the commoners. Because the estates voted separately, the clergy and nobility could outvote the commoners.]

longer having the same advantages, how are the same rights to be preserved? Your harsher climates cause you to have more needs;[99] six months out of the year the public square is unsuitable for standing around; your muted tongues cannot make themselves understood in the open air; you pay more attention to your profits than to your liberty; and you are less fearful of slavery than you are of misery.

What! Can liberty be maintained only with the support of servitude? Perhaps. The two extremes meet. Everything that is not in nature has its drawbacks, and civil society more so than all the rest. There are some unfortunate circumstances where one's liberty can be preserved only at the expense of someone else's, and where the citizen can be perfectly free only if the slave is completely enslaved. Such was the situation in Sparta. As for you, modern peoples, you do not have slaves, but you yourselves are slaves. You pay for their liberty with your own. It is in vain that you crow about that preference. I find more cowardice in it than humanity.

I do not mean by all this that having slaves is necessary, nor that the right of slavery is legitimate, for I have proved the contrary. I am merely stating the reasons why modern peoples who believe themselves free have representatives, and why ancient peoples did not have them. Be that as it may, the moment a people gives itself representatives, it is no longer free; it no longer exists.

All things considered, I do not see that it is possible henceforth for the sovereign to preserve among us the exercise of its rights, unless the city is very small. But if it is very small, will it be subjugated? No. I will show later[100] how the external power of a great people can be combined with the ease of administration and the good order of a small state.

Chapter 16
That the Institution of Government Is Not a Contract

Once the legislative power has been well established, it is a matter of establishing the executive power in the same way. For this latter, which functions only by means of particular acts, not being of the essence of the former, is naturally separate from it. Were it possible for the sovereign, considered as such, to have the executive power, right and fact would be so completely confounded that we would no longer know what is law and what is not. And the body politic, thus denatured, would soon fall prey to the violence against which it was instituted.

---

[99] To adopt in cold countries the luxury and softness of the Orientals is to desire to be given their chains; it is submitting to these with even greater necessity than they did.

[100] This is what I intended to do in the rest of this work, when, in treating external relations, I would have come to confederations. An entirely new subject and its principles have yet to be established.

Since the citizens are all equal by the social contract, what everyone should do can be prescribed by everyone. However, no one has the right to demand that someone else do what he does not do himself. Now it is precisely this right, indispensable for making the body politic live and move, that the sovereign gives the prince in instituting the government.

Several people have claimed that this act of establishment was a contract between the populace and the leaders it gives itself, a contract by which are stipulated between the two parties the conditions under which the one obliges itself to command and the other to obey.[101] It will be granted, I am sure, that this is a strange way of entering into a contract! But let us see if this opinion is tenable.

First, the supreme authority cannot be modified any more than it can be alienated; to limit it is to destroy it. It is absurd and contradictory for the sovereign to acquire a superior. To obligate oneself to obey a master is to return to full liberty.

Moreover, it is evident that this contract between the people and some or other persons would be a particular act. Whence it follows that this contract could be neither a law nor an act of sovereignty, and that consequently it would be illegitimate.

It is also clear that the contracting parties would, in relation to one another, be under only the law of nature and without any guarantee of their reciprocal commitments, which is contrary in every way to the civil state. Since the one who has force at his disposal is always in control of its employment, it would come to the same thing if we were to give the name contract to the act of a man who would say to another, "I am giving you all my goods on the condition that you give me back whatever you wish."

There is only one contract in the state, that of the association, and that alone excludes any other.[102] It is impossible to imagine any public contract that was not a violation of the first contract.

Chapter 17
On the Institution of the Government

What should be the terms under which we should conceive the act by which the government is instituted? I will begin by saying that this act is complex or composed of two others, namely, the establishment of the law and the execution of the law.

---

[101] [This view was widespread in constitutionalist theory, and in the *Discourse on the Origin and Foundations of Inequality among Men* Rousseau describes it as the generally held view. But it is not the view of Hobbes or Locke.]

[102] [Rousseau's target here is Pufendorf, who maintains that there is both a contract of association, which establishes the political community, and a contract of submission, which establishes the government.]

By the first, the sovereign decrees that there will be a governing body established under such and such a form. And it is clear that this act is a law.

By the second, the people name the leaders who will be placed in charge of the government that is being established. And since this nomination is a particular act, it is not a second law, but merely a consequence of the first and a function of the government.

The problem is to understand how there can be an act of government before a government exists, and how the people, which is only sovereign or subject, can in certain circumstances become prince or magistrate.

Moreover, it is here that we discover one of those remarkable properties of the body politic, by which it reconciles seemingly contradictory operations. For this takes place by a sudden conversion of sovereignty into democracy, so that, without any noticeable change, and solely by a new relation of all to all, the citizens, having become magistrates, pass from general to particular acts, and from the law to its execution.

This change of relation is not a speculative subtlety without exemplification in practice. It takes place every day in the English Parliament, where the lower chamber on certain occasions turns itself into a committee of the whole in order to discuss better the business of the sovereign court, thus becoming a simple commission, whereas the moment before it was the sovereign court, so that it later reports to itself, as the House of Commons, the result of what it has just settled in the committee of the whole, and deliberates all over again under one title about what it had already settled under another.

Thus the peculiar advantage of democratic government is that it can be established in actual fact by a simple act of the general will. After this, the provisional government remains in power, if this is the form adopted, or establishes in the name of the sovereign the government prescribed by the law; and thus everything is in accordance with the rule. It is not possible to institute the government in any other legitimate way without renouncing the principles established above.

Chapter 18
The Means of Preventing Usurpations of the Government

From these clarifications, it follows, in confirmation of Chapter 16, that the act that institutes the government is not a contract but a law; that the trustees of the executive power are not the masters of the populace but its officers; that it can establish and remove them when it pleases; that for them there is no question of contracting, but of obeying; and that in taking on the functions the state imposes on them, they merely fulfill their duty as citizens, without in any way having the right to dispute over the conditions.

Thus, when it happens that the populace institutes a hereditary government, whether it is monarchical within a single family or aristocratic within a class of citizens, this is not a commitment it is entering. It is a provisional form that it gives the administration, until the populace is pleased to order it otherwise.[103]

It is true that these changes are always dangerous, and that the established government should never be touched except when it becomes incompatible with the public good. But this circumspection is a maxim of politics and not a rule of law,[104] and the state is no more bound to leave civil authority to its leaders than it is to leave military authority to its generals.

Again, it is true that in such cases it is impossible to be too careful about observing all the formalities required in order to distinguish a regular and legitimate act from a seditious tumult, and the will of an entire people from the clamor of a faction. And it is here above all that one must not grant anything to odious cases[105] except what cannot be refused according to the full rigor of the law. And it is also from this obligation that the prince derives a great advantage in preserving his power in spite of the people, without anyone being able to say that he has usurped it. For in appearing to use only his rights, it is quite easy for him to extend them, and, under the pretext of public peace, to prevent assemblies destined to reestablish good order. Thus he avails himself of a silence he keeps from being broken, or of irregularities he causes to be committed, to assume that the opinion of those who are silenced by fear is supportive of him, and to punish those who dare to speak. This is how the decemvirs, having been first elected for one year and then continued for another year, tried to retain their power in perpetuity by no longer permitting the comitia to assemble. And it is by this simple means that all the governments of the world, once armed with the public force, sooner or later usurp the public authority.

The periodic assemblies I have spoken of earlier are suited to the prevention or postponement of this misfortune, especially when they have no need for a formal convocation. For then the prince could not prevent them without openly declaring himself a violator of the laws and an enemy of the state.

The opening of these assemblies, which have as their sole object the preservation of the social treaty, should always take place through two propositions that can never be suppressed, and that are voted on separately:

---

[103] [The word "provisional" was seized on by the Genevan authorities when they condemned the *Social Contract* as being destructive of all stability in government.]

[104] [Rousseau's word is *droit* (often, as here in the subtitle to the *Social Contract*, "right"). In French, *droit* and *loi* (law) have meanings that overlap much more extensively than law and right in English, so that "law" is often the only possible translation of *droit*. Thus in France one takes a degree *en droit* (in law) and studies in the *faculté de droit* (faculty of law). The French for "the law of nature" is *le droit naturel*, for "the law of nations" it is *le droit des gens*, and for "the law of war" it is *le droit de guerre*.]

[105] ["Odious cases" refers to the principle of Roman law *odia restringenda, favores ampliandi*: when someone claims a right that will have beneficial consequences, the law should be interpreted liberally; but when they claim a right that will have evil ("odious") consequences, the law should be interpreted as narrowly as possible.]

The first: *Does it please the sovereign to preserve the present form of government?*

The second: *Does it please the people to leave its administration to those who are now in charge of it?*[106]

I am presupposing here what I believe I have demonstrated, namely that in the state there is no fundamental law that cannot be revoked, not even the social compact. For if all the citizens were to assemble in order to break this compact by common agreement, no one could doubt that it was legitimately broken. Grotius[107] even thinks that each person can renounce the state of which he is a member and recover his natural liberty and his goods by leaving the country.[108] But it would be absurd that all the citizens together could not do what each of them can do separately.

End of the Third Book

BOOK IV

Chapter 1
That the General Will Is Indestructible

As long as several men together consider themselves to be a single body, they have but a single will, which is concerned with their common preservation and the general well-being. Then all the energies of the state are vigorous and simple; its maxims are clear and luminous; there are no entangled, contradictory interests; the common good is clearly apparent everywhere, demanding only good sense in order to be perceived. Peace, union, equality are enemies of political subtleties. Upright and simple men are difficult to deceive on account of their simplicity. Traps and clever pretexts do not fool them. They are not even clever enough to be duped. When, among the happiest people in the world, bands of peasants are seen regulating their affairs of state under an oak tree[109] and always acting wisely, can one help scorning the refinements of other nations, which make themselves illustrious and miserable with so much art and mystery?

---

[106] [The Genevan authorities took particular offense at this. It looked to them like an invitation to periodic revolutions.]

[107] [Grotius, *Law of War and Peace*, bk. 2, ch. 5, §24. Grotius himself limits this right as Rousseau does in his note.]

[108] On the understanding that one does not leave in order to evade one's duty and to be exempt from serving the homeland at a time when it has need of us. In such circumstances, taking flight would be criminal and punishable; it would no longer be withdrawal, but desertion.

[109] [A reference to the rural cantons of Switzerland.]

A state thus governed needs very few laws; and in proportion as it becomes necessary to promulgate new ones, this necessity is universally understood. The first to propose them merely says what everybody has already felt; and there is no question of either intrigues or eloquence to secure the passage into law of what each has already resolved to do, once he is sure the others will do likewise.

What misleads argumentative types is the fact that, since they take into account only states that were badly constituted from the beginning, they are struck by the impossibility of maintaining such an administration in them. They laugh when they imagine all the foolishness a clever knave or a sly orator could get the people of Paris or London to believe. They do not know that Cromwell would have been sentenced to hard labor by the people of Berne, and the Duke of Beaufort imprisoned by the Genevans.[110]

But when the social bond begins to relax and the state to grow weak, when private interests begin to make themselves felt and small societies begin to influence the large one, the common interest changes and finds opponents. Unanimity no longer reigns in the votes; the general will is no longer the will of all. Contradictions and debates arise, and the best advice does not pass without disputes.

Finally, when the state, on the verge of ruin, subsists only in an illusory and vain form, when the social bond of unity is broken in all hearts, when the meanest interest brazenly appropriates the sacred name of the public good, then the general will becomes mute. Everyone, guided by secret motives, no more expresses his opinion as a citizen than if the state had never existed; and iniquitous decrees having as their sole purpose the private interest are falsely passed under the name of laws.

Does it follow from this that the general will is annihilated or corrupted? No, it is always constant, unalterable, and pure; but it is subordinate to other wills that prevail over it. Each man, in detaching his interest from the common interest, clearly sees that he cannot totally separate himself from it; but his share of the public misfortune seems insignificant to him compared to the exclusive good he intends to make his own. Apart from this private good, he wants the general good in his own interest, just as strongly as anyone else. Even in selling his vote for money he does not extinguish the general will in himself; he evades it. The error he commits is that of changing the thrust of the question and answering a different question from the one he was asked. Thus, instead of saying through his vote, "It is advantageous to the state," he says, "It is advantageous to this man or that party that this or that view should pass." Thus the law of the public order in the assemblies is not so much to maintain the general will there, as to bring it about that it is always questioned and that it always answers.

---

[110] [The Duke of Beaufort (1594–1665) was an illegitimate son of Henry IV; he was twice accused of conspiring to assassinate Richelieu and was exiled, first to Holland and then to England.]

I could present here a number of reflections on the simple right to vote in every act of sovereignty, a right that nothing can take away from the citizens, and on the right to state an opinion, to offer proposals, to divide, to discuss, which the government always takes great care to allow only to its members.[111] But this important subject would require a separate treatise, and I cannot say everything in this one.

Chapter 2
On Voting

It is clear from the preceding chapter that the manner in which general business is taken care of can provide a rather accurate indication of the present state of mores and of the health of the body politic. The more harmony reigns in the assemblies, that is to say, the closer opinions come to unanimity, the more dominant too is the general will. But long debates, dissensions, and tumult betoken the ascendance of private interests and the decline of the state.

This seems less evident when two or more orders enter into its constitution, such as the patricians and the plebeians in Rome, whose quarrels often disturbed the comitia, even in the best of times in the republic. But this exception is more apparent than real. For then, by the vice inherent in the body politic, there are, as it were, two states in one. What is not true of the two together is true of each of them separately. And indeed even in the most tumultuous times, the plebiscites of the people, when the senate did not interfere with them, always passed quietly and by a large majority of votes. Since the citizens have but one interest, the people had but one will.

At the other extreme of the circle, unanimity returns. It is when the citizens, having fallen into servitude, no longer have either liberty or will. Then fear and flattery turn voting into acclamation. People no longer deliberate; either they adore or they curse. Such was the vile manner in which the senate expressed its opinions under the emperors; sometimes it did so with ridiculous precautions. Tacitus observes that under Otho, the senators, while heaping curses upon Vitellius, contrived at the same time to make a frightful noise, so that, if by chance he became master, he would be unable to know what each of them had said.[112]

---

[111] [Rousseau limits the sovereign's right to the right to vote, giving the government a monopoly of proposing legislation and speaking in the assembly. This corresponds to the Genevan constitution, in which the little council controlled the agenda of the general council, and he approves this arrangement in his dedication to the *Discourse on Inequality* and (with reservations) in *Letters Written from the Mountain*. It also corresponds to the Venetian constitution in which the Grand Council voted but did not debate. Rousseau thus makes a major concession to the need to ensure political stability.]

[112] [*Histories*, bk. 1, ch. 85.]

From these various considerations there arise the maxims by which the manner of counting votes and comparing opinions should be regulated, depending on whether the general will is more or less easy to know and the state more or less in decline.

There is but one law that by its nature requires unanimous consent. This is the social compact. For civil association is the most voluntary act in the world. Since every man is born free and master of himself, no one can, under any pretext whatever, place another under subjection without his consent.[113] To decide that the son of a slave is born a slave is to decide that he is not born a man.[114]

If, therefore, at the time of the social compact, there are opponents to it, their opposition does not invalidate the contract; it merely prevents them from being included in it. They are foreigners among citizens. Once the state is instituted, residency implies consent. To inhabit the territory is to submit to sovereignty.[115]

Aside from this primitive contract, the vote of the majority always obligates all the others. This is a consequence of the contract itself. But it is asked how a man can be both free and forced to conform to wills that are not his own. How can the opponents be both free and placed in subjection to laws to which they have not consented?

I answer that the question is not put properly. The citizen consents to all the laws, even to those that pass in spite of his opposition, and even to those that punish him when he dares to violate any of them. The constant will of all the members of the state is the general will; through it they are citizens and free.[116] When a law is proposed in the people's assembly, what is asked of them is not, to be precise, whether they approve or reject the proposition, but whether or not it conforms to the general will that is theirs. Each man, in giving his vote, states his opinion on this matter, and the declaration of the general will is drawn from the counting of votes. When, therefore, the opinion contrary to mine prevails, this proves merely that I was in error, and that what I took to be the general will was not so. If my private opinion had

---

[113] [Cf. Locke, *Two Treatises*, Second Treatise §95, 99.]

[114] [This may be thought to follow from Locke's argument, but Locke never explicitly states this conclusion, and Rousseau is unique among major eighteenth-century political theorists in his systematic opposition to slavery.]

[115] This should always be understood in connection with a free state, for otherwise his family, his goods, the impossibility of claiming asylum, necessity, or violence can keep an inhabitant in a country in spite of himself; and then his sojourn alone no longer presupposes his consent to the contract or to the violation of the contract.

[116] In Genoa, the word *libertas* [liberty] can be read on the front of prisons and on the chains of galley slaves. This application of the motto is fine and just. Indeed it is only malefactors of all social classes who prevent the citizen from being free. In a country where all such people were in the galleys, the most perfect liberty would be enjoyed.

prevailed, I would have done something other than what I had wanted. In that case I would not have been free.

This presupposes, it is true, that all the characteristics of the general will are still in the majority. When they cease to be there, there is no longer any liberty regardless of the side one takes.

In showing earlier how private wills were substituted for the general will in public deliberations, I have given an adequate indication of the possible ways of preventing this abuse. I will discuss this again at a later time. With respect to the proportional number of votes needed to declare this will, I have also given the principles on the basis of which it can be determined. The difference of a single vote breaks a tie vote; a single opponent destroys a unanimous vote. But between a unanimous and a tie vote there are several unequal divisions, at any of which this proportionate number can be fixed in accordance with the condition and needs of the body politic.

Two general maxims can serve to regulate these ratios: one, that the more important and serious the deliberations are, the closer the prevailing opinion should be to unanimity; the other, that the more the matter at hand calls for speed, the smaller the prescribed difference in the division of opinion should be. In decisions that must be reached immediately, a majority of a single vote should suffice. The first of these maxims seems more suited to the laws, and the second to public business. Be that as it may, it is the combination of the two that establishes the ratios that best help the majority to render its decision.

Chapter 3
On Elections

With regard to the elections of the prince and the magistrates, which are, as I have said, complex acts, there are two ways to proceed, namely, by choice or by lots. Both of these have been used in various republics, and at present we still see a very complicated mixture of the two in the election of the Doge of Venice.

"Voting by lot," says Montesquieu, "is of the essence of democracy." I agree, but why is this the case? "Drawing lots," he continues, "is a way of electing that harms no one; it leaves each citizen a reasonable hope of serving the homeland."[117] These are not reasons.

If we keep in mind that the election of leaders is a function of government and not of sovereignty, we will see why the method of drawing lots is more in the nature of democracy, where the administration is all the better the fewer decisions it makes.

In every true democracy the magistracy is not an advantage but a heavy burden that cannot justly be imposed on one private individual rather than

---

[117] [Montesquieu, *Spirit of the Laws*, bk. 2, ch. 2.]

another. The law alone can impose this burden on the one to whom it falls by lot. For in that case, with the condition being equal for all and the choice not depending on any human will, there is no particular application that alters the universality of the law.

In any aristocracy, the prince chooses the prince; the government is preserved by itself, and it is there that voting is appropriate.

The example of the election of the Doge of Venice, far from destroying this distinction, confirms it. This mixed procedure suits a mixed government. For it is an error to regard the government of Venice as a true aristocracy. For although the populace there has no part in the government, the nobility is itself the people. A multitude of poor Barnabites[118] never come[119] near any magistracy and have nothing to show for their nobility but the vain title of excellency and the right to be present at the grand council. Since this grand council is as numerous as our general council in Geneva,[120] its illustrious members have no more privileges than our simple citizens. It is certain that, aside from the extreme disparity between the two republics, the bourgeoisie of Geneva exactly corresponds to the Venetian patriciate. Our natives and inhabitants correspond to the citizens[121] and people of Venice. Our peasants correspond to the subjects on the mainland. Finally, whatever way one considers this republic, apart from its size, its government is no more aristocratic than ours. The whole difference lies in the fact that, since we do not have leaders who serve for life, we do not have the same need to draw lots.

Elections by lot would have few disadvantages in a true democracy, where, all things being equal both in mores and talents as well as in maxims and fortunes, the choice would become almost indifferent. But I have already said there is no such thing as a true democracy.

When choice and lots are mixed, the former should fill the positions requiring special talents, such as military posts. The latter is suited to those positions, such as judicial offices, where good sense, justice, and integrity are enough, because in a well-constituted state these qualities are common to all the citizens.

Neither the drawing of lots nor voting has any place in a monarchical government. Since the monarch is by right the only prince and sole magistrate, the choice of his lieutenants belongs to him alone. When the Abbot of Saint-Pierre proposed multiplying the Councils of the King of France and

---

[118] [This was the name for the poor nobles of Venice, generally said to refer to the area around the Church of St. Barnabas, where they lived, but also presumably a reference to St. Barnabas himself, who sold all he had and gave it to the apostles.]

[119] [The text of the first edition is *approcha* (past tense), but as the rest of the passage is in the present tense this seems likely to be a misprint for *approche* (present tense).]

[120] [The Grand Council had, according to Rousseau in his *Considerations on the Government of Poland*, 1,200 members.]

[121] [The citizens or *cittadini* of Venice, whose status was below that of the nobility (who alone exercised political rights). The citizens had a monopoly of administrative positions.]

electing the members by ballot, he did not realize that he was proposing to change the form of government.[122]

It remains for me to speak of the manner in which the votes are cast and counted in the people's assembly. But perhaps in this regard the chronicle of the Roman system of administration will explain more clearly all the maxims I could establish. It is not beneath the dignity of a judicious reader to consider in some detail how public and private business was conducted in a council made of two hundred thousand men.

Chapter 4
On the Roman Comitia[123]

We have no especially reliable records of the earliest period of Rome's history. It even appears quite likely that most of the things reported about it are fables.[124] And in general the most instructive part of the annals of peoples, which is the history of their founding, is the part we most lack. Experience teaches us every day the causes that lead to the revolutions of empires. But since peoples are no longer being formed, we have almost nothing but conjecture to explain how they were formed.

The customs we find established attest at the very least to the fact that these customs had an origin. Of the traditions that go back to these origins, those that are supported by the greatest authorities and that are confirmed by the strongest reasons should pass for the most certain. These are the maxims I have tried to follow in attempting to find out how the freest and most powerful people on earth exercised its supreme power.

After the founding of Rome, the newborn republic, that is, the army of the founder, composed of Albans, Sabines, and foreigners, was divided into three classes, which took the name *tribus* [thirds or tribes] from this division. Each of these tribes was divided into ten curiae, and each curia into *decuriae*, at the head of which were placed leaders called *curiones* and *decuriones*.

Moreover, from each tribe was drawn a body of one hundred horsemen or knights, called a *century*. It is clear from this that these divisions, being hardly necessary in a market town, originally were exclusively military. But it appears that an instinct for greatness led the small town of Rome to provide itself in advance with a system of administration suited to the capital of the world.

---

[122] [Rousseau, at the instigation of his employer Mme Dupin, wrote at length on the political theory of the Abbot of Saint-Pierre.]

[123] [Rousseau's main sources in this chapter are the *Discourses* of Machiavelli and *De antiquo jure civium Romanorum* (1560) of Sigonius, a little-known work.]

[124] The name *Rome*, which people say comes from *Romulus*, is Greek, and means *force*. The name *Numa* is also Greek, and means *law*. What is the likelihood that the first two kings of that town would have borne in advance names so clearly related to what they did?

One disadvantage soon resulted from this initial division. With the tribes of the Albans[125] and the Sabines[126] always remaining constant, while that of the foreigners[127] grew continually, thanks to their perpetual influx, this latter group soon outnumbered the other two. The remedy that Servius found for this dangerous abuse was to change the division and, in place of the division based on blood, which he abolished, to substitute another division drawn from the areas of the town occupied by each tribe. In place of the three tribes, he made four. Each of them occupied one of the hills of Rome and bore its name. Thus, in remedying the inequality of the moment, he also prevented it from happening in the future. And in order that this division might not be merely one of localities but of men, he prohibited the inhabitants of one quarter from moving into another, which prevented the bloodlines from mingling with one another.

He also doubled the three ancient centuries of horsemen and added to them twelve others, but always under the old names, a simple and judicious means by which he achieved the differentiation of the body of knights from that of the people, without causing the latter to murmur.

To the four urban tribes, Servius added fifteen others called rural tribes, because they were formed from the inhabitants of the countryside, divided into the same number of cantons. Subsequently, the same number of new ones were brought into being, and the Roman people finally found itself divided into thirty-five tribes, a number at which they remained fixed until the end of the republic.

There resulted from this distinction between the tribes of the city and those of the countryside an effect worth noting, because there is no other example of it, and because Rome owed to it both the preservation of its mores and the growth of its empire. One might have thought that the urban tribes soon would have arrogated to themselves power and honors, and would have wasted no time in vilifying the rural tribes. What took place was quite the opposite. The early Romans' taste for country life is well known. They inherited this taste from the wise founder who united liberty with rural and military labors and, so to speak, relegated to the town arts, crafts, intrigue, fortune, and slavery.

Thus, since all the illustrious men in Rome lived in the country and tilled the soil, people became accustomed to look only there for the mainstays of the republic. Since this condition was that of the worthiest patricians, it was honored by everyone. The simple and laborious life of the villagers was preferred to the lazy and idle life of the bourgeois of Rome. And someone who would have been merely a miserable proletarian in the town became a respected citizen as a field worker. It was not without reason, said Varro, that

[125] Ramnenses.
[126] Tatienses.
[127] Luceres.

our great-souled ancestors established in the village the nursery of those robust and valiant men who defended them in time of war and nourished them in time of peace. Pliny says positively that the tribes of the fields were honored on account of the men who made them up; however, cowards whom men wished to vilify were transferred in disgrace to the tribes of the town. When the Sabine Appius Claudius came to settle in Rome, he was decked with honors and inscribed in a rural tribe that later took the name of his family. Finally, freedmen all entered the urban tribes, never the rural ones. And during the entire period of the republic, there was not a single example of any of these freedmen reaching any magistracy, even if he had become a citizen.

This maxim was excellent, but it was pushed so far that it finally resulted in a change and certainly an abuse in the administration.

First, the censors, after having long arrogated to themselves the right to transfer citizens arbitrarily from one tribe to another, permitted most of them to have themselves inscribed in whatever tribe they pleased. Certainly this permission served no useful purpose and deprived the censorship of one of its greatest resources. Moreover, with the great and the powerful having themselves inscribed in the tribes of the countryside, and the freedmen who had become citizens remaining with the populace in the tribes of the town, the tribes in general no longer had either place or territory. On the contrary, they all found themselves so intermixed that the members of each could no longer be identified except by the registers, so that in this way the idea of the word *tribe* shifted from referring to property to referring to persons, or rather it became almost a chimera.

In addition, it happened that since the tribes of the town were nearer at hand, they were often the strongest in the comitia, and sold the state to those who deigned to buy the votes of the mob that composed them.

Regarding the curiae, since the founder had created ten curiae in each tribe, the entire Roman people, which was then contained within the town walls, was composed of thirty curiae, each of which had its temples, its gods, its officials, its priests, and its feasts called *compitalia*, similar to the *paganalia* later held by the rural tribes.

When Servius established this new division, since this number thirty could not be divided equally among his four tribes, and since he did not want to alter it, the curiae became another division of the inhabitants of Rome, independent of the tribes. But there was no question of the curiae either in the rural tribes or among the people that composed them; for since the tribes had become a purely civil establishment and another system of administration had been introduced for the raising of troops, the military divisions of Romulus were found to be superfluous. Thus, even though every citizen was inscribed in a tribe, there were plenty who were not inscribed in a curia.

Servius established still a third division, which bore no relationship to the two preceding ones and which became, in its effects, the most important of all. He divided the entire Roman people into six classes, which he distinguished neither by place nor by person, but by wealth. Thus the first classes were filled by the rich, the last by the poor, and the middle ones by those who enjoyed a moderate fortune. These six classes were subdivided into 193 other bodies called centuries, and these bodies were distributed in such a manner that the first class alone contained more than half of them, and the last contained only one. Thus it was that the class with the smallest number of men was the one with the greatest number of centuries and that the entire last class counted only as a single subdivision, even though it alone contained more than half the inhabitants of Rome.

In order that the people might have less of a grasp of the consequences of this last form, Servius feigned giving it a military air. He placed in the second class two centuries of armorers, and two centuries of artillery in the fourth. In each class, with the exception of the last, he made a distinction between the young and the old, that is to say, between those who were obliged to carry arms and those whose age exempted them by law. This distinction, more than that of wealth, produced the necessity for frequently retaking the census or roll call. Finally, he wished that the assembly would be held in the Campus Martius, and that all those who were of age to serve should come there with their arms.

The reason he did not follow this same division of young and old in the last class is that the populace of which it was composed was not accorded the honor of bearing arms for the homeland. It was necessary to possess a hearth in order to obtain the right to defend it. And of the innumerable troops of beggars who today grace the armies of kings, there is perhaps no one who would not have been disdainfully chased from a Roman cohort, when the soldiers were the defenders of liberty.

In addition there was a distinction in the last class between the *proletarians* and those that are called *capite censi*. The former, not completely reduced to nothing, at least gave citizens to the state, sometimes even soldiers in times of pressing need. As for those who possessed nothing at all and could be reckoned only by counting heads, they were regarded as absolutely worthless, and Marius was the first who deigned to enroll them.

Without deciding here whether this third method of reckoning was good or bad in itself, I believe I can affirm that it could be made practicable only by the simple mores of the early Romans, their disinterestedness, their taste for agriculture, their dislike for commerce and for the passion for profits. Where is the modern people among whom their devouring greed, their unsettled spirit, their intrigue, their continual displacements, their perpetual revolutions of fortunes could allow such an establishment to last twenty years without overturning the entire state? It must also be duly noted that the mores and the censorship, which were stronger than this institution, corrected its defects in Rome, and that a rich man found himself relegated to the class of the poor for having made too much of a show of his wealth.

From all this, it is easy to grasp why mention is almost never made of more than five classes, even though there were actually six. The sixth, since it furnished neither soldiers for the army nor voters for the Campus Martius[128] and was virtually of no use in the republic, was hardly ever counted for anything.

Such were the various divisions of the Roman people. Let us now look at the effect these divisions had on the assemblies. When legitimately convened, these assemblies were called *comitia*. Ordinarily they were held in the Roman forum or in the Campus Martius, and were distinguished as *comitia curiata*, *comitia centuriata*, and *comitia tributa*, according to which of the three forms was the basis on which they were organized. The *comitia curiata* were based on the institution of Romulus, the *comitia centuriata* on that of Servius, and the *comitia tributa* on that of the tribunes of the people. No law received sanction, no magistrate was elected save in the comitia. And since there was no citizen who was not inscribed in a curia, a century, or a tribe, it followed that no citizen was excluded from the right of suffrage and that the Roman people was truly sovereign both de jure and de facto.

For the comitia to be legitimately assembled and for what took place to have the force of law, three conditions had to be met: first, the body or the magistrate who called these assemblies had to be invested with the necessary authority to do so; second, the assembly had to be held on one of the days permitted by law; third, the auguries had to be favorable.

The reason for the first regulation needs no explanation. The second is an administrative matter. Thus the comitia were not allowed to be held on holidays and market days, when people from the country, coming to Rome on business, did not have time to spend the day in the public forum. By means of the third rule, the senate held in check a proud and restless people and appropriately tempered the ardor of seditious tribunes. But these latter found more than one way of getting around this constraint.

The laws and the election of leaders were not the only matters submitted to the judgment of the comitia. Since the Roman people had usurped the most important functions of the government,[129] it can be said that the fate of Europe was decided in its assemblies. This variety of objects gave rise to the various forms these assemblies took on according to the matters on which they had to pronounce.

---

[128] I say *Campus Martius* because it was here that the *comitia centuriata* gathered. In the two other forms of assembly, the people gathered in the *forum* or elsewhere, and then the *capite censi* had as much influence and authority as the first citizens.

[129] [Since, according to Rousseau's political theory, the sovereign people always have the right to reclaim power from the government, the word "usurped" should be read as if in scare quotation marks. The word is evidently not used carelessly, however, as Rousseau repeats it in a reference to this passage in *Letters Written from the Mountain*. Evidently he thought it a mistake for the people to exercise too many of the functions of government.]

In order to judge these various forms, it is enough to compare them. In instituting the curiae, Romulus had intended to contain the senate by means of the people and the people by means of the senate, while he dominated both equally. He therefore gave the people, by means of this form, all the authority of number to balance that of power and wealth that he left to the patricians. But in conformity with the spirit of the monarchy, he nevertheless left a greater advantage to the patricians through their clients' influence on the majority of the votes. This admirable institution of patrons and clients was a masterpiece of politics and humanity, without which the patriciate, so contrary to the spirit of the republic, could not have subsisted. Only Rome had the honor of giving the world this fine example, which never led to any abuse, and which, for all that, has never been copied.

Since this same form of curiae had subsisted under the kings until Servius, and since the reign of the last Tarquin was not considered legitimate, royal laws were generally known by the name *leges curiatae*.

Under the republic, the curiae, always limited to the four urban tribes and including no more than the populace of Rome, were unable to suit either the senate, which was at the head of the patricians, or the tribunes, who, plebeians though they were, were at the head of the citizens who were in comfortable circumstances. The curiae therefore fell into discredit and their degradation was such that their thirty assembled lictors together did what the *comitia curiata* should have done.

The division by centuries was so favorable to the aristocracy that at first it is difficult to see how the senate did not always prevail in the comitia that bears this name and by which the consuls, the censors, and other curule magistrates were elected. In fact, of the 193 centuries that formed the six classes of the entire Roman people, the first class contained 98, and, since the voting was counted by centuries only, this first class alone prevailed in the number of votes over all the rest. When all its centuries were in agreement, they did not even continue to count the votes. Decisions made by the smallest number passed for a decision of the multitude; and it can be said that in the *comitia centuriata* business was settled more by who had the most money than by who had the most votes.

But this extreme authority was tempered in two ways. First, since ordinarily the tribunes, and always a large number of plebeians, were in the class of the rich, they balanced the authority of the patricians in this first class.

The second way consisted in the following. Instead of at the outset making the centuries vote according to their order, which would have meant always beginning with the first, one century was chosen by lot, and that one[130] alone proceeded to the election. After this, all the centuries were called on

---

[130] This century, having been chosen thus by lot, was called *prae rogativa*, on account of the fact that it was the first to be asked for its vote, and it is from this that the word *prerogative* is derived.

another day according to their rank, repeated the same election, and usually confirmed it. Thus the authority of example was removed from rank in order to give it to lot, in accordance with the principle of democracy.

There resulted from this custom still another advantage, namely that the citizens from the country had time between the two elections to inform themselves of the merit of the provisionally named candidate, so that they did not have to vote without knowledge of what was at stake.

But on the pretext of speeding things up, this custom was finally abolished and the two elections were held on the same day.

Strictly speaking, the *comitia tributa* were the council of the Roman people. They were convened only by the tribunes. The tribunes were elected and passed their plebiscites there. Not only did the senate hold no rank in them, it did not even have the right to be present. And since the senators were forced to obey the laws upon which they could not vote, they were less free in this regard than the humblest citizens. This injustice was altogether ill conceived, and was by itself enough to invalidate the decrees of a body to which none of its members were admitted. If all the patricians had been present at these comitia by virtue of the right they had as citizens, having then become simple private individuals, they would not have had a great deal of influence on a form of voting that was tallied by counting heads and where the humblest proletarian had as much clout as the leading figure in the senate.

Thus it can be seen that besides the order that resulted from these various distributions for gathering the votes of so great a people, these distributions were not reducible to forms indifferent in themselves, but each one had effects relative to the viewpoints that caused it to be preferred.

Without going further into greater detail here, it is a consequence of the preceding clarifications that the *comitia tributa* were the most favorable to the popular government, and the *comitia centuriata* most favorable to the aristocracy. Regarding the *comitia curiata*, in which the populace of Rome alone formed the majority, since these were good only for favoring tyranny and evil designs, they fell of their own weight into disrepute, and even the seditious abstained from using a means that made their real intent only too apparent. It is certain that all the majesty of the Roman people is found only in the *comitia centuriata*, which alone were complete, given that the *comitia curiata* lacked the rural tribes, and the *comitia tributa* lacked the senate and the patricians.

As for the manner of collecting the votes, among the early Romans it was as simple as their mores, though not as simple as in Sparta. Each gave his vote in a loud voice, and a clerk marked it down accordingly. The majority vote in each tribe determined the tribe's vote; the majority vote of the tribes determined the people's vote; and the same went for the curiae and the centuries. This custom was good as long as honesty reigned among the citizens and each was ashamed to cast his vote publicly in favor of an unjust proposal or an unworthy subject. But when the people became corrupt and votes were bought, it was fitting that they should cast their votes in secret in order to restrain the buyers through distrust and to provide scoundrels the means of not being traitors.

I know that Cicero condemns this change and attributes the ruin of the republic partly to it.[131] But although I am aware of the weight that Cicero's authority should have here, I cannot agree with him. On the contrary, I think that, by not having made enough changes of this sort, the fall of the state was accelerated. Just as the regimen of healthy people is not suitable for the sick, one should not want to govern a corrupt people by means of the same laws that are suited to a good people. Nothing proves this maxim better than the long life of the Republic of Venice, whose shadow still exists, solely because its laws are suited only to wicked men.

Tablets were therefore distributed to the citizens by means of which each man could vote without anyone knowing what his opinion was. New formalities were also established for collecting the tablets, counting the votes, comparing the numbers, and so on. None of this prevented the integrity of the officials in charge of these functions[132] from often being under suspicion. Finally, to prevent intrigue and vote trafficking, edicts were passed whose sheer multiplicity is proof of their uselessness.

Toward the end of the period of the republic, it was often necessary to have recourse to extraordinary expedients in order to make up for the inadequacy of the laws. Sometimes miracles were alleged. But this means, which could deceive the populace, did not deceive those who governed it. Sometimes an assembly was unexpectedly convened before the candidates had time to carry out their intrigues. Sometimes an entire session was spent on talk, when it was clear that the populace was won over and ready to take the wrong side on an issue. But finally ambition eluded everything; and what is unbelievable is that in the midst of so much abuse, this immense people, by virtue of its ancient regulations, did not cease to choose magistrates, pass laws, judge cases, or expedite private and public business, almost as easily as the senate itself could have done.

Chapter 5
On the Tribunate

When it is not possible to establish an exact proportion between the constitutive parts of the state, or when indestructible causes continually alter the relationships between them, a special magistracy is then established that does not make up yet another body alongside them. This magistracy restores each term to its true relationship to the others, which reinstates each term in its true relationship, and which creates a link or a middle term either between

---

[131] [Cf. Montesquieu, *Spirit of the Laws*, bk. 2, ch. 2.]

[132] Custodes, diribitores, rogatores suffragiorum.

the prince and the people or between the prince and the sovereign, or on both sides at once, if necessary.

This body, which I will call the *tribunate*, is the preserver of the laws and the legislative power. It serves sometimes to protect the sovereign against the government, as the tribunes of the people did in Rome; sometimes to sustain the government against the people, as the Council of Ten now does in Venice; and sometimes to maintain equilibrium between the two, as the ephors did in Sparta.

The tribunate is not a constitutive part of the city and it should have no share in either the legislative or the executive power. But this is precisely what makes its own power the greater. For although it is unable to do anything, it can prevent everything. It is more sacred and more revered as a defender of the laws than the prince who executes them and the sovereign who gives them. This was very clearly apparent in Rome when the proud patricians, who always scorned the entire populace, were forced to bow before a humble official of the people, who had neither auspices nor jurisdiction.

A well-tempered tribunate is the firmest support of a good constitution. But if it has the slightest bit too much force, it undermines everything. As for weakness, there is none in its nature; and provided it is something, it is never less than it ought to be.

It degenerates into tyranny when it usurps the executive power, of which it is merely the moderator, and when it wants to dispense from the laws it ought only to protect.[133] The enormous power of the ephors, which was without danger as long as Sparta preserved its mores, hastened corruption once it had begun. The blood of Agis, who was slaughtered by these tyrants, was avenged by his successor. The crime and the punishment of the ephors equally hastened the fall of the republic; and after Cleomenes, Sparta was no longer anything. Rome also perished in the same way, and the excessive power of the tribunes, which they had gradually usurped, finally served, with the help of the laws that were made to protect liberty, as a safeguard for the emperors who destroyed it. As for the Council of Ten in Venice, it is a bloody tribunal, equally horrifying to the patricians and the people, and which, far from proudly protecting the laws, no longer serves any purpose, after their degradation, beyond that of delivering blows in the dark that no one dares notice.[134]

---

[133] [Rousseau's phrase is *dispenser les loix*. Vaughan and the Pléiade edition interpret this as meaning *administrer les loix* (administer the laws), but I cannot find an equivalent usage in contemporary (or indeed any) dictionaries or elsewhere in Rousseau, and it seems likely that it is a misprint for *dispenser des loix* (dispense from the laws)—a reading adopted by the Hachette edition.]

[134] [This account of contemporary Venice as a species of tyranny follows on a long line of previous commentators, including Montesquieu. See my "Ulysses Bound? Venice and the Idea of Liberty from Howell to Hume," in *Republicanism, Liberty, and Commercial Society*, ed. Wootton (Stanford: Stanford University Press, 1994), 341–67.]

Just like the government, the tribunate is weakened as a result of the multiplication of its members. When the tribunes of the Roman people, who at first were two in number, then five, wanted to double this number, the senate let them do so, certain that one faction could be used to hold the other in check; and this did not fail to happen.

The best way to prevent usurpations by so formidable a body, one that no government has yet made use of, would be not to make this body permanent, but to regulate the intervals during which it would be suppressed. These intervals, which ought not be so long as to allow abuses time to grow in strength, can be fixed by law in such a way that it is easy to shorten them, as needed, by means of extraordinary commissions.

This way seems to me to have no disadvantage, for since, as I have said, the tribunate is not part of the constitution, it can be set aside without doing the constitution any harm; and it seems bound to be effective because a newly reestablished magistrate begins not with the power his predecessor had, but with the power the law gives him.

Chapter 6
On Dictatorship[135]

The inflexibility of the laws, which prevents them from adapting to circumstances, can in certain instances make them harmful and render them the instrument of the state's downfall in time of crisis. The order and the slowness of formal procedures require a space of time that circumstances sometimes do not permit. A thousand eventualities can present themselves, which the legislator has not foreseen, and it is a very necessary bit of foresight to realize that not everything can be foreseen.

It is therefore necessary to avoid the desire to strengthen political institutions to the point of removing the power to suspend their effect. Sparta itself allowed its laws to lie dormant.

But only the greatest dangers can counterbalance the danger of altering the public order, and the sacred power of the laws should never be suspended except when it is a question of the safety of the homeland. In these rare and obvious cases, public safety can be provided for by a special act that confers the responsibility for it on someone who is most worthy. This commission can be carried out in two ways, according to the type of danger.

If increasing the activity of government is enough to remedy the situation, it is concentrated in one or two of its members. Thus it is not the authority of the laws that is altered, but merely the form of their administration. But if the peril is such that the apparatus of the laws is an obstacle to their being protected from it, then a supreme leader is named who silences all the laws and briefly suspends the sovereign authority. In such a case, the general

---

[135] [This chapter is clearly under the influence of Machiavelli, *Discourses*, bk. 1, chs. 34–35.]

will is not in doubt, and it is evident that the first intention of the people is that the state should not perish. In this manner, the suspension of legislative authority does not abolish it. The magistrate who silences it cannot make it speak; he dominates it without being able to represent it. He can do anything but make laws.

The first way was used by the Roman senate when, by a sacred formula, it entrusted the consuls with the responsibility for providing for the safety of the republic. The second took place when one of the two consuls named a dictator,[136] a custom for which Alba had provided Rome the precedent.

In the beginning days of the republic, there was frequent recourse to dictatorship, since the state did not yet have a sufficiently stable basis to be capable of sustaining itself by the force of its constitution. Since the mores at that time made many of the precautions superfluous that would have been necessary in other times, there was no fear either that a dictator would abuse his authority or that he would try to hold on to it beyond his term of office. On the contrary, it seemed that such a great power was a burden to the one in whom it was vested, so quickly did he hasten to rid himself of it, as if a position that stood in the place of the laws would have been too troublesome and dangerous!

Thus it is not so much the danger of its being abused as it is that of its being degraded that makes one criticize the injudicious use of this supreme magistracy in the early days of the republic. For while it was being wasted on elections, dedications, and purely formal proceedings, there was reason to fear that it would become less formidable in time of need, and that people would become accustomed to regard as empty a title that was used exclusively in empty ceremonies.

Toward the end of the republic, the Romans, having become more circumspect, were as unreasonably sparing in their use of the dictatorship as they had formerly been lavish. It was easy to see that their fear was ill founded; that the weakness of the capital then protected it against the magistrates who were in its midst; that a dictator could, under certain circumstances, defend the public liberty without ever being able to make an attack on it; and that Rome's chains would not be forged in Rome itself, but in its armies. The weak resistance that Marius offered Sulla and Pompey offered Caesar clearly demonstrated what could be expected of internal authority in the face of external force.

This error caused them to make huge mistakes, for example, failing to name a dictator in the Catilinian affair. For since this was a question merely of the interior of the town and, at most, of some province in Italy, a dictator, with the unlimited authority that the laws gave him, would have easily quelled the conspiracy, which was stifled only by a coming together of fortuitous events, which human prudence has no right to expect.

---

[136] This nomination was made at night and in secret, as if it were shameful to place a man above the laws.

Instead of that, the senate was content to entrust all its power to the consuls. Whence it happened that, in order to act effectively, Cicero was forced to exceed this power on a crucial point. And although the first transports of joy indicated approval of his conduct, eventually Cicero was justly called to account for the blood of citizens shed against the laws, a reproach that could not have been directed against a dictator. But the eloquence of the consul carried the day. And since even he, Roman though he was, preferred his own glory to his homeland, he sought not so much the most legitimate and safe way of saving the state as he did the way that would get him all the honor for settling this affair.[137] Thus he was justly honored as the liberator of Rome and justly punished as a lawbreaker. However brilliant his recall may have been, it undoubtedly was a pardon.

For the rest, whatever the manner in which this important commission was conferred, it is important to limit a dictatorship's duration to a very short period of time that cannot be prolonged. In the crises that call for its being established, the state is soon either destroyed or saved; and once the pressing need has passed, the dictatorship becomes tyrannical or needless. In Rome, where the dictators had terms of six months only, most of them abdicated before their terms had expired. If the term had been longer, perhaps they would have been tempted to prolong it further, as did the decemvirs with a one-year term. The dictator only had time enough to see to the need that got him elected. He did not have time to dream up other projects.

Chapter 7
On the Censorship

Just as the declaration of the general will takes place through the law, the declaration of the public judgment takes place through the censorship. Public opinion is the sort of law whose minister is the censor, and his task is only to apply it to particular cases, after the example of the prince.

Thus the censorial tribunal, far from being the arbiter of the people's opinion, is merely its spokesman; and as soon as it deviates from this opinion, its decisions are vain and futile.

It is useless to distinguish the mores of a nation from the objects of its esteem, for all these things derive from the same principle and are necessarily intermixed. Among all the peoples of the world, it is not nature but opinion that decides the choice of their pleasures. Reform men's opinions, and their mores will soon become purified all by themselves. Men always love what is good or what they find to be so; but it is in this judgment that they make mistakes. Hence this is the judgment whose regulation is the point at issue.

---

[137] He could not have been sure of this had he proposed a dictator, since he did not dare name himself, and he could not be sure that his colleague would name him.

Whoever judges mores judges honor, and whoever judges honor derives his law from opinion.

The opinions of a people arise from its constitution. Although the law does not regulate mores, legislation is what gives rise to them. When legislation weakens, mores degenerate; but then the judgment of the censors will not do what the force of the laws has not done.

It follows from this that the censorship can be useful for preserving mores, but never for reestablishing them. Establish censors while the laws are vigorous. Once they have lost their vigor, everything is hopeless. Nothing legitimate has any force once the laws no longer have force.

The censorship maintains mores by preventing opinions from becoming corrupt, by preserving their rectitude through wise applications, and sometimes even by making a determination on them when they are still uncertain. The use of seconds in duels, which had been carried to the point of being a craze in the kingdom of France, was abolished by the following few words of the king's edict: "As for those who are cowardly enough to call upon seconds." This judgment anticipated that of the public and suddenly fixed it. But when the same edicts tried to declare that it was also an act of cowardice to fight duels (which of course is quite true, but contrary to common opinion), the public mocked this decision; it concerned a matter about which its mind was already made up.

I have said elsewhere[138] that since public opinion is not subject to constraint, there should be no limitation placed upon the tribunal established to represent it. It is impossible to show too much admiration for the skill with which this device, entirely lost among us moderns, was put into effect among the Romans and even better among the Lacedaemonians.

When a man of bad mores put forward a good proposal in the council of Sparta, the ephors ignored it and had the same proposal put forward by a virtuous citizen. What honor for the one, what shame for the other; and without having given praise or blame to either of the two! Certain drunkards of Samos[139] defiled the tribunals of the ephors. The next day, a public edict gave the Samians permission to be filthy. A true punishment would have been less severe than impunity such as this. When Sparta made a pronouncement on what was or was not decent, Greece did not appeal its judgments.

---

[138] I merely call attention in this chapter to what I have treated at greater length in my *Letter to d'Alembert*.

[139] [Rousseau added the following in the 1782 edition: "They are from another island that the delicacy of our language prohibits me from naming at this time." The copy of the *Social Contract* that Rousseau gave to d'Ivernois has the following note: "They were from Chios and not from Samos, but given the subject matter here, I have never dared employ this word [Chios] in the text. Yet I think I am as bold as anyone; but it is not permitted to anyone to be dirty and coarse, no matter what the subject matter. The French have put so much decency into their language that one can no longer speak the truth while using it." Rousseau was afraid of a pun on the island's name.]

Chapter 8
On Civil Religion[140]

At first men had no other kings but the gods, and no other government than a theocratic one. They reasoned like Caligula, and then they reasoned correctly. A lengthy alteration of feelings and ideas is necessary before men can be resolved to accept a fellowman as a master, in the hope that things will turn out well for having done so.

By the mere fact that God was placed at the head of every political society, it followed that there were as many gods as there were peoples. Two peoples who were alien to one another and nearly always enemies could not recognize the same master for very long. Two armies in combat with one another could not obey the same leader. Thus national divisions led to polytheism, and this in turn led to theological and civil intolerance, which are by nature the same, as will be stated later.

The fanciful notion of the Greeks that they had rediscovered their gods among the beliefs of barbarian peoples arose from another notion they had of regarding themselves as the natural sovereigns of these peoples. But in our day it is a ridiculous bit of erudition that equates the gods of different nations—as if Moloch, Saturn, and Chronos could have been the same god; as if the Phoenicians' Baal, the Greeks' Zeus, and the Romans' Jupiter could have been the same; as if there could be anything in common among chimerical beings having different names!

But if it is asked how in pagan cultures, where each state has its own cult and its own gods, there are no wars of religion, I answer that it was for this very reason that each state, having its own cult as well as its own government, did not distinguish its gods from its laws. Political war was theological as well. The territories of the gods were, so to speak, fixed by national boundaries. The gods of one people had no rights over other peoples. The gods of the pagans were not jealous gods. They divided dominion over the world among themselves. Moses himself and the Hebrew people sometimes countenanced this idea in speaking of the god of Israel. It is true they regarded as nothing the gods of the Canaanites, a proscribed people destined for destruction, and whose land they were to occupy. But note how they spoke of the divinities of

---

[140] [The draft of the *Social Contract* that Rousseau sent his publisher in December 1760 did not contain this chapter. Rousseau described it in a letter of December 23, 1761 as an addition. An early draft is written on the back of the chapter on the legislator (Book I, Chapter 7), and the subject matter of the two is connected in, for example, the thinking of Machiavelli (e.g., *Discourses*, bk. 1, ch. 16). Rousseau will also have had in mind books 24–25 of the *Spirit of the Laws*. On polytheism he had probably read Bernard le Bovier de Fontenelle's *De l'origine des fables* (1724), the article "Fable" in the *Encyclopédie* (by Louis de Jaucourt, published in 1756), and perhaps Hume's *Natural History of Religion* (1757; French translation 1759–1760). If the text is a late addition, the thinking in it was not new; it is summarized in a letter to Voltaire of August 18, 1756. The chapter immediately provoked a storm of controversy.]

neighboring peoples whom they were forbidden to attack! "Is not the possession of what belongs to your god Chamos," said Jephthah to the Ammonites, "lawfully yours? By the same right we possess the lands our victorious god has acquired for himself."[141] It appears to me that here was a clear recognition of the parity between the rights of Chamos and those of the god of Israel.

But when the Jews, while in subjection to the kings of Babylon and later to the kings of Syria, wanted to remain steadfast in not giving recognition to any other god but their own, their refusal, seen as rebellion against the victor, brought them the persecutions we read of in their history, and of which there is no other precedent prior to Christianity.[142]

Since, therefore, each religion was uniquely tied to the laws of the state that prescribed it, there was no other way of converting a people except by enslaving it, nor any other missionaries than conquerors. And with the obligation to change cult being the law of the vanquished, it was necessary to begin by conquering before talking about it. Far from men fighting for the gods, it was, as it was in Homer, the gods who fought for men; each asked his own god for victory and paid for it with new altars. Before taking a fortress, the Romans summoned its gods to leave it. And when they allowed the Tarentines to keep their angry gods, it was because at that point they considered these gods to be in subjection to their own and forced to do them homage. They left the vanquished their gods, just as they left them their laws. A wreath to the Capitoline Jupiter was often the only tribute they imposed.

Finally, the Romans having spread their cult and their gods, along with their empire, and having themselves often adopted the gods of the vanquished by granting to various peoples the right of self-government,[143] the peoples of this vast empire gradually found themselves to have multitudes of gods and cults, which were nearly the same everywhere. And that is how paganism finally became a single, identical religion throughout the known world.

Such were the circumstances under which Jesus came to establish a spiritual kingdom on earth. In separating the theological system from the political system, this made the state cease being united and caused internal divisions that have never ceased to agitate Christian peoples. But since this new idea of an otherworldly kingdom had never entered the heads of the pagans, they

---

[141] *Nonne ea quae possidet Chamos deus tuus, tibi jure debentur?* [Judges 11:24] Such is the text of the Vulgate. Father de Carrières has translated it, "Do you not believe that you have the right to possess what belongs to your god Chamos?" I do not know the force of the Hebrew text; but I see that in the Vulgate Jephthah positively acknowledges the right of the god Chamos, and that the French translator weakened this recognition by adding an "according to you," which is not in the Latin.

[142] It is quite clear that the Phocian War, called the Holy War, was not a war of religion at all. Its objective was to punish sacrileges, and not to make unbelievers submit.

[143] [Rousseau's term is *droit de cité*, which contemporary dictionaries define as the right to elect one's own rulers.]

always regarded the Christians as true rebels who, underneath their hypocritical submission, were only waiting for the moment when they would become independent and the masters, and adroitly usurp the authority they pretended in their weakness to respect. This is the reason for the persecutions.

What the pagans feared happened. Then everything changed its appearance. The humble Christians changed their language, and soon this so-called otherworldly kingdom became, under a visible leader, the most violent despotism in this world.

However, since there has always been a prince and civil laws, this double power has given rise to a perpetual jurisdictional conflict that has made all good polity impossible in Christian states, and no one has ever been able to know whether it is the priest or the master whom one is obliged to obey.

Nevertheless, several peoples, even in Europe or nearby, have wanted to preserve or reestablish the ancient system, but without success. The spirit of Christianity has won everything. The sacred cult has always remained or again become independent of the sovereign and without any necessary link to the body of the state. Mohammed had very sound opinions. He tied his political system together very well, and as long as the form of his government subsisted under his successors, the caliphs, this government was utterly unified, and for that reason it was good. But as the Arabs became prosperous, lettered, polished, soft, and cowardly, they were subjugated by barbarians. Then the division between the two powers began again. Although it is less apparent among the Mohammedans than among the Christians, it is there all the same, especially in the sect of Ali; and there are states, such as Persia, where it never ceases to be felt.

Among us, the kings of England have established themselves as heads of the church, and the czars have done the same. But with this title, they became less its masters than its servants. They have acquired not so much the right to change it as the power to maintain it. They are not its legislators; they are merely its princes. Wherever the clergy constitutes a body,[144] it is master and legislator in its own sphere. Thus there are two powers, two sovereigns, in England and in Russia, just as there are everywhere else.

Of all the Christian writers, the philosopher Hobbes[145] is the only one who clearly saw the evil and the remedy, who dared to propose the reunification

[144] It should be carefully noted that it is not so much the formal assemblies, such as those of France, that bind the clergy together into a body, as it is the communion of the churches. Communion and excommunication are the social compact of the clergy, one with which it will always be the master of the peoples and the kings. All the priests who communicate together [the text reads *communiquent*, but the sense seems to require *communient* (take communion), and one is bound to suspect a slip on the part of Rousseau or his printer] are fellow citizens, even if they should be from the opposite ends of the world. This invention is a political masterpiece. There was nothing like this among the pagan priests; thus they never made up a body of clergy.

[145] [See especially *De Cive*, chs. 6, 17.]

of the two heads of the eagle and the complete restoration of political unity, without which no state or government will ever be well constituted. But he should have seen that the dominating spirit of Christianity was incompatible with his system, and that the interest of the priest would always be stronger than that of the state. It is not so much what is horrible and false in his political theory as what is just and true that has caused it to be hated.[146]

I believe that if the facts of history were developed from this point of view, it would be easy to refute the opposing sentiments of Bayle and Warburton, the one holding that no religion is useful to the body politic, while the other maintains, to the contrary, that Christianity is its firmest support.[147] We could prove to the first that no state has ever been founded without religion serving as its base, and to the second that Christian law is at bottom more injurious than it is useful for the strong constitution of the state. To succeed in making myself understood, I need only give a bit more precision to the excessively vague ideas about religion that are pertinent to my subject.

When considered in relation to society, which is either general or particular,[148] religion can also be divided into two kinds, namely, the religion of the man and that of the citizen. The first—without temples, altars, or rites and limited to the purely internal cult of the supreme God and to the eternal duties of morality—is the pure and simple religion of the Gospel, the true theism, and what can be called natural divine law.[149] The other, inscribed in a single country, gives it its gods, its own titulary patrons. It has its dogmas, its rites, its exterior cult prescribed by laws. Outside the nation that practices it, everything is infidel, alien, and barbarous to it. It extends the duties and rights of man only as far as its altars. Such were all the religions of the early peoples, to which the name of civil or positive divine law can be given.

There is a third sort of religion, which is more bizarre. In giving men two sets of legislation, two leaders, and two homelands, it subjects them to contradictory duties and prevents them from being simultaneously devout men and citizens. Such is the religion of the Lamas and of the Japanese, and

---

[146] Notice, among other texts, in Grotius' letter to his brother, dated April 11, 1643, what this learned man approves of and what he criticizes in the [Hobbes'] book *De Cive*. It is true that, prone to being indulgent, he appears to forgive the author for his good points for the sake of his bad ones. [Rousseau knew of this letter from Barbeyrac's edition of Grotius' *Law of War and Peace*. In it Grotius approves of what Hobbes says about monarchy and disapproves of what he says about religion—the opposite of Rousseau's view.] But not everyone is so merciful.

[147] [Bayle, *Diverse Thoughts on the Comet* (1682); Warburton, *Divine Legation of Moses* (1737–1741), or rather, presumably, the French translation of *The Alliance between Church and State*.]

[148] [The general society is the society of all human beings; the particular society is the political community.]

[149] [Rousseau's most famous account of this true Christianity is to be found in "The Profession of Faith of the Savoyard Vicar," which appears within *Émile*.]

such is Roman Christianity. It can be called the religion of the priest. It leads to a kind of mixed and unsociable law that has no name.

Considered from a political standpoint, these three types of religion all have their faults. The third is so evidently bad that it is a waste of time to amuse oneself by proving it. Whatever breaks up social unity is worthless. All institutions that place man in contradiction with himself are of no value.

The second is good in that it unites the divine cult with love of the laws and in that, in making the homeland the object of its citizens' admiration, it teaches them that all service to the state is service to its tutelary god. It is a kind of theocracy in which there ought to be no pontiff other than the prince and no priests other than the magistrates. To die for one's country is, then, to become a martyr; to violate its laws is to be impious; to subject a guilty man to public execration is to deliver him to the wrath of the gods: *sacer estod*.[150] However, it is bad in that, being based on error and lies, it deceives men, makes them credulous and superstitious, and drowns the true cult of the divinity in an empty ceremony. It is also bad when, on becoming exclusive and tyrannical, it makes a people bloodthirsty and intolerant, so that men breathe only murder and massacre, and believe they are performing a holy action in killing anyone who does not accept their gods. This places such a people in a natural state of war with all others, which is quite harmful to its own security.

Thus there remains the religion of man or Christianity (not that of today, but that of the Gospel, which is completely different). Through this holy, sublime, true religion, men, in being the children of the same God, all acknowledge one another as brothers, and the society that unites them is not dissolved even at death.

But since this religion has no particular relation to the body politic, it leaves laws with only the force the laws derive from themselves, without adding any other force to them. And thus one of the great bonds of a particular society remains ineffectual. Moreover, far from attaching the hearts of the citizens to the state, it detaches them from it as from all the other earthly things. I know of nothing more contrary to the social spirit.[151]

We are told that a people of true Christians would form the most perfect society imaginable. I see but one major difficulty in this assumption, namely that a society of true Christians would no longer be a society of men.

I even say that this supposed society would not, for all its perfection, be the strongest or the most durable. By dint of being perfect, it would lack a bond of union; its destructive vice would be in its very perfection.

---

[150] ["Let him be cursed."]

[151] [Later, Rousseau clarified that here he meant "contrary to the spirit of any particular society or political community," not "contrary to the spirit of the general society of all human beings."]

Each man would fulfill his duty; the people would be subject to the laws; the leaders would be just and moderate, the magistrates would be upright and incorruptible; soldiers would scorn death; there would be neither vanity nor luxury. All of this is very fine, but let us look further.

Christianity is a completely spiritual religion, concerned exclusively with things heavenly. The homeland of the Christian is not of this world. He does his duty, it is true, but he does it with a profound indifference toward the success or failure of his efforts. As long as he has nothing to reproach himself for, it matters little to him whether everything is going well or poorly down here. If the state is flourishing, he hardly dares to enjoy the public felicity, for fear of becoming puffed up with his country's glory. If the state is in decline, he blesses the hand of God that weighs heavily on his people.

For the society to be peaceful and for harmony to be maintained, every citizen without exception would have to be an equally good Christian. But if, unhappily, there is a single ambitious man, a single hypocrite, a Catiline, for example, or a Cromwell, he would quite undoubtedly gain the upper hand on his pious compatriots. Christian charity does not readily allow one to think ill of one's neighbors. Once he has discovered by some ruse the art of deceiving them and of laying hold of a part of the public authority, behold a man established in dignity! God wills that he be respected. Soon, behold a power! God wills that he be obeyed. Does the trustee of this power abuse it? He is the rod with which God punishes his children. It would be against one's conscience to expel the usurper. It would be necessary to disturb the public tranquility, use violence, and shed blood. All this accords ill with the meekness of a Christian. And after all, what difference does it make whether one is a free man or a serf in this vale of tears? The essential thing is getting to heaven, and resignation is but another means to that end.

What if a foreign war breaks out? The citizens march without reservation into combat; none among them dreams of deserting. They do their duty, but without passion for victory; they know how to die better than how to be victorious. What difference does it make whether they are the victors or the vanquished? Does not providence know better than they what they need? Just imagine the advantage a fierce, impetuous, and passionate enemy could draw from their stoicism! Set them face to face with those generous peoples who were devoured by an ardent love of glory and homeland. Suppose your Christian republic is face to face with Sparta or Rome. The pious Christians will be beaten, crushed, and destroyed before they realize where they are, or else they will owe their safety only to the scorn their enemies will conceive for them. To my way of thinking, the oath taken by Fabius' soldiers was a fine one. They did not swear to die or to win; they swore to return victorious. And they kept their promise. Christians would never have taken such an oath; they would have believed they were tempting God.

But I am deceiving myself in talking about a Christian republic; these terms are mutually exclusive. Christianity preaches only servitude and dependence.

Its spirit is too favorable to tyranny for tyranny not to take advantage of it at all times. True Christians are made to be slaves.[152] They know it and are hardly moved by this. This brief life has too little value in their eyes.

Christian troops, we are told, are excellent. I deny this. Is someone going to show me some? For my part, I do not know of any Christian troops. Someone will mention the crusades. Without disputing the valor of the crusaders, I will point out that, far from being Christians, they were soldiers of the priest; they were citizens of the church; they were fighting for its spiritual country that the church, goodness knows how, had made temporal. Properly understood, this is a throwback to paganism. Since the Gospel does not establish a national religion, no holy war is possible among Christians.

Under the pagan emperors, Christian soldiers were brave. All the Christian authors affirm this, and I believe it. This was a competition for honor against the pagan troops. Once the emperors were Christians, this competition ceased. And when the cross expelled the eagle, all Roman valor disappeared.

But leaving aside political considerations, let us return to right and determine the principles that govern this important point. The right that the social compact gives the sovereign over the subjects does not, as I have said, go beyond the limits of public utility.[153] The subjects, therefore, do not have to account to the sovereign for their opinions, except to the extent that these opinions are of significance to the community. Now it is of great consequence to the state that each citizen have a religion that causes him to love his duties. But the dogmas of that religion are of no interest to either the state or its members, except to the extent that these dogmas relate to morality and to the duties that the one who professes them is required to fulfill toward others. Each man can have in addition such opinions as he pleases, without it being any of the sovereign's business to know what they are. For since the other world is outside the province of the sovereign, whatever the fate of subjects in the life to come, it is none of its business, as long as they are good citizens in this life.

---

[152] [Cf. Machiavelli, *Discourses*, bk 2, ch. 2.]

[153] "In the republic," says the Marquis d'Argenson, "each man is perfectly free with respect to what does not harm others." [D'Argenson's *Considerations on the Government of France* circulated widely in manuscript but was first published by Rey (Rousseau's publisher) in 1764, partly, one presumes, because of Rousseau's praise of it. This sentence does not appear in the published text, which is taken (as Rey admits) from a faulty manuscript. Of course, since the text was unpublished and d'Argenson had died in 1757, Rousseau was also free to play fast and loose with d'Argenson's text.] This is the invariable boundary. It cannot be expressed more precisely. I have been unable to deny myself the pleasure of occasionally citing this manuscript, even though it is unknown to the public, in order to pay homage to the memory of a famous and noteworthy man, who, even as a minister, retained the heart of a true citizen, along with just and sound opinions on the government of his country.

There is, therefore, a purely civil profession of faith, the articles of which it belongs to the sovereign to establish, not exactly as dogmas of religion, but as sentiments of sociability, without which it is impossible to be a good citizen or a faithful subject.[154] While not having the ability to obligate anyone to believe them, the sovereign can banish from the state anyone who does not believe them. It can banish him not for being impious but for being unsociable, for being incapable of sincerely loving the laws and justice, and of sacrificing his life, if necessary, for his duty. If, after having publicly acknowledged these same dogmas, a person acts as if he does not believe them, he should be put to death; he has committed the greatest of crimes: he has lied before the laws.

The dogmas of the civil religion ought to be simple, few in number, precisely worded, without explanations or commentaries. The existence of a powerful, intelligent, beneficent divinity that foresees and provides; the life to come; the happiness of the just; the punishment of the wicked; the sanctity of the social contract and of the laws—these are the positive dogmas.[155] As for the negative dogmas, I am limiting them to just one, namely, intolerance. It is part of the cults we have excluded.

Those who distinguish between civil and theological intolerance are mistaken, in my opinion. Those two types of intolerance are inseparable. It is impossible to live in peace with those one believes to be damned. To love them would be to hate God, who punishes them. It is absolutely necessary to either reclaim them or torment them. Whenever theological intolerance is allowed, it is impossible for it not to have some civil effect;[156] and once it does, the

---

[154] Caesar, speaking in Catiline's defense, tried to establish the dogma of the mortality of the soul. To refute him, Cato and Cicero did not waste time philosophizing. They contented themselves with showing that Caesar spoke like a bad citizen and advanced a doctrine that was injurious to the state. In fact, this was what the Roman senate had to judge, and not a question of theology.

[155] [Locke in his *Letter Concerning Toleration* (1689) had similarly denied toleration to atheists, but Rousseau goes further in making the sanctity of the social contract an article of required belief.]

[156] Marriage, for example, being a civil contract, has civil effects without which it is impossible for a society even to subsist. Suppose then that a clergy reaches the point where it ascribes to itself alone the right to permit this act (a right that must necessarily be usurped in every intolerant religion). In that case, is it not clear that in establishing the authority of the church in this matter, it will render ineffectual that of the prince, who will have no more subjects than those whom the clergy wishes to give him? Is it not also clear that the clergy—if master of whether to marry or not to marry people according to whether or not they accept this or that doctrine, according to whether or not they accept or reject this or that formula, according to whether they are more or less devoted to them, if it behaves prudently and holds firm—will alone dispose of inheritance, offices, the citizens, the state itself, which could not subsist if composed solely of bastards? But, it will be said, abuses will be

sovereign no longer is sovereign, not even over temporal affairs. Thenceforward, priests are the true masters; kings are simply their officers.

Now that there no longer is and never again can be an exclusive national religion, tolerance should be shown to all those who tolerate others, as long as their dogmas contain nothing contrary to the duties of a citizen. But whoever dares to say, "Outside the church there is no salvation" ought to be expelled from the state, unless the state is the church and the prince the pontiff. Such a dogma is good only in a theocratic government; in all other forms of government it is ruinous. The reason why Henry IV is said to have embraced the Roman religion should make every decent man, and above all any prince who knows how to reason, leave it.[157]

Chapter 9
Conclusion

After laying down the true principles of political right and attempting to establish the state on this basis, it remains to support the state by means of its external relations, which would include the laws of nations—commerce; the

---

appealed; summonses and decrees will be issued; the church's income will be seized. What rubbish! If it has a little—I will not say courage but—good sense, the clergy will let all this happen and carry on regardless. It will serenely allow the appeals, the summonses, the decrees, and the seizures, and it will end up master. It is not, it seems to me, a big sacrifice to abandon a part when one is sure of securing the whole. [Rousseau wrote a lengthy first version of this note in his draft of the *Social Contract* (Pléiade ed., 3:343–44). In it he describes the Protestants of France—who had been subjected to prolonged persecution since the revocation of the Edict of Nantes in 1685 and were forbidden to marry (since legal marriages required participation in the Catholic sacrament of the Mass) and thus, because children born out of wedlock could not inherit, unable to pass on their property to their children—as "reduced to the most horrible situation in which ever a people has found itself since the beginning of the world." It seems he then wrote a second version of the note referring to the case of the Protestant clergyman Rochette and the three brothers Grenier (on which, see David D. Bien, "Imagining the Huguenot Minority in Old Regime France," in *The Construction of Minorities*, ed. André Burguière and Raymond Grew [Ann Arbor: University of Michigan Press, 2001], 65–88, at 80–81). Then, when the four were executed in Toulouse on February 19, 1762, and when his book was in press, he substituted the present version. Finally he asked his publisher to reprint the sheet without the note, so that first editions of the *Social Contract* exist in two states, with and without the final version of the note (letters to Rey, March 11, 14, 18, and 25, 1762). Rousseau's motive in attempting to withdraw the note was evidently his fear of the reaction of the French authorities. It is worth bearing in mind that this question touched him directly: once he converted back to Protestantism in 1754 it became impossible for him to marry his companion Thérèse Levasseur; they went through a "ceremony" of marriage, which had no legal force, in 1768. Voltaire's *Treatise on Toleration*, which protested against the persecution of Protestants, was published in 1763.]

[157] [Henry IV is supposed to have decided to become a Catholic because Protestant theologians acknowledged that he could be saved while being Catholic, while Catholic theologians denied that he could be saved while being Protestant. Catholicism was thus, Henry claimed, the safest bet. Thus he converted because the Catholics were more intolerant than the Protestants.]

law of war and conquests; public law, leagues, negotiations, treaties, and so on.[158] But all that forms a new subject that is too vast for my nearsightedness. I should always have set my sights on things that are nearer at hand to me.

END

---

[158] [Rousseau's text has a comma after "law of nations," and commas between each item in the list; but the list that follows consists of three elements of the law of nations, so the punctuation has been revised to convey his sense.]

The State of War

The bulk of Rousseau's manuscript for "The State of War" was published first in 1896 and repeatedly thereafter. A further fragment was discovered in 1965 and published first in 1967. However, it was not until 1987 that Grace G. Roosevelt established the correct order of the text and the relationship of the parts to the whole. This edition, therefore, follows her reconstruction.[1] The text was drafted in the mid-1750s, between completion of the second Discourse *and work on the* Social Contract, *and it must originally have formed part of the larger project that Rousseau abandoned when he decided to publish the* Social Contract. *The text is crucial for understanding the extent to which Rousseau's political theory results from a close engagement with Hobbes.*

D.W.

---

[1] [Grace G. Roosevelt, "A Reconstruction of Rousseau's Fragments on the State of War," *History of Political Thought* 8 (1987): 225–44; Roosevelt, *Reading Rousseau in the Nuclear Age* (Philadelphia: Temple University Press, 1990).]

THE STATE OF WAR

I open the books on rights and morals, I listen to the scholars and legal experts, and, moved by their "thought-provoking" arguments, I deplore the miseries of nature, I admire the peace and justice established by the civil order, I bless the wisdom of public institutions, and I console myself for being a man by viewing myself as a citizen. Well instructed as to my duties and my happiness, I close the book, I leave the classroom, and I look around me. I see poor wretches groaning under an iron yoke, the human race crushed by a handful of oppressors, a starving mass of people overcome by pain and hunger, whose blood and tears the rich drink in peace, and everywhere the strong armed against the weak with the formidable power of the laws.

All this occurs peacefully and without resistance. It is the tranquility of the companions of Ulysses imprisoned in the Cyclops' cave waiting to be devoured. One can but groan and be quiet. Let us draw an eternal veil over these objects of horror. I lift my eyes and look off in the distance. I see fires and flames, countrysides deserted, and towns sacked. Wild men, where are you dragging these poor wretches? I hear a horrible racket. What an uproar! What cries! I draw near. I see a scene of murders, ten thousand men slaughtered, the dead piled up in heaps, the dying trampled underfoot by horses, everywhere the image of death and agony. This then is the fruit of these peaceful institutions! Pity and indignation rise up from the depths of my heart. Ah, barbarous philosopher! Read us your book on a battlefield!

What human feelings would not be moved by these sad objects? But being human and pleading the cause of humanity are no longer permitted. Justice and truth must be bent to the interest of the strongest—this is the rule. The people grant neither pensions nor jobs nor university chairs nor appointments to academies. What reason could there be for protecting them? Magnanimous princes, I speak in the name of the literary community; oppress the people with a clear conscience; we expect everything from you alone. As far as we are concerned, the people are good for nothing.

How would so weak a voice make itself heard over such self-serving out-cries? Alas, I should keep quiet, but surely the voice of my heart could pierce so sad a silence? No; without entering into the disgusting details that would be taken for satires only because they are true, I will confine myself, as I have always done, to examining human institutions in relation to their principles, to correcting, if possible, the false ideas that self-interested authors give us about them, and at least to ensuring that injustice and violence do not shamelessly appropriate the name of right and equity.

As I consider the condition of the human species, the first thing I notice is a manifest contradiction in its constitution, which makes it always irresolute.

Man to man, we live in a civil state and are subject to laws; people to people, each enjoys natural freedom; this is what makes our situation fundamentally worse than if these distinctions were unknown. For living in both the social order and the state of nature, we are subject to the inconveniences of both without finding safety in either. It is true that the perfection of the social order consists in the conjunction of force and law; but for this to be the case, law must govern force. Nevertheless, according to the received ideas regarding the absolute independence of princes, force alone, speaking to citizens in the guise of law and to foreigners in the guise of reason of state, deprives the latter of the power and the former of the will to resist, so that everywhere the vain name of justice serves merely as a shield for violence.

As for what is commonly called "the right of nations," it is certain that, for lack of sanction, these laws are but chimeras that are even weaker than the law of nature. This latter at least speaks to the heart of individuals. On the contrary, as for the right of nations, since it has no other guarantee than its usefulness to the one who submits to it, its decisions are respected only to the extent that self-interest confirms them. In the mixed condition in which we find ourselves, regardless of which one of the two systems one prefers, by doing too much or too little we have done nothing, and we have placed ourselves in the worst state possible. This, it seems to me, is the real origin of public calamities.

Let us briefly contrast these ideas with the horrible system of Hobbes, and we will find, completely contrary to his absurd doctrine, that the state of war is far from being natural to man; rather, war is born of peace, or at least of the precautions men have taken to assure themselves a lasting peace. But, before entering into this discussion, let us try to explain what it . . .[2]

[Who could have imagined without shuddering the mad system of the natural war of each against all? What a strange animal he must be who would believe his good is bound up with the destruction of his entire species! And how can one conceive that this species, so monstrous and so detestable, could last even two generations? Yet this is how far the desire or rather the rage to establish despotism and passive obedience has led one of the finest geniuses who ever lived.[3] So ferocious a principle was worthy of its purpose.

The state of society that constrains all our natural inclinations cannot, for all that, annihilate them. Despite our prejudices and despite ourselves, they continue to speak to us in the depths of our hearts and often bring us back to the true, which we abandon to pursue chimeras. If this mutual and destructive enmity were an essential part of our constitution, it would therefore still continue to make itself felt and would put us, despite ourselves, at odds with one another, cutting across all social bonds. The frightful hatred of humanity would eat away at man's heart. He would grieve at the birth of his

---

[2] [Rousseau crossed out the four paragraphs that follow in his manuscript.]
[3] [I.e., Thomas Hobbes.]

own children; he would rejoice at the death of his brothers; and, on finding someone asleep, his first movement would be to kill him.

The benevolence that causes us to take part in the happiness of our fellowmen, the compassion that identifies us with the one who suffers and distresses us at his pain, would be sentiments unknown and directly contrary to nature. A sensitive and compassionate man would be a monster; and we would naturally be what we have a great deal of difficulty becoming amid the depravation that pursues us.

In vain would the sophist say that this mutual enmity is not innate and immediate but is based on the struggle that inevitably follows from each individual's right to all things. For the sentiment of this alleged right is no more natural to man than the war that he causes to arise from it.]

I have already said and I cannot repeat too often that the error of Hobbes and of the philosophers is to confuse natural man with the men they have before their eyes, and to transfer into one system a being that can thrive only in another. Man wants his well-being and everything that can contribute to it; that is indisputable. But naturally this well-being of man is confined to what is physically necessary; for when he has a healthy soul and his body does not suffer, what is there, consistent with his constitution, that is lacking for him to be happy? He who has nothing desires little; he who commands no one has little ambition. But a surplus awakens greed; the more one gets, the more one desires. He who has much wants to have everything; and the mad passion for universal monarchy has never tormented the heart of anyone but a great king. Such is the march of nature; such is the development of the passions. A superficial philosopher observes souls kneaded and fermented a hundred times in the leaven of society and believes he has observed man. But to know him well, one needs to know how to disentangle the natural development of his sentiments, and it is not among the inhabitants of a city that one should look for the first feature of nature imprinted on the human heart.

Thus this analytical method leads to nothing but abysses and mysteries, where the wisest understand the least. Ask why mores are corrupted in proportion as minds are enlightened; unable to find the cause, they will have the nerve to deny the fact. Ask why savages brought among us share neither our passions nor our pleasures and take no interest in all that we desire with great fervor. They will never explain it, or they will explain it only by my principles. They know only what they see, and they have never seen nature. They know perfectly well what a city dweller from London or Paris is; but they will never know what a man is.

But even if it were true that this unlimited and ungovernable greed were as developed in all men as our sophist claims, it would still not produce that state of universal war of each against all, of which Hobbes dares to sketch the odious picture. This unbridled desire to appropriate everything is incompatible with that of destroying all of one's fellowmen; and the victor who, having killed everyone, had the misfortune to remain alone in the world, would enjoy nothing in it for precisely the reason that he would have everything. What are even riches good for, if not to be spent? What use to him is possessing the entire universe if he is its only inhabitant? What? Will his stomach devour all the fruits of the earth? Who will gather for him the crops from all parts of the world? Who will carry word of his empire into the vast wildernesses in which he will never live? What will he do with his treasures, who will consume his provisions, before whose eyes will he display his power? I know. Instead of massacring everyone, he will put them all in irons, at least in order to have slaves. This immediately changes the whole state of the question; and since it is no longer a question of destroying, the state of war is abolished. Let the reader here suspend his judgment. I will not forget to return to this point.

Man is naturally peaceable and timid; at the slightest danger his first movement is to flee; he becomes warlike only by dint of habit and experience. Honor, self-interest, prejudices, vengeance—all the passions that can make him brave perils and death—are alien to him in the state of nature. It is only after having entered into society with another man that he decides to attack someone else, and it is only after having been a citizen that he becomes a soldier. That does not demonstrate strong inclinations to wage war with all his fellowmen. But I am pausing too long over a system as revolting as it is absurd and that has already been refuted a hundred times.

There is then no general war between man and man; and the human species was not formed merely for mutual self-destruction. It remains to consider the accidental and particular war that can arise between two or more individuals.

If the natural law were inscribed only in human reason, it would hardly be capable of directing most of our actions, but it is also engraved in the heart of man in indelible characters, and it is there that it speaks to him more forcefully than do all the precepts of the philosophers; it is there that it cries out to him that he is not allowed to sacrifice the life of his fellowman except to preserve his own, and there that it makes him feel horror at spilling human blood not in anger, even when he finds himself obliged to do so.

I find it conceivable that in the quarrels that can arise in the state of nature and where there is no one to arbitrate, an irritated man could sometimes kill another, either openly or by surprise. But if this were a genuine war, imagine the strange position this same man would have to be in if he could preserve his own life only at the expense of someone else's; and if by virtue of a relation established between them it were necessary for one to die so that the other might live. War is a permanent state that presupposes constant relations, and these relations rarely obtain between man and man, where everything between individuals is in a continual flux that constantly changes relations and interests. Thus the subject of a dispute arises and ceases at almost the same moment, a quarrel begins and ends in a single day, and there can be fights and murders but never or very rarely lengthy enmities and wars.

In the civil state, where the life of all citizens is within the power of the sovereign and where no one has the right to dispose of his own life or that of another, the state of war cannot obtain any more than among individuals; and as for duels, provocations, cartels, calls to one-on-one combat, aside from the fact that they were an illegitimate and barbarous abuse of an entirely military constitution, they did not result in a genuine state of war but in a private affair that was resolved within a limited time and place, such that, for a second fight to take place, a fresh call to arms was needed. An exception to this must be made for the private wars that were suspended by short-lived truces that were called "The Peace of God" and that were sanctioned by the Institutions of Saint Louis. But this case is unique in history.

One could ask further whether the kings who are de facto independent of human power could initiate among themselves personal and private wars independent of those of the state. This question is certainly an idle one, for, as everyone knows, princes are not in the habit of sparing others in order to expose themselves to danger. Moreover, this question depends on another question that it is not for me to decide, namely, whether or not the prince is himself subject to the laws of the state; for if he is subject to them, his person is tied to the state and his life belongs to it, just like that of the least citizen. But if the prince is above the laws, he lives in the pure state of nature and need not account for any of his actions either to his subjects or to anyone else.

On the Social State

We now enter into a new order of things. We will see men, united by an artificial concord, assemble to cut one another's throats and all the horrors of war arise from the efforts made to prevent war. But, first of all, it is important to formulate more precise notions about the essence of the body politic than has been done until now. The reader should take note of the fact that it is a question here not so much of history and facts as of right and justice and that I examine things in terms of their nature rather than in terms of our prejudices.

From the first society formed, the formation of all the others necessarily follows. One must either be part of it or unite to resist it. One must either imitate it or allow oneself to be swallowed up by it.

Thus the entire face of the earth is changed; everywhere nature has disappeared; everywhere human art has taken its place; independence and natural liberty have given way to laws and slavery; there is no longer a free being; the philosopher looks for a man and no longer finds one. But it is vain to think that nature can be annihilated; it springs up again and appears where it was least expected. The independence that is taken away from men finds refuge in societies, and these great bodies, left to their own impulses, produce shocks that are more terrible in proportion as their mass exceeds that of individuals.

But, it will be said, since each of these bodies has such a solid foundation, how is it possible for them ever to collide? Should not their own constitution keep them in an eternal peace between themselves? Are they required, like men, to go looking outside for whatever provisions they need? Have they not within themselves all that is necessary for their preservation? Are competition and trade an inevitable source of discord, and is not the fact that the inhabitants in all the countries of the world existed before there was commerce insurmountable proof that they could subsist without it?

End of the chapter: There is no war between men; there is war only between states.

To this I could be satisfied with answering with facts and then I would have no rebuttal to fear, but I have not forgotten that I am reasoning here about the nature of things and not about events that can have a thousand particular causes independent of the common principle. But let us carefully consider the constitution of bodies politic, and although each one could, strictly speaking, see to its own preservation, we will find that their mutual relations are nevertheless more intimate than those among individuals. For man fundamentally has no necessary relation with his fellowmen; he can subsist in full vigor without their assistance; he needs not so much the attentions of man as the fruits of the earth; and the earth produces more than is necessary to feed all its inhabitants. Add to this that man's force and size has a limit set by nature that he cannot exceed. From whatever perspective he looks at himself, he finds all of his faculties limited. His life is short; his years are numbered. His stomach does not increase in size along with his wealth, his passions increase in vain, his pleasures have their limits, his heart is limited like everything else, his capacity for enjoyment is always the same. He may well fancy he is becoming bigger; he remains forever small.

On the contrary, the state, being an artificial body, has no determinate measure; the size proper to it is indefinite, and it can always increase it. It feels weak as long as there are others that are stronger than itself. Its security, its preservation demand that it make itself more powerful than all its neighbors. It cannot become larger, feed itself, flex its muscles except at their expense, and if there is no need for it to look for its subsistence outside itself, it constantly looks outside itself for new members who might give it a more resolute firmness. For the inequality of men has limits imposed by the hands of nature, but the inequality of societies can grow without cease until a single society absorbs all the others.

Thus, since the size of the body politic is purely relative, it is ceaselessly forced to compare itself in order to know itself; it depends on everything that surrounds it, and it has to take an interest in everything occurring around it, for it would be impossible to remain within itself without gaining or losing anything. Its becoming small or great, weak or strong depends on whether its neighbor expands or contracts and grows stronger or weaker. Finally, its very solidity, by making its relations more stable, means that it produces a more certain result in all of its actions and renders all of its quarrels more dangerous.

It appears that people have taken on the task of turning upside down all true ideas of things. Everything inclines natural man to rest; eating and sleeping are the only needs he knows; and only hunger pries him from his torpor. He is represented as a ferocious creature, always ready to torment his fellowmen on account of passions of which he has no knowledge. By contrast, those passions that are aroused within the bosom of society by everything that can inflame them are considered nonexistent. A thousand writers have dared to say that the body politic is without passions and that there is no other reason of state aside from reason itself. As if it were not apparent, on the contrary, that the essence of society consists in the activity of its members and that a state without movement would be nothing but a dead body. As if all the histories of the world did not show us that the best constituted societies are also the most active and the continual action and reaction, internal as well as external, of their members did not attest to the vigor of the entire body.

The difference between human art and the work of nature makes itself felt in its effects. Citizens call themselves limbs of the state, but they cannot unite themselves to it in the way that true limbs are joined to a body. It is impossible to bring it about that each of them does not have an individual and separate existence by means of which he can be sufficient unto himself for his own preservation. The nerves are less sensitive, the muscles have less strength, all the ties are more slack, the least accident can break up everything.

Considering how inferior the public force in the aggregate of the body politic is to the sum total of private forces, how much friction, so to speak, there is in the working of the entire machine, it is apparent then that, all things being equal, the weakest man has more force for his own preservation than the most robust state has for its own.

For this state to last, the liveliness of its passions must supplement the liveliness[4] of its movements, and its will must enliven itself by as much as its power tapers off. This is the law of self-preservation that nature itself establishes among the species and that maintains them all despite their inequality. This too, one might say in passing, is the reason small states have proportionately more vigor than large ones, for public sensitivity[5] does not increase with territory; the more the territory expands, the more the will weakens, the more the movements become feeble, and this great body, overcome by its own weight, sinks down, languishes, and shrivels away.

[4] [Rousseau evidently meant "the lack of liveliness" or "the torpor."]
[5] [The sense of community.]

[War and the State of War]

After having seen the earth become covered with new states, after having discovered a general relationship among them that tends to their mutual destruction, it remains for us to see what exactly constitutes their existence, their well-being, and their life, in order then to discover the kinds of hostilities by which they can attack and harm one another.

It is from the social pact that the body politic receives its unity and its "common self."[6] Its government and its laws make its constitution more or less robust. Its life is in the hearts of the citizens; their courage and their mores make it more or less durable. The only actions that it performs freely and that can be imputed to it are dictated by the general will, and it is by the nature of these actions that one can judge whether the being that produces them is well- or ill-constituted.

Thus, as long as there exists a common will to observe the social pact and the laws, this pact continues to subsist, and as long as this will manifests itself through outward acts, the state is not annihilated. But without ceasing to exist, it can find itself at a point of either vigor or decline, from which—be it weak, healthy, or sick, and tending either to destroy or to strengthen itself—its well-being can grow or change in an infinite number of ways, almost all of which depend on it. This immense detail is not part of my subject, but here is a summary that has a bearing on it.

The General Idea of War between One State and Another

The principle of life of the body politic and, so to speak, the heart of the state, is the social pact, which, as soon as it is wounded, immediately dies, falls down, and dissolves. However, this pact is not a charter on parchment that can be destroyed simply by being torn up; it is inscribed in the general will, and it is there that it is not easily annulled.

Therefore, since it is impossible at first to smash the whole, it is gotten at through its parts; if the body is invulnerable, the limbs are wounded in order to weaken it; if it cannot be deprived of existence, at least its well-being is reduced; if it is impossible to reach the seat of life, then what preserves it is destroyed; an attack is made on the government, the laws, mores, goods, possessions, men. When everything that preserves it is annihilated, the state must eventually perish.

All these means are or can be used in a war of one power against another, and they are also frequently the conditions imposed by the victors in order to continue harming the vanquished once they have been disarmed.

---

[6] [Its corporate identity.]

For the object of all the evil that is inflicted on one's enemy by war is to force him to endure having even more evil done to him by peace. There is not a single type of these kinds of hostilities of which history does not provide examples. I need not speak of the economic contributions in the form of commodities or provisions or about territory seized or inhabitants moved elsewhere. Even an annual tribute of men is not all that rare. Without going back to Minos and the Athenians, it is widely known that the emperors of Mexico attacked their neighbors only in order to have captives to sacrifice, and in our own day the wars the kings of Guinea fight among themselves and their treaties with the peoples of Europe have as their sole object tribute and slave trafficking. It is not difficult to substantiate the claim that sometimes the purpose and effect of war is to pervert the constitution of the enemy state.

The republics of Greece attacked each other less in order to deprive one another of freedom than to change the form of their government, and they changed the government of the vanquished only to hold them more effectively in their dependence. The Macedonians and all the other conquerors of Sparta always placed great importance on abolishing the laws of Lycurgus, and the Romans believed they could show no greater sign of clemency toward a subject people than to leave it its own laws. It is also widely known that one of the maxims of their politics was to foster among their enemies and cast out from among themselves the effeminate and sedentary arts that enervate and soften men. "Leave their angry gods to the Tarentines," said Fabius when he was asked to bring to Rome the statues and paintings that adorned Tarentum; and the first signs of decadence in Roman morals is rightly imputed to Marcellus for not having followed the same policy in Syracuse. So true is this that a clever conqueror sometimes does more harm to the vanquished by what he leaves them than by what he takes away from them, and that, by contrast, a greedy usurper often harms himself more than his enemy by the evil that he does him indirectly. This influence of mores has always been regarded as most important by truly enlightened princes. The only punishment Cyrus imposed on the rebellious Lydians was a soft and effeminate life, and the manner in which the tyrant Aristodemus went about keeping the inhabitants of Cumae in a state of dependence is too curious not to be related. . . .

What the State of War Is[7]

These examples are sufficient to give an idea of the various means by which a state can be weakened and of those whose use seems permitted by war in order to harm one's enemy; as for the treaties, which are the preconditions for one or more of these means, what basically are such types of peace except a war

---

[7] [Omitted here is a fairly lengthy passage that is crossed out in the manuscript. The argument is restated in a briefer form in the passage that follows.]

continued with all the more cruelty since the vanquished enemy no longer has the right to defend himself? I will speak about this elsewhere.

Add to all this the palpable displays of ill will that are indicative of the intent to do harm, such as refusing to a power the titles due to it, misrepresenting its rights, rejecting its claims, depriving its subjects of the freedom to trade, stirring up enemies against it, or, finally, infringing on the right of nations in respect to it on any pretext whatsoever.

Not all of these various ways of hurting a body politic are equally practicable or equally useful to the one who makes use of them, and those that work to our own advantage and the disadvantage of the enemy are naturally preferred. Land, money, men, all the spoils that can be appropriated thus become the principal objects of mutual hostilities. As this base greed imperceptibly changes people's ideas of things, war finally degenerates into pillage, and those who began as enemies and warriors gradually become tyrants and thieves.

So as not to adopt unthinkingly these changes in ideas, let us start by fixing our own ideas by means of a definition and try to make it so simple that it would be impossible to misuse it.

I therefore call war between one power and another the effect of a mutual, steady, and manifest inclination to destroy the enemy state, or at least to weaken it, by all means possible. This inclination put into action is war properly so called; as long as it remains in a state of inaction, it is merely the "state of war."

I foresee an objection: since according to me the state of war is natural between powers, why does the inclination from which war results need to be made manifest? To this I answer that I was speaking previously about the natural state; that I am speaking here of the legitimate state; and that later on I will show how, in order to make it legitimate, war needs a declaration.

Fundamental Distinctions

I beg my reader not to forget that I am not investigating what makes war advantageous to the one who wages it but what makes it legitimate. Being just almost always has a cost. Is one therefore exempted from being so?

If there never were and never could be a genuine war between individuals, who then are those between whom it takes place and who can really call themselves enemies? I answer that they are public persons. And what is a public person? I answer that it is that moral being that is called "sovereign," which has been given its existence by the social pact, and all of whose wills bear the name "laws." Let us here apply the above distinctions; as for the effects of war, the sovereign may be said to be the one doing the damage and the state the one suffering it.

If war takes place only between moral beings, then there is no need to attack real men, and war can be waged without depriving anyone of his life. But this requires an explanation.

If we look at things solely in terms of a strict understanding of the social pact, then land, money, men, and everything included within the confines of the state belong to it without reservation. But since the rights of society, being founded on those of nature, cannot abolish them, all these objects need to be considered in a twofold relation, namely, the soil as both public territory and as the patrimony of private individuals; goods as belonging in one sense to the sovereign and in another sense to the owners; the inhabitants as citizens and as men. Basically, since the body politic is only a moral person, it is merely a construction of reason.[8] Take away the public convention, and right away the state is destroyed without the slightest change in all that comprises it; and never will all the conventions of men know how to change anything in the physical makeup of things. What then is it to wage war on a sovereign? It is to attack the public convention and all that results from it; for the essence of the state consists exclusively in that. If the social pact could be broken with a single stroke, right away there would be no more war; and with that single stroke the state would be killed, without a single man dying. Aristotle says that in order to authorize the cruelties inflicted upon the helots in Sparta, the ephors, on taking charge, solemnly declared war on them. This declaration was as superfluous as it was barbarous. The state of war necessarily existed between them solely because they were the masters and the others were the slaves. Without doubt, since the Lacedaemonians killed the helots, the helots had every right to kill the Lacedaemonians.

---

[8] [Rousseau's term is *être de raison*, which corresponds to the scholastic *ens rationis*. See *Social Contract*, note 30.]

Index